Lecture Notes
in Business Information Processing   139

Series Editors

Wil van der Aalst
  Eindhoven Technical University, The Netherlands
John Mylopoulos
  University of Trento, Italy
Michael Rosemann
  Queensland University of Technology, Brisbane, Qld, Australia
Michael J. Shaw
  University of Illinois, Urbana-Champaign, IL, USA
Clemens Szyperski
  Microsoft Research, Redmond, WA, USA

W0080467

Geert Poels (Ed.)

Enterprise Information Systems of the Future

6th IFIP WG 8.9 Working Conference, CONFENIS 2012
Ghent, Belgium, September 19-21, 2012
Revised Selected Papers

 Springer

Volume Editor

Geert Poels
Ghent University
Faculty of Economics and Business Administration
Department of Management Information Science
and Operations Management
Ghent, Belgium
E-mail: geert.poels@ugent.be

ISSN 1865-1348   e-ISSN 1865-1356
ISBN 978-3-642-36610-9   e-ISBN 978-3-642-36611-6
DOI 10.1007/978-3-642-36611-6
Springer Heidelberg Dordrecht London New York

Library of Congress Control Number: 2013931188

ACM Computing Classification (1998): J.1, H.4, H.3.5

© IFIP International Federation for Information Processing 2013
This work is subject to copyright. All rights are reserved, whether the whole or part of the material is
concerned, specifically the rights of translation, reprinting, re-use of illustrations, recitation, broadcasting,
reproduction on microfilms or in any other way, and storage in data banks. Duplication of this publication
or parts thereof is permitted only under the provisions of the German Copyright Law of September 9, 1965,
in ist current version, and permission for use must always be obtained from Springer. Violations are liable
to prosecution under the German Copyright Law.
The use of general descriptive names, registered names, trademarks, etc. in this publication does not imply,
even in the absence of a specific statement, that such names are exempt from the relevant protective laws
and regulations and therefore free for general use.

Typesetting: Camera-ready by author, data conversion by Scientific Publishing Services, Chennai, India

Printed on acid-free paper

Springer is part of Springer Science+Business Media (www.springer.com)

Preface

Enterprise information systems of the future – evolving toward more performance through transparency and agility. The theme of CONFENIS 2012, the 6th International IFIP TC8 WG 8.9 Conference on Research and Practical Issues in Enterprise Information Systems, held in Ghent (Belgium) during September 19–21, 2012, emphasized two evolutions in the domain of enterprise information systems. The first evolution is the development of more open systems, e.g., the creation of interoperation between systems from collaborating organizations or the composition of systems from standard modules and packages offered by different vendors. The second evolution is the move toward more flexible systems; meaning easily configurable and adaptable systems based on service-oriented software architectures, the software as a service business model, cloud-computing infrastructures, and software product line approaches. Apart from these industry evolutions, we have also witnessed a rediscovery of the design science tradition in enterprise information systems research. Design science is where the origin of our academic discipline lies; however, the last few decades have seen enterprise information systems researchers move away from their core object of study (i.e., the system) toward the study of the environment in which the system resides (i.e., the organization and its users). Fully embracing novel and exotic research methods, paradigms, and theories originating in the social sciences, the enterprise information system became for many researchers a black box of which the design was left to computer scientists and was considered outside the realm of enterprise information systems research. Luckily, times are changing.

With CONFENIS 2012 we heartily wished to support the revisiting of design science research in enterprise information systems. With full respect for the pluralistic and open-minded spirit of the IFIP TC8 WG 8.9 Enterprise Information Systems community, we especially welcomed in our call for papers novel design science research contributions. We explicitly called for technical or evaluation papers on methods, techniques, and technologies to make enterprise information systems more transparent (e.g., research on enterprise modeling, ontology and architecture that would 'open up' the structure and behavior of enterprise systems) as well as more empirically driven research and theoretical, conceptual, or even visionary papers on how flexible enterprise information system solutions can foster business agility and innovation.

Our call was responded to with the submission of 53 contributions, including completed research papers, work-in-progress papers, experience reports, and visionary/conceptual papers. After a rigorous review process of 3 months, facilitated by the EasyChair conference management system, we finally selected 25 papers, of which 10 full-length papers and 15 short papers, to be published in this LNBIP volume.

These 25 papers present a well-balanced mix between the more traditional social sciences and the more novel (or reactionary as its opponents would claim) design science paradigms in enterprise information systems research. Moreover, they include practitioner-oriented and practice–originating contributions, reminding us of the relevance of our discipline and the applied nature of its research. Topics addressed by the accepted papers fall into three categories, ranging from a broad to narrow views on enterprise information systems research:

- Researching information systems in business, with topic areas such as enterprise modeling, business process management, and business process mining
- Researching enterprise information systems from a management or organization perspective, with topic areas including management of enterprise systems, business intelligence, service innovation, decision support and negotiation, and strategic planning of enterprise systems
- Researching design, implementation, and offering of ERP systems, with as topic areas ERP system design methodologies, case studies and worldwide experiences in implementing ERP systems, and ERP systems as a service

Not included in the volume, but an essential part of the CONFENIS 2012 academic program, were the talks by invited speakers. Bill McCarthy of Michigan State University, founder of the Resource-Event-Agent semantic data model for accounting information systems, which is instrumental to the development of integrated enterprise information systems, gave a talk on "The REA-Invention of Double Entry Bookkeeping — Moving Accounting Back to the Center of Enterprise Information Architectures". Hajo Reijers of the Eindhoven University of Technology provided us with novel insights into "The Process of Process Modeling" while Carol Brown of Stevens Institute of Technology widened our view with her talk on "Enterprise Systems in Healthcare: Leveraging What We Know from Other Industries."

The success of a conference is a joint effort in which the Program Chair's contribution is nothing more than a drop in the ocean. First and foremost, we thank the director and staff members of the Economic Council of the province of East Flanders (EROV) for their enthusiasm, dedication, and excellent work in organizing this conference. I personally wish to thank my esteemed colleague, Dirk Deschoolmeester, Emeritus Professor of Ghent University and representative for Belgium in IFIP TC8, for bringing the CONFENIS conference to Ghent. Further, we sincerely thank the members of the Program Committee for their careful and timely review of the submissions. Most importantly, we thank the authors for submitting high-quality papers to CONFENIS 2012. We are proud to present in this LNBIP volume, which is the result of their hard labor.

September 2012   Geert Poels

Organization

Program Committee

Geert Poels	Ghent University (Chair), Belgium
Jan Claes	Ghent University, Belgium
Frederik Gailly	Vrije Universiteit Brussel, Belgium
Shangming Zhou	University of Wales, Swansea, UK
Björn Johansson	Lund University, Sweden
Petr Doucek	University of Economics, Prague, Czech Republic
Bjarne Rerup Schlichter	Århus School of Business, Denmark
Jan Devos	Ghent University Association, Belgium
Nguyen Manh Tuan	Ho Chi Minh City University of Technology, Vietnam
Jan Pries-Heje	Roskilde University, Denmark
Sohail Chaudhry	Villanova University, USA
A Min Tjoa	Vienna University of Technology, Austria
Maria Raffai	Szechenyi Istvan University, Hungary
Lisa Seymour	University of Cape Town, South Africa
Rogerio Atem De Carvalho	Instituto Federal Fluminense, Brazil
Guido Geerts	University of Delaware, USA
Jingzhi Guo	University of Macau, P.R. China
Monique Snoeck	KU Leuven, Belgium
Susan Foster	Monash University, Australia
Peggy Chaudhry	Villanova University, USA
Parthasarathy Sudhaman	Thiagarajar College of Engineering, India
Bee Hua Goh	National University of Singapore, Singapore
Lars Taxén	Linköping University, Sweden
Victor Romanov	Russian Plekhanov University, Russia
Michael Rosemann	Queensland University of Technology, Australia
Flavia Santoro	NP2Tec / UNIRIO, Brazil
Rob Kusters	OU / TUE, The Netherlands
Renato Campos	UNESP, Brazil
Young Moon	Syracuse University, USA
Charles Møller	Aalborg University, Denmark
Lu Liu	Beihang University, China
Joachim Schuler	Pforzheim University, Germany
Torben Tambo	Aarhus University, Denmark

Per Svejvig   Aarhus University, Denmark
Frantisek Sudzina   Aarhus University, Denmark
Jens Ove Riis   Aalborg University, Denmark
Ana Paula Costa   Federal University of Pernambuco, Brazil
Luc Chalmet   Ghent University, Belgium
Muthu Ramachandran   Leeds Metropolitan University, UK
Steven De Haes   Antwerp Management School, Belgium
Paul Gemmel   Ghent University, Belgium
Dirk Deschoolmeester   Ghent University, Belgium
Lene Pries-Heje   The IT University of Copenhagen, Denmark

Additional Reviewers

David L. Olson   University of Nebraska-Lincoln, USA
Carlos Francisco Simões Gomes   Universidade Federal Fluminense, Brazil

Table of Contents

Full Papers

Short Papers

Process Innovation: Redesigning an Enterprise Backbone System

Joachim Van den Bergh and Stijn Viaene

Joachim.VandenBergh@vlerick.com

Abstract. This case study covers the story of a process reengineering effort at Belgacom Mobile, the largest Belgian mobile telecommunications operator. It describes how a smart combination of theoretical concepts can lead to process innovation, and product innovation. The process innovation effort consisted of a large automation pillar and the rebuilding of the enterprise backbone system SPOMS. Architectural principles were applied to allow the redesigned process to be flexible and capable of dealing with newly emerging SIM card types and technological advances. The sub-processes will be orchestrated by the process owner who controls the entire process from a process dashboard. This case shows the potential benefits of Business Process Management (BPM), IT-enabled innovation and Product Factory. The redesigned SIM card ordering process thus provides a sustainable answer to the ever shortening life-cycle of products and technologies, SIM cards in particular, and the call for process flexibility in fast changing environments.

The contribution of this project to the general understanding IT-enabled innovation lies in the innovative approach. Namely, product and process were separated from each other by means of Production Process ID creation. The redesigned SIM card ordering process thus provides a sustainable answer to the ever shortening life-cycle of products and technologies, SIM cards in particular. The redesigned sub-processes are orchestrated by the process owner who controls the entire process from a process dashboard. In terms of performance improvement, the project resulted in (1) increased process flexibility (2) and consistency, (3) dramatically shortened lead-times and (4) better control over the process.

Keywords: IT-enabled innovation, Business Process Management, Flexibility, Process Design, Process Innovation, Enterprise systems.

1 Introduction

In order to survive and thrive in a highly competitive business environment, organizations need to be in control of their business processes. Moreover, organizations that find themselves in a sector with galloping technological developments experience the necessity of flexible processes characterized by a high degree of product independence [1]. Belgacom Mobile, market leader in the Belgian mobile telecommunications market, finds itself in such a position and is continuously pressured by the smaller challengers in the market. Furthermore, the mobile

G. Poels (Ed.): CONFENIS 2012, LNBIP 139, pp. 1–17, 2013.
© IFIP International Federation for Information Processing 2013

telecommunications sector is known to develop at a rapid pace, driven by technological advances. It is, therefore, crucial for Belgacom Mobile to be capable of managing and optimizing its business processes and on top of that keeping them adaptable to emerging technologies with the support of a reliable enterprise IT system.

The severe fight for the customer due to the market situation results in large promotional marketing campaigns, for example inclusion of free SIM cards with popular magazines. These campaigns are typically dependent on temporary trends and needed quick response from the back office processes producing and supplying the SIM cards. Simultaneously new types of SIM cards are being introduced as a result of technological advances, requiring to be embedded in the existing process structure.

Due to these circumstances the SIM card ordering process at Belgacom Mobile, a core business process for the company, was under increasing pressure. In 2006 the supply chain management team realised that the process and its supporting technology SPOMS (SIM card Purchasing Order Management System) needed a thorough reengineering. Most of the expertise on the old tool had left the company and furthermore it was starting to become clear that the process was not as flexible and agile as required to react on requests from the marketing department. Lastly, the process as it was, posed an impediment for product innovation because it needed reworking for each and every new type of SIM card that was being introduced. Some decisive action to set this situation right was necessary. After several rounds of proposals an innovative solution came to light to automate and simplify the SIM card order process.

As stated in the official business case document the objective was to "reengineer the current SIM card order management process to make the process future-proof, efficient and flexible". Whereas at first, they had a mere automation of the existing process in mind – it was very labour intensive – over time the mindset shifted towards an approach that emphasised both process reengineering and automation. Based on the business case developed by the supply chain team, stressing the numerous benefits of reengineering, and the risk associated with not doing the project, the project received a 'MUST DO' label from the review committee. Thus the project became a high strategic priority and gained access to the necessary resources.

This case study is specifically intended to formulate an empirically evidenced answer to these research questions, validating the existing body of knowledge and theory on IT-enabled process innovation and enterprise systems: How does IT support enterprise processes in turbulent environments? Does a combination of BPM and SOA truly deliver superior business results? What are the key success factors in an IT-enabled process innovation effort?

The originality of the final project set-up presents this case as the perfect example for showcasing IT-enabled process innovation. First, relevant concepts of BPM, IT-enabled innovation, architecture and process-specific terms are situated. Next, the context, business case and set-up for the project are described. Subsequently, the project's main features and particularities are outlined. To conclude, the results of the Belgacom Mobile project are presented and the learning points and contributions are explained.

2   Theoretical Background

2.1   Processes and Flexibility: An Architectural Approach

Flexibility is generally defined as the ability to adapt to different circumstances. It is one of the main goals of process management since flexible processes are appreciated assets to deal with changing market demands. IT infrastructure needs to allow such flexibility in business processes. Process management systems are according to Weske [2] narrowing the gap between business objectives and the technology that is there to help achieving those goals. Notwithstanding the fact that IT systems have shown to be capable of enhancing process flexibility there are mixed feelings towards their role in all this. Especially the widespread implementations of diverse ERP systems have led to discussion. One could argue that adapting processes in such a way that they would fit the prescribed ERP software reference processes is hardly a practice that promotes process flexibility. If an organisation manages its processes well, they can be considered as a source of competitive advantage. On the other hand there is a tendency towards the use of industry best practices and reference models, turning certain processes more and more into a commodity. Working on process innovation expectedly results in superior business processes that differentiate an organisation from its competitors.

Process flexibility comes with two major requirements as stated by Stohr and zür Mühlen [3]: "First, there must be a capability to develop new processes and change existing processes rapidly and inexpensively, and secondly process work must be flexible within the scope of a given process design." The former implies that (new) processes must be designed in such a way that they can be deployed rapidly. Several enterprise process management systems now provide the ability to transform process models into executable processes. The underlying technology is crucial since it must allow for interoperability with other internal and external IT applications. Thus, new processes can easily connect to other systems and reuse parts of existing processes as services that can be invoked.

With regard to the SPOMS project, both the Supply Chain Manager and the external consultants involved in the project agreed that an architectural approach was best suited for this particular project. Specifically, Service Oriented Architecture (SOA) is said to bring various advantages to business processes [4, 5]. Numerous blogs, vendor reports and white papers have spread the belief that SOA and BPM are two sides of the same coin and that both approaches deliver the best results when combined [6, 7, 8].

SOA was defined as a "component model that interrelates the different functional units of an application, called 'services', through well-defined interfaces and contracts between these services. The interface is defined in a neutral manner that should be independent of the hardware platform, the operating system, and the programming language in which the service is implemented" [9]. Loose coupling and reusability of services are the cornerstones of the interest in SOA as a means to make business processes more agile, a condition for sustainable success in today's business environments. Both legacy systems and newly developed applications can be formulated as a set of services as well as external systems [10]. Each business process can call on these services when needed. SOA requires the set-up of a new architectural layer of abstraction – at the service level – between processes and systems. Loose coupling stands for the fact that the service requester should not be aware of the structure that underpins the requested service [11]. A recent literature study showed that SOA literature has exponentially increased in the last few years [12]. In another study Becker et al. [13] concluded that SOA adoption is still in its early phase.

Turbulent business environments call for adequate approaches to provide robust IT support for business processes. El Sawy and Pavlou [14] stated that "using an SOA and web services is an effective way of conserving IT investments because it removes the need for massive integration and re-integration expenditures when requirements change". The flexibility of modular business processes and supporting IT systems lies in the quick adaptation capabilities when the business environment changes, and in this way affects the business processes. However, SOA implementation involves several challenges. First of all, identifying and defining services could pose a problem to organizations. Another challenge of SOA is the involvement of the business in the process [15]. Therefore alignment between business and ICT is a key success factor for SOA implementation. Finally, SOA should never be a strategy in its own right, but should be a decision to support the organizational strategy [16].

Business Process Management (BPM) is an essential capability for many organizations. It provides a horizontal view of an organization's core business processes and the organization's capability of managing, improving and controlling these processes [17]. Zairi [18] defines BPM as "a structured approach to analyses and continually improve fundamental activities such as manufacturing, marketing, communications and other major elements of a company's operation." Over the past years, the potential benefits of BPM have repeatedly been addressed in management literature. Among the reported benefits we note: increased process efficiency [19], higher speed-to-market, cost effectiveness, enterprise process coordination [17], and strategic alignment [18, 20, 21]. One of the key factors in this case is the benefit of increased organizational flexibility: *"The documentation, improvement and automation of these processes as a result of various competitive and regulatory pressures should lessen the internal rigidity of organizations. Processes also serve as the link between an organization and its business partners. To the extent that inter-organizational processes are improved, documented and automated, one would expect that the ability of the firm to interact flexibly in its environment should be improved"*[3].

2.2   IT-Enabled Process Innovation

As IT becomes ubiquitous in society and companies it is inherently important for processes as well. In some environments process innovation relies on the potential to adapt within the underlying IT infrastructure. IT systems and infrastructure therefore need to be designed in such a way that it enhances an organisation's capability to innovate. Any process innovation effort needs to take into account the IT infrastructure it impacts as a factor that could either enable or hamper the chances to succeed. Mitchell and Zmud [22] incorporate under IT infrastructure all "enabling technologies, sourcing arrangements, and policies that form an intricate system of information-related activities." Getting a hold of such a system is quite difficult if its parts are scattered over a multitude of both internal and external parties. Each particular element could potentially make or break redesign efforts. So therefore, when the opportunity arises IT infrastructure should be designed in such a way that they enable rather than obstruct process innovation. Designing a robust business process goes often hand in hand with reviewing and redesigning major parts of the IT infrastructure which in itself can be an innovation [22]. In the SPOMS case the IT presence was undeniable and obviously the former IT infrastructure was not at all enabling innovation, rather the opposite. Therefore the IT department was involved early on leading to a solution that was not only supported but also driven by multiple departments - including IT - where all involved parties acknowledged that the IT infrastructure to be developed had to be not only efficient in the short term but also enabling growth and innovation in the long term. The infrastructure has thus become a dynamic capability [23] for Belgacom Mobile, allowing them to adapt to future market requirements.

Fig. 1. IT-enabled process innovation (adapted from Davenport, 1993)

Investing in IT backbone systems has a positive impact on the process innovation capability. Research by Kim and Kim [24] has shown that investing in IT to deal with dynamic business markets provides a competitive advantage through enhancing a firm's ability to innovate internal processes. Organisations that are able to adapt processes flexibly to changing environments hold an advantage over their less flexible competitors. These insights correspond with the statements by Stohr and zür Mühlen [3] that process flexibility allows organisations to "rapidly assume new competitive positions and to act proactively to achieve competitive advantage". A combination of optimised processes and smart supporting IT systems should result in opportunities to innovate service and product delivery, and to compete in fast changing environments. Process flexibility can help an organisation to deliver new products or services to the market as fast as possible and to react swiftly on market changes [3].

According to Davenport [17] IT has an impact on process innovation in several ways. IT brings opportunities to eliminate human labour from a process, to capture process information to better understand the process, to change the sequence of the process or enable parallel activities, to track the status of the process, to improve process analysis and decision making, to coordinate a complex process, to coordinate between tasks and processes, to capture and distribute knowledge and, finally, to eliminate intermediaries from the process. Many of these opportunities are supported by the SPOMS case.

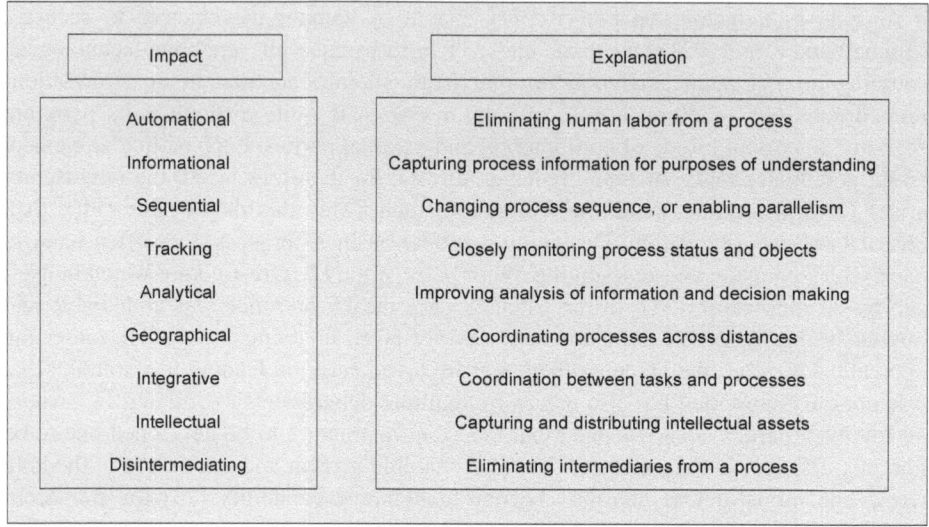

Impact	Explanation
Automational	Eliminating human labor from a process
Informational	Capturing process information for purposes of understanding
Sequential	Changing process sequence, or enabling parallelism
Tracking	Closely monitoring process status and objects
Analytical	Improving analysis of information and decision making
Geographical	Coordinating processes across distances
Integrative	Coordination between tasks and processes
Intellectual	Capturing and distributing intellectual assets
Disintermediating	Eliminating intermediaries from a process

Fig. 2. IT impact on process innovation (adapted from Davenport, 1993)

On the other hand Davenport [17] admits that IT can be a constraint for process efficiency and innovation. The SPOMS case shows that, if IT systems become too complex for example, they pose a barrier for the performance of the process. The SPOMS IT systems landscape is very complex and dispersed. It is often difficult, expensive and time-consuming to replace all legacy systems by a new one but that can be dealt with in an elegant way by opting for an architectural approach where the process is supported by an orchestrating instance (in this case the SPOMS dashboard) communicating with existing legacy systems and using them as a service.

Apart from technological conditions, a number of other conditions needs to be in place. Business processes are unlikely to be efficient and/or flexible if there is no clearly defined ownership, if the processes are not transparent, etc. A typical symptomatic problem, especially in larger organisations, is that all subsystems – i.e. departments, geographic regions, business units – act as islands in the organisation although they are supposed to function as one system. The issue gets even more of a barrier if business processes involve many 3rd party interventions, as in the SPOMS case [25]. Ever since large organisations have existed specialisation and integration have to be balanced. Working on process innovation should start from there. Process innovation efforts should not focus on mere automations of processes but on clarifying activities and roles and organising and optimising the allocation and execution of those. Hence, process innovation projects are both organisational adaptations and an IT infrastructure supporting that particular business process [22].

3   IT-Enabled Process Innovation at Work: SPOMS

For Belgacom Mobile, flexible and efficient core processes are a strategic objective. In order to be effective, a redesign effort should reconsider process activities and resources, and how they are conceived, planned and implemented [26]. Davenport [17] categorizes redesign projects as process innovations *"when they produce radically new configurations of assets and activities"*. If the innovation effort is characterized by a high degree of information technology (IT) involvement, it is described as 'IT-enabled innovation'.

In the SPOMS case, the need to drastically innovate the process and its underlying IT system was obvious. The burning platform for initiating the project was the imminent risk of a system breakdown, with considerable consequences for the entire ordering process and hence for the overall position of Belgacom Mobile in a highly competitive market with mobile customers. Given the evident need, the project could be approached simultaneously as an opportunity to make the SIM card future-proof, thanks to a flexible and scalable design. Business processes in an environment such as the business environment in which Belgacom Mobile operates, with a multitude of supporting IT systems, are highly interdependent. In such circumstances *"IT alters the ways in which people work and execute business processes, both within the enterprise and with business partners and customers"*[14]. As far as Belgacom is concerned, IT investments serve three purposes, which indicate the intended benefits accruing from IT: firstly, IT is an enabler for *running* the business (enabler); next, IT can help to *grow* the business (scalability); and lastly, IT has the ability to *transform* the business (flexibility). The SPOMS case could be regarded as an investment supporting each of these purposes.

Table 1. Three IT purposes at Belgacom (Source: Presentation by Mr Scott Alcott, Executive VP Operations, Belgacom Group, 22/02/2010, [27])

Short- **term**	**Run the business:** An indicator of how much of the IT resource is consumed and focused on the *continuing operation* of the business. This largely covers maintenance, renewal, and capacity-related expenditure.
	Grow the business: An indicator of how much of the IT resource is consumed and focused on *developing and enhancing* IT systems *in support of business growth* (typically organic growth). New projects are captured in this category.
Mid- **term**	**Transform the business:** An indicator of how much of the IT resource is consumed and focused on implementing technology systems that *support new business models, structurally reduce the total cost of ownership and create sustained efficiencies.*

3.1   The SPOMS Project

The SPOMS project scope included a myriad of processes, starting from master data creation in an ERP software module, up to the hand-over of the SIM card data to the Order Management System and IT integration domains, while incorporating many third parties outside Belgacom Mobile, such as SIM suppliers, product suppliers, logistics providers, Mobile Virtual Network Enablers (MVNEs)[1] and Direct Mobile Virtual Network Operators (MVNOs)[2]. Together these processes constitute the supply chain process for ordering SIM cards at Belgacom Mobile.

The SIM card supply chain process at Belgacom Mobile, as it formerly existed, still involved a lot of manual operations. SCM administrators were responsible for monitoring the entire process, keeping a spreadsheet overview based on a purchase order number reference, generated by the ERP software. Next, they had to send out a spreadsheet file with procurement details to a number of third parties such as distributors, suppliers, and packagers, each requiring different types of files. Therefore they had to rework the response file to the proper layout and in most cases send this new file by e-mail to the addressee. Generating these files manually was a time-consuming practice, leaving ample room for errors. Depending on the SIM card type, the procurement process could also differ, which further complicated the follow-up of the entire process. Errors could easily go unnoticed and remain unreported. Moreover, each party involved in the process had different ways of communicating with Belgacom Mobile. The process for special commercial campaigns had a total lead time of 3 months (i.e. from start-up of the campaign until stock is available to launch on the market). Finally, the process capacity was a limiting factor for the sales volume of SIM cards by Belgacom Mobile.

The imminent danger of a failure in the complex tangle of applications and entities posed a real threat to the business continuity of Belgacom Mobile. Errors in this core process could severely damage Belgacom's reputation and brand image. The emergency of the situation prompted Belgacom Mobile to assign a 'MUST DO' label to the SPOMS project, meaning it had strategic value for the company and was high on the priority agenda. The IT department and the marketing department agreed from the start that reengineering of SPOMS was a necessity and lent their full support to this project. The Supply Chain Manager and the external agency that was hired to execute the project opted from the start for an architectural end-to-end approach. Therefore, an IT project architect was involved in the project team early on. With reference to the 'old' process, the Supply Chain Manager stressed the urgent need for radical change: "We are currently facing a serious risk of business continuity failure. At the time, the market was growing and customers were becoming more demanding in terms of lead time. Frankly, I do not think we would have been able to cope much longer. We simply could not scale, let alone be more flexible." The SIM card Product Manager, being the main internal customer of SPOMS, acknowledges this: "At the

---

[1] MVNE: Mobile Virtual Network Operators enable the activation of the SIM cards on the network. This party needs to receive the technical information through an electronic file. Belgacom Mobile performs the procurement of the SIM cards, but the MVNE activates the SIM cards on the network.

[2] MVNO: A Mobile Virtual Network Operator is a provider of SIM cards that actually uses Belgacom Mobile services to operate. These operators receive SIM cards with a specific design from the logistics provider through the SIM card ordering process, but they do not receive the SIM card data in an electronic format. They are called virtual as they do not operate themselves, but use Belgacom Mobile as provider while using their own branding.

marketing side we were welcoming every attempt to considerably reduce the time-to-market for card introductions.

The business case for the SPOMS project included the following objectives:

1. Integration of the many departments and business partners
2. Reducing manual operations
3. Standardization
4. Decreasing total lead time
5. Increasing production process capacity

The basis for the set-up of SPOMS was inspired by several theoretical principles. These principles served as a general guideline for successfully redesigning and automating the process.

- Making the solution flexible to allow for adaptation to future requirements and reuse of existing components using the principles of Service-Oriented Architecture (SOA), web services and object-oriented programming where possible.
- Centralized approach to process governance and ownership, using a dashboard to act as a 'process orchestrator'.
- Making the processes product independent, thus building a product factory, to allow flexibility in designing new products in the day-to-day product innovation at Belgacom Mobile.

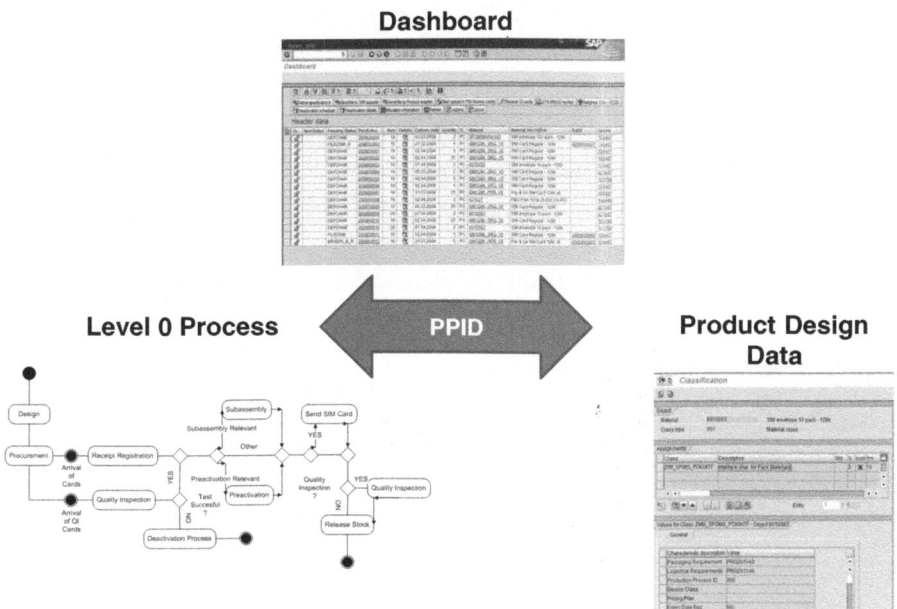

Fig. 3. Belgacom Mobile SIM card ordering process reengineering project overview

The SPOMS project presents two new features that are being introduced as innovations to the former process: the creation of a level zero process map as a representation of the as-is situation of the SIM card ordering and activation process (see figure 3), and the creation of the SPOMS dashboard in order to provide the user with an overview of all current purchase orders in the process (see figure 3).

3.2   An Architected Process Solution

First of all, the as-is process was critically examined and completely redesigned. The newly developed process model was described at the highest level by a generic level zero process that can be applied to all existing SIM cards types and can easily be adapted when new SIM card types are being introduced. Using the level zero process contributed to simplifying the SIM card ordering process and capturing all necessary steps in the entire business flow, regardless of the type of SIM card. This enabled Belgacom Mobile to separate the processes from the products, thus increasing effectiveness and enabling the definition of new products with specific process flows.

The idea behind the SPOMS concept was to create one general flow - the so-called level zero process - that can be applied in all cases and to all production processes (see figure 4). Because not every step in the level zero process needed to be performed for all of the production processes, guidelines had to be developed to indicate what steps were relevant in which cases. These decision points are saved in production process templates. For each production process ID, the actions to be performed are identified beforehand. When a SIM card resource or SIM pack is defined as a material in the ERP software, a production process ID needs to be assigned to it. This enables SPOMS to decide which paths to follow when ordering these materials.

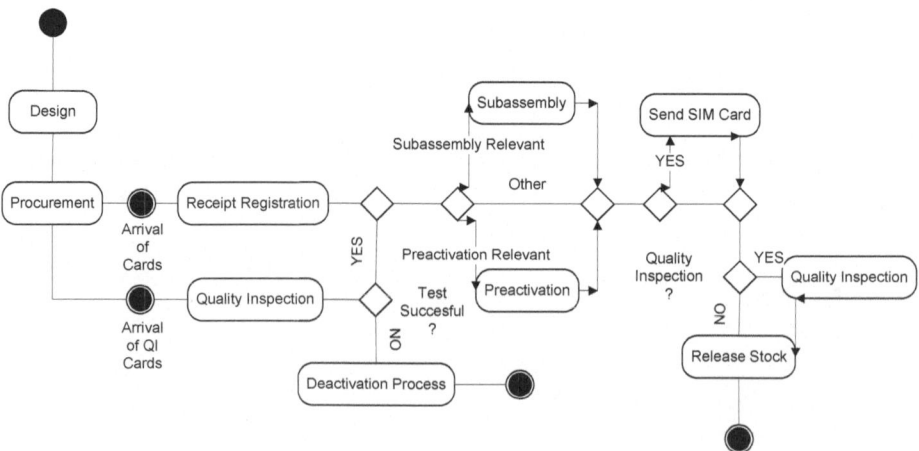

Fig. 4. The Level 0 Belgacom SIM card ordering process

The Logistics Manager explains the new process as follows: "This new process is nothing like the old one. Before, we had no real overview of the status of orders for new cards, responsibilities were not centralized, and everyone seemed to be constantly working in fire-fighting mode. We managed to reengineer what used to be a very complex and burdensome business process with a lot of manual interventions to an almost fully automated, streamlined and transparent process that not only interconnects internal departments but also some external partners."

3.3   Centralized Process Governance

Secondly, the installation of a dashboard was an important project milestone. The purpose of the dashboard was to provide a single screen overview of all purchase orders currently in progress and to become the primary tool for steering the process. The dashboard would provide the tools for one-click generation of the input files for suppliers, starting the pre-activation scheduling, adding order-specific characteristics such as serial numbers, et cetera. Every step of the SIM card ordering process has been added as a status to the dashboard, which enables the user to view up-to-date and accurate status information for each purchase order item line.

The SPOMS dashboard is the core component of the SPOMS solution. It is the heart of SPOMS, from which most of the functionalities in the process can be accessed in an easy and intuitive way. The dashboard acts as a 'process orchestrator', and is the leading application triggering actions throughout the entire process by means of web services. The dashboard also keeps track of the status of interfaces and actions in the ERP system and in related internal and external systems. All interfaces that leave or enter SPOMS update the relevant dashboard statuses for the individual purchase order items.

The dashboard is the main tool for Logistics to perform the day-to-day follow-up of the SIM card procurement process, as it shows the status in ordering, production, quality testing and delivery of SIM cards and SIM products (or packs). The SPOMS dashboard was conceived as a native ERP transaction screen, retaining the same look and feel as the other ERP transactions.

The main purposes of the SPOMS dashboard can be summarized as follows:

- To be the main tool for the SIM card purchasing follow-up on a daily basis, visualizing the purchase order item status throughout the entire process.
- To be the orchestrator of the SIM card ordering process, triggering all the actions needed to complete the process.

Integrating the level zero process and the dashboard functionality, however, implied an optimisation of the current master data creation procedure. For each SIM card production process type (PPID), a template was prepared specifying the dashboard functionalities and statuses that are relevant for that particular template. For each newly developed SIM card, the template already defines which process steps the card will have to go through. Furthermore, the technical approach adopted for the SPOMS project assured that all the SIM card data formatting and mediation required by the level zero process to interface with other technical components of Belgacom Mobile and the various third parties, are performed correctly and in a secure way.

3.4   Project Implementation Challenges

Due to the complexity of the systems integration, the project presented multiple challenges. On the architectural level, two major challenges had to be addressed. First and foremost, data consistency had to be carefully safeguarded between all of the integrating systems. Secondly, all sub-processes needed to be aligned and the possibility to initiate, follow up and perform error handling had to be integrated. In order to cope with these challenges, the decision was made to adopt a process orchestration or centralized process approach, rather than a decentralized process approach. Process orchestration implies that the process is fully controlled and organized from one central location, and that every action/service reports back to the process controller. As shown in figure 1, for the SIM card ordering process, all actions are initiated and followed up in the SIM Card Ordering Dashboard, which acts as the process controller.

This orchestrated way of working for SPOMS provides the following advantages:

- A status overview in the ERP system was established showing the current process phase. Every process step taken in a different environment reports back to the controller dashboard as soon as that process step is completed or when an error occurs. This ensures that the processes are perfectly aligned as there is one central controller controlling the entire process.
- New actions can only be initiated from the controller dashboard. As a result decisions regarding the process flow to be followed can only be made from one central point, instead of having other systems performing consecutive actions and reporting back only after a number of actions have been completed.
- Errors are immediately reported to the controller, which allows commencing error handling in a virtually online mode.

"We in marketing are now completely responsible for the SIM card ordering management process," stresses the SIM card Product Manager. "Not only do we control the process input, we can also reconfigure it for new SIM card types. If anything, the innovated SPOMS process has put an end to the situation where the responsibility for errors was shunted back and forth between departments. With the SPOMS dashboard we can monitor the status of the outstanding orders in real time, and the system warns us immediately when there is a problem somewhere along the chain. Now, we can manage the entire process in a much more focused way."

4   Accomplishments: IT-Enabled Innovation Rewarded

The performance of the redesigned and automated process was reviewed in May 2009. Data gathered from January to April 2009 were compared with data collected over the same period in 2008. As the renewed SPOMS went live in October 2008, it was considered that enough time had elapsed to gain experience and further refine the process before starting the comparison. The old and new SPOMS were compared based on the following criteria:

4.1   Increased SIM Card Production Capacity

The total number of SIM cards introduced onto the market after creation of a purchase order, has remained the same. The reason for this can be found in the market demand, which has slowed down because of the economic crisis. Nonetheless, we note that the process capacity has increased substantially.

The architectural approach provides for flexible up- and downscaling without any hassle. Development of new applications is far easier in service-oriented environments because these allow for flexible reuse of service components (Weske, 2007).

4.2   Shorter Lead Time from Purchase Order Creation Until Ready for Delivery to the Market

The lead time of the entire production process was reduced significantly. For every 100,000 SIM cards produced, 23 working days have been gained, i.e. a lead time reduction of approximately 1 month per 100,000 cards. This time saving is the result of a reduction of the time needed to develop and send the SIM card production request file to the SIM supplier. In the redesigned SPOMS no manual intervention is needed to create the request file, as opposed to the former SPOMS.

The Supply Chain Administrator can now give priority to marketing actions if needed. In 2008, for every preactivation a ticket had to be created for requesting this preactivation and time-consuming communication was needed in order to update the schedule. This has now been automated and centralized at the level of the process owner, who makes the decisions and manages the entire process. Next to the process optimization by the scheduler, also the capacity of the preactivation system has increased.

4.3   Shorter Total Lead Time of Marketing Actions, from Defining a New Card Layout Until Ready for Delivery to the Market

Given the shorter production lead time (see above), the total lead time is also considerably reduced. When considering the total lead time of marketing actions, we note that in 2008 a marketing action was initiated 3 months before the planned deadline, whereas in 2009 an action could still be approved until 6 weeks before the scheduled date. The reasons for this are the shorter production lead time on one the hand (reduction of 1 month), and the faster definition of the card, which is now a transparent process that can be carried out by means of master data creation, on the other hand.

4.4   Reduction of Workload in the Supply Chain Department

Within the supply chain team an 80% reduction of FTE involvement in SPOMS has been realized, allowing FTEs to be reallocated to other activities in the department. Furthermore, the automation of the entire process has also significantly reduced the workload in all other departments involved, because the process is far less complex and error-prone than before.

In general, due to the shorter total lead time, Belgacom Mobile can respond much faster to market demands for promotional actions, which benefits overall competitiveness. Secondly, the internal stress level, caused by barely being able to meet the deadlines of a marketing action, has dropped noticeably. This is mainly the result of the shorter total lead time, which allows for a better planning and faster go-to-market, smoother communication between all parties and reduced manual follow-up of actions.

5   Lessons Learned

5.1   Lesson 1: The Product Factory for Process Flexibility

During the reengineering project, some important lessons were learned that may prove valuable for future process reengineering projects. First of all, a major breakthrough was realized by separating product and process by means of the Product Factory concept. The key benefit of this approach is long-term process flexibility, which allows for product innovation without consequently having to change the process or having to install a new process. The reusability of the solution concept for other applications is another added bonus that comes with the application of SOA.

5.2   Lesson 2: Combining Process Thinking (BPM) and Architecture (SOA) for IT-Enabled Process Innovation

Secondly, the SPOMS case at Belgacom clearly highlights the potential of a process-oriented approach combined with architectural principles. The Logistics Manager comments: "This project has really convinced me of the importance of process thinking and architecting for this company. It was remarkable to see project participants ponder the impact of the decisions we made throughout the SPOMS project on other departments (even beyond the ones involved in the project) – which is quite unique. Some of this end-to-end thinking has led us to add additional peripheral processes to the original scope of the project." He adds: "Our choice for an architected approach has enabled us to unravel the enormous complexity of this business process. The investment in business process modeling has resulted in transparency, which helped us to make sure that we did not overlook any important aspects. The architectural approach we adopted provided the necessary scalability and flexibility. It did take almost a year to map all of the requirements, but this effort certainly paid off in terms of efficiency and sustainability."

5.3   Lesson 3: Project Management

In terms of project management the project lived up to the expectations. The scope remained virtually unchanged during the entire project, and the project was completed on time and even on budget. Critical to this success were the well formulated business requirements, the strong business case, and great collaboration between all of the parties involved. As the project sponsor, the Logistics Manager made sure that the initial project scope and architecture were not compromised by superfluous 'nice-to-haves'. The SIM card Product Manager testifies to this: "Indeed, from a marketing perspective we tend to push for more features all the time. But the project sponsor was always there to challenge the necessity of these extras from the viewpoint of the initial business case and verified if they really fitted within the solution architecture. This resulted in a solution that is highly efficient, but can still be leveraged for future use." The IT Project Architect responsible for designing and implementing a solid technical solution, agrees: "This was one of these projects that was actually completed on time, on budget and without major scope adjustments. The fact that a sound business case and analysis were developed and carried out prior to the project launch really proved worthwhile. We knew why we were doing it and what we were getting ourselves into."

6   Conclusion

Over the years, Belgacom Mobile's market position has come under increasing pressure due to fierce competition and changing customer demands. As the Telco sector is highly turbulent and known for its fast technological advances, flexible people and processes are crucial for keeping up with the competition. For marketing purposes it is extremely important to be able to launch SIM card campaigns as quickly as possible. In addition, the risk of process failure may affect Belgacom Mobile's brand image and market position. The SIM card order management process is therefore a core process for Belgacom Mobile and its reliable functioning is therefore an asset to the company as a whole.

The Logistics Manager sums up the achievements of the SPOMS project: "We have put a lot of hard work in SPOMS. We have prepared exceptionally well with a very strong team of people combining different backgrounds. The result is a truly versatile and solid new business process supported by tools that enable the front-line staff to provide the efficiency and flexibility our markets require. This IT-enabled business process innovation is actually the result of a combination of end-to-end thinking, team work, results orientation and, last but not least, an architectural approach to support not just sustainability of a technical solution but also design freedom for product managers."

This paper contributes to the general understanding of combining an architectural approach with BPM in the frame of IT-enabled improvement projects. Managers gain a deeper insight into how process reengineering can enhance process flexibility and thus create room for product innovation generating benefits that go beyond mere internal efficiency gains. In general, due to the reduced total lead time, Belgacom Mobile can respond more quickly to market demands for promotional actions. This has strengthened the company's competitive position. In terms of project management, the SPOMS project stands out because it was completed on time and on budget, without major scope adjustments. Moreover, project insiders indicated a close collaboration between several business departments and the IT department as a key factor to the project's success. Ultimately, the new SPOMS process promises to deliver not only operational benefits, but also maximum process flexibility for new products to be introduced, which is one of the main drivers in the turbulent telecommunications sector. Furthermore, this case provides evidence of the business value of IT-enabled process innovation and BPM investments, a missing link in literature.

Acknowledgements. The authors wish to thank Belgacom Mobile executives Johan Verbeeck, Pascal Masuit, John-David Hendrickx, Scott Alcott and Laurent Claus for their valuable contributions to this work and for the possibility to look into this exceptional case. Furthermore we express our gratitude to Bert Van Genechten, a Delaware consultant.

References

1. Becker, J., Kugeler, M., Rosemann, M.: Process Management: A Guide for the Design of Business Processes. Springer, Berlin (2004)
2. Weske, M.: Business Process Management: Concepts, Languages, Architectures. Springer, Heidelberg (2007)
3. zür Muehlen, M., Stohr, E.A.: Business Process Management: Impact on Organizational Flexibility. Global Journal of Flexible Systems Management 9(4), iii–v (2008)
4. Beimborn, D., Nils, J., Weitzel, T.: Drivers and Inhibitors of SOA Business Value – Conceptualizing a Research Model. In: Proceedings of the Fourteenth Americas Conference on Information Systems, Toronto, Canada (August 2008)
5. Trkman, P., Kovačič, A., Popovič, A.: SOA Adoption Phases: A Case Study. Business & Information Systems Engineering 3(4), 211–220 (2011)
6. Behara, G.K.: BPM and SOA: a strategic alliance. BP Trends (May 2006)
7. Carter, S.: The role of Business Process Management in SOA. DM Review 17(5) (2007)
8. Malinverno, P., Hill, J.B.: BPM and SOA are better together. Gartner Research Report (2007)
9. Walker, L.: IBM business transformation enabled by service-oriented architecture. IBM Systems Journal 46(4), 651–667 (2007)
10. Brahe, S.: BPM on Top of SOA: Experiences from the Financial Industry. In: Alonso, G., Dadam, P., Rosemann, M. (eds.) BPM 2007. LNCS, vol. 4714, pp. 96–111. Springer, Heidelberg (2007)
11. Conlon, S.J., Hale, J.G., Lukose, S., Strong, J.: Information Extraction Agents For Service Oriented Architecture Using Web Service Systems: A Framework. Journal of Computer Information Systems 48(3), 74–83 (2008)
12. Sidorova, A., Isik, O.: Business process research: a cross-disciplinary review. Business Process Management Journal 16(4), 566–597 (2010)
13. Becker, A., Widjaja, T., Buxmann, P.: Value Potentials and Challenges of Service-Oriented Architectures. Business & Information Systems Engineering 3(4), 199–210 (2011)

14. El Sawy, O.A., Pavlou, P.A.: IT-Enabled Business Capabilities for Turbulent Environments. MIS Quarterly Executive 7(3), 139–150 (2008)
15. Bell, A.E.: From the Front Lines DOA with SOA. Communications of the ACM 51(10), 27–28 (2008)
16. Baskerville, R., Cavallari, M., Hjort-Madsen, K., Pries-Heje, J., Sorrentino, M., Virili, F.: Extensible Architectures: The Strategic Value of Service-Oriented Architecture in Banking. In: Proceedings of the 13th European Conference on Information Systems, Regensburg, Germany (2005)
17. Davenport, T.H.: Process Innovation: Re-engineering Work Through Information Technology. Harvard Business School Press, Boston (1993)
18. Zairi, M.: Business process management: a boundaryless approach to modern competitiveness. Business Process Management Journal 3(1), 64–80 (1997)
19. Harmon, P.: Business Process Change: A guide for business managers and BPM and Six Sigma professionals, 2nd edn. MK Publishers (2007)
20. Lee, R.G., Dale, B.G.: Business Process Management: a review and evaluation. Business Process Management Journal 4(3), 214–225 (1998)
21. Hammer, M., Champy, J.: Reengineering the corporation, 1st edn. Harper Business, New York (1993)
22. Mitchell, V.L., Zmud, R.W.: The effects of coupling IT and work process strategies in redesign projects. Organization Science 10, 424–438 (1999)
23. Eisenhardt, K., Martin, J.: Dynamic Capabilities: what are they? Strategic Management Journal 21(10/11), 1105–1121 (2000)
24. Kim, J.W., Kim, E.W.: The Impacts of IT Investment Directions and Strategies of Supply Chain Management Implementing Enterprises on Business Performance. International Journal of Business Research 9(4), 126–137 (2009)
25. Lawrence, P.R., Lorsch, J.W.: Differentiation and Integration in Complex Organizations. Administrative Science Quarterly 12(1), 1–47 (1967)
26. Damanpour, F.: Organizational innovation: a meta-analysis of effects of determinants and moderators. Academy of Management Journal 34(3), 555–590 (1991)
27. Alcott, S.: Presentation by Mr. Scott Alcott, Executive VP Operations. Belgacom Group, at a 'We Invite for You' session (February 22, 2010)

IT Landscape Management Using Network Analysis

Daniel Simon[1] and Kai Fischbach[2]

[1] Department of Information Systems and Information Management, University of Cologne
simon@wim.uni-koeln.de
[2] Chair in Information Systems and Social Networks, University of Bamberg
kai.fischbach@uni-bamberg.de

Abstract. Dependency analyses have become crucial in today's enterprise architecture practices, which usually face complex IT landscapes with highly interdependent applications. In such environments, a deep understanding of the application's context is essential to determine its qualities and project its further evolution. However, method support for making this context a tangible IT landscape management part and thus facilitating quantitative decision making still seems expandable. Based on the representation as a network of applications and their relations of data exchange, this paper therefore suggests ways to support the IT landscape's examination through network analysis. We develop this approach based on a combination of theoretical explanations, past empirical findings, and experiences taken from the architecture practices of four sample organizations. We illustrate and evaluate our approach with a short case study. Our approach, developed and illustrated in close alignment with insights from actual practice, thus offers ideas and advice for researchers and practitioners alike.

Keywords: IT landscape management, enterprise architecture management, dependency analysis, network analysis, network centrality

1   Introduction

Complex information technology (IT) landscapes of hundreds or even thousands of business and infrastructure applications (cf. [1]) have become commonplace in many organizations. As a result, applications today, more than ever before, cannot be treated individually; rather, they can be fully understood only in the context of their environment – a basic principle of systems thinking [2]. As an interwoven system of applications (cf. [3]), that is, as a specific "collection of components organized to accomplish ... a set of functions" [1], the IT landscape is thus subject to a variety of inherent relations and dependencies. Together, these interrelationships form an essential part of the overall architecture of such a system, which represents its "fundamental concepts or properties ... in its environment embodied in its elements, relationships, and the principles of its design and evolution" [4].

For a managed evolution of the constituents of the business and IT landscape, including their interdependencies, many organizations have thus implemented enterprise architecture (EA) management practices. Relevant techniques for these

G. Poels (Ed.): CONFENIS 2012, LNBIP 139, pp. 18–34, 2013.
© IFIP International Federation for Information Processing 2013

practices include, in particular, regular "neighbourhood analyses" [5] for evaluating applications in their current state, while considering their position in the overall IT environment, and for preparing for architectural impacts across the IT landscape in case of intended application changes, especially of those with high system relevance.

Although the importance of such dependency analyses is now recognized, they seem only partially implemented in EA practices, as Aier et al. [6] discovered in their state-of-the-art survey of EA professionals. In their conclusion, they call for greater methodical support for such analyses. Therefore, the creation of a greater operationalization of systems thinking in EA management, that is, the ability to make more "tangible" the context of relationships and, in particular, the interaction of specific parts with the whole, may need to come to the core of future research.

At the same time, network analysis (NA) comes into more widespread use to explore complex phenomena, for example, at the social, political, economic, and organizational levels. This includes, for example, the interpretation of network structures to discover collaboration patterns within and across organizational boundaries and then correlate these patterns with the performance of individuals or entire groups. In line with the holistic nature of systems thinking, NA is based on the assumption that actors (represented as nodes) are interdependent and that relations (represented as edges) between actors provide access to specific resources [7].

With that in mind, similar considerations can be made at the level of IT applications that support the business tasks of specific users. In fact, one may view the IT landscape as a network of applications (the actors) linked by their inter-dependencies (the edges); the emergent structure reflects dependencies in the work of different stakeholders in the enterprise and manifests their patterns of collaboration.

In this paper, we thus introduce NA into the examination of IT landscapes and explore the research question of how NA measures can support IT landscape management (IT LM). Our findings show that using such metrics from NA may contribute significantly to an increased understanding of applications and their context and substantiate assessments at several points in the IT LM process. Our study thus contributes to the advancement of IT LM method support motivated above.

The remainder of this paper is structured as follows. Section 2 surveys earlier research into the use of NA for IT LM purposes. Section 3 provides the paper's conceptual foundation and introduces relevant NA measures. Section 4 then develops our theoretical concept and discusses the metrics' meaningfulness in IT LM. In Section 5, we put these theoretical thoughts to the test and present the case of an insurance company, the IT landscape of which we studied using NA to gain insights into certain properties both of specific applications and the landscape as a whole. We close the paper with our conclusions and an outlook on future work in Section 6.

2 Related Work

There is little research dealing with the application of NA means to IT LM. The works closest to ours are those of Dreyfus and Iyer [8, 9] and Iyer et al. [10], who also adopt a network perspective on IT architecture. Given limited resources, they argue, it is important to identify a subset of components of the overall architecture (macro architecture) that are to be controlled or actively managed. They distinguish between intrinsically important components that may, for example, support critical business tasks, represent large investments, or have a large number of users and thus are most often the focus of decision makers, and components that are important because of their positions in the larger network of interdependent components. They call the latter architectural control points, the control of which allows decision makers to influence the evolution of the architecture toward ongoing support of the business goals. These architectural control points, however, are considered moving targets given regular changes in the architecture. So, this is where active management is needed; in their studies, the authors (among others) find that architectural thinking in the form of rules guiding the emergence reduces the decline in control of key nodes.

According to the authors, these key nodes, which may adversely affect the network as a whole if they fail, can be identified using network centrality measures (also see [11]). In addition, the authors argue that NA can help enterprise architects identify the shared core, that is, the set of components used by most other components, and also the best decomposition of a set of components that minimizes dependencies across architectural clusters while maximizing dependencies within a cluster. Aier and Schönherr [12] focus on the latter in greater detail and present an algorithm-based modeling approach that adopts NA concepts to define service domains and support the design of a service-oriented architecture.

All in all, though, the use of NA in IT LM has not yet been made systematic and has not been detailed in terms of which network centrality measures can help gain what insights into the IT landscape and single applications. That lack is what motivating our research. We ground our study in the work of Simon et al. [13], which offers a framework for IT LM and suggests, among other things, a set of basic dimensions for application analysis, including risk, value, and complexity.

3   Conceptual Foundation: Measures of Network Analysis

Before exploring the use of NA in IT LM, we here set the conceptual foundation of our work, introducing basic concepts of NA and clarifying their meaning in our context. Rooted in graph theory, NA conceptualizes and visualizes structures that emerge from any interaction or connection as networks and allows a quantitative analysis of the network nodes' relationships (cf. [7]).

As indicated, the representation of the IT landscape as a network of nodes and edges is central to our approach. Nodes represent applications, which we consider executable software components that support business functions [1, 9]; edges represent relationships and interdependencies between applications. In general, these relationships can take different forms, that is, there are multiple possible definitions of what constitutes a link (cf. [14]). For example, links may indicate the same vendor or supporting technology of different software components; alternatively, they may also represent physical interfaces between applications. In our interpretation, edges represent data exchange/flow; as such, they can be considered logical interfaces between applications. In this model, two nodes are linked if they exchange data; in other words, one application depends on the other application for data.

In this study, we use different centrality measures to examine both the characteristics of such a network as a whole, that is, the structural patterns of interaction between applications, and the role and distinctive position of individual applications within the overall landscape (exemplary real-life figures are provided in Section 5).

Degree centrality (C_D) represents the number of relations of a given node and thus indicates the degree of "activity" [7, 15, 16] of applications within the IT landscape. Formally, it can be defined as follows:

$$C_D(i) = \sum_j x_{ij} \tag{1}$$

where x_{ij} equals 1 if there is a link between applications i and j, and $x_{ij} = 0$ otherwise. Using directed ties, we can also distinguish in-degree (C_{In-D}) and out-degree centrality (C_{Out-D}) and thus account for the extent to which an application provides or consumes data.

Closeness centrality (C_C) measures the geodesic distance of a given node to all other nodes in the network [7, 15, 16]. The node that can reach all other nodes in the fewest steps is most central. C_C can be formalized as

$$C_C(i) = \frac{1}{\sum_j d_{ij}} \tag{2}$$

where d_{ij} is the number of links in a shortest path from application i to j ($i \neq j$).

Betweenness centrality (C_B) represents the "number of shortest paths that pass through a given node" [7, 15, 16] and therefore indicates whether an application plays some kind of a gatekeeper function, controlling data exchange in the overall network. In mathematical terms, it can be written as

$$C_B(i) = \sum_{j,k} \frac{g_{jik}}{g_{jk}} \tag{3}$$

where g_{jk} denotes the number of shortest paths from application j to k ($j, k \neq i$), and g_{jik} is the number of shortest paths from application j to k passing through application i. Normalization results in values of between 0 and 1. In contrast to C_D, C_B thus also considers indirect relationships in the network, since here the position between other nodes is relevant.

The consideration of indirect relationships is also true for eigenvector centrality (C_E), which quantifies the extent to which nodes are connected to other central nodes in the network [17]. For computing this measure for a given node, the relationships to other nodes are thus weighed based on these nodes' centralities:

$$C_E(i) = \frac{1}{\lambda} \sum_j x_{ij} C_E(j) \tag{4}$$

where $x_{ij} = 1$ if applications i and j are connected, and $x_{ij} = 0$ otherwise, and λ is the largest eigenvalue of the adjacency matrix X.

Eventually, we also consider overall graph density (as the number of edges divided by the maximum number of edges in a full graph), modularity (as the number of edges falling within groups minus the expected number in an equivalent network with edges placed at random) [18], and the clustering coefficient (the average fraction of a node's neighbors that are also neighbors of one another) [19] as global measures for gaining insights into the IT landscape as a whole.

4   The Role of Network Analysis in IT Landscape Management

Based on the representation of applications and their data exchange as a network of nodes and (directed) edges, we now theorize about application scenarios of NA in IT LM and the role of the network metrics just discussed. Two main inputs provided the basis for this exploration, namely a thorough analysis of the literature and information extracted from four architecture practices (see below), both of which we used to first identify and structure activities and variables to be examined in IT LM. To figure out the potential role of NA metrics, we employ a combination of theoretical explanations (i.e., logical reasoning), empirical findings from the literature (e.g., the relationship between application costs and the number of interdependencies), and own empirical evidence about application evaluation (e.g., complexity is typically measured by the number of applications and dependencies) as captured in the personal experiences of the first author (cf. [20]), who has direct knowledge of the architecture practices of a sample of four organizations in the insurance, banking, pharmaceuticals, and public sectors (two operating worldwide, and the others focusing on the German market). In terms of the empirical reasoning, we thus base our discussion on a meaningful combination of convenience sampling (sample selected from this author's practice) and purposive sampling (sample of organizations of different types, e.g., industry sector, size, and geographic scope) [21] to point to opportunities to incorporate means of NA in architectural activities. The four reference practices have an age of at least two years and are part of IT organizations employing between 500 and 1400 people. They also had defined EA processes in which IT LM was part of the scope.

Metrics may play an important role in IT LM; this is in line with De Marco [22], who writes that "you cannot control what you cannot measure." In general, the NA measures introduced represent reasonable instruments in the given context, as they meet the required properties for IT LM metrics identified in [23]: they are basically well understood and have a communicable meaning (see preceding section). This allows for achieving the main goal of using metrics [23]: the communication of actual facts regarding the status quo and future potential. Specifically, the NA measures allow an evaluation that is objective in nature and considers related elements from the overall context rather than relying on subjective ratings by individual experts.

Architectural views and evaluations are of crucial relevance in several EA management tasks, and at different levels of abstraction (cf. [1, 24]). Scenarios of using network measures and views for characterizing the IT landscape and its applications may thus exist across the entire EA lifecycle through which EA elements are driven: documentation; analysis; planning and decision making; implementation; and governance [5, 13]. We explore this in detail in the following subsections.

4.1   IT Landscape Documentation

As for architectural documentation, it is common practice to partition and refine the overall EA into more detailed domain architectures that cover specific segments (e.g., marketing and sales) of the enterprise and allow the distribution of architectural work in large enterprises. Within the limited scope of these domain architectures, dedicated domain architects may also become responsible for further architecture developments [1, 25]. However, the accountability still remains at the level of the enterprise architect; larger changes within the IT landscape of a specific domain may affect the overall enterprise or may be subject to interdependencies with other domains.

Once a strategic initiative at the domain level results in issuance of a request for architecture work that involves a further development of the domain's IT landscape, typically starting with the documentation of the current state, two of our reference practices thus check the extent to which the enterprise architect needs to be involved in that endeavor. The involvement may be restricted to certain governance activities, but may also require close participation in the IT LM process. Criteria being checked to determine the degree of EA involvement include, for example, the domain landscape's complexity, as indicated by the number of applications and dependencies, and the initiative's cross-functional character, as represented by the existence of applications that are used across several business processes and organizational units.

In practice, this check is often completed using rough and subjective estimations; given the above criteria, NA measures may represent more reliable indicators. Assuming that cross-functional applications (e.g., enterprise resource planning) are part of the landscape's shared core and thus are connected to many other applications either directly or at least indirectly, C_C seems a reasonable measure for indicating the initiative's cross-functional character as it can capture the mean distance of an application to all others. Depending on the number of applications with a C_C value that exceeds a pre-defined threshold, the decision about the EA involvement could be made. In addition, one would evaluate the landscape's complexity; there, the average C_D value of the domain's applications, that is, the average number of their relations (cf. [26]), seems an appropriate measure, given the relevance of the number of dependencies for this criterion.

If there is already a documented state of the domain landscape, C_C and C_D can be calculated in a pre-state of actual IT LM activities so that enterprise architects can already be involved in the documentation phase (in this case, restricted to updating activities) if considered necessary due to high centrality values; otherwise, the involvement check would be completed once one has passed through this phase.

With a documented state of the overall landscape, one can also check whether the clusters that may have emerged in the actual network of applications are consistent with the pre-defined structure of domains, which are most often derived based on means of functional decomposition [27] and should thus group close to each other those elements that are cohesive and related [24, 25] (e.g., recruiting and human resource development). As a result, there should be maximal dependencies within a domain, but minimal dependencies across different domains. This can be validated by using network views of the IT landscape and by calculating, for example, the sum of the edges within a domain compared to the sum of the edges to components of other domains. An alternative is to calculate average C_C at the intra-domain level and compare it to the inter-domain value. In addition, one may use global modularity, which indicates the number of communities within the network, and the clustering coefficient, which considers how nodes are embedded in their neighborhood and thus provides an overall indication of the network clustering.

If the actual clusters represented by the existing relationships and derived from NA are not at all in line with the domain structure, one may not have achieved the best decomposition, that is, one that allows a relatively independent management with a clear scope of responsibility. By applying the approach depicted in [12] and removing edges with highest C_B (as the number of shortest paths between pairs of vertices that run along it) until separate communities emerge, one may find a more suitable structure. However, an inconsistency between the domain structure and any results from NA may not necessarily reflect an improper decomposition, but may also point to a state, in which there are some domains with several redundant applications and thus more relations to other domains if there was only one of these applications in place. This leads us to the next main step in the process – the IT landscape's analysis.

4.2   IT Landscape Analysis

Generally, analyzing the current IT landscape aims at capturing the condition of both the landscape as a whole and each application individually. It has been acknowledged that the overall landscape's condition is determined to a significant degree by its complexity and modifiability [13, 28]. Landscape complexity is related closely to the overall number of interdependencies within the landscape [14, 28]. Similarly, landscape modifiability can be explained by the average coupling between applications, that is, the average number of relationships of service consumption and provision [26]. To quantify these qualities, network density and average C_D thus seem simple but promising instruments that could help in establishing adequate metrics at the landscape level, which apparently have not yet permeated practice [5], as also reflected in our sample.

NA metrics may also serve as reasonable indicators for some of the attributes that are relevant for individual application analysis [13]. Applications are typically analyzed in terms of their associated risks. Therefore, one may differentiate between risk cause (i.e., factors that increase the probability of the risk event), risk event (i.e., the risk itself, associated with a certain probability), and risk impact [1, 29, 30]. In simple terms, the risk event describes an application failure in terms of its availability (including, e.g., performance, reliability), confidentiality, and integrity, or, from a long-term perspective, states of insufficient maintainability and modifiability/ adaptability to keep the application performing as expected and required and able to adapt to changing requirements [1, 31, 32, 33]. The risk impact can be manifold; in terms of the effects of non-availability, the insurance reference practice distinguishes productivity, monetary, and immaterial losses (negative impact on, e.g., customer satisfaction, image, or regulatory compliance), together denoted as the criticality of IT applications. For each dimension, applications are rated using a simple ordinal scale, the stages of which represent some sort of risk classes within this dimension.

What is not considered explicitly in these figures, however, is the context of a given application. Obviously, when applications occupy a central position in relation to their context of related applications, they can influence their environment (maybe even the network as a whole) negatively [32]. To estimate such impacts in terms of the scope of failure, network centrality measures thus seem appropriate instruments. One way of operationalizing possible effects of application failure on other applications is C_{Out-D}, which represents the number of applications that the given application must provide with data; actually, the average value may indicate the extent to which the overall landscape is prone to failure propagation. C_E may offer more specific insights into potential negative effects, taking into account the centrality of the related applications themselves; for example, the failure of an application that provides presumably central applications such as customer relationship management and contract management with data may be more severe than that of one primarily related to rather peripheral applications such as travel expense accounting. Eventually, using C_B allows the identification of applications whose failure could have a negative affect on the coaction of other applications or entire clusters of applications (consider, for example, an inventory management application, which may be required to have a working process from order management to billing); in the worst case, the failure of applications of high C_B could result in clusters falling apart. Network metrics can thus serve to give adequate consideration to an application's context in risk impact analysis and to complement the single-application-centric analysis of criticality with context-related variables represented by network centralities (in the example above, possibly by establishing another dimension with a dedicated network impact factor).

The cause of the risk also seems related closely to the context in which a given application operates. On the one hand, this is due to the influence other applications may exert on an application in terms of the data it consumes, as indicated by C_{In-D}. So, failures of other applications that provide certain data may, in turn, contribute to the risk of a given application, due to its availability or performance that might be negatively affected. On the other hand, the flexibility of application change may also be influenced by connections, whether ingoing or outgoing, to other applications [13, 28]. This has also been observed in [11], where it is shown that increased component coupling, as a measure of the degree of dependency between one software component and all others, is associated with decreased flexibility. For the purpose of measurement, C_D works as a direct indicator, whereas C_C may be used alike, as it indicates a component's distance to all others and thus its extent of being coupled.

Another attribute for which the network position is relevant is the cost of an application. According to [14], application costs are affected significantly by the number of the application's interdependencies (the higher the interdependencies, the higher its operations and maintenance costs). In line with these insights, an application's C_D appears to be a helpful indicator for evaluating costs; while it does not provide cost figures itself, it may be used to provide a proper indication. This seems reasonable, particularly where detailed cost calculations are not part of the scope of EA activities or are difficult to obtain from IT controlling, for example, due to a different level of abstraction used for controlling purposes – a challenge that one reference practice faces in particular. A straightforward alternative could be to group applications into C_D classes and use this classification as a type of cost indicator.

Application value is a particularly important attribute for analysis, because it is only when an application is critical to success that weaknesses in other aspects such as technical health or operational performance may become particularly relevant [5]. In general, application value can be analyzed along different dimensions such as strategic (e.g., support of business strategy) (cf. [34]), operational (e.g., cycle time reductions) and financial (e.g., contribution to revenue generation) dimensions [13] – an approach basically shared by two of our reference practices. As for the operational dimension, C_B seems an adequate evaluation metric given that applications can be considered especially valuable if they occupy a central position within one (or several) business process(es) and may, for example, somewhat control the data exchange therein. This offers an alternative to the approach of our sample insurance company, for example, where we found a scale used for measuring the operational application value, ranging from "the support of only a small part of process steps" to "the support of all relevant process steps" but without consideration of the application's power of control.

The strategic fit of an application is another attribute, where a current state may be measured by network characteristics. This is because today's strategic directives most often embrace some statements representing a certain pursuit of standardization; this is the case in our four sample practices, where we also find this reflected in their architecture principles (as the general rules and guidelines of architecture work [1]). These may conflict with the existence of several applications with many interrelationships, as represented by their C_D; at least in networks that include representations of elements such as an enterprise service bus (ESB) as nodes, such high C_D values point to a high number of remaining peer-to-peer interfaces (as the use of an ESB would typically suggest an encapsulation of individual interdependencies).

Table 1. Application analysis and the role of network metrics

Application attributes	Role of network metrics for application analysis
Risks	• Out-C_D quantifies the number of applications possibly affected by application failure (i.e., the scope of direct failure propagation). • In-C_D quantifies the number of applications, which in case of failure may affect a given application. • C_D and C_C indicate the state of modifiability of a given application. • C_B quantifies, given the failure of an application, the threat of other applications or entire clusters impeded in their coaction. • C_E quantifies the threat of central applications affected by application failure.
Costs	• C_D indicates the cost associated with a given application.
Value	• C_B indicates applications that control data flow within one or across several business processes.
Strategic fit	• C_D may indicate applications that are not compliant with strategic directives that stipulate standardization and homogeneity.
Technical complexity	• C_D may indicate the number of physical interfaces of an application.

For the same reason, C_D may also support analysis of an application's technical health, because one of the factors that determine the technical health is complexity [13]. It can (among others) be explained by the application's number of (physical) interfaces (cf. [28]), which is also one of the main criteria our sample insurance provider considers to determine the future prospects of an application from a technical perspective. As this number may be related to the number of links in the representing network (see above), C_D may also be considered a reasonable health indicator.

Table 1 summarizes the potential role of network metrics in IT landscape analysis.

4.3   IT Landscape Planning and Decision Making

To approach any issues discovered in the analysis stage, the succeeding planning of the future IT landscape typically involves defining alternative scenarios, which are weighed against one another to determine the desired option [5, 13]. This is also how our sample organizations proceed. Evaluation of this sort includes the scenario costs, risks, and time constraints [5]. Therefore, it is also necessary to consider the effects of changes captured within a scenario across the IT landscape [1, 13]. If there are plans to take action in terms of the application lifecycle, for example, a "simple" upgrade to a new application release may require others to be upgraded before (cf. [35, 36]).

Our reference practices basically aim to keep the scenario evaluation rather simple and mostly use ordinal scales for their ratings; again, this is where NA measures may provide added value, since they are straightforward to use and meaningful alike. Risks can come from potential negative impacts of the planned change of an IT landscape element on others. So, modifications of positionally important applications could expose the organization to significant risks. Such risks can be indicated by C_D, given the number of related applications it represents. C_E may take this even further, since it allows for a focus on impacts on applications that are themselves central. In addition, C_B allows a more differentiated approach to scenario risk evaluation; it may pinpoint applications that could adversely affect the coaction of other applications or entire clusters that could fall apart, given their position between others. Eventually, it is C_D that can apparently also help evaluate scenarios in terms of time and costs. It can indicate necessary efforts of adapting other applications or their interfaces due to changes of a particular application; this is because it explicates the number of related applications that might also be modified in result (though it does not say anything about the quality of these related changes).

Once the evaluation has led to the selection of a favored scenario, this target landscape is typically compared to the current one to identify gaps between these states. According to common practice, these gaps are then consolidated and assigned to projects aimed at closing them [1, 34]. Other demands or project ideas that may have been brought from other business units into project portfolio management need to be integrated in this planning of projects [5]. Enterprise architects typically help refine the scope of potential projects, check their effects on the architectural landscape, and bring the insights gained by surveying their architectural content (e.g., applications, their dependencies, and affected business functions) into the assessment of project proposals in terms of criteria such as costs, risks, and value and into the synchronization of projects changing the same or related elements [1, 24, 27, 34, 35].

Using network centrality measures, the enterprise architect may bring new qualities into these project evaluations; in fact, consideration may also be given not only to architectural objects affected directly by a project (typically depicted in a project context diagram), but also those affected indirectly because they are related to an object in project scope. In this way, NA metrics help operationalize a project impact check, considering the network position of the architectural content of a project.

4.4   Implementation of Target IT Landscape

Once projects for implementing the target landscape are defined and initiated, the EA function needs to assure that adequate and conformant architectural solutions are designed, for example, by sending off solution architects to accompany the projects. However, not every project may need to be monitored in such detail, and resources may also be limited. To determine which architectural project support is most appropriate (e.g., regular compliance reviews, ongoing participation) [1], three of our sample organizations conduct a check of architectural relevance. Among other criteria, they check the complexity of the project architecture, which our sample bank gauges by the number of interfaces of the components to be implemented and the resulting number of affected components.

Again, for this measurement of topologic complexity, C_D of the applications in scope of the project seems a reasonable indicator, since it quantifies the number of affected components; as such, it can facilitate the architectural relevance check (cf. [37]). It can also be visualized in system context diagrams. However, it could well be that one project affects several rather small applications while another affects only a few, but large, applications. That is why the use of C_E should be considered as well.

The subsequent processes of solution architecture design, that is, the component design at the micro-architectural level that occurs within the designated projects for implementing the target landscape, can also be informed by NA metrics (cf. [36]). For example, they may indicate whether design principles such as coupling and cohesion are sufficiently realized and help ensure that resources are allocated primarily to critical modules (cf. [38]); further details are beyond the scope of this paper though.

4.5   Governance of IT Landscape Management

Across the above fields of activity within IT LM (i.e., from documentation to implementation), it is crucial to assure ongoing architectural governance [1]. This includes the measurement of results, which is of particular importance since it provides the basis for justifying and selling the value of an EA function in the long run – a challenge that EA practitioners increasingly face today [39].

The EA charter [1] is a fundamental basis for any governance activities; it defines the mission, vision, goals, objectives, and key performance indicators (KPIs). So, this is where the measurement of success finds its variables and instruments. Two of our sample organizations have established such a charter. In the pharmaceutical organization, two specific objectives defined in the charter are a minimal number of dependencies between applications and between technology components. The number of individual peer-to-peer application interfaces and the average number of dependencies to other technology components are used as the corresponding KPIs.

With that in mind, (average) C_D apparently manifests as a suitable metric for governance purposes as well (note that edges in the network should represent physical relationships to measure the number of peer-to-peer interfaces; at the logical level, relationships of data exchange remain the relevant aspect to be represented by edges).

In the next section, we present the case of an insurance company and our use of NA to study its IT landscape to provide some evaluation of our approach (the case description was reviewed and validated by the organization).

5   Case Study: An Application of the Approach to Practice

The enterprise we studied is a German insurance company that is a key player in the markets for household, liability, and car insurance. An EA practice was established in 2009, embedded predominantly in the IT department (of about 250 employees) with five enterprise IT architects, about twenty solution architects, and the architecture board and architecture review board as the decision-making bodies for strategic and solution architecture issues, respectively. EA processes were defined, including for architecture documentation and analyses, target architecture planning, project portfolio evaluations, and compliance assessments. In 2010, a toolbox of templates and checklists for solution architecture design was developed. Likewise, a standards management framework was introduced. At the same time, considerable efforts were undertaken to capture an initial state of the IT landscape, resulting in a map of business and infrastructure applications and their relationships of data exchange. What still remained to be substantiated are methods and techniques to support the regular IT LM process. To help evaluate our concept and create new insights for its IT LM practices, the organization thus provided us with the above landscape map. We imported the corresponding file into Gephi, an open-source software tool for graph and network analysis [40]. The resulting network of applications showed numerous interrelationships. In total, the network comprised 338 nodes and 859 edges, accounting for a density of 0.008 and modularity of 0.49; average C_D was 5.08.

On that basis, we computed C_D, C_B, and C_E of the network's applications (as the organization asked for a focus on only a few metrics). Armed with these metrics, we went into discussions with the lead enterprise IT architect, one of his fellow enterprise IT architects, and the IT architect who had created the draft IT landscape map. We compared the computation results with intuitive notions about the applications that are most critical, valuable, prone to failure, complex, costly, and difficult to adapt. We asked the architects to suggest a few applications to which they would ascribe these properties, and later presented the top-ten applications according to each metric.

This stimulated considerable discussion among the architects. Some figures were obvious to them, that is, some of the applications indicated to be most central by the metrics were also those they had assumed to represent key applications. In fact, all metrics indicated the same three applications to be most central: a premium collection, claims (e.g., C_{Out-D}=39, C_{In-D}=35, C_B=0.22, C_E=0.81), and policy application (with a much higher C_{In-D} (=38) than C_{Out-D} (=13)). It was also interesting to see that the participants had assigned at least one application to each of the above properties that also showed up among those with highest C_D. This seems in line with our theory about the supporting role of C_D in application analysis.

In contrast, other insights were less expected. C_B indicated, for example, a sales support application to be significant (C_B=0.12) that did not have a high C_D at all. Upon further discussion, the architects were able to justify that this application was important because it allowed the automatic forwarding of application data, which plays a crucial role in achieving high quantities of new policies per day. This fosters our suggestion about the potential role of C_B in criticality and value assessments of applications, as it may allow the incorporation of new facets into such analyses.

The C_B data also identified one financial accounting application as central (C_B=0.1) that had been considered especially valuable by the architects themselves; this means they can also substantiate initially subjective valuations. Notably, this application also had a high C_{In-D}, but a rather low C_{Out-D}. This let us to conclude that a considerable C_{In-D} may also point to a certain value; examples may be business intelligence and premium collection applications that collect, aggregate, and process data from many different sources to support activities of great strategic or monetary relevance.

Using C_E also led us to further insights beyond those gained by using C_D; for example, it identified a family insurance application as positionally important (C_E of 0.38) that also did not have a high C_D. So, while each metric was considered helpful, C_B and C_E brought unexpected insights and helped us capture non-intuitive findings. C_{In-D} turned out to add another dimension into the assessment of application value.

When checking the network values for selected applications that did not appear in the top-ten lists, we also identified an application scenario of NA in IT LM that we had not previously considered in our approach. This is because the architects found applications that showed unexpectedly low centrality values (or even seemed to be disconnected), which raised the question of whether this actually represents reality or whether information about some links in the network was still missing. Network metrics thus also help resolve questions of data quality and aid in reviewing architectural documentation in terms of its correctness and completeness.

All in all, the nature of discussion changed quickly from the simple examination of raw counts to broader concerns of analysis and usage-oriented issues. It was acknowledged that the network metrics could support different aspects of IT LM, as represented by the EA lifecycle introduced above. Particular value was seen how they supported checking new demands or projects in terms of their architectural relevance.

Despite this value, we found some limitations and needs for extensions during the discussions. One interesting point concerned the possibility of weighting the edges to increase the meaningfulness of the analysis. On the one hand, one could quantify the edges in terms of frequency of data exchange. An impact of failure of an application with several connections might be less relevant if, for example, data are transferred only once a year over these connections. On the other hand, a qualitative weighting of edges also seems reasonable to account for their relevance to any critical business processes. Concerns were also raised regarding the meaningfulness of C_B if the relevant network path is subject to several media disruptions. More generally, in- and outgoing links of a node with a high C_B could refer to separate business processes; in such a case, any failure may have no immediate impact. The architects concluded that any indications that the NA measures provide should be analyzed in further detail.

Final words of attention came out of the discussions regarding the semantics of the network's elements. In particular, this relates to the question of what actually constitutes an IT landscape's node. A differentiation between business and infrastructure applications and their representation in separate networks was considered reasonable. As such, the former network would represent the real data sources and sinks, which are the ones that are more likely meaningful to the business. Brokering applications such as integration buses are of minor relevance to the business and their inclusion in one and the same network may thus complicate communication.

Another question was the level of abstraction at which a network should be spanned: this could be either the level of aggregated building blocks (cf. [1]) or of the individual parts. In the latter case, larger applications would be represented by several nodes in the network, which seems reasonable if one knows about the dependencies at that level of application modules. One further issue then arose in the discussions, which was the question of what actually defines a module such that it would be represented by a node in the network. It was opined that for a module to be considered a separate component, one should generally be able to procure, build, install, and operate that module independently from any others (this is also in line with [9]).

Altogether, we found qualitative support for our approach with this case study, and could even extend it at some points on that basis. We also encountered some area where further development is needed to advance the approach.

6   Conclusion and Outlook

With this study, we have uncovered the potential role of NA in IT LM (as requested by this paper's research question). There are several benefits of using NA metrics across the EA lifecycle. As for documentation, they can support the check for EA involvement in domain initiatives, and also the review of documentation in terms of its quality; in the analysis, network metrics can then help gain specific insights into the risks, costs, value, strategic fit, and technical complexity of applications. In other words, the metrics may alert enterprise architects of weaknesses and of applications in which one should invest to mitigate risks and ensure value. When it comes to IT landscape planning, the use of network metrics can support the evaluation of transformation scenarios and related projects in terms of any impacts. The support of architectural relevance checks also makes network metrics relevant in the implementation phase. Finally, governance may also be facilitated by the use of such metrics; in this regard, they help measure the IT LM performance.

In line with systems thinking, the NA metrics presented thus enable a simplified and objective evaluation of applications in consideration of their context of related applications. One of the main use cases are application risk assessments, in which C_C,

C_B, and C_E complement C_D such that they allow a more differentiated examination of dependencies. As such, these metrics uncover specific insights and should be used in combination with other methods to verify potential areas of action. Our empirical findings obtained through the case study support and, to some degree, extend our concept; however, they also point to aspects that should be the subject of further research, such as the weighting of edges.

Our results have value despite the study's limitations. For the development of our approach, we could not make use of a fully representative sample, from which we could infer universal statements about the entire organizational population, although we could take advantage of our use of purposive sampling. Likewise, the case study used for testing our approach in practice is limited to one sample organization, in which IT LM has yet to be completely implemented using the network metrics.

Our study could thus be extended in various ways in the future. First, the extension of our sample seems a promising way to move the research process along. An essential future step thus would be to apply the approach iteratively in a number of real-life cases to verify its applicability and uncover further areas for improvement. These cases should also incorporate the requirements already gathered in our case study. Moreover, the set of NA metrics could be widened to include other instruments that facilitate identifying an entire group of critical applications (cf. [10]), which would collectively have the greatest (and most disruptive) reach in the network. With respect to decision making in IT LM, human aspects could be given greater consideration to include the cost of changing what is in the heads of users.

All in all, we believe this study offers ideas and advice for academics and practitioners alike. Aside from the academic value that lies in the understanding of our concept, this study also provides a foundation on which to draw in the future in terms of the further development of method support for IT LM; as indicated, further research and empirical findings is required to validate and extend the findings. For practitioners, our approach should help them scrutinize dependencies in the IT landscape and serve as a conceptual guideline for applying NA metrics as a quantitative basis for activities across the EA lifecycle. This is supported by this study's use of cases, which illustrate IT LM peculiarities in practice and helped build and test our approach. We can thus conclude with a recommendation for EA tool vendors to make their tools able to compute NA metrics (beyond C_D) so that they actually become integral in IT LM in practice.

References

1. The Open Group: TOGAF Version 9. Van Haren Publishing, Netherlands (2009)
2. Gharajedaghi, J.: Systems Thinking: Managing Chaos and Complexity, A Platform for Designing Business Architecture. Morgan Kaufmann, USA (2011)
3. Bernus, P., Schmidt, G.: Architectures of information systems. In: Bernus, P., Mertins, K., Schmidt, G. (eds.) Handbook on Architectures of Information Systems. Springer (2006)
4. International Organization for Standardization, ISO/IEC/IEEE 42010:2011, Systems and software engineering – Architecture description, http://www.iso-architecture.org/42010/

5. Niemann, K.D.: From enterprise architecture to IT governance. Vieweg, Wiesbaden (2006)
6. Aier, S., Riege, C., Winter, R.: Unternehmensarchitektur – Literaturüberblick und Stand der Praxis. Wirtschaftsinformatik 50(4), 292–304 (2008)
7. Otte, E., Rousseau, R.: Social network analysis: a powerful strategy, also for the information sciences. J. Inf. Sci. 28(6), 441–453 (2002)
8. Dreyfus, D., Iyer, B.: Architectural control and emergent architecture: a network perspective. Boston University Working Paper (2005)
9. Dreyfus, D., Iyer, B.: Enterprise Architecture: A Social Network Perspective. In: 39th HICSS (2006)
10. Iyer, B., Dreyfus, D., Gyllstrom, P.: A Network-based View of Enterprise Architecture. In: Saha, P. (ed.) Handbook of Enterprise Systems Architecture in Practice. IGI Global (2007)
11. Dreyfus, D., Wyner, G.M.: Digital Cement: Software Portfolio Architecture, Complexity, and Flexibility. In: 17th AMCIS (2011)
12. Aier, S., Schönherr, M.: Integrating an enterprise architecture using domain clustering. In: Trends in Enterprise Architecture Research 2007, pp. 23–30 (2007)
13. Simon, D., Fischbach, K., Schoder, D.: Application Portfolio Management – An Integrated Framework and a Software Tool Evaluation Approach. CAIS 26, 35–56 (2010)
14. Mocker, M.: What is complex about 273 applications? Untangling application architecture complexity in a case of European Investment Banking. In: 42nd HICSS (2009)
15. Wasserman, S., Faust, K.: Social Network Analysis: Methods & Applications. CUP (1994)
16. Freeman, L.C.: Centrality in Social Networks. Soc. Netw. 1, 215–239 (1978/1979)
17. Bonacich, P.: Some unique properties of eigenvector centrality. Soc. Netw. 29, 555–564 (2007)
18. Newman, M.E.J.: Modularity and community structure in networks. Natl. Academy Sci. 103(23), 8577–8582 (2006)
19. Uzzi, B., Spiro, J.: Collaboration and Creativity: The Small World Problem. American J. Sociology 111(2), 447–504 (2005)
20. Webster, J., Watson, R.T.: Analyzing the Past to Prepare for the Future. MIS Q 26 (2002)
21. Teddlie, C., Yu, F.: Mixed Methods Sampling: A Typology with Examples. J. Mixed Methods Res. 1, 77–100 (2007)
22. De Marco, T.: Controlling software projects. Yourdon Press, New York (1982)
23. Buckl, S., Ernst, A.M., Lankes, J., Matthes, F., Schweda, C.M.: State of the Art in Enterprise Architecture Management. TU Munich, Chair for Informatics 19, Germany (2009)
24. Buckl, S., Ernst, A.M., Lankes, J., Matthes, F.: Enterprise Architecture Management Pattern Catalog. TU Munich, Chair for Informatics 19, Germany (2008)
25. Bruls, W.A.G., van Steenbergen, M., Foorthuis, R.M., Bos, R., Brinkkemper, S.: Domain Architectures as an Instrument to Refine Enterprise Architecture. CAIS 27, 517–540 (2010)
26. Vasconcelos, A., Sousa, P., Tribolet, J.: Information System Architecture Evaluation: From Software to Enterprise Level Approaches. In: 12th Eur. Conf. on IT Evaluation (2005)
27. Hanschke, I.: Strategic IT Management. Springer, Berlin (2010)
28. Vasconcelos, A., Sousa, P., Tribolet, J.: Information System Architecture Metrics: an Enterprise Engineering Evaluation approach. Electron J. Inf. Syst. Eval. 10(1), 91–122 (2007)
29. OGC: Managing Successful Projects with PRINCE 2. The Stationery Office Ltd. (2009)
30. Sherer, S.A., Alter, S.: Information Systems Risks and Risk Factors: Are They Mostly about Information Systems? CAIS 14, 29–64 (2004)

31. BSI, Bundesamt für Sicherheit in der Informationstechnik,
    `https://www.bsi.bund.de`
32. Jordan, E., Silcock, L.: Beating IT Risks. Wiley, Hoboken (2005)
33. Maizlish, B., Handler, R.: IT Portfolio Management Step-by-Step. Wiley, Hoboken (2005)
34. Quartel, D., Steen, M.W.A., Lankhorst, M.: Application and project portfolio valuation using EA and business requirements modelling. Enterp. Inf. Syst. 6(2), 189–213 (2012)
35. Saat, J.: Zeitbezogene Abhängigkeitsanalysen der Unternehmensarchitektur. In: MKWI 2010, pp. 119–130 (2010)
36. Jönsson, P.: The Anatomy – An Instrument for Managing Software Evolution and Evolvability. In: 2nd Int. Workshop on Softw. Evolvability, pp. 31–37 (2006)
37. Buckl, S., Ernst, A.M., Matthes, F., Schulz, C., Schweda, C.M.: Constructing an Enterprise-specific Radar System for Assisted Project Surveillance. In: MSI 2009, pp. 33–47 (2009)
38. Zimmermann, T., Nagappan, N.: Predicting defects using network analysis on dependency graphs. In: 30th Int. Conf. on Softw. Engineering, pp. 531–540 (2008)
39. Schelp, J., Stutz, M.: A Balanced Scorecard Approach to Measure the Value of Enterprise Architecture. In: Trends in Enterprise Architecture Research 2007, pp. 5–11 (2007)
40. Bastian, M., Heymann, S., Jacomy, M.: Gephi: An Open Source Software for Exploring and Manipulating Networks. In: Int. Conf. on Weblogs & Social Media, pp. 361–362 (2009)

SaaS ERP Adoption Intent: Explaining the South African SME Perspective

Julian Faasen[1], Lisa F. Seymour[1], and Joachim Schuler[2]

[1] Information Systems Department, University of Cape Town, Private Bag,
Rondebosch 7700, South Africa
Lisa.Seymour@uct.ac.za
[2] Pforzheim University, Tiefenbronnerstrasse 65,
75175 Pforzheim, Germany
Joachim.Schuler@hs-pforzheim.de

Abstract. This interpretive research study explores intention to adopt SaaS ERP software within South African SMEs. Semi-structured interviews with participants from different industry sectors were performed and seven multidimensional factors emerged explaining the current reluctance to adoption. While, improved IT reliability and perceived cost reduction were seem as benefits they were dominated by other reasons. Reluctance to adopt was attributed to systems performance and availability risk; sunk cost and satisfaction with existing systems; data security risk; loss of control and lack of vendor trust; and finally functionality fit and customization limitations. The findings provide new insights into the slow SaaS ERP adoption in South Africa and provide empirically supported data to guide future research efforts. Findings can be used by SaaS vendors to address perceived shortcomings of SaaS ERP software.

Keywords: Software as a Service, Cloud computing, Enterprise Resource Planning, SaaS ERP, South African SME, Information Systems adoption.

1 Introduction

Small and medium enterprises (SMEs) are major players in every economy and make a significant contribution to employment and Gross Domestic Product (GDP) [1]. In the past, many organizations were focused on local markets, but have been forced to respond to competition on a global level as well [2]. The role of the SME in developing countries such as South Africa is considered critical in terms of poverty alleviation, employment creation and international competitiveness [3]. However, resource limitations have made it difficult for many smaller organizations to enter new markets and compete against their larger counterparts. Thus SMEs in all countries are forced to seek innovative ways to become more efficient and competitive within a marketplace rife with uncertainty. Adoption of Information Systems (IS) is viewed as a way for SMEs to become more competitive and to drive business benefits such as cost reduction, improved profitability, enhanced customer service, new market growth opportunities and more efficient operating relationships

G. Poels (Ed.): CONFENIS 2012, LNBIP 139, pp. 35–47, 2013.
© IFIP International Federation for Information Processing 2013

with trading partners [4]. Many organizations have adopted Enterprise Resource Planning (ERP) software in an attempt to achieve such benefits.

ERP software facilitates the integration of cross-functional business processes in order to improve operational efficiencies and business performance. If used correctly, ERP software can drive bottom-line results and enhance competitive advantage. Whilst most large organizations world-wide have managed to acquire ERP software [5], it has been reported that many SMEs have been unwilling to adopt ERP software due to the high cost and risk involved [6]. However, an alternative to on-premise enterprise software has been made possible with the advent of the Software as a Service (SaaS) model.

SaaS as a subset of cloud computing involves the delivery of web-based software applications via the internet. SaaS is essentially an outsourcing arrangement, where enterprise software is hosted on a SaaS vendor's infrastructure and rented by customers at a fraction of the cost compared with traditional on-premise solutions. Customers access the software using an internet browser and benefit through lower upfront capital requirements [7], faster deployment time [8]; [9], improved elasticity [10], flexible monthly installments [11] and more predictable IT budgeting [8]; [12]. Countering these benefits are concerns around software reliability, data security [12]; [13]; [14] and long-term cost savings [15]. Customization limitations [16] and integration challenges [10] are considered major concerns relating to SaaS offerings. Furthermore, concerns relating to data security and systems availability have raised questions as to the feasibility of SaaS for hosting mission-critical software.

Despite the perceived drawbacks of SaaS, Gartner suggests that SaaS ERP solutions are attracting growing interest in the marketplace [17]. Traditional ERP vendors such as SAP have begun expanding their product ranges to include SaaS-based offerings. The success of Salesforce's SaaS CRM solution provides further evidence that the SaaS model is capable of delivering key business functionality. However, the adoption of SaaS ERP software has been reported as slow [17] and appears to be confined to developed countries. Despite the plethora of online content promoting the benefits of SaaS ERP software, there is a lack of empirical research available that explains the slow rate of adoption. Thus, the purpose of this study is to gain an understanding of the reluctance to adopt SaaS ERP software within South African SMEs. This research is considered important as SaaS is a rapidly growing phenomenon with widespread interest in the marketplace. Furthermore, this study aims to narrow the research gap by contributing towards much-needed empirical research into SaaS ERP adoption.

2   Literature Review

A number of pure-play SaaS vendors as well as traditional ERP providers are offering ERP software via the SaaS model. Krigsman [18] summarized the major SaaS ERP vendors and offerings and found that many are offering the major six core modules: Financial Management, Human Resources Management, Project Management, Manufacturing, Service Operations Management and Supply Chain Management.

However, according to Aberdeen Group, only nine SaaS vendors actually offered pure SaaS ERP software and services [19]. A Forrsights survey found that 15% of survey participants were planning adoption of SaaS ERP by 2013 [20]. However, two-thirds of those firms were planning to complement their existing on-premise ERP software with a SaaS offering. Only 5% of survey participants planned to replace most/all of their on-premise ERP systems within 2 years (from the time of their survey). These findings provide evidence of the slow rate of SaaS ERP adoption. It should also be noted that popular SaaS ERP vendors such as Netsuite and Epicor were not yet providing SaaS ERP products in South Africa during the time of this study in 2011.

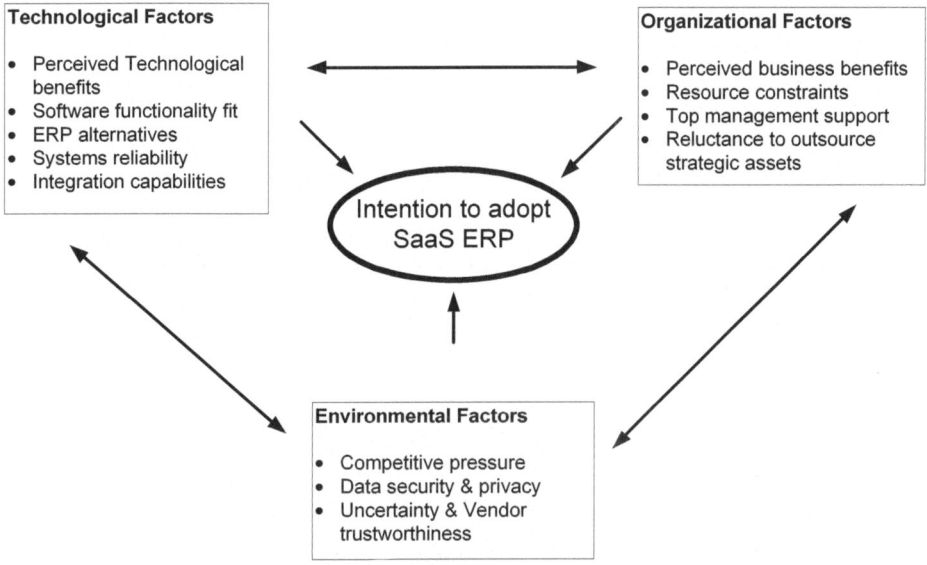

Fig. 1. Model derived from the broad literature

Given the scarcity of SaaS ERP literature, a literature review of the factors potentially influencing this slow adoption was performed based on prior studies relating to on-premise ERP adoption, IS adoption, SaaS, ASP and IS outsourcing (Figure 1). The major factors identified are structured according to the Technology-Organization Environment (TOE) framework [21]. For parsimonious reasons only these factors that were confirmed from our results are discussed in the results section of this paper.

3   Research Method

The primary research question was to identify why South African SMEs are reluctant to consider the adoption of SaaS ERP. Given the lack of research available an inductive interpretive and exploratory approach was deemed appropriate. The study also contained deductive elements as past research was used to generate an initial model. Walsham [22] posits that past theory in interpretive research is useful as a means of creating a sensible theoretical basis for informing the initial empirical work. To reduce the risk of relying too heavily on theory, a significant degree of openness to the research data was maintained through continual reassessment of initial assumptions [22].

Non-probability purposive sampling [23] was used to identify suitable organizations to interview and ethics approval from the University was obtained prior to commencing data collection. The sample frame consisted of South African SMEs with between 50 and 200 employees [24]. One participating organization contained 250 employees and was included due to difficulties finding appropriate interview candidates. SMEs in different industry segments were targeted to increase representation. Furthermore, SMEs that operated within traditional ERP-focussed industries (e.g. manufacturing, logistics, distribution, warehousing and financial services, etc.) were considered to improve the relevance of research findings. The majority of participants interviewed were key decision makers within their respective organizations to accurately reflect the intention to adopt SaaS ERP software within their respective organizations. Table 1 provides a summary of company and participant demographics.

Table 1. Company and Participant Demographics

Company code	Participant Code	Position	Experience	Industry	Employees
A	A1	Digital Director	10 years +	Book publishing & distribution	250
A	A2	IT Operations Manager	17 Years	Book publishing & distribution	250
B	B	Head of IT	20 years +	Financial Services	120
C	C1	Chief Operating Officer	20 years +	Specialized Health Services	50
C	C2	IT Consultant	7 years +	Specialized Health Services	50
D	D	Financial Director	20 years +	Freight Logistics Provider	200
E	E	Managing Director	20 years +	Medical Distribution	137

Data was collected using semi-structured interviews with questions which were initially guided by a priori themes extracted from the literature review. However, the researcher practised flexibility by showing a willingness to deviate from the initial research questions in order to explore new avenues [25].

Data analysis was conducted using the general inductive approach, where research findings emerged from the significant themes in the raw research data [26]. To enhance the quality of analysis member checking, thick descriptions, code-recode and audit trail strategies [27] were employed.

4   Data Analysis and Discussion

During interviews, it was apparent that the term "ERP" was sometimes used to represent functionality provided by a number of disparate systems. Thus the term ERP was used in terms of how the participant's companies used their business software collectively to fulfil the role of ERP software. Table 2 below provides an overview of the software landscape for each of the companies interviewed. Companies used a combination of off-the-shelf, bespoke, vertical ERP or modular ERP applications.

In this study, intention to adopt SaaS ERP software is defined as the degree to which the organization (SME) considers replacing all or most of their on-premise enterprise software with SaaS ERP software. SaaS ERP was defined as web-based ERP software that is hosted by SaaS ERP vendors and delivered to customers via the internet. The initial engagement with participants focussed primarily on multi-tenant SaaS ERP offerings, implying that a single instance of the ERP software would be shared with other companies.

Table 2. Software landscape for companies interviewed

Current Software Landscape	Company code				
	A	B	C	D	E
Using industry-specific ERP software	Yes	No	No	No	No
Using component-based ERP software	No	No	Yes	Yes	Yes
Using off-the-shelf software	Yes	Yes	Yes	Yes	Yes
Using Bespoke (customized) software	Yes	Yes	Yes	Yes	No
Implementation of ERP software in progress	No	Yes	No	No	No

At the time of this study SaaS ERP was not easily available from vendors in South Africa. Irrespective of the availability, none of the companies interviewed had an intention of adopting SaaS ERP software in the future. However, one participant suggested a positive intention towards adoption of SaaS applications: "Microsoft CRM is available on the SaaS model...that's the way companies are going and we are seriously considering going that way" (Participant B). His company was in the process of planning a trial of SaaS CRM software. However, Participant B's organization was also in the process implementing on-premise ERP software. The findings are inconsistent with global Gartner and Forrsights surveys which reported a willingness and intention to adopt SaaS ERP software within small and mid-sized organizations [28]; [20].

The main objective of this research was to explore the factors that impacted the reluctance to consider SaaS ERP software adoption within South African SMEs. The following 7 themes emerged and are discussed in the following sections:

1. Perceived cost reduction (driver)
2. Sunk cost and Satisfaction with existing system (inhibitor)
3. Systems performance and availability risk (inhibitor)

4. Improved IT reliability (driver)
5. Data security risk (inhibitor)
6. Loss of control and Vendor trust (inhibitor)
7. Functionality Fit and Customization Limitations (inhibitor)

4.1 Perceived Cost Reduction

In line with the literature cost reductions were envisaged in terms of initial hardware and infrastructure [30]; [31]; [10] and were perceived as having a positive effect on intention to adopt SaaS ERP. However, participants also referred to the high cost of maintaining their on-premise ERP applications and potential long term operational cost savings with SaaS ERP.

"..it's the ongoing running costs, support and maintenance, that makes a difference" (Participant B).

However, these high costs were often justified in terms of the value that their on-premise systems provided:

"...if it's considered important then cost is very much a side issue" (Participant D).

4.2 Sunk Cost and Satisfaction with Existing Systems

The intention to adopt SaaS ERP was negatively affected by sunk cost and satisfaction with their existing systems. This was the 2nd most dominant theme. Sunk cost represents irrecoverable costs incurred during the acquisition and evolution of their existing IT systems.

"...if you're company that's got a sunk cost in ERP...the hardware and staff and training them up...what is the benefit of moving across to a SaaS model?" (A1).

"...if we were starting today with a clean slate, with not having a server room full of hardware, then definitely...SaaS would be a good idea" (D)

Satisfaction with existing systems relates to the perception of participants that their existing enterprise software was fit for purpose.

"...whenever you've got a system in place that ticks 90% of your boxes and it's reliable...why change, what are we going to gain, will the gain be worth the pain and effort and the cost of changing" (A1).

The effect of sunk costs towards SaaS ERP adoption intent could not be verified within academic literature but is consistent with the 2009 Aberdeen Group survey, where organizations showed reluctance towards adoption due to past investment in IT [28]. Both sub-themes were also related to a lack of perceived benefits towards changing to alternatives such as SaaS ERP.

"...you're constantly investing in the current system and you're depreciating those costs over three, five, years. So... if you've got those sunk costs...even if you could save 30% you'd have to weigh it up around the investment" (A1).

This is in agreement with research which states that organizations adopt technology innovations only if they consider the technology to be capable of addressing a perceived performance gap or to exploit a business opportunity [32].

4.3   System Performance and Availability Risk

Concerns over systems performance and availability risk were the dominant reasons for the reluctance to adopt SaaS ERP. This was commented on by all participants. Systems performance and availability risk concerns were primarily related to bandwidth concerns in South Africa. More specifically, bandwidth cost, internet latency limitations and bandwidth reliability (uptime) were considered factors which impacted the performance and availability of SaaS ERP solutions, thus impacting adoption intent. These findings are in line with literature which suggests that systems performance and availability concerns have a negative impact on ASP adoption [33] and SaaS adoption [34].

"The cheapest, I suppose is the ADSL, with 4MB lines, but they tend to fall over, cables get stolen" (Participant D).

"They can't guarantee you no downtime, but I mean there are so many factors locally that they've got no control of. You know, you have a parastatal running the bulk of our bandwidth system" (E)

Systems performance and availability was associated with the risk of losing access to mission-critical systems and the resulting impact on business operations. Although bandwidth has become cheaper and more reliable in South Africa over the past decade, organizations and SaaS vendors are still faced with a number of challenges in addressing the risks associated with performance and availability of SaaS ERP software.

4.4   Improved IT Reliability

Most participants felt that SaaS ERP would be beneficial as a means of providing them with improved reliability of their core business software due to sophisticated platform technology, regular software updates, more effective backups and better systems redundancy. These sub-themes were considered major benefits of SaaS ERP software for SMEs interviewed. The perceived benefits of redundancy, backing up and received software updates were expressed as follows:

"I think it will be a safer option ...if they've got more expensive infrastructure with redundancy built in" (C1).

"...the other advantage is in terms of backing up and protecting of data...at least that becomes somebody else's responsibility" (E). "...it's probably more often updated...because it's been shared across a range of customers; it has to really be perfect all the time" (A1).

The benefit of improved IT reliability becomes more evident when one considers many SMEs often lack the required skills and resources to manage their on-premise enterprise systems effectively [35]; [36] thus making on-demand sourcing models such as SaaS more attractive:

"...having ERP software in-house that you maintain...does come with huge human resource constraint's." and "I'm not in the business of managing ERP systems, I'm in the business of book publishing and distribution...SaaS ERP makes all the sense in the world...you focus on just using it for your business rather than you run the product as well" (A1).

4.5   Data Security Risk

Data security concerns were the fourth most dominant explanation and were related to concerns around the security and confidentiality of business information hosted on SaaS vendor infrastructure. Senior management provided the majority of responses. Data security concerns related to external hacking, risks from inside the SaaS vendor environment and from other clients sharing the infrastructure.

"...somebody somewhere at some level has got to have access to all of that information and it's a very off-putting factor for us" (E).

"they've got a large number of other clients accessing the same servers" (D)

This confirms data security risk as one of the major inhibitors of SaaS ERP adoption [6], [12], [13]; [10]. Issues relating to vendor control over privileged access and segregation of data between SaaS tenants [29] appear to be strong concerns. Whilst SaaS vendors claim that their solutions are more secure, SaaS is generally considered suitable for applications with low data security and privacy concerns [34]. Ensuring that sufficient data security mechanisms are in place is also critical in terms of regulatory compliance when moving applications into the cloud [11]. South African organizations would also need to consider the new Protection of Personal Information Act.

4.6   Loss of Control and Lack of Vendor Trust

A number of participants associated SaaS ERP with a loss of control over their software and hardware components. They also raised concerns around trusting vendors with their mission-critical software solutions. This was the 3rd most dominant theme, with the majority of responses coming from senior management:

"...if they decide to do maintenance...there's nothing we can do about it...you don't have a choice" (C2).

"...they sort of cut corners and then you end up getting almost a specific-to-SLA type of service" (A2).

"Obviously the disadvantage is the fact that you are putting a lot of trust in another company and you've got to be sure that they are going to deliver because your entire business now is running on the quality of their staff, their turnaround times" (A1).

Participants felt that being reliant on vendors introduced risk that may affect the performance, availability and security of their mission critical applications. This is related to literature suggesting that organizations prefer in-house systems due to the risk of losing control over mission critical applications [34]. The linkage between lack of vendor trust and two other themes, systems performance and availability risk and data security risk, are consistent with Heart's [13] findings.

In this study, systems performance and availability risk was primarily related to bandwidth constraints (cost, internet latency and reliability). Thus, in the context of this study, the vendor trust aspect is very much related to SaaS vendors to ensure data security and ISPs to ensure internet connectivity uptime.

4.7   Functionality Fit and Customization Limitations

Functionality fit refers to the degree to which ERP software matches the organizations functionality requirements. This was the least dominant concern with three participants raising concerns around lack of flexibility of SaaS ERP software due to concerns around the ability to customize the software.

"...it's got enhanced modules like book production....it gets quite complex, so that's for instance one of the modules that's quite niche that you don't get in typical ERP...I think if you were starting from scratch and you had nothing, the benefit would be that if we put (current ERP software) in, the product and the people who put it in for you understand the industry whereas...but would there be anyone within SAP or Oracle who really understands the book industry?" (A).

"I think the disadvantages are flexibility...most of them won't allow too much of customization" (B).

"They do have a certain amount of configurability in the program...but when it comes down to the actual software application, they (ERP vendor) say this is what you get...and if you want to change, that's fine but then we'll make the change available to everybody...so you lose your competitive advantage" (D).

Functionality fit is considered an important factor which effects on-premise ERP software adoption [6] [37]. There are a limited number of vendors providing pure SaaS ERP software services [36] and SaaS ERP vendors are providing core ERP modules that cater for a wider market segment [18]. However, niche organizations that require highly specific functionality may find SaaS ERP software unsuitable, since the SaaS ERP business process logic may not fit their organization's functionality requirements.

Customization of ERP software is viewed as a means of accommodating the lack of functionality fit between the ERP software and the organization's functionality requirements, however, customization is limited within multi-tenancy SaaS ERP software [10]; [16].

Organizations could adopt SaaS ERP to fulfil standard functionality (accounting, warehousing, etc) whilst retaining in-house bespoke software to deliver specific functionality required but then integration complexity could become an issue. Various integration options are available for SaaS users. Platform as a service (PaaS) solutions provided by SalesForce.com (using Force.com and AppExchange) provide organizations with opportunities for purchasing 3rd party plugins that address integration needs [9]. However, changes to the SaaS software (e.g. software upgrades or customization) could break 3rd party interfaces [12]. Alternatively, organizations can make use of the standard web application programming interfaces (APIs) provided by the SaaS solution providers [16]; [12]. This enables SaaS vendors to continuously provide updates to functionality without breaking existing integrations [12]. However, these integration solutions have raised concerns around data security since multiple customers are transacting via the same web APIs [38].

5 Conclusion

The purpose of this research was to investigate reluctance by South African SMEs to consider the SaaS ERP business model. The following 7 themes emerged, in order from most significant to least, based on the participant perceptions, personal experience and organizational context (Figure 2).

1. Systems performance and availability risk (inhibitor)
2. Sunk cost and Satisfaction with existing system (inhibitor)
3. Loss of control and Vendor trust (inhibitor)
4. Data security risk (inhibitor)
5. Improved IT reliability (driver)
6. Perceived cost reduction (driver)
7. Functionality Fit and Customization Limitations (inhibitor)

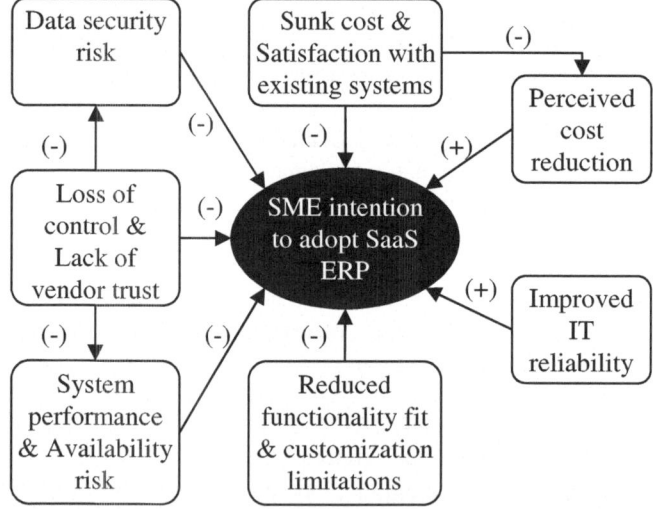

Fig. 2. An explanation of SME reluctance to adopt SaaS ERP. Negative effects are indicated by a negative sign (-) and positive effects by a positive sign (+).

Reluctance to adopt SaaS ERP was predominantly attributed to system performance and availability risk; data security risk; and loss of control and lack of vendor trust. Furthermore, loss of control and lack of vendor trust was found to increase the risks associated with systems performance and availability and the risks associated with data security. Thus organizations believed that in-house systems afforded them more control over their mission-critical software.

The presence of sunk costs appeared to negatively affect their perceptions towards the degree of cost reduction gains on offer with SaaS ERP software. Satisfaction with existing systems was associated with a lack of perceived benefits towards SaaS ERP software (why should we change when our current systems work?).

There was an acknowledgement that the SaaS ERP model would provide improved IT reliability but it also would come with reduced functionality fit and customization limitations.

Lack of control and vendor trust concerns dominate in the South African environment and this is exacerbated by high risks of unavailability attributed to the poor network infrastructure of the country. Concerns regarding cable theft were even reported. The findings in this study are not necessarily representative of all organizations in South Africa and due to the lack of SaaS ERP vendor presence in South Africa, it is reasonable to assume that South African organizations lack sufficient awareness around SaaS ERP software capabilities and this may have introduced a significant degree of bias.

By providing empirically supported research into SaaS ERP adoption, this research has attempted to narrow the research gap and to provide a basis for the development of future knowledge and theory. SaaS vendors in particular may be able to benefit through comparing these findings with their own surveys and establishing new and innovative ways to address the inhibitors of SaaS ERP adoption intent.

These research findings suggest similarities between the satisfaction with existing systems factor and the diffusion of innovations (DOI) model construct "relative advantage". Other data segments (not included within this paper) also suggest a possible relationship with two other DOI constructs "observability" and "trialability". Therefore the use of DOI theory for future research into SaaS ERP adoption might improve understanding.

References

1. Seethamraju, R., Seethamraju, J.: Adoption of ERPs in a medium-sized enterprise-A case study. In: ACIS 2008 Proceedings, vol. 887 (2008)
2. Shehab, E., Sharp, M., Supramaniam, L., Spedding, T.: Enterprise resource planning: An integrative review. Business Process Management Journal 10(4), 359–386 (2004)
3. Berry, A., von Blottnitz, M., Cassim, R., Kesper, A., Rajaratnam, B., Van Seventer, D.E.: The Economics of Small, Medium and Micro Enterprises in South Africa, Trade and Industrial Policy Strategies, Johannesburg (2002)
4. Premkumar, G.: A meta-analysis of research on information technology implementation in small business. Journal of Organizational Computing and Electronic Commerce 13(2), 91–121 (2003)
5. Klaus, H., Rosemann, M., Gable, G.G.: What is ERP? Information Systems Frontiers 2(2), 141–162 (2000)
6. Buonanno, G., Faverio, P., Pigni, F., Ravarini, A., Sciuto, D., Tagliavini, M.: Factors affecting ERP system adoption: A comparative analysis between SMEs and large companies. Journal of Enterprise Information Management 18(4), 384–426 (2005)
7. Feuerlicht, G., Govardhan, S.: SOA: Trends and directions. Systems Integration, 149–155 (2009)
8. Benlian, A.: A transaction cost theoretical analysis of software-as-a-service (SAAS)-based sourcing in SMBs and enterprises. In: ECIS 2009 Proceedings, Paper 4 (2009)
9. Deyo, J.: Software as a service (SaaS): A look at the migration of applications to the web (2008), http://www.isy.vcu.edu/~jsutherl/Info658/SAAS-JER.pdf (retrieved May 7, 2011)

10. Xin, M., Levina, N.: Software-as-a Service Model: Elaborating Client-Side Adoption Factors. In: ICIS 2008 Proceedings, vol. 86 (2008)
11. Armbrust, M., Fox, A., Griffith, R., Joseph, A.D., Katz, R., Konwinski, A., Lee, G., Patterson, D., Rabkin, A., Stoica, I., Zaharia, M.: A view of cloud computing. Communications of the ACM 53(4), 50–58 (2010)
12. Hai, H., Sakoda, S.: SaaS and integration best practices. Fujitsu Scientific and Technical Journal 45(3), 257–264 (2009)
13. Heart, T.: Who Is out there? Exploring Trust in the Remote-Hosting Vendor Community. In: ECIS Proceedings, Paper 2 (2007)
14. Kern, T., Willcocks, L.P., Lacity, M.C.: Application service provision: Risk assessment and mitigation. MIS Quarterly Executive 1(2), 113–126 (2002)
15. Hestermann, C., Anderson, R. P., Pang, C.: Magic quadrant for midmarket and tier 2-oriented ERP for product-centric companies. Gartner, Inc. (2009), http://www.wellpointsystems.com/pdf/GartnerMagicQuadrantforE RPMay2009.pdf (retrieved May 7, 2011)
16. Chong, F., Carraro, G.: Architecture strategies for catching the long tail. MSDN Library, Microsoft Corporation (2006)
17. Hestermann, C., Montgomery, N., Pang, C.: Magic quadrant for ERP for Product-Centric Midmarket Companies. Gartner, Inc. (2010), http://sme.news-sap.com/files/ 2011/01/SAP-vol2art5.pdf (retrieved September 20, 2011)
18. Krigsman, M.: The 2011 focus experts' guide to enterprise resource planning. Focus Group, pp. 1–24 (2010), http://www.focus.com/research/erp/2011- focus-experts-guide-enterprise-resource-planning-1/ (retrieved May 7, 2011)
19. Wailgum, T.: SaaS ERP Has Buzz, But Who Are the Real Players (2010), http://www.cio.com/article/572463/ (retrieved September 22, 2011)
20. Kisker, H.: ERP Grows Into The Cloud: Reflections From SuiteWorld 2011 (2011), http://blogs.forrester.com/holger_kisker/11-05-16- erp_grows_into_the_cloud_reflections_from_suiteworld_2011 (retrieved September 22, 2011)
21. Tornatzky, L.G., Fleischer, M.: The process of technological innovation. Lexington Books, Lexington (1990)
22. Walsham, G.: Interpretive case studies in IS research: Nature and method. European Journal of Information Systems 4(2), 74–81 (1995)
23. Saunders, M., Lewis, P., Thornhill, A.: Research methods of business students, 5th edn. Pearson Education/Prentice Hall, London (2009)
24. Small Business Act 102 (1996), http://www.info.gov.za/acts/1996/a102-96.pdf
25. Myers, M.D., Newman, M.: The qualitative interview in IS research: Examining the craft. Information and Organization 17(1), 2–26 (2007)
26. Thomas, D.R.: A general inductive approach for analyzing qualitative evaluation data. American Journal of Evaluation 27(2), 237 (2006)
27. Anfara, V.A., Brown, K.M., Mangione, T.L.: Qualitative analysis on stage: Making the research process more public. Educational Researcher 31(7), 28 (2002)
28. Aberdeen group: SaaS ERP: Trends and observations (2009), http://www.plex.com/download/AberdeenSaaSERPTrendsandObserva tions.pdf

29. Brodkin, J.: Gartner: Seven cloud-computing security risks (2008),
    http://www.infoworld.com/d/security-central/gartner-seven-
    cloud-computing-security-risks-853?page=0,1
30. Kaplan, J.: SaaS survey shows new model becoming mainstream. Cutter Consortium Executive Update 6(22) (2005)
31. Torbacki, W.: SaaS–direction of technology development in ERP/MRP systems. Archives of Materials Science 58, 58 (2008)
32. Premkumar, G., Roberts, M.: Adoption of new information technologies in rural small businesses. Omega: The International Journal of Management Science 27(4), 467–484 (1999)
33. Lee, H., Kim, J., Kim, J.: Determinants of success for application service provider: An empirical test in small businesses. International Journal of Human-Computer Studies 65(9), 796–815 (2007)
34. Benlian, A., Hess, T., Buxmann, P.: Drivers of SaaS-Adoption–An empirical study of different application types. Business & Information Systems Engineering 1(5), 357–369 (2009)
35. Kamhawi, E.M.: Enterprise resource-planning systems adoption in Bahrain: Motives, benefits, and barriers. Journal of Enterprise Information Management 21(3), 310–334 (2008)
36. Ramdani, B., Kawalek, P.: SMEs & IS innovations adoption: A review and assessment of previous research. Academia Revista Latinoamericana De Administración (39), 47–70 (2007)
37. Markus, M.L., Tanis, C.: The enterprise systems experience-from adoption to success. Framing the Domains of IT Research: Glimpsing the Future through the Past 173, 173–207 (2000)
38. Sun, W., Zhang, K., Chen, S.-K., Zhang, X., Liang, H.: Software as a Service: An Integration Perspective. In: Krämer, B.J., Lin, K.-J., Narasimhan, P. (eds.) ICSOC 2007. LNCS, vol. 4749, pp. 558–569. Springer, Heidelberg (2007)

Sub-process Discovery: Opportunities for Process Diagnostics

Raykenler Yzquierdo-Herrera, Rogelio Silverio-Castro, and Manuel Lazo-Cortés

Faculty 3, University of the Informatics Sciences. Habana, Cuba
{ryzquierdo,Silverio,manuelslc}@uci.cu

Abstract. Most business processes in real life are not strictly ruled by the information systems that support them. This behavior is reflected in the traces stored by information systems. It is useful to diagnose in early stages of business process analysis. Process diagnostics is part of the process mining and it encompasses process performance analysis, anomaly detection, and inspection of interesting patterns. The techniques developed in this area have problems to detect sub-processes associated with the analyzed process and framing anomalies and significant patterns in the detected sub-processes. This proposal allows to segment the aligned traces and to form representative groups of sub-processes that compose the process analyzed. The tree of building blocks obtained reflects the hierarchical organization that is established between the sub-processes, considering main execution patterns. The proposal allows greater accuracy in the diagnosis. Based on the findings, implications for theory and practice are discussed.

Keywords: Business process, process diagnostics, process mining, trace alignment.

1 Introduction

Most enterprises and businesses use information systems to manage their business processes [1]. Enterprise Resource Planning systems, Supply Chain Management systems, Customer Relationship Management systems, and systems for Business Process Management themselves are few of the examples that could be mentioned. Information systems register actions in the form of traces as a result of executing instances or cases of a business process. The discovery of processes from the information contained in the traces is part of process mining or workflow mining [2, 3]. The discovery of the process model based on traces allows comparisons with the prescribed or theoretical model. Recent research works describe process mining application as support to the "operationalization" of the enterprise processes. "The idea of process mining is to discover, to monitor, and to improve real processes (i.e., not assumed processes) by extracting knowledge from event logs readily available in today's information systems" [4].

Most business processes in real life are not strictly ruled by the information systems on the background. This means that although there is a notion of a process,

G. Poels (Ed.): CONFENIS 2012, LNBIP 139, pp. 48–57, 2013.
© IFIP International Federation for Information Processing 2013

actors can get away from it, or even ignore it completely. In these environments, it may be wise to start a process improvement or to establish a process quality control to discover the actual running process [5-7].

It is useful to diagnose in early stages of business process analysis. Process diagnostics is part of process mining and it encompasses process performance analysis, anomaly detection, and inspection of interesting patterns [8]. Diagnosis provides a holistic view of the process, the most significant aspects of it and of the techniques that can be useful in further analysis.

The techniques developed in this area have problems to detect sub-processes associated with the analyzed process and framing anomalies, and significant patterns in the detected sub-processes [6, 8].

This proposal allows to segment the aligned traces and to form representative groups of sub-processes that compose the analyzed process. The tree of building blocks obtained reflects the hierarchical organization that is established between the sub-processes, considering main execution patterns. On each case, the building blocks created allows to group segments of the traces which can be significant for analysis.

The rest of this paper is organized as follows: section 2 introduces some related works; in section 3, methodological approach is presented. Furthermore, in section 4, real environment proposed algorithm's application and its results are discussed. Finally, conclusions are given in section 5.

2   Related Works

Among the most used techniques on log visualization, Dotted chart analysis can be found [9]. This technique is a "Gantt charts analogous technique, showing a `helicopter view' of the event log and assisting in process performance analysis by depicting process events in a graphical way, and primarily focuses on the time dimension of events" [8]. Business analysis is manually made from the dotted chart. Manual inspection and comprehension of the dotted chart becomes cumbersome and often infeasible to identify interesting patterns over the use of logs with medium to large number of activities (within few tens to hundreds).

Other commonly used visualization technique is Stream scope visualization. It is based on the event class correlations [10]. Using stream scope visualization, patterns of co-occurring events may be easily recognized by their vicinity. However, the technique is restricted by its unavailability to provide a holistic view of the event log although it visualizes each trace separately.

The use of tandem arrays and maximal repeats to capture recurring patterns within and across the traces is proposed by Bose and Van der Aalst [11]. This work has two limitations, the number of uncovered patterns can be enormous, and the patterns uncovered are atomic (the dependencies/correlations between patterns need to be discovered separately).

The Conformance checking allows to detect inconsistencies/deviations between a process model and its corresponding execution log [12, 13]. Conformance checking as a trend has inherent limitations in its applicability, especially for diagnostic purposes.

It assumes the existence of a preceding process model. However, in reality, process models are either not present or if present are incorrect or outdated [6].

At this point research works that arise with interesting patterns and anomalies detection were shown. Further on, focus will be pointed to sub-processes detection. In this sense, investigations that obtain cluster activity in the analyzed process can be mentioned, which can be useful to understand the context of certain anomalies. These research works are not highly recommended for real environments either is difficult to know the relationship established between the activities that form a group [5, 14]. Those techniques do not provide a holistic view of the process. The Fuzzy Miner discovery technique allows to obtain cluster activities, but it considers that each activity belongs to a single node [15].

The insufficiency for detecting sub-processes makes it complicated, in many occasions, to contextualize detected aspects and to understand its causes. This limitation prevails on the work developed by Van der Aalst and Bose (2012) [8] despite the fact that these authors agree this research yields the best obtained results in diagnostics by making possible to identify recurring patterns and provides a comprehensive holistic view of the process.

3   Methodological Approach

Initially, authors present a set of necessary definitions for a better understanding of the proposal.

Definition 1 (Business process): A business process consists of a set of activities that are performed in coordination in an organizational and technical environment. These activities jointly realize a business goal. Each business process is enacted by a single organization, but it may interact with business processes performed by other organizations [16]. ∎

Definition 2 (Sub-process): A sub-process is just an encapsulation of business activities that represent a coherent complex logical unit of work. Sub-processes have their own attributes and goals, but they also contribute to achieving the goal of the process. A sub-process is also a process and, an activity, its minimal expression. ∎

A process can be decomposed into multiple sub-processes using the following workflow patterns:

- Sequence: two sub-processes are arranged sequentially, if one occurs immediately after the other sub-process.
- Choice (XOR or OR): two sub-processes are arranged as options in a decision point; if on each case or process instance only one (XOR) or both in any order (OR) occur.
- Parallelism: two sub-processes are arranged in parallel if both occur simultaneously.
- Loop: A loop occurs when a sub-process is repeated multiple times.

Sub-processes can be decomposed into other sub-processes until the level of atomic activity. This allows building a tree where each level has a lower level of abstraction.

Definition 3 (Trace and event log). Let Σ denote the set of activities. Σ^+ is the set of all non-empty finite sequences of activities from Σ. Any $T \in \Sigma^+$ is a possible trace. An event log $\mathcal{L}$ is a multi-set of traces [8]. ∎

Definition 4 (Building block and decomposition into building blocks): Let us denote by S the set of all sub-processes that compose the process P, $\mathcal{L}$ the event log that represents the executed instances of P, $\mathcal{A}$ is the matrix obtained in trace alignment from $\mathcal{L}$, and Q is the set of all sub-matrices over $\mathcal{A}$ (Traces Alignment uses the technique developed by Bose and Van der Aalst (2012)[8]).

Let us denote by Q' the set of sub-matrices that represent the sub-processes of S, such that $Q' \subseteq Q$. Let C^i, C^j, $C^{j+1} \in Q'$, the sequence relationship between two sub-processes represented by C^j and C^{j+1} is denoted by $C^j >' C^{j+1}$. Analogously the choice relationship is denoted by $C^j \#' C^{j+1}$ and the parallelism relationship by $C^j \|' C^{j+1}$. The loop over C^j is denoted by $(C^j)^*$.

Let $s_i \in S$ the process represented by a matrix $C^i \in Q'$ and composed by the sequence of sub-processes represented by $C^j,..., C^{j+k}$ then matrix C^i and the set $\{C^j,..., C^{j+k}\}$ are called *building blocks*. The sub-processes represented by $\{C^j,...,C^{j+k}\}$ are related in one way (sequence, parallelism, OR-XOR or loop). ∎

General steps of the proposal are presented below.

3.1   Trace Alignment

Starting from a workflow log, traces are aligned following the algorithm developed by Bose and Van der Aalst [8]. With the result of aligned traces a file that represents the matrix $\mathcal{A}$ is generated. Trace alignment is a representation of the activities according to a relative order of occurrence and considering cases structure. The order established between activities allows identifying a group of workflow patterns.

3.2   Pre-Processing Aligned Traces

Incomplete cases are determined as cases which do not meet the process end-event. Incomplete cases have gaps ("-") in the columns for the process final activities. These cases can be treated or eliminated; afterwards, traces can be re-aligned. Moreover, trace alignment can be modified in order to assure each column is occupied by a single task.

3.3   Tree of Building Blocks

The algorithm for determining the tree of building blocks is the following.

Algorithm 1. Determining the tree of building blocks
Input: Matrix $\mathcal{A}$
Output: Tree of building blocks
1: Create an empty tree
2: Create a building block C^i and it is associated with
   the root node of the generated tree. $C^i = \mathcal{A}$
3: **if** C^i is not a row matrix **then**
4:   $CL = Sequence\text{-}Search(C^i)$. /*$CL$ is a list of obtained
   building blocks*/
5:   **if** $|CL| < 1$ **then**
6:     $CL = Loop\text{-}Search(C^i)$
7:     **if** $|CL| < 1$ **then**
8:       $CL = XOR\text{-}OR\text{-}Search(C^i)$
9:       **if** $|CL| < 1$ **then**
10:         $CL = Parallelism\text{-}Search(C^i)$
11:         **if** $|CL| < 1$ **then**
12:           $CL = Hidden\text{-}Sequence\text{-}Search(C^i)$
          Endif
        Endif
      Endif
    Endif
13: **For** each building block i from CL **do**
14:   i is modified. /* the repeated row and the columns
   that contain only gap from the building block are
   eliminated */
15:     Add i as a child node of root node (C^i)
16:     Apply the Algorithm 1 starting from 3 to i
17:   **if** tree obtained in the previous step • $\emptyset$ **then**
18:     Add to i, as children, the children nodes of the
   root of tree obtained in the step 16
    Endif
  EndFor
  Else
19: Return an empty tree
  Endif
20: Return the generated tree

The procedures *Sequence-Search*, *Loop-Search*, *XOR-OR-Search*, *Parallelism-Search* and *Hidden-Sequence-Search* are described below.

Sequence-Search: The purpose of this proceeding is to determine if the building block (as input) is a process that can be decomposed by a sequence of sub-processes. If the de-composition is possible, it returns a list of detected building blocks, otherwise it returns an empty list. Sequentially ordered sub-processes can be clearly identified. These are separated by one or more activities that appear to occupy an entire column each. Sometimes these activities may not be identified because they could not be mapped in the event log.

Loop-Search: The purpose of this proceeding is to determine if the building block (as input) represents a sub-process repetition. If the de-composition is possible, it returns a list with one building block, otherwise it returns an empty list. To determine if a building block that represents a sub-process repetition is necessary to identify the initial activity of that specific sub-process. This initial activity can be kept to separate sequences of activities. Those identified sequences constitute the rows of the new building block. Repeated sequences are discarded.

XOR-OR-Search: The purpose of this proceeding is to determine if the building block (as input) is a process that can be decomposed by a choice of sub-processes (OR or XOR). If the de-composition is possible, it returns a list of building blocks detected, otherwise it returns an empty list.

Firstly, authors search the de-composition by XOR. To determine the building blocks that represent options (XOR) in a decision point disjoint sets are constructed with the activities which form the analyzed building block. Originally, there is a set of activities to each building block row; later on, the sets that intersect with some activity are joined. If there is more than one set at the end of this process, then building blocks that represent each of resultant options are created. Otherwise, if there is only one set, then the search to identify the de-composition by OR is performed. In order to do this, base sequences are determined. A base sequence is a row of a building block that is not composed entirely by the join of other rows. Sequences that contain common activities belong to the same set.

Parallelism-Search: The purpose of this proceeding is to determine if the building block (as input) is a process that can be decomposed by a parallelism of sub-processes. If the de-composition is possible, it returns a list of detected building blocks, otherwise it returns an empty list. To determine the building blocks that represent parallel sub-processes, disjoint sets are identified with the activities which form the analyzed building block. Activities belonging to different sets are in parallel, while activities belonging to one specific set are related by other workflow pattern. If more than one set is obtained as result, then the building blocks are formed from these parallel sub-processes.

Hidden-Sequence-Search: The purpose of this proceeding is to determine if the building block (as input) is a process that can be decomposed by a sequence of sub-processes. If the de-composition is possible, it returns a list of detected building blocks, otherwise it returns an empty list.

In this case, it is assumed that the activity or activities which define the sequentially ordered sub-processes are not recorded in the traces. Consequently, possible solutions (de-composition scenarios) are determined considering the issues set out below.

- Each building block that forms a solution can be decomposed by XOR, OR, loop or parallelism.
- The solutions are evaluated and the best are selected, taking into account within the evaluation that formed building blocks decrease the amount of broken loops and parallelisms (e.g. a broken loop is evident when an activity appears multiple times

in a row in the analyzed building block; then different instances of the referred activity make appearance on different new building blocks instead a same new building block).

4   Applying the Proposal in a Real Environment and Discussion

The technique presented in section 3 has been implemented and the traces of module Management of Roles from National Identification System (SUIN) were analyzed. The SUIN is a system developed by the Cuban Ministry of Interior in conjunction with the Cuban University of Informatics Sciences. The event log did allow determining anomalies in the selected process (31 cases, 804 events, 52 events classes and 3 types of events). The first step was to apply the trace alignment technic developed by Van der Aalst and Bose (2012) [8]. Fig. 1 shows the obtained alignment from the event log.

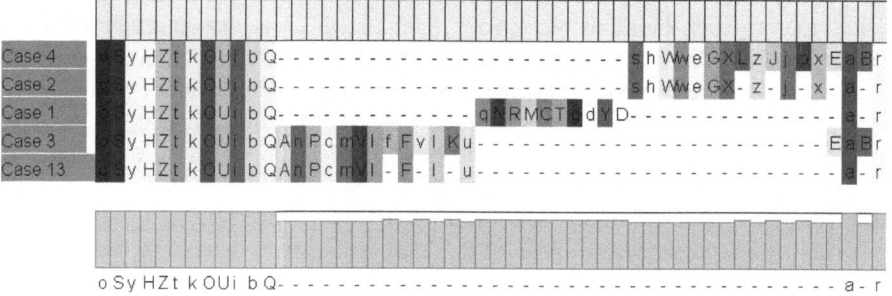

Fig. 1. Trace alignment

The proposal was applied to obtained a matrix from the alignment (Fig. 1) and afterwards the tree of building blocks, as shown in Fig. 2 (left panel), was obtained.

It can be noticed that: the obtained tree of building blocks may be expanded until all nodes become leaves or until they can no more be decomposed. The edges have different colors to differentiate the used workflow pattern; this is also indicated by a text message in each case (SEQUENCE, XOR, HIDDEN_SEQUENCE).

On Fig. 2 it appears the BB_2_4 building block selected (circle enclosed) which corresponds to the final decomposition resultant sub-process of BB_1_1. The BB_2_4 building block was chosen because it makes it possible to know how the process end. It also contains two cases, the first with frequency of 12 and a second with frequency of 19. This information can be appreciated in the middle table shown on figure 2, which corresponds to each case's occurrence frequency. Neither case's occurrence frequency nor activities' occurrence frequency are used in Algorithm 1, but they are incorporated in the developed tool to make process diagnosis easier.

The first BB_2_4 case is associated to the activity B which represents the event *Roles Management* activity *fault*. It is relevant this process failed 12 of the 31 executed times, representing a 38.7% of faults. Consequently failure causes on the process tested were sought.

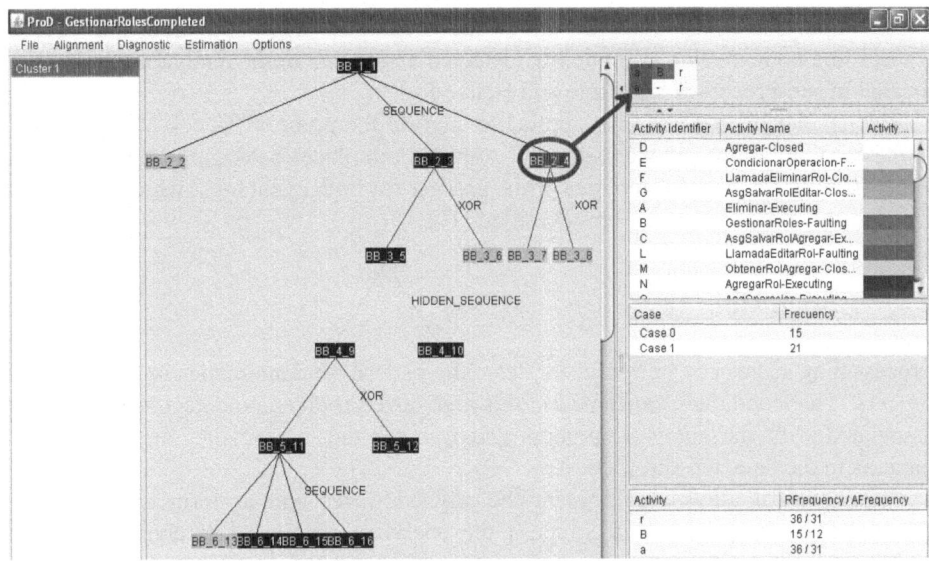

Fig. 2. Process de-composition

The origin of faults was searched on BB_2_3, which includes possible actions related to add, edit or delete a role. From the BB_2_3 de-composition two building blocks are obtained, the BB_3_5 and BB_3_6, both of them representing choice options. BB_3_6 represents the *Create Role* sub-process and it does not contain any B activity, which indicates that this building block had no influence in the process failure. From the BB_3_5 de-composition two new building blocks are obtained. In which the BB_4_10 represents the *Edit Role* and *Delete Role* sub-processes end-event. In BB_4_10 the event failure appears, it indicates that the failure lays on the sub-processes *Edit Role* and *Delete Role*. Detailed analysis of the Building block BB_4_9 and its de-composition was performed in order to determine the sequence of activities that led to failures in the *Edit Role* sub-process (represented by BB_5_11) and Delete Role sub-process (represented by BB_5_12). This detected sequence of activities is useful for future warnings prior to the possibility of a failure. Authors were able to identified specific cases in which failures occurred. Knowing the cases and events where the failure took place, the involved users were identified.

The technique developed by the authors, as well as the technique developed by Van der Aalst and Bose (2012) [8] allows detecting interesting patterns and provides a holistic view of the process. The proposal also allows detection of sub-processes that compose the analyzed process. The detected sub-processes enclose anomalies and interesting patterns, something that is not satisfied by the techniques discussed in section 2.

Another advantage of the present research is that it combines the cases and activities occurrence frequency analysis with the staged analysis from correctly structured sequence events on sub-processes. This contributes to the understanding of the failure causes and therefore a subsequent possible process improvement.

An important contribution of this work is that the anomalies detected can be framed in a context. For example, the detected anomalies in the analyzed process are located in sub-processes Edit Role and Delete Role.

The developed tool was also applied to analyze the process "Check Management" in the bar Gulf View and the restaurant Aguiar, both places belonging to the National Hotel (Cuba). Main characteristics of the process for both event logs, which supported the auditing of the process, were identified [17].

5   Conclusion

Process diagnostics can be useful for detecting patterns and anomalies in the analyzed process. The techniques developed in this area have problems to detect sub-processes associated with the analyzed process and framing those anomalies and significant patterns in the detected sub-processes.

This proposal allows to segment the aligned traces and to form representative groups of sub-processes that compose the analyzed process. The obtained tree of building blocks reflects the hierarchical organization that is established between the sub-processes, considering main execution patterns. On each case, the building blocks created allow to group segments of the traces which can be significant for analysis.

The proposal allows detecting interesting patterns and provides a holistic view of the process. Another advantage of the present research is that the interesting patterns detected can be framed in a context. The discovery of sub-processes that compose the analyzed process, its dependencies and correlations allow greater accuracy in the diagnosis. All this is possible thanks to the combination of the cases and activities occurrence frequency analysis with the staged analysis from correctly structured sequence events on sub-processes.

References

1. Hendricks, K.B., Singhal, V.R., Stratman, J.K.: The impact of enterprise systems on corporate performance: A study of ERP, SCM, and CRM system implementations. Journal of Operations Management 25(1), 65–82 (2007)
2. Agrawal, R., Gunopulos, D., Leymann, F.: Mining Process Models from Workflow Logs. In: Schek, H.-J., Saltor, F., Ramos, I., Alonso, G. (eds.) EDBT 1998. LNCS, vol. 1377, pp. 469–483. Springer, Heidelberg (1998)
3. Cook, J.E., Wolf, A.L.: Discovering Models of Software Processes from Event-Based Data. ACM Transactions on Software Engineering and Methodology, 215–249 (1998)
4. van der Aalst, W.M.P.: Process Mining. Discovery, Conformance and Enhancement of Business Processes. Springer, Heidelberg (2011)
5. van Dongen, B.F., Adriansyah, A.: Process Mining: Fuzzy Clustering and Performance Visualization. In: Rinderle-Ma, S., Sadiq, S., Leymann, F. (eds.) BPM 2009 Workshops. LNBIP, vol. 43, pp. 158–169. Springer, Heidelberg (2010)
6. Jagadeesh Chandra Bose, R.P., van der Aalst, W.M.P.: Trace Alignment in Process Mining: Opportunities for Process Diagnostics. In: Hull, R., Mendling, J., Tai, S. (eds.) BPM 2010. LNCS, vol. 6336, pp. 227–242. Springer, Heidelberg (2010)

7. Song, M., Günther, C.W., van der Aalst, W.M.P.: Trace Clustering in Process Mining. In: Ardagna, D., Mecella, M., Yang, J. (eds.) BPM 2008 Workshops. LNBIP, vol. 17, pp. 109–120. Springer, Heidelberg (2009)
8. Bose, R.P.J.C., van der Aalst, W.M.P.: Process diagnostics using trace alignment: Opportunities, issues, and challenges. Inf. Syst. 37(2), 117–141 (2012)
9. Song, M., van der Aalst, W.M.P.: Supporting process mining by showing events at a glance. In: 17th Annual Workshop on Information Technologies and Systems, WITS (2007)
10. Günther, C.W.: Process Mining in Flexible Environments. Eindhoven University of Technology, Eindhoven (2009)
11. Jagadeesh Chandra Bose, R.P., van der Aalst, W.M.P.: Abstractions in process mining: A taxonomy of patterns. In: Dayal, U., Eder, J., Koehler, J., Reijers, H.A. (eds.) BPM 2009. LNCS, vol. 5701, pp. 159–175. Springer, Heidelberg (2009)
12. Rozinat, A., van der Aalst, W.M.P.: Conformance checking of processes based on monitoring real behavior. Inf. Syst. 33(1), 64–95 (2008)
13. Adriansyah, A., van Dongen, B.F., van der Aalst, W.M.P.: Towards Robust Conformance Checking. In: zur Muehlen, M., Su, J. (eds.) BPM 2010 Workshops. LNBIP, vol. 66, pp. 122–133. Springer, Heidelberg (2011)
14. Aalst, W.M.P.V.D., Rubin, V., Verbeek, H.M.W., Dongen, B.F.V., Kindler, E., Günther, C.W.: ProcessMining: A Two-Step Approach to Balance Between Underfitting and Overfitting. Software and Systems Modeling 9(1), 87–111 (2009)
15. Günther, C.W., van der Aalst, W.M.P.: Fuzzy Mining – Adaptive Process Simplification Based on Multi-perspective Metrics. In: Alonso, G., Dadam, P., Rosemann, M. (eds.) BPM 2007. LNCS, vol. 4714, pp. 328–343. Springer, Heidelberg (2007)
16. Weske, M.: Business Process Management. Concepts, Languages, Architectures, Ed. S.-V.B, Heidelberg (2007)
17. González, L., Suárez, M.: Procedure for the application of process mining techniques in auditing processes (Degree). Faculty of Industrial Engineering, Polytechnic Institute José Antonio Echeverría, Havana, Cuba (2012)

A Proposal of Effort Estimation Method for Information Mining Projects Oriented to SMEs

Pablo Pytel[1,2,3], Paola Britos[4], and Ramón García-Martínez[2]

[1] PhD Program on Computer Science, Computer Science School,
National University of La Plata, Buenos Aires, Argentina
[2] Information Systems Research Group, National University of Lanus,
Buenos Aires, Argentina
[3] Information System Methodologies Research Group,
Technological National University at Buenos Aires, Argentina
[4] Information Mining Research Group, National University of Rio Negro
at El Bolson, Río Negro, Argentina
{ppytel,paobritos}@gmail.com, rgarcia@unla.edu.ar

Abstract. Software projects need to predict the cost and effort with its associated quantity of resources at the beginning of every project. Information Mining projects are not an exception to this requirement, particularly when they are required by Small and Medium-sized Enterprises (SMEs). An existing Information Mining projects estimation method is not reliable for small-sized projects because it tends to overestimates the estimated efforts. Therefore, considering the characteristics of these projects developed with the CRISP-DM methodology, an estimation method oriented to SMEs is proposed in this paper. First, the main features of SMEs' projects are described and applied as cost drivers of the new method with the corresponding formula. Then this is validated by comparing its results to the existing estimation method using SMEs real projects. As a result, it can be seen that the proposed method produces a more accurate estimation than the existing estimation method for small-sized projects.

Keywords: Effort Estimation method, Information Mining, Small and Medium-sized Enterprises, Project Planning, Software Engineering.

1   Introduction

Information Mining consists in the extraction of non-trivial knowledge which is located (implicitly) in the available data from different information sources [1]. That knowledge is previously unknown and it can be useful for some decision making process [2]. Normally, for an expert, the data itself is not the most relevant but it is the knowledge included in their relations, fluctuations and dependencies. Information Mining Process can be defined as a set of logically related tasks that are executed to achieve [3], from a set of information with a degree of value to the organization, another set of information with a greater degree of value than the initial one [4]. Once the problem and the customer's necessities are identified, the Information Mining Engineer selects the Information Mining Processes to be executed. Each Information

G. Poels (Ed.): CONFENIS 2012, LNBIP 139, pp. 58–74, 2013.
© IFIP International Federation for Information Processing 2013

Mining Process has several Data Mining Techniques that may be chosen to carry on the job [5]. Thus, it can be said that, Data Mining is associated to the technology (i.e. algorithms from the Machine Learning's field) while Information Mining is related to the processes and methodologies to complete the project successfully. In other words, while Data Mining is more related to the development tasks, Information Mining is closer to Software Engineering activities [6]. However, not all the models and methodologies available in Software Engineering can be applied to Information Mining projects because they do not handle the same practical aspects [7]. Therefore, specific models, methodologies, techniques and tools need to be created and validated in order to aid the Information Mining practitioners to carry on a project.

As in every Software project, Information Mining projects begin with a set of activities that are referred as project planning. This requires the prediction of the effort with the necessary resources and associated cost. Nevertheless, the normal effort estimation method applied in Conventional Software Development projects cannot be used at Information Mining projects because the considered characteristics are different. For example COCOMO II [8], one of the most used estimation method for Conventional Software projects, uses the quantity of source code lines as a parameter. This is not useful for estimating an Information Mining project because the data mining algorithms are already available in commercial tools and then it is not necessary to develop software. Estimation methods in Information Mining projects should use more representative characteristics, such as, the quantity of data sources, the level of integration within the data and the type of problem to be solved. In that respect, only one specific analytical estimation method for Information Mining projects has been found after a documentary research. This method called Data Mining Cost Model (or DMCoMo) is defined in [9]. However, from a statistical analysis of DMCoMo performed in [10], it has been found that this method tends to overestimate the efforts principally in small-sized projects that are usually required by Small and Medium-sized Enterprises [11].

In this context, the objective of this paper is proposing a new effort estimation method for Information Mining projects considering the features of Small and Medium-sized Enterprises (SMEs). First, the estimation method DMCoMo is described (section 2), and the main characteristics of SMEs' projects are identified (section 3). Then an estimation method oriented to SMEs is proposed (section 4) comparing its results to DMCoMo method using real projects data (section 5). Finally, the main conclusions and future research work are presented (section 6).

2   DMCoMo Estimation Method

Analytical estimation methods (such as COCOMO) are constructed based on the application of regression methods in the available historical data to obtain mathematical relationships between the variables (also called cost drivers) that are formalized through mathematical formulas which are used to calculate the estimated effort. DMCoMo [9] defines a set of 23 cost drivers to perform the cost estimation which are associated to the main characteristics of Information Mining projects. These cost drivers are classified in six categories which are included in table 1 as specified in [9]. Once the values of the cost drivers are defined, they are introduced in the mathematical formulas provided by the method. DMCoMo has two formulas which have been defined by linear regression with the information of 40 real projects of different business types (such as marketing, meteorological projects and medical projects). The first formula uses all 23 cost drivers as variables (formula named MM23) and it should be used when the project is well defined; while the second formula only uses 8 cost drivers (MM8) and it should be used when the project is partially defined. As a result of introducing the values in the corresponding formula, the quantity of men x month (MM) is calculated.

Table 1. Cost Drivers used by DMCoMo

Category	Cost Drivers
Source Data	− Number of Tables (NTAB) − Number of Tuples (NTUP) − Number of Table Attributes (NATR) − Data Dispersion (DISP) − Nulls Percentage (PNUL) − Data Model Availability (DMOD) − External Data Level (DEXT)
Data Mining Models	− Number of Data Models (NMOD) − Types of Data Model (TMOD) − Number of Tuples for each Data Models (MTUP) − Number and Type of Attributes for each Data Model (MATR) − Techniques Availability for each Data Model (MTEC)
Development Platform	− Number and Type of Data Sources (NFUN) − Distance and Communication Form (SCOM)
Techniques and Tools	− Tools Availability (TOOL) − Compatibility Level between Tools and Other Software (COMP) − Training Level of Tool Users (NFOR)
Project	− Number of Involved Departments (NDEP) − Documentation (DOCU) − Multisite Development (SITE)
Project Staff	− Problem Type Familiarity (MFAM) − Data Knowledge (KDAT) − Directive Attitude (ADIR)

But, as it has been pointed out by the authors, the behaviour of DMCoMo in projects outside of the 90 and 185 men x month range is unknown. From a statistical analysis of its behaviour performed in [10], DMCoMo always tends to overestimates the estimated efforts (i.e. all project estimations are always bigger than 60 men x month). Therefore, DMCoMo could be used in medium and big-sized projects but it is not useful for small-sized projects. As these are the projects normally required by Small and Medium-sized Enterprises, a new estimation method for Information Mining projects is proposed considering the characteristics of small-sized projects.

3   SMEs' Information Mining Projects

According to the Organization for Economic Cooperation and Development (OECD) Small and Medium-sized Enterprises (SMEs) and Entrepreneurship Outlook report [12]: "SMEs constitute the dominant form of business organization in all countries world-wide, accounting for over 95 % and up to 99 % of the business population depending on country". However, although the importance of SMEs is well known, there is no universal criterion to characterise them. Depending on the country and region, there are different quantitative and qualitative parameters used to recognize a company as SMEs. For instance, at Latin America each country has a different definition [13]: while Argentina considers as SME all independent companies that have an annual turnover lower than USD 20,000 (U.S. dollars maximum amount that depends on the company's activities), Brazil includes all companies with 500 employees or less. On the other hand, the European Union defines as SMEs all companies with 250 employees or less, assets lower than USD 60,000 and gross sales lower than USD 70,000 per year. In that respect, International Organization for Standardization (ISO) has recognized the necessity to specify a software engineering standard for SMEs and thus it is working in the ISO/IEC 29110 standard "Lifecycle profiles for Very Small Entities" [14]. The term 'Very Small Entity' (VSE) was defined by the ISO/IEC JTC1/SC7 Working Group 24 [15] as being "an entity (enterprise, organization, department or project) having up to 25 people".

From these definitions (and our experience), in this paper an Information Mining project for SMEs is demarcated as a project performed at a company of 250 employees or less (at one or several locations) where the high-level managers (usually the company's owners) need non-trivial knowledge extracted from the available databases to solve a specific business problem with no special risks at play. As the company's employees usually do not have the necessary experience, the project is performed by contracted outsourced consultants. From our experience, the project team can be restricted up to 25 people (including both the outsourced consultants and the involved company staff) with maximum project duration of one year.

The Information Mining project's initial tasks are similar to a Conventional Software Development project. The consultants need to elicit both the necessities and desires of the stakeholders, and also the characteristics of the available data sources within the organization (i.e. existing data repositories). Although, the outsourced consultants must have a minimum knowledge and experience in developing Information Mining projects, they might or not have experience in similar projects on the same business type which could facilitate the tasks of understanding the organization and its related data. As the data repositories are not often properly documented, the organization's experts should be interviewed. However, experts are normally scarce and reluctant to get involved in the elicitation sessions. Thus, it is required the willingness of the personnel and the supervisors to identify the correct characteristics of the organization and the data repositories. As the project duration is quite short and the structure of the organization is centralized, it is considered that the elicited requirements will not change.

On the other hand, the Information and Communication Technology (ICT) infrastructure of SMEs is analysed. In [16] it is indicated that more than 70% of Latin

America's SMEs have an ICT infrastructure, but only 37% have automated services and/or proprietary software. Normally commercial off-the-shelf software is used (such as spread-sheets managers and document editors) to register the management and operational information. The data repositories are not large (from our experience, less than one million records) but implemented in different formats and technologies. Therefore, data formatting, data cleaning and data integration tasks will have a considerable effort if there is no available software tools to perform them because ad-hoc software should be developed to implement these tasks.

4   Proposed Effort Estimation Method Oriented to SMEs

For specifying the effort estimation method oriented to SMEs, first, the cost drivers used to characterize a SMEs' project are defined (section 4.1) and then the corresponding formula is presented (section 4.2). This formula has been obtained by regression using real projects information. From 44 real information mining projects available, 77% has been used for obtaining the proposed method's formula (section 4.2) and 23% for validation of the proposed method (section 5). This means that 34 real projects have been used for obtaining the formula and 10 projects for validation.

These real Information Mining projects have been collected by researchers from the Information Systems Research Group of the National University of Lanus (GISI-DDPyT-UNLa), the Information System Methodologies Research Group of the Technological National University at Buenos Aires (GEMIS-FRBA-UTN), and the Information Mining Research Group of the National University of Rio Negro at El Bolson (SAEB-UNRN). It should be noted that all these projects had been performed applying the CRISP-DM methodology [17]. Therefore, the proposed estimation method can be considered reliable only for Information Mining projects developed with this methodology.

4.1   Cost Drivers

Considering the characteristics of Information Mining projects for SMEs indicated in section 3, eight cost drivers are specified. Few cost drivers have been identified in this version because, as explained in [18], when an effort estimation method is created, many of the non-significant data should be ignored. As a result the model is prevented from being too complex (and therefore impractical), the irrelevant and co-dependent variables are removed, and the noise is also reduced. The cost drivers have been selected based on the most critical tasks of CRISP-DM methodology [17]: in [19] it is indicated that building the data mining models and finding patterns is quite simple now, but 90% of the effort is included in the data pre-processing (i.e. "Data Preparation" tasks performed at phase III of CRISP-DM). From our experience, the other critical tasks are related to "Business Understanding" phase (i.e. *"understanding of the business' background"* and *"identifying the project success"* tasks). The proposed cost factors are grouped into three groups as follows:

4.1.1   Cost Drivers Related to the Project

- *Information Mining objective type (OBTY)*
  This cost driver analyses the objective of the Information Mining project and therefore the type of process to be applied based on the definition performed in [5]. The allowed values for this cost drivers are indicated in table 2.

Table 2. Values of OBTY cost driver

Value	Description
1	It is desired to identify the rules that characterize the behaviour or the description of an already known class.
2	It is desired to identify a partition of the available data without having a previously known classification.
3	It is desired to identify the rules that characterize the data partitions without a previous known classification.
4	It is desired to identify the attributes that have a greater frequency of incidence over the behaviour or the description of an already known class.
5	It is desired to identify the attributes that have a greater frequency of incidence over a previously unknown class.

- *Level of collaboration from the organization (LECO)*
  The level of collaboration from the members of the organization is analysed by reviewing if the high-level management (i.e. usually the SME's owners), the middle-level management (supervisors and department's heads) and the operational personnel are willing to help the consultants to understand the business and the related data (specially in the first phases of the project). If the Information Mining project has been contracted, it is assumed that at least the high-level management should support it. The possible values for this cost factor are shown in table 3.

Table 3. Values of LECO cost drivers

Value	Description
1	Both managers and the organization's personnel are willing to collaborate on the project.
2	Only the managers are willing to collaborate on the project while the rest of the company's personnel is indifferent to the project.
3	Only the high-level managers are willing to collaborate on the project while the middle-level manager and the rest of the company's personnel is indifferent to the project.
4	Only the high-level managers are willing to collaborate on the project while middle-level manager is not willing to collaborate.

4.1.2   Cost Drivers Related to the Available Data

- *Quantity and type of the available data repositories (AREP)*
  The data repositories to be used in the Information Mining process are analysed (including data base management systems, spread-sheets and documents among others). In this case, both the quantity of data repositories (public or private from

the company) and the implementation technology are studied. In this stage, it is not necessary to know the quantity of tables in each repository because their integration within a repository is relatively simple as it can be performed with a query statement. However, depending on the technology, the complexity of the data integration tasks could vary. The following criteria can be used:

– If all the data repositories are implemented with the same technology, then the repositories are compatible for integration.

– If the data can be exported into a common format, then the repositories can be considered as compatible for integration because the data integration tasks will be performed using the exported data.

– On the other hand, if there are non-digital repositories (i.e. written paper), then the technology should not be considered compatible for the integration. But the estimation method is not able to predict the required time to perform the digitalization because it could vary on many factors (such as quantity of papers, length, format and diversity among others).

The possible values for this cost factor are shown in table 4.

Table 4. Values of AREP cost driver

Value	Description
1	Only 1 available data repository.
2	Between 2 and 5 data repositories compatible technology for integration.
3	Between 2 and 5 data repositories non-compatible technology for integration.
4	More than 5 data repositories compatible technology for integration.
5	More than 5 data repositories no-compatible technology for integration.

- *Total quantity of available tuples in main table (QTUM)*
  This variable ponders the approximate quantity of tuples (records) available in the main table to be used when applying data mining techniques. The possible values for this cost factor are shown in table 5.

Table 5. Values of QTUM cost driver

Value	Description
1	Up to 100 tuples from main table.
2	Between 101 and 1,000 tuples from main table.
3	Between 1,001 and 20,000 tuples from main table.
4	Between 20,001 and 80,000 tuples from main table.
5	Between 80,001 and 5,000,000 tuples from main table.
6	More than 5,000,000 tuples from main table.

- *Total quantity of available tuples in auxiliaries tables (QTUA)*
  This variable ponders the approximate quantity of tuples (records) available in the auxiliary tables (if any) used to add additional information to the main table (such as a table used to determine the product characteristics associated to the product ID of the sales main table). Normally, these auxiliary tables include fewer records than the main table. The possible values for this cost factor are shown in table 6.

Table 6. Values of QTUA cost driver

Value	Description
1	No auxiliary tables used.
2	Up to 1,000 tuples from auxiliary tables.
3	Between 1,001 and 50,000 tuples from auxiliary tables.
4	More than 50,000 tuples from auxiliary tables.

- *Knowledge level about the data sources (KLDS)*
  The knowledge level about the data sources studies if the data repositories and their tables are properly documented. In other words, if a document exits that defining the technology in which it is implemented, the characteristics of the tables' fields, and how the data is created, modified, and/or deleted.

  When this document is not available, it should be necessary to hold meetings with experts (usually in charge of the data administration and maintenance) to explain them. As a result the project required effort should be increased depending on the collaboration of these experts to help the consultants.

  The possible values for this cost factor are shown in table 7.

Table 7. Values of KLDS cost driver

Value	Description
1	All the data tables and repositories are properly documented.
2	More than 50% of the data tables and repositories are documented and there are available experts to explain the data sources.
3	Less than 50% of the data tables and repositories are documented but there are available experts to explain the data sources.
4	The data tables and repositories are not documented but there are available experts to explain the data sources.
5	The data tables and repositories are not documented, and the available experts are not willing to explain the data sources.
6	The data tables and repositories are not documented and there are not available experts to explain the data sources.

4.1.3   Cost Drivers Related to the available Resources

- *Knowledge and experience level of the information mining team (KEXT)*
  This cost driver studies the ability of the outsourced consultants that will carry out the project. Both the knowledge and experience of the team in similar previous projects are analysed by considering the similarity of the business type, the data to be used and the expected goals. It is assumed that when there is greater similarity, the effort should be lower. Otherwise, the effort should be increased.

  The possible values for this cost factor are shown in table 8.

- *Functionality and usability of available tools (TOOL)*
  This cost driver analyses the characteristics of the information mining tools to be utilized in the project and its implemented functionalities. Both the data preparation functions and the data mining techniques are reviewed.

  The possible values for this cost factor are shown in table 9.

Table 8. Values of KEXT cost driver

Value	Description
1	The information mining team has worked with similar data in similar business types to obtain the same objectives.
2	The information mining team has worked with different data in similar business types to obtain the same objectives.
3	The information mining team has worked with similar data in other business types to obtain the same objectives.
4	The information mining team has worked with different data in other business types to obtain the same objectives.
5	The information mining team has worked with different data in other business types to obtain other objectives.

Table 9. Values of TOOL cost driver

Value	Description
1	The tool includes functions for data formatting and integration (allowing the importation of more than one data table) and data mining techniques.
2	The tool includes functions for data formatting and data mining techniques, and it allows importing more than one data table independently.
3	The tool includes functions for data formatting and data mining techniques, and it allows importing only one data table at a time.
4	The tool includes only functions for data mining techniques, and it allows importing more than one data table independently.
5	The tool includes only functions for data mining techniques, and it allows importing only one data table at a time.

4.2   Estimation Formula

Once the values of the cost drivers have been specified, they were used to characterize 34 information mining projects with their real effort[1] collected by co-researchers as indicated before. A multivariate linear regression method [20] has been applied to obtain a linear equation of the form used by COCOMO family methods [8]. As a result, the following formula is obtained:

$$PEM = 0.80\,OBTY + 1.10\,LECO - 1.20\,AREP - 0.30\,QTUM - 0.70\,QTUA$$
$$+ 1.80\,KLDS - 0.90\,KEXT + 1.86\,TOOL - 3.30 \qquad (1)$$

where *PEM* is the effort estimated by the proposed method for SMEs (in men x month), and the following cost drivers: information mining objective type (*OBTY*), level of collaboration from the organization (*LECO*), quantity and type of the available data repositories (*AREP*), total quantity of available tuples in the main table (*QTUM*) and in auxiliaries tables (*QTUA*), knowledge level about the data sources (*KLDS*), knowledge and experience level of the information mining team (*KEXT*), and functionality and usability of available tools (*TOOL*). The values for each cost driver are defined in tables 2 to 9 respectively of section 4.1.

---

[1] The real projects data used for regression is available at:
    http://tinyurl.com/bm93wol

5   Validation of the Proposed Estimation Method

In order to validate the estimation method defined in section 4, the data of other 10 collected information mining projects is used to compare the accuracy of the proposed method with both the real effort with the effort estimated by DMCoMo method. A brief description of these projects with their applied effort (in men x months) are shown in table 10.

Table 10. Data of the information mining projects used for the validation

#	Business Objectives	Information Mining Objectives	Real Effort (men x month)
P1	The business objective is classifying the different types of cars and reviewing the acceptance of the clients, and detecting the characteristics of the most accepted car.	The process of discovering behaviour rules is used.	2.41
P2	As there is not big increment in the middle segment, the company wants to gain market by attracting new customers. In order to achieve that, it is required to determine the necessities of that niche market.	The process of discovering behaviour rules is used.	7.00
P3	The high management of a company have decided to enhance and expand their market presence by launching a new product. The new concept will be proclaimed as a new production unit which aimed to create more jobs, more sales and therefore more revenue.	The processes of discovering behaviour rules and weighting of attributes are used.	1.64
P4	It is necessary to identify the customer behaviour in order to understand which type of customer is more inclined to buy any package of products. The desired objective is increasing the level of acceptance and sales of product packages.	The process of discovering behaviour rules is used.	3.65
P5	The objectives of the project are performing a personalized marketing campaign to the clients, and locating the ads in the most optimal places (i.e. the places with most CTR).	The process of discovery group-membership rules is used.	9.35
P6	Perform an analysis of the causes why the babies have some deceases when they are born, considering the economic, social and educational level, and also the age of the mother	The processes of discovering behaviour rules and weighting of attributes are used.	11.63
P7	The help desk sector of a governmental organization employs software system to register each received phone call. As a result, it is possible to identify a repairing request, a change or bad function of any computer in order to assign a technical who will solve the problem.	The process of discovering group-membership rules is used.	6.73
P8	The objective is improving the image of the company to the customers by having a better distribution service. This means finding the internal and external factors of the company that affect the delay of the orders to be delivered to customers.	The process of discovering group-membership rules is used.	5.40
P9	The purpose is achieving the best global technologies, the ownership of independent intellectual property rights, and the creation of an internationally famous brand among the world-class global automotive market.	The processes of discovering group-membership rules and weighting of the attributes are used.	8.38
P10	It has been decided to identify the key attributes that produce good quality wines. Once these attributes are detected, they should improve the lesser quality wines.	The processes of discovering behaviour rules and weighting of attributes are used.	1.56

Using the collected project data, the values of the DoCoMo's cost drivers are defined to calculate the corresponding estimation method. Both the formula that uses 8 cost factors (MM8 column) and the formula that uses the 23 cost factors (MM23 column) are applied obtaining the values shown in table 11.

Table 11. Effort calculated by DMCoMo method

#	MM23 (men x month)	MM8 (men x month)	NTAR	NTUP	NATR	DISP	PNUL	DMOP	DEXT	NMOP	TMOP	MTUP	MATR	MTEC	NFUN	SCOM	TOOL	COMP	NFOR	NDEP	DOCU	SITE	KDAT	ADIR	MFAM
P1	94.88	84.23	1	1	7	1	0	1	1	1	0	1	1	1	3	1	1	3	3	4	5	3	4	1	3
P2	51.84	67.16	0	1	1	1	1	4	0	2	1	1	2	1	1	1	1	5	3	2	2	1	3	1	5
P3	68.07	67.16	0	1	1	1	1	1	0	2	1	1	2	1	1	1	1	0	3	2	3	1	3	1	5
P4	111.47	118.99	3	5	5	2	2	2	1	3	3	3	3	5	3	0	1	2	3	1	2	0	2	4	3
P5	122.52	110.92	1	3	3	2	1	5	2	3	1	3	3	3	2	1	1	1	1	4	2	2	4	2	1
P6	81.36	80.27	0	1	1	1	2	1	2	2	1	1	2	1	1	1	1	0	1	1	2	1	1	1	5
P7	92.49	96.02	1	1	1	1	2	1	2	2	3	1	2	4	1	1	1	1	3	3	2	3	2	2	3
P8	89.68	116.87	2	0	3	4	1	0	0	1	1	0	3	1	0	1	1	4	2	0	2	0	1	6	0
P9	98.74	97.63	0	1	1	1	1	1	2	2	4	1	2	1	1	1	1	3	3	4	5	3	3	1	4
P10	103.13	105.32	0	1	1	1	1	0	2	2	4	1	2	4	2	1	1	2	1	2	5	3	2	1	4

Similarly, the same procedure is performed to calculate the effort applying the formula specified in section 3.2 for the proposed estimation method oriented to SMEs (PEM column) as shown in table 12.

Table 12. Effort calculated by the proposed estimation method oriented to SMEs

#	OBTY	LECO	AREP	QTUM	QTUA	KLDS	KEXT	TOOL	PEM (men x month)
P1	1	1	3	3	1	3	2	3	2,58
P2	1	1	1	3	1	3	5	5	6,00
P3	4	1	1	3	3	2	5	3	1,48
P4	1	4	3	5	1	1	2	3	1,68
P5	3	2	2	5	2	3	1	5	9,80
P6	4	1	1	2	1	1	5	5	5,10
P7	3	2	1	4	1	1	2	3	3,78
P8	1	4	1	3	2	1	1	3	4,88
P9	5	1	1	3	3	3	4	5	8,70
P10	4	1	2	2	1	1	4	3	1,08

Finally, in table 13 the estimated efforts are compared with the real effort of each project (REf column) are compared. The efforts calculated by the DMCoMo method (MM8 and MM23 columns) and the proposed method for SMEs (PEM column) are indicating with their corresponding error (i.e. the difference between the real effort and the values calculated by each method). Also, the Relative Error for the estimation of the proposed method is shown (calculated as the error divided by the real effort).

Table 13. Comparison of the calculated efforts (in men x month)

#	REf	DMCoMo				PROPOSED METHOD		
		MM8	REf - MM8	MM23	REf - MM23	PEM	REf - PEM	Relative Error
P1	2.41	84.23	-81.82	94.88	-92.47	2,58	-0.17	-7.2%
P2	7.00	67.16	-60.16	51.84	-44.84	6,00	1.00	14.3%
P3	1.64	67.16	-65.52	68.07	-66.43	1,48	0.16	9.8%
P4	3.65	118.99	-115.34	111.47	-107.82	1,68	1.97	54.0%
P5	9.35	110.92	-101.57	122.52	-113.17	9,80	-0.45	-4.8%
P6	11.63	80.27	-68.65	81.36	-69.73	5,10	6.53	56.1%
P7	6.73	96.02	-89.29	92.49	-85.76	3,78	2.95	43.8%
P8	5.40	116.87	-111.47	89.68	-84.28	4,88	0.52	9.6%
P9	8.38	97.63	-89.26	98.74	-90.36	8,70	-0.33	-3.9%
P10	1.56	105.32	-103.75	103.13	-101.56	1,08	0.48	30.9%

Table 13. *(Continued)*

#	REf	DMCoMo				PROPOSED METHOD		
		MM8	REf - MM8	MM23	REf - MM23	PEM	REf - PEM	Relative Error
Average Error		88.68		85.64		1.46		
Error Variance		380.28		428.99		3.98		

This comparison is reflected in a boxplot graph (figure 1) where the behaviour of the real and calculated efforts are shown by indicating the minimum and maximum values (thin line), standard deviation range (thick line) and average value (marker).

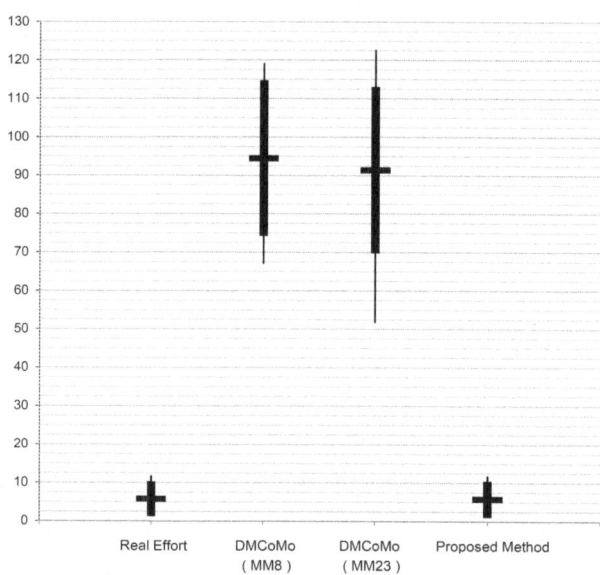

Fig. 1. Boxplot graph comparing the behaviour of the Real Effort with the efforts calculated by DMCoMo and by the proposed estimation method for SMEs

When analysing the results of the DMCoMo method from table 13, it can be seen that the average error is very big (approximately 86 men x months for both formulas) with an error standard deviation of about ± 20 men x months respectively. DMCoMo always tends to overestimate the effort of the project (i.e. the error values are always negative) with a ratio greater than 590% (less difference for the project #6). This behaviour can be seen also graphically in figure 1. In addition, all estimated values are bigger than 60 men x months, which is the maximum threshold value previously identified for SMEs projects. From looking at these results, the conclusions of [9] are confirmed: DMCoMo estimation method is not recommended to predict the effort of small-sized information mining projects.

On the other hand, when the results of the proposed method for SMEs are analysed, it can be seen that the average error is approximately 1.46 men x months with
an error standard deviation of approximately ± 2 men x months. In order to study the
behaviour of the proposed method with the real effort a new boxplot graph is presented in figure 2. From this second boxplot graph, it seems that the behaviour of the
proposed method tends to underestimate the real effort behaviour. There are similar
minimum values (i.e. 1.56 men x months for the real effort and 1.08 men x months for
the proposed method), maximum values (i.e. 11.63 men x months for REf and 9.80
for PEM), and averages (i.e. 5.77 and 4.51 men x months respectively).

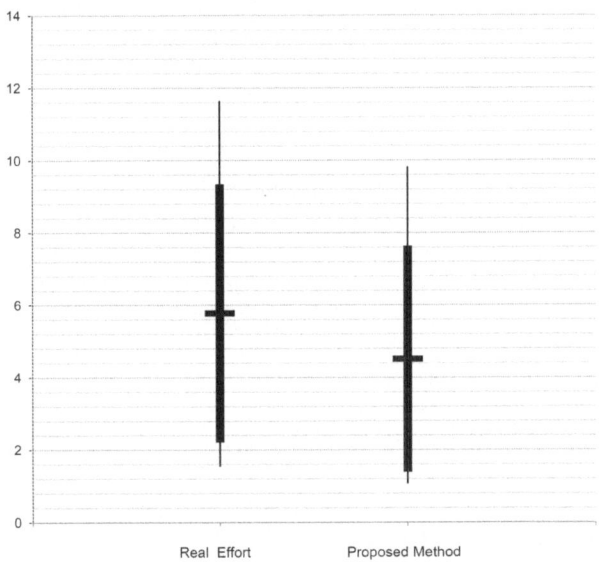

Fig. 2. Boxplot graph comparing the behaviour of the Real Effort with the effort calculated by
the proposed estimation method for SMEs

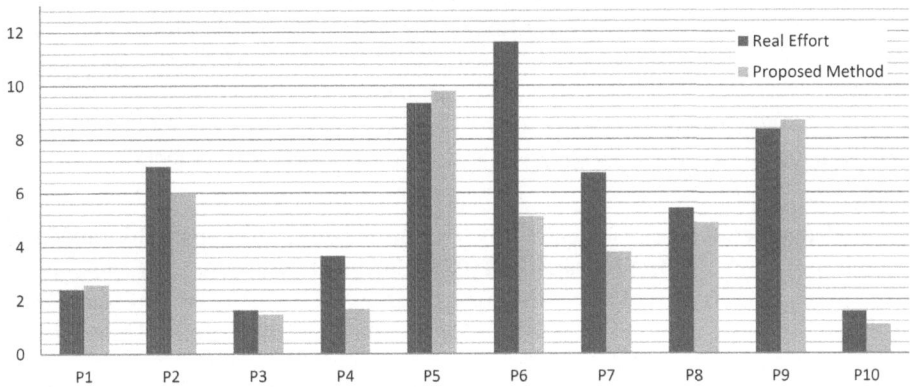

Fig. 3. Bar graph comparing for each project the Real Effort (REf) and the effort calculated by
the proposed estimation method for SMEs (PEM)

Finally, if the real and estimated efforts of each project are compared using a chart graph (figure 3), it can be seen that the estimations of the proposed method are not completely accurate:

— Projects #1, #3, #5, #8 and #9 have estimated efforts with an absolute error smaller than one men x month and a relative error lower than 10%.
— Projects #2 and #10 have an estimated effort smaller than the real one with a relative error lower than 35%. In this case, the average error is about 0.74 men x months with a maximum error of one men x months (project #2).
— At last, projects #4, #6 and #7 have an estimated with a relative error greater than 35% (but lower than 60%). In this case, the maximum error is nearly 7 men x months (project #6) and an average error of 3.81 men x month.

6   Conclusions

Software projects need to predict the cost and effort with its associated quantity of resources at the beginning of every project. The prediction of the required effort to perform an Information Mining project is necessary for Small and Medium-sized Enterprises (SMEs). Considering the characteristics of these projects developed with the CRISP-DM methodology, an estimation method oriented to SMEs has been proposed defining seven cost drivers and formula.

From the validation of the proposed method, it has been seen that that the proposed method produces a more accurate estimation than the DMCoMo method for small-sized projects. But, even though the overall behaviour of the proposed method is similar to real project behaviour, it tends to perform a little underestimation (the average error is smaller than 1.5 men x month). It can be highlighted that 50% of estimations have a relative error smaller than 10%, and the 20% have a relative error between 11% and 35%. For the rest of estimations, the relative error is smaller than 57%. Nevertheless, in all cases the absolute error is smaller than 7 men x months. These errors could be due to the existence of other factors affecting the project effort which have not been considered in this version of the estimation method.

As future research work, the identified issues will be studied in order to provide a more accurate version of the estimation method oriented to SMEs by studying the dependency between the cost drivers and then adding new cost drivers or redefining the existing ones. Another possible approach is modifying the existing equation formula by using an exponential regression with more collected real project data.

Acknowledgements. The research reported in this paper has been partially funded by research project grants 33A105 and 33B102 of National University of Lanus, by research project grants 40B133 and 40B065 of National University of Rio Negro, and by research project grant EIUTIBA11211 of Technological National University at Buenos Aires.

Also, the authors wish to thank to the researchers that provided the examples of real SMEs Information Mining Projects used in this paper.

References

1. Schiefer, J., Jeng, J., Kapoor, S., Chowdhary, P.: Process Information Factory: A Data Management Approach for Enhancing Business Process Intelligence. In: Proceedings 2004 IEEE International Conference on E-Commerce Technology, pp. 162–169 (2004)
2. Stefanovic, N., Majstorovic, V., Stefanovic, D.: Supply Chain Business Intelligence Model. In: Proceedings 13th International Conference on Life Cycle Engineering, pp. 613–618 (2006)
3. Curtis, B., Kellner, M., Over, J.: Process Modelling. Communications of the ACM 35(9), 75–90 (1992)
4. Ferreira, J., Takai, O., Pu, C.: Integration of Business Processes with Autonomous Information Systems: A Case Study in Government Services. In: Proceedings Seventh IEEE International Conference on E-Commerce Technology, pp. 471–474 (2005)
5. Garcia-Martinez, R., Britos, P., Pollo-Cattaneo, F., Rodriguez, D., Pytel, P.: Information Mining Processes Based on Intelligent Systems. In: Proceedings of II International Congress on Computer Science and Informatics (INFONOR-CHILE 2011), pp. 87–94 (2011) ISBN 978-956-7701-03-2
6. García-Martínez, R., Britos, P., Pesado, P., Bertone, R., Pollo-Cattaneo, F., Rodríguez, D., Pytel, P., Vanrell, J.: Towards an Information Mining Engineering. En Software Engineering, Methods, Modeling and Teaching. Sello Editorial Universidad de Medellín, pp. 83–99 (2011) ISBN 978-958-8692-32-6
7. Rodríguez, D., Pollo-Cattaneo, F., Britos, P., García-Martínez, R.: Estimación Empírica de Carga de Trabajo en Proyectos de Explotación de Información. Anales del XVI Congreso Argentino de Ciencias de la Computación, pp. 664–673 (2010) ISBN 978-950-9474-49-9
8. Boehm, B., Abts, C., Brown, A., Chulani, S., Clark, B., Horowitz, E., Madachy, R., Reifer, D., Steece, B.: Software Cost Estimation with COCOMO II. Prentice-Hall, Englewood Cliffs (2000)
9. Marbán, O., Menasalvas, E., Fernández-Baizán, C.: A cost model to estimate the effort of data mining projects (DMCoMo). Information Systems 33, 133–150 (2008)
10. Pytel, P., Tomasello, M., Rodríguez, D., Pollo-Cattaneo, F., Britos, P., García-Martínez, R.: Estudio del Modelo Paramétrico DMCoMo de Estimación de Proyectos de Explotación de Información. In: Proceedings XVII Congreso Argentino de Ciencias de la Computación, pp. 979–988 (2011) ISBN 978-950-34-0756-1
11. García-Martínez, R., Lelli, R., Merlino, H., Cornachia, L., Rodriguez, D., Pytel, P., Arboleya, H.: Ingeniería de Proyectos de Explotación de Información para PYMES. In: Proceedings XIII Workshop de Investigadores en Ciencias de la Computación, pp. 253–257 (2011) ISBN 978-950-673-892-1
12. Organization for Economic Cooperation and Development: OECD SME and Entrepreneurship Outlook 2005. OECD Publishing (2005), doi: 10.1787/9789264009257-en
13. Álvarez, M., Durán, J.: Manual de la Micro, Pequeña y Mediana Empresa. Una contribución a la mejora de los sistemas de información y el desarrollo de las políticas públicas, CEPAL - Naciones Unidas, San Salvador (2009), http://tinyurl.com/d5zarna
14. International Organization for Standardization: ISO/IEC DTR 29110-1 Software Engineering - Lifecycle Profiles for Very Small Entities (VSEs) - Part 1: Overview. International Organization for Standardization (ISO), Geneva, Switzerland (2011)
15. Laporte, C., Alexandre, S.Y., Renault, A.: Developing International Standards for VSEs. IEEE Computer 41(3), 98–101 (2008)

16. Ríos, M.D.: El Pequeño Empresario en ALC, las TIC y el Comercio Electrónico. Instituto para la Conectividad en las Américas (2006), http://tinyurl.com/c97qkjd
17. Chapman, P., Clinton, J., Keber, R., Khabaza, T., Reinartz, T., Shearer, C., Wirth, R.: CRISP-DM 1.0 Step by step BI guide Edited by SPSS (2000), http://tinyurl.com/crispdm
18. Chen, Z., Menzies, T., Port, D., Boehm, D.: Finding the right data for software cost modeling. IEEE Software 22(6), 38–46 (2005), doi:10.1109/MS.2005.151
19. Domingos, P., Elkan, C., Gehrke, J., Han, J., Heckerman, D., Keim, D., et al.: 10 challenging problems in data mining research. International Journal of Information Technology & Decision Making 5(4), 597–604 (2006)
20. Weisberg, S.: Applied Linear Regression. John Wiley & Sons, New York (1985)

Measuring the Impact of Suspension on the Process Enactment Environment during Process Evolution

Pieter Hens[1], Monique Snoeck[1], and Manu De Backer[1,2,3]

[1] KU Leuven, Dept. of Decision Sciences and Information Management,
Naamsestraat 69, 3000 Leuven, Belgium
[2] Universiteit Antwerpen, Dept. of Management Information Systems,
Prinsstraat 13, 2000 Antwerpen, Belgium
[3] Hogeschool Gent, Dept. of Management and Informatics,
Kortrijksesteenweg 14, 9000 Gent, Belgium

Abstract. Current workflow management systems implement the ability to automatically execute predefined process models. However, processes change over time and therefore a redeployment process has to be implemented to propagate changes into the running process enactment environment. One of the necessary steps in change propagation is to suspend the current process execution. This suspension does however decrease availability of the workflow management system, increases downtime and implicitly also decreases scalability. In this paper we provide a quantification of the impact of suspension on the runtime process enactment environment and experimentally evaluate this impact, hereby providing a better insight in suspension impact. Furthermore two suspension techniques are compared and a discussion is provided in which situations, which suspension technique is beneficial.

Keywords: Workflow Enactment, Process Evolution, High Availability Systems.

1   Introduction

Workflow management systems allow for the automated coordination and support of business processes. A business process represents the organizational flow of control and information from one process entity to another. By using an executable business process modeling language to describe the process (like BPMN2.0 [1] or BPEL [2]), a *process engine* can be used to read, interpret, deploy and execute the predefined process model [3]. However, due to changing business requirements, unexpected situations, changing environmental conditions, etc., the system should support the continuous restructuring and redeployment of the deployed process model. A current challenge for any workflow management system is to be able to respond effectively to these process changes.

Two types of runtime process changes can be identified: *ad-hoc change* and *evolutionary change* or *process evolution* [4]. The former handles case or instance

G. Poels (Ed.): CONFENIS 2012, LNBIP 139, pp. 75–89, 2013.
© IFIP International Federation for Information Processing 2013

specific changes and the latter handles case-independent, process model restructuring. In the rest of this paper we restrict ourselves to evolutionary changes. Process evolution means that over time the currently running process model is changed and this modified model has to be deployed in the runtime architecture. Process evolution is typically supported in a workflow management system by adopting a versioning mechanism. As shown in figure 1, each process instance is linked to its corresponding process model (schema) version. This allows new process model versions to be deployed over time. After (re-)deployment, each new process instantiation request is handled with the newest (most current) schema version. In order to also support process changes which not only affect new, but also already running process instances, it is required to migrate running process instances to the new process schema version. When deploying a new schema version, it is determined, according to a specific correctness criterion [5], which running process instances can migrate to the newest version and which can not. Migration is done by simple relinking the process instance and schema version (see figure 1), hereby propagating the change to the running process instances. In more detail, each deployment of a new process schema version undergoes the following steps:

1. Suspend the enactment of all process instances;
2. Determine which process instances can migrate;
3. Deploy the new version and migrate the identified process instances; and
4. Resume the process enactment

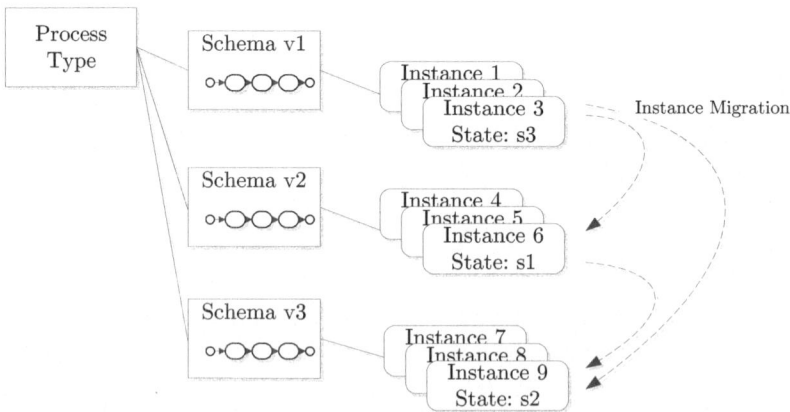

Fig. 1. Versioning and instance migration in a workflow management system

Suspension is necessary, because state based knowledge is required to determine if a process instance can migrate. Globally, instance migration can happen when the current execution state of the process instance is compliant with the new process schema. If the process instance is not suspended, the execution state of the instance can change during the deployment process, resulting in a possibly inconsistent system's execution state (i.e. instances which are not able to migrate are migrated nonetheless). A first objective of this paper is to examine how this suspension affects the process enactment environment during process evolution. Especially if lots of process instances have to be inspected to determine process instance migration, process enactment suspension creates a possibly unwanted downtime of the system during process evolution. This downtime could be problematic for systems which need to be highly available. For example, the foreign exchange market is a continuous market which accepts orders 24 hours a day. The processes behind these trading systems therefore have to be highly available and downtime should be limited to a minimum. Because of the necessary suspension, changing a process model and deploying it in the runtime environment disrupts the process execution, and therefore the business (e.g. trading). In which way the suspension during process evolution disrupts the enactment environment is however not yet investigated. This paper provides a better insight into the impact of suspension on the process enactment environment. The focus of this research is on process evolution for high availability systems.

Because suspension during process evolution can be harmful to some systems, we also investigate if a different approach to process evolution can be beneficial for those systems. Typically, process instances are suspended in their entirety, no matter the execution state of the instance. We call this *global suspension* (see the example in the top part of figure 2). Global suspension means that the process engine controlling the process instances is suspended, therefore suspending every running process instance and halting any state change in those instances. In a previous project we introduced a technique which enables, in contrast to global suspension, *partial suspension* of a process enactment [6]. Partial suspension allows the suspension of only specific parts of the process model, where the rest of the process can keep executing. The process engine is therefore not suspended in its entirety, but is still allowed to control specific parts of the process model. The bottom part of figure 2 shows an example of partial suspension. This suspension technique has the obvious advantage that during process evolution, some parts of the process model are not suspended and therefore do not experience downtime. A second goal of this paper is therefore to investigate how the reduced downtime resulting from the partial suspension technique impacts the enactment environment and how this compares to the impact when using global suspension. Moreover we discuss if using a different approach to suspension during process evolution can actually improve the availability and scalability of a high availability workflow management system. To the best of our knowledge this is the first research which evaluates a suspension technique for process enactment.

We can formulate our research questions as follows:

RQ(1) What is the impact of suspension on the runtime processes during process evolution?

> **RQ(a)** What is the impact of global suspension on the runtime processes during process evolution?
>
> **RQ(b)** What is the impact of partial suspension on the runtime processes during process evolution?

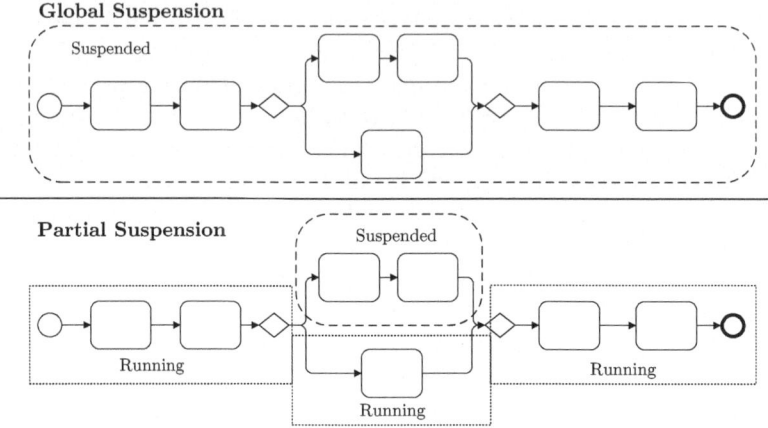

Fig. 2. Global versus partial suspension of the process enactment

RQ(2) Does a high availability process system benefit from using a different technique for process evolution (e.g. partial suspension)?

The contributions of this paper include the definition of four variables which measure the impact of suspension on the process enactment environment (section 4) and a provision of a better insight into the impact of suspension on the process enactment environment, varying over different system variables (section 4.1, 4.2 and 4.3). First, some background is provided in instance migration and the partial suspension technique (section 2). The paper concludes with a discussion of the benefits and disadvantages of partial and global suspension (section 5).

2   Background

In the experiments that investigate the impact of suspension on the enactment environment, both global and partial suspension is used. This allows the comparison of traditional process evolution with another suspension technique. In order to perform the experiments, we need a criterion that determines which process instances are able to migrate and we need a test environment that allows to (globally and partially) suspend, resume and migrate processes.

To determine which process instance is able to migrate, a migration criterion needs to be employed. For this purpose we used the change region technique introduced by van der Aalst [7]. The change region defines a region of states in the process model, computed from the old and new schema version. Figure 3 shows an example process model with two versions and their change region. A process instance with an execution state residing inside the change region is not able to migrate. If it resides outside the region, it is able to migrate. The deployment manager therefore checks the execution state of each (suspended) process instance and migrates any instance accordingly.

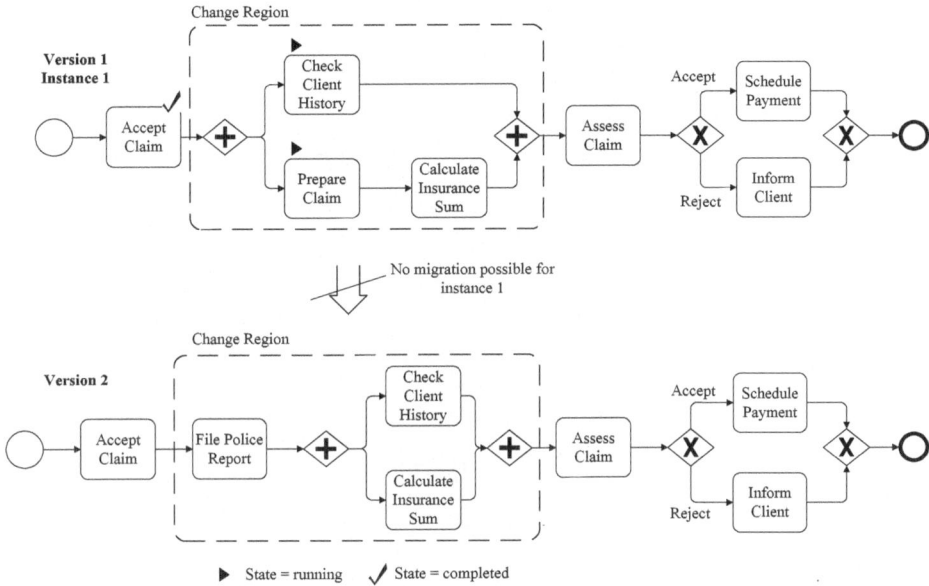

Fig. 3. Two versions of an insurance claim handling process

To implement partial suspension, a different method for process enactment has to be used. In a previous project we developed an approach to fragmented process enactment [8]. A process model is fragmented into logically different pieces, where each fragment is executed on its own, dedicated process engine (see figure 4). This fragmentation facilitates the fine grained control of the process model enactment. Each fragment's execution can be suspended, resumed, inspected and changed independently of others. For process evolution, this means that only a (sufficient) part of the process model execution can be suspended during model redeployment, in stead of the model in its entirety. In [6], we propose a process evolution protocol for the fragmented enactment environment and provide a method to determine the minimal part of the process model which needs to be suspended during process evolution. For the example in figure 3 the minimal fragments (tasks) that need to be suspended are the tasks *check client history, prepare claim, calculate insurance sum* and *accept claim*. All other parts of the model are still able to execute during redeployment, i.e. a process instance which reached an execution state not belonging to the suspended fragments can keep executing. For figure 3 this means that a process instance that resides in a state where task *assess claim* is being executed is still able to move to an execution state where *schedule payment* or *inform client* is triggered (the execution of this instance is not halted during process evolution).

Note that when a process instance is suspended, *process control* is suspended, not the actual work items (tasks) in the process. Already started tasks can finish their execution, regardless of the state of the process model enactment. Suspension therefore means that control (token) transfer in the process enactment is

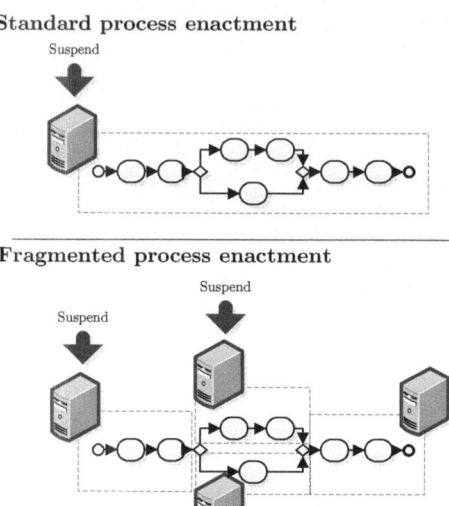

Fig. 4. Traditional and fragmented process enactment

halted (i.e. no new task executions are triggered), but already existing task instances can keep running. For example, a task "boat shipment" is not suspended during process evolution, but the state change in the process instance indicating the completion of the shipment task is not permitted.

For a further elaboration of the fragmented execution and the change region evolution protocol we refer to [6].

3   Experimental Setup

To analyze the impact of *partial (but sufficient) suspension* and *global suspension* on the enactment environment during process evolution, experiments are performed with our own implemented execution environment[1]. The effect of global and partial suspension is analyzed, varying over: process instantiation rate (section 4.1), task execution time (section 4.2) and position of the change in the process model (section 4.3). For each configuration, the throughput (process instance completions per time unit) is measured. To exclude randomness (from the Java program execution, CPU scheduling, etc.) each experimental configuration is run 3 times. The average throughput of these 3 runs is used for the further analysis. In the experimental setup we assume unlimited resources[2], to exclude

---

[1] The execution environment is implemented in Java and run on an Intel Core 2 Duo, 2.66GHz, with 4GB RAM configuration.

[2] This is simulated by not letting tasks perform any actual work (e.g. no SOAP call to a web service), but *'sleep'* through their designated task time. The execution environment itself has a sufficient performance to handle a large amount of simultaneous process instances and therefore does not interfere with the measurements [8].

performance issues of process coordination [8]. This way we only measure the influence of the suspension technique on the process execution. In all but one experiments the two versions of the insurance claim handling process model as shown in figure 3 is used as experimental model (since this model is also used in earlier work [6]).

Throughput of the process enactment is measured for a certain time period, in which the following two steps are performed:

1. Deploy version 1 of the insurance claim handling process; and
2. At a fixed time ($t = 6$), version 2 of the insurance claim handling process is deployed into the running enactment environment. This triggers the process evolution steps as described in the introduction. The change region and suspension criteria are calculated; the process enactment is suspended; the new model is deployed; any possible running process instances are migrated and the enactment is resumed again.

Note that, since we focus on high availability and continuous systems, the (independent) clients continue sending process instantiation requests during the process evolution deployment process (at a specified request rate).

4   Analysis

Figure 5 shows the throughput measured over time for both global and partial suspension during process evolution. Time is indicated in units (tu), throughput is measured per time unit and the client sends a constant number of requests per time unit ($rptu$). From the graph we can identify four disparity variables, quantifying the impact of suspension on the process enactment environment:

(1) suspension-start indicating when the effect of suspension is noticeable in throughput;
(2) suspension-base indicating the lowest throughput during process evolution;

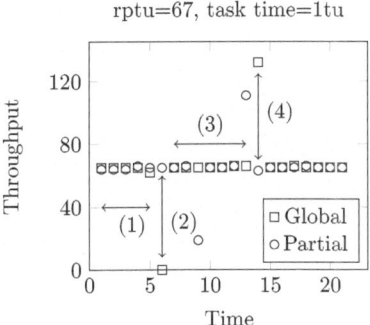

Fig. 5. Throughput over time for a process execution where a process change happens at time 6

(3) catchup-time indicating the time needed to handle any backlog buildup and revert back to the standard (average) throughput; and

(4) backlog-summit indicating the highest throughput during process evolution, i.e. the backlog that formed during suspension.

In figure 5 we see that the suspension-base with global suspension equals zero. This will always be the case, since the entire process execution is suspended, thus not allowing any process instances to complete over a certain time period. For partial suspension, the suspension-base never reaches zero, as the environment is still able to complete some process instances during suspension (since not every fragment is suspended, see section 2). Similarly, the backlog that is created during suspension is noticeably smaller for partial suspension. Another prominent difference is that the effect of suspension is only visible at a later time for partial suspension than for global suspension. The catchup-time is therefore also smaller for partial suspension.

In the next sections, we vary over different configurations, investigating how these four variables fluctuate, comparing partial and global suspension. Since in some configurations, the throughput is much more irregular than the example shown in figure 5, we capture the four variables (dispersion of the throughput during process evolution) by means of the *Mean Absolute Deviation (MAD)*[3]:

$$D = \frac{1}{n} \sum_{i=1}^{n} |x_i - m(X)| \tag{1}$$

where $m(X)$ equals the average throughput under normal conditions (standard execution, no suspension and process evolution). The MAD is calculated for the entire time period of the experiment (20tu in this case). In the case of figure 5, $D(global) = 6.75$ and $D(partial) = 4.81$. A higher value means a bigger dispersion, and therefore a bigger throughput irregularity during process evolution.

4.1   Effect of RPTU on Suspension Throughput

To test the effect of varying process instantiation rate (or *system load*) on the throughput during process evolution, an experiment is set up that enacts the insurance claim handling process and where a change as described in section 3 is initiated. Throughput is measured for each time interval and the experiment is rerun for different process instantiation rates.

Figure 6 shows the depth of the suspension (suspension-base) for each request rate, for partial suspension as well as for global suspension. As already mentioned, the suspension-base for global suspension is always zero, no matter

---

[3] Note that MAD is closely related to standard deviation, also measuring dispersion. We have chosen MAD, because it gives a more comprehensible (descriptive) dispersion score. MAD can however not be used in mathematical statistics, which is no problem because we only use the dispersion scores for a relative comparison. For a discussion on MAD we refer to [9].

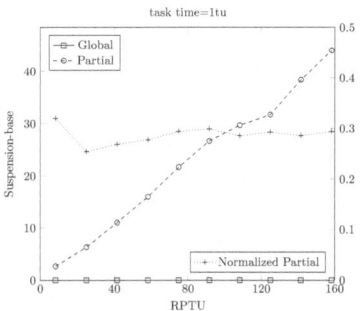

Fig. 6. Suspension-base with varying request rate

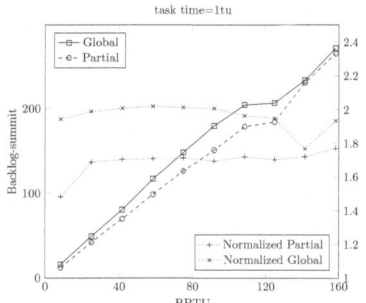

Fig. 7. Backlog-summit with varying request rate

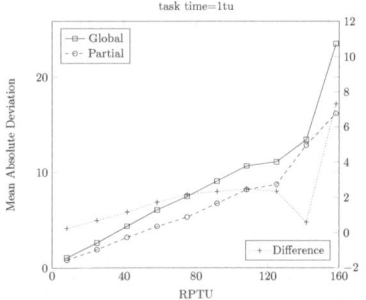

Fig. 8. Mean Absolute Deviation of throughput with varying RPM and constant task time

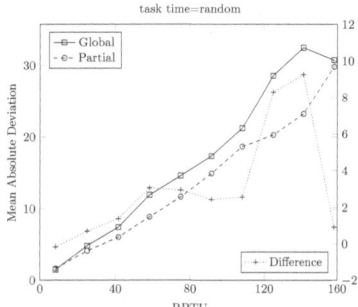

Fig. 9. Mean Absolute Deviation of throughput with varying RPM and random task time

the request rate. For partial suspension, we notice an increase in the minimum throughput during process evolution as the request rate increases. This is a consequence of the increased process instantiation rate. Since more requests are sent per time unit, more instances can also be completed per time unit. Under the assumption of unlimited resources (see section 3), the suspension-base increases linearly with respect to request rate. For limited resources, throughput will reach a maximum at a certain load (request rate) and the suspension-base will flatten out at higher request rates. See [8] and [10] for process execution performance tests.

To evaluate if rptu has a relative effect on the suspension-base, the normalized values of the suspension-base for partial suspension are also depicted on figure 6. From the normalized values we can conclude that the suspension-base does not increase or decrease, relative to the request rate. The same conclusions can be drawn for the backlog-summit (see figure 7). At higher request rates, the backlog will be bigger (since more process instantiations are requested during suspension). However, relative to the request rate, the backlog-summit stays constant for either partial and global suspension.

Figure 8 shows the MAD for partial and global suspension. Here we can conclude that partial suspension has a slight advantage over global suspension, i.e. the process throughput is less irregular during process evolution, using the partial suspension technique. This advantage is however not dependent on request rate. In general, the throughput during process evolution is fairly resilient against varying request rates for both partial and global suspension techniques.

The previous results are all experiments performed where each task has a similar, constant task time. This is not realistic as every task execution can have a different duration (even within the same process instance), which is especially true for human tasks. To inspect the influence of different task times, figure 9 shows the MAD for the same experiment, but with random task times (random per task, per instance). Although the MAD is higher, the conclusions are similar to the experiments with constant task times. There is no influence of request rate on throughput during process evolution and partial suspension undergoes a smaller throughput irregularity than global suspension. Further experiments are therefore done with a constant task time, so that any randomness will not interfere with the results.

Suspension-start and catchup-times are in this case not reported because they stay constant at any request rate.

4.2   Effect of Task Times on Suspension Throughput

In this section we evaluate the effect of task execution times on the throughput during process evolution. An experiment is set up with the same configuration as in the previous section with the difference that we vary over task times and not process instantiation rate (rptu=70).

Figure 10 and 11 show the throughput during process enactment and process evolution, for a task timing of $\frac{1}{5}$tu and a timing of 2.6tu. The big difference between the two throughput measurements is the much higher dispersion when the task time is bigger (Figure 11). In stead of one drop in throughput and one increase to handle the backlog, there is an entire range of drops and increases until the process enactment stabilizes again (catchup). This is especially apparent for the global suspension. As the process gets suspended, the throughput drops to zero at time t, at time $t+1$ the throughput increases to $\pm$ the backlog-summit and drops again to zero at time $t+2$. This alternation continues until the enactment stabilizes. Figure 12 explains why this phenomenon happens. During suspension, each task is still able to finish its execution, only the process engine is suspended (see section 2). This means that, during suspension, a backlog of control flow tokens which need to be transferred to the next task in the process model is created for each task in the model (see figure 12). Once the process enactment is resumed, the backlog is transferred in its entirety to the next task in the process flow (each token buffer is shifted one place to the right). Hereafter, each task will handle the received backlog in its entirety and simultaneously (process instances are handled in parallel). Since task execution takes a significant amount of time

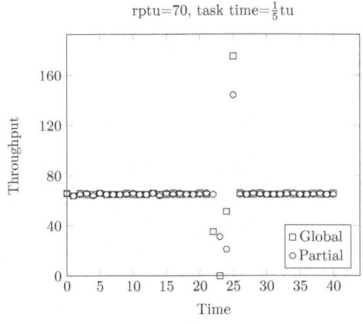

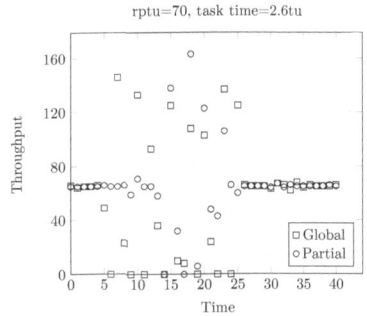

Fig. 10. Throughput over time, with task execution time=$\frac{1}{5}$tu

Fig. 11. Throughput over time, with task execution time=2.6tu

($2.6tu$), throughput drops to zero in the first time period after resumption (no process instances are completing, since there are still tasks left to be done). When the tasks finish execution of the backlog, the token buffer is again shifted one place to the right in the process model. For the last task in the model, this means that the respective process instances are completed. A higher throughput is therefore measured (all instances in the last task's backlog finish simultaneously). This alternation continues until every created backlog per task is handled.

Figure 13 shows the MAD with varying task times and an rptu of 70. The absolute difference between global suspension and partial suspension is also depicted. From the incline of the difference graph we see that there is a larger effect of increasing task times on throughput irregularity for global suspension than partial suspension. The larger the task timings, the larger the relative benefit of using partial suspension as a suspension technique in process evolution.

4.3 Effect of the Change Position on Suspension Throughput

To measure the effect of the change position in the process model, we used the test model shown in figure 14. The change propagated in the enactment system is a task deletion, resulting in the partial suspension of two tasks, the deleted task and the task in the upward flow (see section 2). Throughput is measured for each change propagation: deletion of task A, deletion of task B, etc.

Figure 15 shows the throughput when a change happens in the beginning of the process model (task A is deleted) and figure 16 shows the throughput when a change happens at the end of the process model (task G is deleted). The difference in suspension-start for the partial suspension technique is clearly noticeable from these two graphs. When a change happens in the beginning of the process flow, the effect of the suspension is visible in throughput at a later time than when the change happens at the end of the process flow. Figure 17 provides an overview of suspension-start across varying change positions. The shifting suspension-start for partial suspension is due to the fact that when the suspension zone is at the beginning of the process model, every process instance

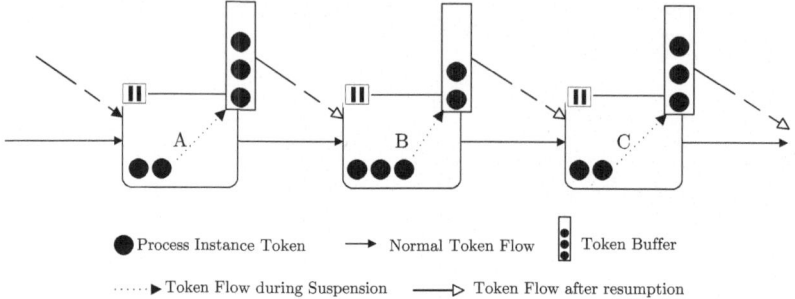

Fig. 12. The reason for alternating suspension-base/summit with larger task execution times

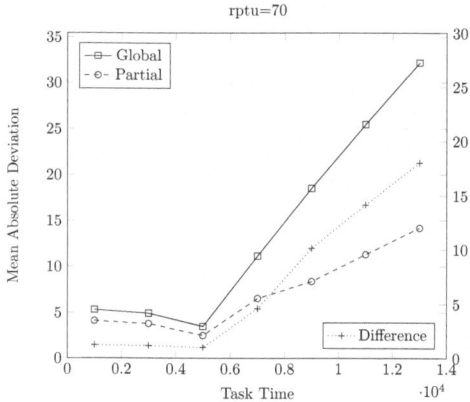

Fig. 13. Mean Absolute Deviation of throughput with varying task time

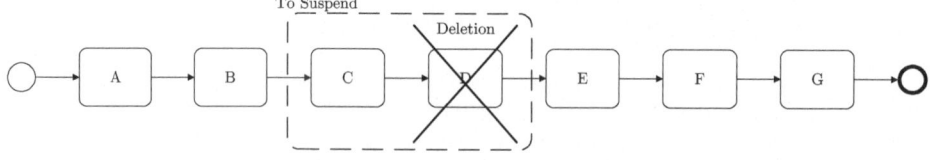

Fig. 14. Test model for measuring the effect of the change position on suspension throughput

already past the suspension zone can still complete without any downtime (the effect is only noticeable at a later time). When the suspension zone is at the end of the process model, almost every running process instance is *blocked* by the suspended fragments (the effect is immediately visible).

The MAD for each change position configuration is however always the same (figure 18). Suspension-start varies according to the change position, but the catch-up time, suspension-base and backlog-summit are constant.

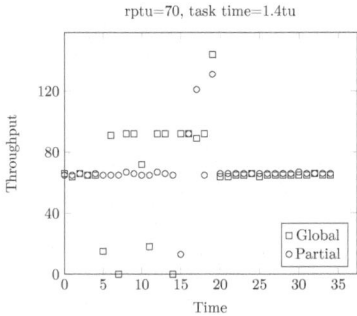

Fig. 15. Throughput over time, with a change at the beginning of the process flow (delete A)

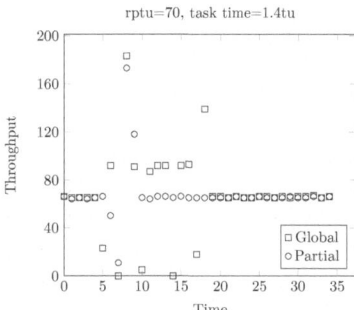

Fig. 16. Throughput over time, with a change at the end of the process flow (delete G)

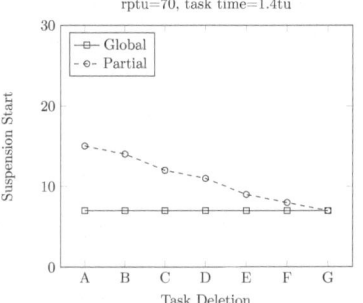

Fig. 17. Suspension-start with varying change position

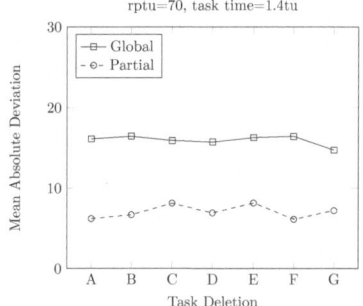

Fig. 18. Mean Absolute Deviation of throughput with varying change region position

5   Discussion

In the previous section we measured throughput during process evolution, quantifying the impact suspension has on process enactment. Comparing the results we see that with the partial suspension technique, throughput experiences a smaller irregularity than when using global suspension. Indeed, partial suspension leaves room for process instances to still complete and execute, even when the system is suspended. This decreases downtime of the overall process enactment environment. For increasing task times, partial suspension even has an increasing relative advantage over global suspension. In both the other cases, changing request rate and changing position, the relative advantage of partial suspension is constant (but existing nonetheless).

Besides reduced downtime, another advantage of partial suspension observed in the experiments is a diminished backlog buildup. Backlog buildup and an irregular execution can be problematic for less scalable systems. In a real-life scenario, resources are limited and if the backlog grows larger, more process instances have to be handled simultaneously. At heavy loads the performance of process execution degrades and throughput drops [10]. In [8] we show that already at 83rptu, a process engine significantly loses performance and has trouble catching up. A high backlog buildup will therefore decrease performance, further increasing the irregularity during process evolution.

There is thus an advantage of using the partial suspension technique, but it can be argued that it remains fairly small. The process evolution protocol is rather quick, which limits the downtime (suspension time) of the enactment. In our experiments, the catchup-time when using global suspension is $\pm$ 2 minutes (for 10 second task timings). At some point in time throughput equals zero for global suspension, but the downtime stays limited to a very small time period. The advantages of partial suspension are therefore limited to systems which satisfy the following assumptions: high availability is required, there is a continuous client request rate and process evolution is performed during this (busy) process enactment. In the introduction we already gave one example of such a system: the foreign exchange market, which satisfies all the assumptions. Other systems could satisfy the assumptions on specific (unforeseen) moments and benefit from the partial suspension technique in these situations. For example, in a Short Message Service (SMS) [11] process implemented by a telecommunications company, it is defined that after each SMS sent a confirmation of receipt is sent back to the sender of that SMS. During high loads of the network (e.g. big events, natural disasters [12], ...), the company may want to disable the confirmation SMS, and therefore has a need to change the implemented process during process enactment. Since availability is important in these situations, the downtime caused by process evolution should be limited. In this specific case is partial suspension during process evolution beneficial.

The benefits of partial suspension are therefore only limited to very specific environments, but it can be very valuable on these systems.

6   Conclusion and Future Research

In this paper we investigated the impact of suspension on the process enactment environment when process evolution is needed. A better insight in the effect of suspension is provided by defining four variables which quantify this effect: suspension-start, suspension-base, catchup-time and backlog-summit. During suspension, process throughput drops and a backlog is created which increases the load on the enactment system. Furthermore we compared two different suspension techniques for process evolution: global suspension and partial suspension. The partial suspension technique has a reduced impact on the process enactment environment, provides for a smaller downtime and decreases the backlog buildup. These benefits are however only profitable in very limited situations: high availability systems that have a continuous process instantiation request rate. For these systems, the partial suspension technique can be very valuable. In other cases the advantages of partial suspension do not outweigh the overhead of implementing the technique in the workflow management system.

This paper is focused on evolutionary changes. Future research involves investigating the impact of ad-hoc, case-specific changes. Is the change impact of updating a case-specific scenario similar to the impact of propagating a case-independent change?

References

1. Object Management Group: Bpmn 2.0 (June 2010),
   http://www.omg.org/cgi-bin/doc?dtc/10-06-04
2. Oracle: Bpel process manager (May 2010),
   http://www.oracle.com/technology/products/ias/bpel/index.html
3. van der Aalst, W.M.P., ter Hofstede, A.H.M., Weske, M.: Business Process Management: A Survey. In: van der Aalst, W.M.P., ter Hofstede, A.H.M., Weske, M. (eds.) BPM 2003. LNCS, vol. 2678, pp. 1–12. Springer, Heidelberg (2003)
4. Weber, B., Sadiq, S., Reichert, M.: Beyond rigidity–dynamic process lifecycle support. Computer Science Research and Development 23(2), 47–65 (2009)
5. Rinderle, S., Reichert, M., Dadam, P.: Correctness criteria for dynamic changes in workflow systems–a survey. Data & Knowledge Engineering 50(1), 9–34 (2004)
6. Hens, P., Snoeck, M., De Backer, M., Poels, G.: Process evolution in a distributed process execution environment. Submitted for International Journal on Information System Modeling and Design (2012)
7. van der Aalst, W.: Exterminating the dynamic change bug: A concrete approach to support workflow change. Information Systems Frontiers 3(3), 297–317 (2001)
8. Hens, P., Snoeck, M., De Backer, M., Poels, G.: An autonomous distributed system for business process execution. Submitted for Information Systems (2011)
9. Gorard, S.: Revisiting a 90-year-old debate: the advantages of the mean deviation. British Journal of Educational Studies 53(4), 417–430 (2005)
10. Nanda, M., Chandra, S., Sarkar, V.: Decentralizing execution of composite web services. ACM SIGPLAN Notices 39(10), 170–187 (2004)
11. Peersman, C., Cvetkovic, S., Griffiths, P., Spear, H.: The global system for mobile communications short message service. IEEE Personal Communications 7(3), 15–23 (2000)
12. Ministery of Internal Affairs and Communications (Japan): Maintaining communications capabilities during major natural disasters and other emergency situations (2011), http://www.soumu.go.jp/main_content/000146938.pdf

User Perceptions, Motivations and Implications on ERP Usage: An Indian Higher Education Context

Jyoti M. Bhat, Bhavya Shroff, and Rajendra K. Bandi

Indian Institute of Management, Bangalore, India
{jyoti.bhat,bhavya.ps,rbandi}@iimb.ernet.in

Abstract. Globally ERP implementation in higher education (HE) sector has been increasing with universities under pressure to improve their performance and efficiency. Most of the studies related to ERP implementation in higher education are related to the factors which influence the success of ERP implementation or failures across various universities especially in the US and Australia. There is limited study of ERP implementation in HE institutes from a user perspective. Indian HE institutions have just started adopting ERP and there is no study available related to the Indian universities. In this paper we study the employee perceptions, motivations and use of ERP and the implications to the organization objectives. We study the ERP implementation in an Indian HE institute and provide a descriptive case study which can serve as a real life example for HE institutes in India and other developing countries planning to implement Enterprise Systems.

Keywords: Case study, Motivations, User perceptions, ERP implementation, Higher education.

1 Introduction

Enterprise Resource Planning (ERP) is an integrated management tool in the form of software packages which are implemented in organizations to integrate all the existing organizational systems and functions [1]. The implementation of ERP is one of the most pervasive change activities that organizations have brought in during the last decade. There are several factors on which the outcome of any technology implementation depends, including activities of decision makers and on how end users respond to those activities [2]. ERP systems have been introduced into higher education (HE) sector to improve and integrate the management and administration processes in student registration, human resources systems and financial processing [1]. But in educational institutes the ERP system implementation has been problematic due to lack of ERP implementation expertise and IT resources [3].

Globally there has been an increase in ERP adoption in higher education institutions and the HE ERP market has shown rapid growth and consolidation in the recent years [4]. While it is accepted that ERP in HE is different from implementing ERP in the corporate settings [5, 6], existing academic literature studying ERP implementation in HE is limited. Literature covers the drivers for ERP adoption in

G. Poels (Ed.): CONFENIS 2012, LNBIP 139, pp. 90–105, 2013.
© IFIP International Federation for Information Processing 2013

universities and HE sector such as modernization of systems, need for greater flexibility and usability, business process reengineering, integration of data and systems, risk avoidance and reduced maintenance [6, 7], and the issues with ERP implementation such as organizational issues related to decision-making process, management support, change management practices, project management issues, privacy & security issues and impact of organizational culture [1, 8].

Indian education institutions have started adopting IT for administration and teaching. ERP adoption in Indian HE has recently picked up and differs from that in universities in other countries on aspects like IT management capabilities of the HE institution, lack of IT exposure of the administrative staff, organizational structure, vendor experience, and implementation support in the Indian IT market. For instance, many of the senior administrative staff in educational institutions are not exposed to computer usage and introduction of ERP systems requires considerable training for the staff.

In this paper we study the ERP implementation in an Indian higher education institution. The focus of the study is on employee perceptions, motivations and use of ERP and the implication to the organizational goals. We first provide the theoretical background and the research question. Next, the case study is presented by providing details of the research method followed by an overview of the case study organization. We discuss the detailed case analysis along with the findings, followed by the conclusions.

2   Theoretical Background and Research Question

ERP systems were initially designed, to support common organizational functions like payroll, human resource management, materials management, accounting, etc. As ERP was extended to new contexts like public sector, higher education, and services industry, new modules have been added to cater to the industry specific needs and operations [5]. In the context of HE, ERP systems provide a different set of administrative and academic functionalities like handling admissions of students (e.g. processing student application forms, candidate short-listing, fee processing), course enrollments, student data management (e.g., attendance tracking, grade information), course management (e.g. enrollment, feedback on courses), asset management(e.g., contracts, grants), library systems, financial systems, alumni management and research networks [5] [9]. Hence the context of HE offers unique set of requirements and challenges for the ERP implementation.

The complexity and the wide ranging impact of ERP implementation make it an organizational change initiative rather than just a technology implementation effort. Hence, Hong and Kim [10] state organizational resistance to change as one of the critical success factors (CSF) for ERP implementation. User resistance to ERP and IS systems and strategies for managing them have been studied by various researchers [11, 12]. Studies capturing the difference in perception among decision makers and end users with respect to effective implementation activities are limited [13]. As compared to corporates, educational institutes depend on boardroom consensus rather than managerial prerogative [14] and a distributed authority structure [15]. McCredie and Updegrove [16], based on their experience in US institutions, highlight the need to develop decision-making frameworks in HE institutions specifically to assist ERP implementations, as consensus based decision making does not work in ERP projects. Other inefficiencies in ERP implementation due to HE organization structures are lack of communication among units, lack of transparency of responsibilities and business processes [17]. The critical success factors [15, 18] and factors leading to unsuccessful and ineffective ERP implementation in HE institutes [8] have been discussed by researchers.

Siau and Messersmith [19] highlight the need to focus on the end-users who hold the key to ERP implementation success, especially in public institutions. Through a qualitative content analysis, they find that during ERP implementation in HE, special attention needs to be paid to stakeholder participation, internal and external communication and business process reengineering. Their study also finds that motivating employees intrinsically is of great benefit to universities making significant organizational changes (like ERP implementation), especially when they cannot financially afford other motivational facilities. Abugabah and Sanzogni [20] provide a detailed literature survey of ERP implementation in HE and find that, while most studies of ERP focus on the technical issues or implementation processes, studies of user perspectives are less evident in literature. They point out the need to shift research attention to more important elements such as users, task and system and how these can increase the benefits of ERP. The behavioural intention of a user's acceptance of information system can be well defined by 'Technology Acceptance Model' (TAM) [21, 22]. According to TAM, the behavioural intention to accept any technology depends on two key beliefs, the perceived usefulness and the ease of use [21]. Perceived usefulness is an individual's subjective probability of how an information system application can enhance his or her job performance, whereas ease of use is the degree to which user feels the system to be free of effort.

For any implementation, end user satisfaction is an important measure of the success of the respective system [23, 24]. The difference between the implementation perception of end user and management level employee is evident at all developmental stages as users have conflicting information requirements and end users do not have any power on system design [25]. It is very important for the decision makers that they ensure end user involvement in the system development process [18]. Several stakeholders involved in ERP implementation, including top management, project manager, team leaders, trainers, end user, consultants and vendors [13] may have their own interests in ERP implementation [26].The absence of a shared understanding of project benefits may contribute to implementation difficulties. Also, ERP systems have the potential to dramatically alter jobs and business processes [27].

Huang and Palvia [28] identify differences in the ERP implementation issues in advanced and developing countries. At the macro level, issues of ERP implementation in developing countries are infrastructure, economic growth, and government regulations; and at the organization level, low IT maturity, small size of firms, lack of process management and BPR experience. They find that in India and China, organizations lack a culture that regards computers as a pervasive way of doing business. Soh, Kein & Tay-Yap [29] suggest that cultural 'misfit' i.e., gap between the functionality in the ERP package and the requirements of the adopting organizations may be higher in Asia because the business models and processes embedded in most

ERP packages reflect European and U.S. industry practices. Studies exist which look at the modifications required to transfer and adapt ERP systems built for developed countries to the socio-organizational conditions of developing countries [30, 31]. Plant and Willcocks [32] extend the work related to the critical success factors of ERP by Somers & Nelson [33] and find that the CSFs differ by country and context.

The literature review while highlighting the importance of user participation, their motivation and perceptions for the successful adoption of ERP, identifies the need for ERP studies from a user perspective. The existing research studies on CSF also bring out the differences in CSF priorities based on national and cultural issues.

Our research objective is to study the ERP implementation in the Indian HE scenario from a user perspective. The broad research question we are addressing is: Does the Indian HE context offer uniqueness for ERP implementation? The paper explores this in terms of administrative and management work practices, perceptions of the administrative and academic work-force about ERP, decision-making and change management.

3   Research Method

The research method adopted is that of a case study. This qualitative method has been chosen since it helps investigate a contemporary situation within its real life context. The primary intent of the case study is to understand the perceptions and motivations of the staff and management about the ERP implementation in the Indian HE institution. A single descriptive case study was conducted of a leading business school in India. The single case study approach was used to provide a richer understanding of the situation and not to test any theory [34]. As the study was to understand the employee perceptions and capture the contextual complexity, data was collected through semi-structured open-ended interviews rather than administering a questionnaire. The method helped to get the direct reports of attitudes and perceptions of the interviewees and achieve depth in the study.

The sampling method employed for the interviews was what Marshall and Rossman [35] classify as 'elite interviewing', "a specialized case of interviewing that focuses on a particular type of interviewee" (p: 94) "considered to be the influential, the prominent, and the well-informed people in an organization" (p: 83). While this method can give rise to 'elite bias', it has been ensured that the interviewees include those from various levels within the organization to 'represent various "voices"' [36].The ERP Chairperson was the key informant who provided information regarding the goals and motivations of ERP implementation at the Institute, the product evaluation, selection, implementation approach, plan, progress and challenges in the ERP implementation. He also assisted the study by providing a list of key people involved in the ERP project and the primary users and units within the Institute. The choice of respondents was made by the researchers to ensure coverage across different units, roles and employment experience with the Institute. The ERP program manager, an independent consultant, responsible for the ERP implementation program was identified as another key informant. A phase-wise ERP implementation approach was being adopted in the Institute, with each phase covering different administrative departments and academic program offices. Administrative Officers (AO) and staff from different departments who were involved in the implementation were contacted for data collection. The interviews were conducted over three months from September 2011 to Nov 2011, around two years after the first phase of implementation. The researchers interviewed twelve interviewees involved in various roles of AO, admissions officer and staff at various program offices and functional departments. Each interview session lasted 90 to150 minutes. At least two researchers were present during each interview and notes were taken by two researchers to ensure completeness and data accuracy. The initial assumptions of the researchers that are based on theory and inputs from ERP Chairperson have been put to test by constant questioning of these assumptions during the interpretive analysis of transcripts.

4   Background

Established in the early 70s, the case organization – an Indian graduate business school (referred to as GBS in this paper), has since built on its base of highly accomplished faculty, world class infrastructure and motivated student body and is one of the premier institutes for management education and research. Currently the Institute offers four MBA equivalent programs, in addition to a doctoral program. All programs are highly rated and GBS alumni occupy senior managerial and academic positions across the globe. The other programs include Executive Education Programs (EEP), international programs jointly offered with foreign universities and courses for entrepreneurs and family businesses. In addition to the research conducted by the individual faculty members in the various Areas, GBS has 10 research centres focusing on different aspects of management and different sectors.

GBS being a quasi-government organization, has to adhere to many of the policies and directives from the Ministry of Human Resource Development (HRD) of Indian government pertaining to employees' recruitment and compensation, students' intake and registration, organization structure and processes. However, the Institute operations are handled independently within this broad framework. GBS is only a graduate business school and hence the administrative structure is different from that found in other typical universities. The Institute is headed by a Director, a position held for a specific period of time after which (s)he continues to be a faculty. The faculty members are entrusted with additional management and administrative responsibilities generally of 2-year duration. Some of the posts include Dean (Academic), Dean (Administration), and Chairperson of the respective Program, etc. Each program chairperson is assisted by an Administrative Officer, who also reports to the Chief Administrative Officer (CAO). The Institute's administration activities are handled by the various AOs along with the supervisors and other staff. GBS's organization can be viewed as being purely administrative (facility management, estate maintenance, travel etc.), academic administration (library, computer centre, placement cell) and purely academic (the programs, faculty research). An illustrative organizational chart is presented below.

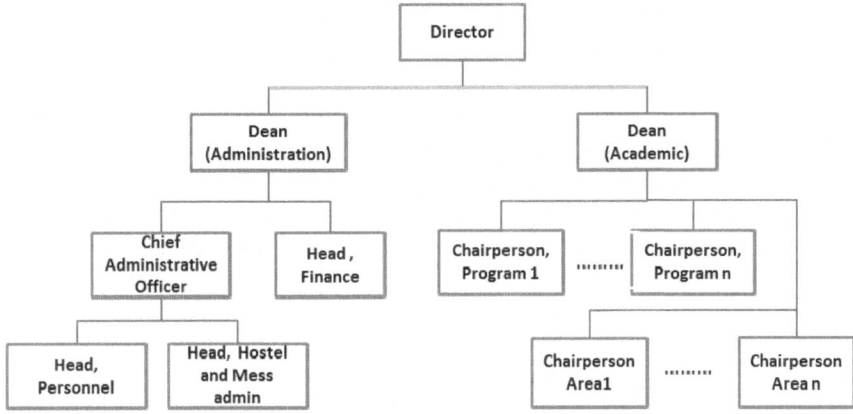

Fig. 1. Organization Structure of GBS

There are no formal job descriptions or roles and responsibilities defined within GBS. Between the three levels of officer, supervisor and staff, the tasks are distributed through consensus within the team. It is expected that the staff handle responsibilities ranging from day to day logistics, data entry, consolidation, answering queries, to other official work. The officers assist the Chairpersons in managing the programs and are involved in making decisions related to a program. They provide the necessary information and reports related to the program to the Director and the Board of Governors.

Many of the administrative staff have been with the Institute since the early days of the Institute and much longer than the faculty. Many of them have completed their terminal education decades back and have up-skilled themselves to handle the changes in day-to-day work. The administration processes were largely manual, using spread sheets and documents. There is very little formal documentation of these processes as they have evolved over time. Coupled with this, most of the staff is due to retire in the next few years taking with them the tacit knowledge and organizational know-how of the processes and the policies. GBS does not plan to replace the outgoing employees with new recruits, in line with the Ministry of HRD's prescriptions to reduce staff strength. GBS currently has about 2000 students, 200 staff, 30 interns and consultants, 85 contract employees and 120 faculty members. The Institute is comfortable with outsourcing and has outsourced most of the support services like housekeeping maintenance, catering, IT infrastructure support, etc.

4.1   IT at GBS (Graduate Business School)

GBS does not have an in-house IS team. All the IT infrastructure and support operations have been outsourced and are handled by the onsite IT vendor staff with supervision from the GBS IT Manager. Prior to ERP, most of the administration processes were islands of automation with some paper-based manual processes, creating a dependency on the specific individuals in terms of knowledge of work processes. Not every employee had access to desktop computers till a few years prior to ERP implementation. Usage of software applications was on a need basis and distributed across the departments. Finance and Accounts departments and Payroll used a popular desktop based third party package. Library had acquired a library management system; student registration was handled by another local software product. Spread sheets (MS-Excel) were used for storing, communicating and analyzing data in most departments and programs.

The processes for fee payment and obtaining clearances from the accounts departments, HR processes like leave and employee records management, were all handled manually. Student feedback collection and analysis, course scheduling, resource allocation etc., were all manual paper-based processes. The information on the utilization and availability of resources at a given point of time was not available easily.

GBS has executive positions for various support functions like finance, administration, and personnel, but has not recognized the need for such a role for Information Systems (IS). Whenever any queries or decisions related to IS come up, the Institute management looks towards the faculty in the IS department for assistance. Hence when the ERP initiative was envisaged by the management, there was a significant handicap about who will lead the implementation team.

5   ERP Implementation Context

GBS's initial attempt at ERP was in 2006, when ERP in HE was just gaining traction with universities, and vendors were very actively increasing their product footprint into the HE areas. Though a contract was initiated with one of the leading ERP vendors, the project was abandoned due to organizational dynamics and lack of consensus on decisions related to product choice, budget, implementation approach, etc [16]. The current ERP implementation initiative was championed by the Dean (Administration) when he took charge in 2008 and he was supported by the Institute Director who had recently joined GBS. In line with the GBS's vision of being a world class institution providing world class infrastructure, using a process-centric approach, leveraging technology for optimal utilization of resources was one of the main drivers.

During the last decade the scale, scope and complexity of administration at GBS has increased tremendously with increase in student intake and introduction of new programs. Administrative complexity is in the form of number of programs and electives offered, scheduling of faculty lectures, management and co-ordination of the teaching infrastructure, managing student registration, fees, attendance, grades and feedback of increasing number of students across varied courses and programs. While the human bandwidth was being challenged, expectations from the Institute's board, students, applicants and other stakeholders were increasing continuously with respect to the services, productivity and responsiveness of the Institute.

An analysis of the HR system by the Dean in 2008 revealed that about 60% of the administrative workforce would retire in the next five years. Program Chairpersons and faculty have limited knowledge of the administrative processes. There were issues related to aging workforce, retention of organizational process knowledge and sustenance of administrative process improvements. GBS also realized that there were issues with documentation and standardization of procedures across the various programs. Organizational data was in silos and was highly person-dependent. Regular reporting was missing and hence there were no reports to look at if there was a need to understand any situation.

'Data was in islands'. – Dean (administration)

5.1 ERP Selection and Implementation Process

A team consisting of the Finance head, CAO and a few faculty members was formed for the ERP product evaluation and vendor selection. It was decided that the software provider should also handle the implementation. The current vendor was chosen based on the responses to the request for proposal sent to the leading ERP vendors in the HE space. The product evaluation exercise was very detailed. Process scripts were written for some of the key GBS processes using inputs from the program chairpersons and department heads and provided to the vendor. The vendor later provided a demo of the various features of the ERP software to GBS staff. Collectively the groups agreed that ERP was good but nobody knew how it affected them. There was an 18 month lead time between the product decision and the actual signing of the contract as there were still some contemplations about the product.

An implementation committee consisting of Finance head, ERP Chairperson (who is an IS faculty member), an external ERP consultant and vendor member was formed to oversee the implementation process. Neither the vendor's Indian team nor the GBS implementation committee had sufficient and relevant implementation experience. Added to this, there were issues with vendor's competencies to implement and readiness to start as this was their first HE ERP implementation in India. While the vendor has implementation expertise available globally, this being their first implementation in South Asia, there was very little implementation expertise in their Indian team. Once the implementation was initiated several other people-related issues came up like inability of users to attend training sessions due to their work load; resistance to double data entry (current system and ERP system) for data validation runs; hesitance to share knowledge.

The Dean recruited contract hires to handle the extra workload of double data entry. People motivated towards using ERP were roped in to maintain the implementation momentum. Regular status reporting and weekly meetings were conducted to induce peer pressure on the lagging departments. But there were no defined goals related to ERP implementation for departments and individuals.

GBS adopted a phased ERP implementation approach and the first phase went live in December 2009 within 6 months of the initial training to the staff. While the implementation is currently being expanded to other units with more functionality, there are instances of user resistance visible across the Institute. Some of the staff who were identified as ERP friendly and early adopters say that the ERP is not very useful and they continue doing their work in Excel and upload data to ERP at the end.

5.2 Communication

Lack of communication regarding ERP implementation and progress is glaringly obvious in GBS. No formal communication mechanisms have been setup by the management. It is assumed that communication will flow down through the hierarchy and reporting channels. There has been no communication from the senior management in the Institute regarding the objectives of ERP, the challenges and issues which may come up during implementation and the support which will be provided to the staff. There was a mention of ERP in the fortnightly newsletter when it was first deployed. The weekly meetings conducted during the early stages of ERP implementation have also stopped. Almost all the people interviewed mentioned that they knew about ERP from their informal networks. This increased the ambiguity and misinformation related to ERP.

"ERP implementation information was not communicated to the employees because strategically the team did not want oppositions from the time of implementation itself. Also how could most of the employees have helped apart from informing what they are doing?" – external ERP consultant

6   Analysis of the Case

The case analysis reveals many interesting details related to ERP implementation, some which are specific to the Indian context keeping the end user in perspective. We analyze the motivations, user perceptions and implications under the following broad categories: (1) Motivation for ERP adoption (2) User perceptions during ERP implementation (3) Changed job characteristics (4) Technical issues and decisions.

6.1   Motivation for ERP Adoption

The motivation for GBS management for ERP adoption was driven by the then existing organizational context and external environment influences. The main drivers for ERP implementation were:

- Handle administration complexity by centralizing the administration processes across programs and automation of processes using ERP
- Retention of organizational process knowledge and ensure continuity in efficiency improvements in administration
- Meet the rising expectations from all stakeholders
- Provide shared access to data for decision support

Except for organizational knowledge retention which is unique to GBS, the other drivers are in common with most ERP implementations in HE [6, 7]. There was also the implicit goal of reducing the administrative staff by bringing in automation. This would be achieved by not replacing the staff who retire, rather than through downsizing, though this was not explicitly communicated to the employees

Users have different motivations for adopting (or not adopting) ERP based on individual perceptions, attitudes and interests.

"…. have used PeopleSoft in my previous organization and know that ERP will bring down my workload drastically. I am able to focus on other activities related to student affairs…" – Admin associate at a program office

"....with my software background, I was open to ERP as I hoped it would automate most of the processes and reduce the data entry requirements..." - Admin staff at one of the programs which was the initial adopter of ERP

"We have been told to implement ERP and so we will. ... I have heard from my friends in other organizations that ERP will make my work easy......" - Officer at one of the departments

".....I was interested to learn about this ERP and took the initiative to understand what it involved..." - Admin staff at one of the programs which was the initial adopter of ERP

"....people were worried about layoffs, as they thought that bringing in a technology may lead to reduction in manpower. A few of the older employees were unwilling to accept the ERP as they did not want to learn..." – Supervisor at Finance Department

These views reflect the influence of age, prior exposure to IT, benefits visualized from ERP, superior and peer influence, misinformation and insecurity. These factors have been identified by previous researchers when studying Theory of planned behavior (TPB), technology adoption behaviours and decisions in TAM [37, 38, 39].

6.2   User Perceptions during ERP Implementation

The implementation team opined that they took all efforts including custom building the functionality in some cases to ensure product suitability to GBS processes and thorough testing and parallel runs before going live.

But the staff feels that the system is not suited for their needs.
"...This product is suited for US Universities. Indian Institutes are different. The vendor people can't understand our concepts...."
"....You can't expect me to change myself to fit into the box you have provided; the ERP has to be customized to suit our processes...."
"...Different programs have different validation requirements (for applications)and the ERP team does not understand this."

In addition to this perception of misfit between the ERP system and existing processes, the staff also perceives that they were not involved in the ERP selection and implementation process.
"... for the initial implementation, the requirements were not obtained from the users."
"...all our requirements were initially channeled through the ERP consultant to the vendor's development team. The consultant is not an ERP expert. Now with direct interaction we can see that our requirements are being considered..."
" ...They (Vendor) showed us some screens, but no one asked us how we process our forms..."
"....I was not actively involved in requirements phase and there was no direct coordination between vendor and me"
"Training was not done properly. ...The training was provided after a long time"

In order to avoid personality clashes between the external consultant and AOs, the vendor's development staff started interacting directly with the GBS staff during the implementation phase. A positive outcome of this was that the initial perception of the staff related to lack of involvement in the process [40] was addressed to some extent by these interactions.

6.3   Changed Job Characteristics

With the introduction of ERP most of the junior staff within the Institute mentioned that their workload has reduced as many of the tasks are fully automated. They are younger and more open to ERP and experience higher job satisfaction since they can do more value adding work. They are now able to devote time to address students' issues, offer more services like manage student clubs, handle course bidding process etc., and focus on other administrative activities that were neglected before. Some of them believe that in future each program office would be able to operate with just two members (an Officer and an Associate). However, the perceptions of the officers differ in this aspect, they feel that the ERP system will not be able to handle the various complexities of the processes and that human intervention is required in many cases. This view of the officers may be because they perceive loss of power and autonomy due to loss of control on program level information and decision making, similar to what Markus [41] observed when centralized processes were implemented using information systems. With the new processes in ERP and easy access to integrated data for the decision making, the senior staff may feel their contribution to productivity is reduced [42]. There also seems to be a minor power struggle within the program offices.

"...they view it as power moving to juniors working with ERP ... but many of them are not willing to learn ERP as they are nearing retirement..." – Junior Staff

With many of the employees retiring in the next few years, lack of job descriptions and the changes in tasks of the administrative staff due to ERP implementation, GBS can explore job (re)design considering its objective of optimal utilization of resources [27]. Formal job definition is required as ERP mandates it due to access and control flows built in the system. There may be a clash between the informal reporting structures and responsibilities currently practiced and the formal reporting structure required by ERP.

6.4   Technical Issues and Decisions

At GBS the level of customization of the process in the ERP package was decided based on the department type: no customization for purely administrative functions; minimal customization for academic administration; and high customization for purely academic functions. Many of the users were not fully aware of the customization criteria as there was no communication on what they can expect. Hence the users assumed that the functionality offered by ERP would have procedures, formats and templates that they currently used. They expected the flexibility of reports and data access similar to what they were exposed to with spread sheets.

The ERP applications were designed by considering data security, control and data integrity. This meant that users would not be able to access data which was not relevant to them. The users were confused as to why data which was available in the system cannot be shared with them. Any data requirement other than what the standard reports offered, invited questions from the development team and had to go through an approval from the ERP committee, but no explicit policies related to data security and privacy were communicated. This was also a cause for user dissatisfaction since the system introduced control in every operation by standardizing procedures. Certain reports which were one-off type of reports were not available as standard reports which led to user perception that the reports are not flexible. Some of the ERP friendly users learnt that queries could be built to generate one-time reports. As most of the data collection was automated, the need for data access for the staff became redundant, but they were not able to appreciate the reasons. For e.g., employee leave records are automated and all leave history can be viewed by the employee. Personnel department does not need to maintain the paper forms of leave application; hence all personnel department members do not have access to employees' leave records.

Some of the staff mentioned that analysis results provided by ERP do not match the manual process outputs. But on verification with the ERP committee it was found that the reason for mismatch was due to the shortcomings of the Excel based analysis. Some decisions which were taken by junior staff while working on Excel macros are issues which impact calculations, but were previously not obvious. For e.g., if a cell is left blank for a score, when taking the weighted average, should it be considered as not applicable or as zero? If taken as zero, which was usually the case in excel, it would change the mean and other parameters of the measure. Similar issues which were perceived as technical shortcomings or defects in the ERP were actually policy decisions consciously taken by the ERP committee team with approval from the Dean (Administration).

But other technical glitches and shortcomings added to the employee frustration. The initial screens were not user friendly as the focus of the ERP team was more on automating the process first and improving usability later. Due to the phased implementation approach some of the departments have only been doing data entry and have not seen the benefits of their efforts. Some complained that the system has not yet stabilized and goes offline sometimes creating doubts related to data storage.

"...all my leave records are in the system. I do not know whether the data will be safe in ERP 30 years from now, when I retire. So I keep a paper based copy of all the records..." - a staff member from personnel department.

The training appears to have been focused on how to do data entry and not on using the ERP system for processing and task execution.

"I was given training for 3 months on how to enter the data. But not on how I can see the reports or get information about the employee records."

Given the lack of IT awareness and limited exposure to IT systems and ERP, training from an end-user perspective may reduce many of the concerns and apprehensions of the staff with respect to ERP.

7   Discussion

The ERP implementation at GBS is currently on with a few functions and processes yet to be addressed. Hence maintaining positive perceptions and motivations towards ERP usage is critical for the ERP implementation. We find that most of the reasons for user resistance are linked to the perceptions built during the course of the ERP implementation process. Many of the users mentioned that their initial expectations of ERP which lead to their adoption of ERP, were not met and now they feel that ERP is not very useful. The reasons for employees' resistance which Jiang et al. [11] summarize were visible in GBS - change in job content, loss of status, altered interpersonal relationships, loss of power, change in decision-making approach, uncertainty / unfamiliarity / misinformation and job insecurity.

As negative perceptions can spread through peer influences when there is no communication from senior management [37], the ERP committee at GBS will have to adopt strategies to promote user acceptance and address the various perceptions and reasons for user resistance. Lectchinskaia et.al [18] identify stakeholder participation as the most important CSF among the 22 CSFs they have deduced from their meta-analysis of CSFs.

We discuss below some of the study findings which are unique to GBS and the Indian context and recommend practices for ERP implementation.

- *Implicit goals for ERP implementation affecting user perceptions:* GBS motivation of handling the issues of aging workforce and knowledge retention through ERP implementation appears to be unique. GBS actions due to the implicit goal of reducing staff, evident through low communication to staff (about ERP rollout), hiring temporary staff for data entry, focus on functionality rather than usability, has an impact on user perceptions. GBS needs to evaluate the negative impact of these actions on its long-term goal.
- *Organization structure affecting the long-term perspective of ERP:* Given the phased approach taken up by GBS, the 2-3 year tenure of the various senior management positions is affecting the long-term success of the ERP implementation. Specific goals and responsibility for the ERP adoption needs to be assigned to different roles in the organization.
- *Aging workforce issues hindering ERP implementation:* The senior-user buy-in and participation may be minimal or absent as they perceive themselves as becoming redundant and having to re-skill themselves. GBS needs to address this issue as the goal of knowledge retention requires senior-users participation in the ERP implementation.
- *The ERP product not a good 'fit' to the Indian HE context*: When evaluating non-India based ERP package for the Indian HE institute, the product evaluation and vendor selection exercise has to include requirements related to cultural fit, terminology, language, etc.
- *Absence of in-house IS team creating conflicts:* As there is no in-house IS group in GBS, the external ERP consultant holds an important position as the ERP implementation program manager. This is creating conflicts as the staff views

him as a barrier to getting their requirements across to the development team. Frequent communication and other interventions by GBS management will help reduce these conflicts and provide support to the program manager role.

- *User training needs to be customized to the level of awareness:* Some employees feared loss of data and doubted correctness of data in ERP systems. The low IT maturity and computer awareness of the user demands that the user training address many aspects of ERP system. For e.g. training on data storage and accessibility to build users trust in the security and stability of the data within the system, extent of flexibility provided by ERP to the user, etc.

- *Lack of data related policies creating confusion:* Users could not understand why there were not given access to certain data and reports. As ERP brings in the ability for data consolidation and aggregation across the organization, data access and control has to be explicitly defined and implemented in the system. Policies related to data security, data privacy and data usage should be defined and communicated to all users. BPR, change in organizational structure and responsibilities is usually identified as important CSFs for ERP, but data related policies have not been explicitly mentioned.

8   Conclusions

When an information system is introduced in an organization, 'one of the most fundamental results is that the system is either used or not used' [43]. The study revealed that there are variations in the level of ERP usage by the end-users. The study focused on the motivation that led to usage of the system, the perceptions and challenges that downplayed the intended usage of the system and differences in adoption by staff at various levels. Many of the findings in the study align with issues identified in other ERP implementations in higher education institutes globally. Some of the issues identified in the case study are due to specific characteristics of Indian HE institutes like absence of IT management capabilities in the HE institution, lack of IT exposure of the administrative staff, vendor experience & implementation support in the Indian IT market and HE organizational structure. The finding related to the need for defining explicit data related policies during ERP implementation is applicable in all scenarios and has not been discussed in prior literature.

The study also identified certain issues which are unique to the Indian context and provided inputs to handle them, and can serve as a real life example for other HE institutes in India. Additionally, many of the aspects related to Indian HE would be found in other developing country institutes and the findings can be applied to those contexts as well.

References

1. Von Hellens, L., Nielsen, S., Beekhuyzen, J.: Qualitative case studies on implementation of enterprise wide systems. Idea Group, Hershey (2005)
2. Lewis, L.K., Seibold, D.R.: Innovation modification during intra-organizational adoption. Academy of Management Review 18(3), 22–54 (1993)

3. Esteves, J., Pastor, J.: Enterprise resource planning system research: An annotated bibliography. Communications of the Association for Information Systems 7(8), 1–52 (2001)
4. Harris, M., Lowendahl, J.M., Zastrocky, M.: Magic Quadrant for Higher Education Administrative Suites, Gartner Report. Gartner (2008)
5. Pollock, N., Cornford, J.: ERP Systems and the University as a "unique" organisation. Information Technology and People 17(1), 31–52 (2004)
6. King, P.: The promise and Performance of Enterprise Systems in Higher Education, Respondent Summary. ECAR Respondent Summary (2002), http://net.educause.edu/ir/library/pdf/ecar_so/ers/ers0204/EKF0204.pdf (retrieved April 20, 2012)
7. Oliver, D., Romm, C.: ERP systems: the route to adoption. In: Proceedings of Americas Conference on Information Systems, AMCIS, Long-Beach, CA, pp. 1039–1044 (2000)
8. Beekhuyzen, J.M.: Organizational culture and enterprise resource planning (ERP) systems implementation. Unpublished Thesis, Griffith University, Brisbane, Qld, Australia (2001)
9. Zornada, L., Velkavrh, T.B.: Implementing ERP in Higher Education Institutions. In: 27th International Conference on Information Technology Interfaces, Cavtat, Croatia (2005)
10. Hong, K.K., Kim, Y.G.: The critical success factors for ERP implementation: an organizational fit perspective. Information & Management 40, 25–40 (2002)
11. Jiang, J.J., Muhanna, W.A., Klein, G.: User resistance and strategies for promoting acceptance across system types. Information & Management 37(1), 25–36 (2000)
12. Shang, S., Su, T.: Managing User Resistance in Enterprise Systems Implementation. In: Americas Conference on Information Systems, pp. 149–153 (2004)
13. Gyampah, K.A.: ERP implementation factors A comparison of managerial and end-user perspectives. Business Process Management Journal 10(2), 171–183 (2004)
14. Gates, K.F.: Evaluating the North American pilot for SAP's campus management system. In: Von Hellens, L., Nielsen, S., Beekhuyzen, J. (eds.) Qualitative Case Studies on Implementation of Enterprise Wide Systems, pp. 192–210. Idea Group, Hershey (2005)
15. Rabaa'i, A.: Identifying Critical Success Factors of ERP Systems at the Higher Education Sector. In: Proc.of the 3rd International Symposium on Innovation in Information & Communication Technology (ICIICT 2009), Amman, Jordan, December 15-17, pp. 133–147 (2009)
16. McCredie, J., Updegrove, D.: Enterprise System Implementations: Lessons from the Trenches. CAUSE/EFFECT 22(4), 1–10 (1999)
17. Sprenger, J., Klages, M., Breitner, M.: Cost-Benefit Analysis for the Selection, Migration, and Operationof a Campus Management System. Business Informatics and Systems Engineering 2(4), 219–231 (2010)
18. Lechtchinskaia, L., Uffen, J., Breitner, M.H.: Critical Success Factors for Adoption of Integrated Information Systems in Higher Education Institutions – A Meta-Analysis. In: AMCIS 2011 Proceedings (2011)
19. Siau, K., Messersmith, J.: Analyzing ERP Implementation at a Public University Using the Innovation Strategy Model. International Journal of Human-Computer Interaction 16(1), 57–80 (2002)
20. Abugabah, A., Sanzogni, L.: Enterprise Resource Planning (ERP) System in Higher Education: A literature Review and Implications. World Academy of Science, Engineering and Technology 71 (2010)
21. Davis, F.: Perceived usefulness, perceived ease of use, and user acceptance of information technology. MIS Quarterly 13(3), 319–334 (1989)

22. Venkatesh, V., Davis, F.D.: A Theoretical Extension of the Technology Acceptance Model: Four Longitudinal Field Studies. Management Science 46(2), 186–204 (2000)
23. Delone, W., McLean, E.R.: Information systems success: the quest for the dependent variable. Information Systems Research 3(1), 60–95 (1992)
24. Wixom, B.H., Todd, P.A.: A theoretical integration of user satisfaction and technology acceptance. Information Systems Research 16(1), 85–102 (2005)
25. Frantz, S.: Perceptions of selected administrators regarding Enterprise Planning software implementation best practices, and the relationship between these perceptions and selected variables. Unpublished Doctoral Thesis, The University of Southern Mississippi (2001)
26. Goodwin, M.: Tales of Resistance in an Australian University. In: von Hellens, L., Nielsen, S., Beekhuyzen, J. (eds.) Qualitative Case Studies on Implementation of Enterprise Wide Systems. Idea Group, Hershey (2005)
27. Morris, M.G., Venkatesh, V.: Job characteristics and job satisfaction: understanding the role of enterprise resource planning system implementation. MIS Quarterly 34(1), 143–161 (2010)
28. Huang, Z., Palvia, P.: ERP implementation issues in advanced and developing countries. Business Process Management Journal 7(3), 276–284 (2001)
29. Soh, C., Kien, S.S., Tay-Yap, J.: Cultural Fits and Misfits: Is ERP a Universal Solution? Communications of the ACM 41(4), 47–51 (2000)
30. Jarvenpaa, S.L., Leidner, D.E.: An Information Company in Mexico: Extending the resource-based view of the firm to a developing country context. Information Systems Research 9(4), 342–361 (1998)
31. He, X.: The ERP Challenge in China: A resource-based perspective. Information Systems Journal 14, 153–167 (2004)
32. Plant, R., Willcocks, L.: Critical Success Factors in International ERP Implementations: A Case Research Approach. Journal of Computer Information Systems 47(3), 60–70 (2007)
33. Somers, T.M., Nelson, K.: The Impact of Critical Success Factors across the Stages of Enterprise Resource Planning Implementations. In: Proceedings of the 34th Hawaii International Conference on System Sciences (HICSS-3), Maui, Hawaii (2001)
34. Yin, R.: Case study research: Design and methods, 3rd edn., vol. 5. SAGE, Thousand Oaks (2003)
35. Marshall, C., Rossman, G.B.: Designing qualitative research. Sage, Thousand Oaks (1995)
36. Myers, M.D., Newman, M.: The qualitative interview in IS research: Examining the craft. Information and Organization 17(1), 2–26 (2007)
37. Morris, M.G., Venkatesh, V.: Age differences in technology adoption decisions: implications for a changing work force. Personnel Psychology 53, 375–403 (2000)
38. Janson, M.A., Woo, C.C., Smith, L.D.: Information systems development and communicative action theory. Information & Management 25, 59–72 (1993)
39. de Jager, P.: Communicating in times of change. Journal of Systems Management, 28–30 (1994)
40. Mumford, E.: Human values and the introduction of technological change. Manchester Business School Review 3(2), 13–17 (1979)
41. Markus, M.L.: Power, politics, and MIS implementation. Communications of the ACM 26(6), 430–444 (1983)
42. Smith, H.A., McKeen, J.D.: Computerization and management: a study of conflict and change. Information & Management 22, 53–64 (1992)
43. Silver, M.S., Markus, L., Beath, C.: The Information Technology Interaction Model: A Foundation for the MBA Core Course. MIS Quarterly 19(3), 361–390 (1995)

Understanding the ERP System Use in Budgeting

Wipawee Uppatumwichian

Department of Informatics, Lund University, Ole Römers väg 6, 22363 Lund, Sweden
wipawee.uppatumwichian@ics.lu.se

Abstract. This paper investigates the enterprise resource planning (ERP) system use in budgeting in order to explain how and why ERP systems are used or not used in budgeting practices. Budgeting is considered as a social phenomenon which requires flexibility for decision-making and integration for management controls. The analysis at the activity levels, guided by the concept of 'conflict' in structuration theory (ST), suggests that ERP systems impede flexibility in decision-making. However, the systems have the potential to facilitate integration in management controls. The analysis at the structural level, guided by the concept of 'contradiction' in ST, concludes that the ERP systems are not widely used in budgeting. This is because the systems support the integration function alone while budgeting assumes both roles. This paper offers the ERP system non-use explanation from an ulitarian perspective. Additionally, it calls for solutions to improve ERP use especially for the integration function.

Keywords: structuration theory, budgeting, ERP system, IS use.

1   Introduction

The advance in information system (IS) technologies has promised many improved benefits to organisations [1, 2]. However such improvements are often hindered by unwillingness to accept new IS technologies [3, 4]. This results in IS technology non-use [5] and/or workaround [6, 7] and, inevitably moderate business benefits. For this reason, a traditional IS use research has been well-established in the discipline [8] to investigate how and why users use or not use certain IS technologies.

In the field of accounting information system (AIS), previous research has indicated that there is a limited amount of research as well as understanding on the use of enterprise resource planning (ERP) systems to support management accounting practices [9-12]. Up to now, the available research results conclude that most organisations have not yet embraced the powerful capacity of the ERP systems to support the management accounting function [4, 13, 14]. Many studies have reported a consistent limited ERP use in management accounting function using data from many countries across the globe such as Egypt [15], Australia [16], Finland [4, 17-19] and Denmark [20]. Several researchers have in particular called for more research contributions on the ERP system use in management accounting context, and especially on how the systems might be used to support the two key functions in

G. Poels (Ed.): CONFENIS 2012, LNBIP 139, pp. 106–121, 2013.
© IFIP International Federation for Information Processing 2013

manegement accounting: decision-making and management control functions [10, 12, 21]. This paper responds to that call by uncovering the ERP systems use in budgeting. In relation to other management accounting activities, budgeting is considered to be the most suitable social phenomenon under investigation. This is because budgeting is a longstanding control procedure [22] which continues to soar in popularity among modern organisations [23]. In addition, it assumes the dual roles of decision-making and management control [24].

Budgeting is considered as a process undertaken to achieve a quantitative statement for a defined time period [25]. A budget cycle can be said to cover activities such as (1) budget construction, (2) consolidation, (3) monitoring and (4) reporting. The levers of control (LOC) framework [26] suggests that budgeting can be used interactively for decision-making and diagnostically for management control. This is in line with modern budgeting literature [24, 27] whose interpretation is that budgeting assumes the dual roles. However, the degree of combination between these two roles varies according to management's judgements in specific situations [26]. This dual role requires budgeting to be more flexible for decision-making yet integrative for management control [28].

Given the research gaps addressed and the flexible yet integrative roles of budgeting, this paper seeks to uncover how the ERP systems are used in budgeting as well as to explain why the ERP systems are used or not used in budgeting.

This paper proceeds as follows. The next section provides a literature review in the ERP system use literature with regard to the integration and flexibility domains. Section 3 discusses the concepts of conflict and contradiction in structuration theory (ST) which is the main theory used. After that, section 4 deliberates on the research method and case companies contained in this study. Subsequently, section 5 proceeds to data analysis based on the conflict and contradiction concepts in ST in order to explain how and why ERP systems are used or not used in budgeting. Section 6 ends this paper with conclusions and research implications.

2   The ERP Literature Review on Flexibility and Integration

This section reviews ERP literatures based on the integration and flexibility domains as it has been previously suggested that budgeting possesses these dual roles. It starts out with a brief discussion on what the ERP system is and its relation to accounting. Later it proceeds to discuss about incompatible conclusions in the literature about how the ERP system can be used to promote flexibility and integration.

The ERP system, in essence, is an integrated cross-functional system containing many selectable software modules which span to support numerous business functions that a typical organisation might have such as accounting and finance, human resources, and sales and distributions [12]. The system can be considered as a *reference model* which segments organisations into diverse yet related functions through a centralised database [29]. The ERP system mandates a rigid business model which enforces underlying data structure, process model as well as organisational structure [30] in order to achieve an ultimate integration between business operation and IS technology [31].

The ERP system has become a main research interest within the IS discipline as well as its sister discipline, the AIS research, since the inception of this system in the early 1990s [4, 12]. Indeed, it can be said that AIS gives rise to the modern ERP system because accounting is one of the early business operations that IS technology is employed to hasten the process [32]. A research finding [13] posits that the ERP systems require implementing organisations to set up the systems according to either 'accounting' or 'logistic' modes which forms a different control locus in organisations. Such indication strongly supports the prevailing relationship that accounting has in connection to the modern ERP system.

In relation to the flexibility domain, research to date has provided a contradictory conclusion on the relationship between the ERP system and flexibility. One research stream considers the ERP system to impose a stabilising effect on organisations because of the lack of flexibility in relation to changing business conditions [7, 16, 17, 20, 33, 34]. Akkermans et al. [35], for example, report that leading IT executives perceive the ERP system as a hindrance to strategic business initiatives. The ERP system is said to have low system flexibility which does not correspond to the changing networking organisation mode. This line of research concludes that a lack of flexibility in ERP system can post a direct risk to organisations because the ERP system reference model is not suitable to business processes [34, 36]. In addition, the lack of flexibility results in two possible lines of actions from users: (1) actions in the form of inaction, that is, a passive resistance not to use the ERP systems [5], or (2) actions to reinvent the systems or a workaround [7]. The other stream of research maintains that ERP system implementation improve flexibility in organisations [2, 37-39]. Shang and Seddon [2], for example, propose that the ERP system contributes to increased flexibility in organisational strategies. This is because a modular IT infrastructure in the ERP system allows organisations to cherry pick modules which support their current business initiatives. In the same line, Brazel and Dang [37] posit that ERP implementation allows more organisational flexibility to generate financial reports. Cadili and Whitley [39] support this view to a certain extent as they insert that the flexibility of an ERP system tends to decrease as the system grows in size and complication.

With regard to the integration domain, a similar contradictory conclusion on the role of ERP to integration is presented in the literature. One stream of research posits that the reference model embedded in the ERP system [29], which enforces a strict data definition across organisational units through a single database, enables integration and control [2, 14, 19, 37, 38]. Some of the benefits mentioned in the literature after an ERP implementation are: reporting capability [37], information quality [40], decision-making [38] and strategic alliance [2]. Another stream of research tends to put a serious criticism toward the view that ERP implementation will enable organisational integration. Quattrone and Hopper [41], for example, argue that the ERP system is at best a *belief* that activities can be integrated by making transactions visible and homogenous. Dechow and Mouritsen [13] explicitly support this view by indicating that: "[The] ERP systems do not define what integration is and how it is to be developed". They argue that it is not possible to manage integration around the ERP systems, or any other IS systems. Regularly, any other means of integration but IS is more fruitful for organisational integration and control, such as a lunch room observation. In many cases, it is argued that integration can only be achieved through a willingness to throw away some data and integrate less information [31].

3 Theoretical Background

A review of IS use research [8] has indicated that there are three main *explanatory views* which are widely used to explain IS use research. First the ulitarian view holds that users are rational in their choice of system use. This stream of research often employs a technology acceptance model [3] or a media richness theory [42] to explain system use. Second the social influence view deems that social mechanisms are of importance in enforcing system use in particular social contexts [43]. The third and the last contingency view [44] explains that people decide to use or not to use systems through personal characteristics and situational factors. Factors such as behavioural control [6], as well as skills and recipient attributes [45] serve as explanations to system use/non-use.

Being aware about these theoretical alternatives in the literature, the author chooses to approach this research through the lens of ST. It is convinced that the theory has a potential to uncover ERP use based on the ulitarian view. ST is appealing to the ERP system use study because the flexible yet integrative roles of budgeting fit into the contradiction discussion in social sciences research. It has been discussed that most modern theories along with social practices represent contradictions in themselves [46]. Anthony Giddens, the founder of ST, explicitly supports the aforementioned argument. He writes: "don't look for the functions social practices fulfil, look for the contradiction they embody!" [47].

The heart of ST is an attempt to treat human actions and social structures as a duality rather than a dualism. To achieve this, Giddens bridges the two opposing philosophical views of *functionalism* and *interpretivism*. Functionalism holds that social structures are independent of human actions. Interpretivism, on the contrary, holds that social structures exist only in human minds. It is maintained that structures exist as human actors apply them. They are the medium and outcome of human interactions. ST is appealing to IS research because of its vast potential to uncover the interplay of people with technology [48, 49].

This paper focuses particularly on one element of ST, which is the concept of conflict and contradiction. According to Walsham [5], this concept is largely ignored in the literature as well as in the IS research. Giddens defines *contradiction* as "an *opposition* or *disjunction* of structural principles of social systems, where those principles operate *in terms of each other* but at the same time *contravene one another*" [47]. To supplement contradiction which occurs at the structural level, he conceptualises *conflict,* which is claimed to occur at the level of social practice. In his own words, conflict is a "struggle between actors or collectives expressed as definite social practices" [47]. Based on the original writing, Walsham [5] interprets conflicts as the *real activity* and contradiction as the *potential basis for conflict* which arises from structural contradictions.

This theorising has immediate application to the study of ERP systems use in budgeting. It is deemed that the flexibility (in decision-making) and integration (in management control) inherent in budgeting are the *real activities* that face business controllers in their daily operations with budgeting. Meanwhile, ERP systems and budgeting are treated as two different social structures [50] which form the *potential basis for conflict* due to the clash between these structures. The next section discusses the research method and the case organisations involved in this study.

4   Research Method and Case Description

This study employs an interpretative case study method according to Walsham [51]. The primary research design is a multiple case study [52] in which the researcher investigates a single phenomenon [53], namely the use of ERP systems in budgeting. This research design is based on rich empirical data [52, 54], therefore it tends to generate better explanation in respond to the initial research aim to describe and explain ERP system use in budgeting.

Eleven for-profit organisations from Thailand are included in this study. To be eligible for the study, these organisations meet the following three criteria. First they have installed and used an ERP system for finance and accounting functions for at least two years to ensure system maturity [55]. Second, they employ budgeting as the main management accounting control. Third they are listed on a stock exchange to ensure size and internal control consistency due to stock market regulations [12].

This research is designed with triangulation in mind [56] in order to improve the validity of research findings. Based on Denzin [57]'s triangulation typologies, the methodological triangulation is applied in this study. Interviews, which are the primary data collection method, are conducted with twenty-one business controllers in eleven profit-organisations in Thailand in autumn 2011. These interviews are conducted at interviewee's locations. Therefore data from several other sources such as internal documentations and system demonstrations are available to the researcher for the methodological triangulation purpose. The interview follows a semi-structured format which lasts for approximately one to two hours on average. Interview participants are business controllers who are directly responsible for budgeting as well as IS technologies within organisations. Interview participants are for example chief financial controller (CFO), accounting vice president, planning vice president, accounting policy vice president, management accounting manager, business analyst, and business intelligent manager. Appendix 1 provides an excerpt of the interview guide. All interview participants have been working for the current organisations for a considerable amount of time which ranges between two to twenty years. Therefore it is deemed that they are knowledgeable of the subject under investigation. All interviews are recorded, transcribed and analysed in Nvivo8 data analysis software. Coding is performed following the inductive coding technique [56] using a simple two-level theme; an open-ended general etic coding followed by a more specific emic coding in order to allow a maximum interwoven within data analysis. Appendix 2 provides an example of the coding process performed in this research.

With regard to the case companies, the organisations selected represent core industries of Thailand such as the energy industry (Cases A-C), the food industry (Cases D-G) and the automobile industry (Cases H and I). The energy group is the backbone of Thailand's energy production chain, which accounts for more than half of the country's energy demands. The food industry group includes business units of global food companies and Thai food conglomerates which export foods worldwide. The automobile industry group is directly involved in the production and distribution chains of the world's leading automobile brands. For the two remaining cases, Case J is a Thai business unit of a global household electronic appliance company. Case K is a Thai hospitality conglomerate which operates numerous five-star hotels and luxury serviced apartments throughout the Asia Pacific region. In terms of IS technologies, all of these companies employ both ERP and spreadsheets (SSs) for budgeting functions. However, some have access to additional BI applications. Some companies employ off-the-shelf BI solutions for budgeting purpose such as the Cognos BI systems. Nevertheless some companies choose to develop their own BI systems in collaboration with IS/IT consultants. This type of in-house BI is referred to as "own BI". Table 1 provides a clear description of each case organisation. The next section presents data analysis obtained from these organisations.

Table 1. Case company description

Case	Main Activities	Owner	ERP	SSs	BI
A	Power plant	Thai	SAP	Yes	Magnitude
B	Oil and Petrochemical	Thai	SAP	Yes	Cognos
C	Oil refinery	Thai	SAP	Yes	-
D	Frozen food processor	Thai	SAP	Yes	-
E	Drinks and dairy products	Foreign	SAP	Yes	Magnitude
F	Drinks	Foreign	SAP	Yes	Own BI
G	Agricultural products	Thai	BPCS	Yes	-
H	Truck	Foreign	SAP	Yes	-
I	Automobile parts	Thai	SAP	Yes	Own BI
J	Electronic appliances	Foreign	JDE	Yes	Own BI
K	Hotels and apartments	Thai	Oracle	Yes	IDeaS

5   Analysis

The analysis is presented based on the theoretical section presented earlier. It starts with the 'conflict' between (1) the ERP system and flexibility and (2) the ERP system and integration at the four budgeting activity levels. These two sections aim to explain how the ERP systems are used or not used in budgeting. Later on, the paper proceeds to discuss the 'contradiction' between the ERP system and budgeting at a structural level in order to suggest why the ERP system are used or not used to support budgeting activities.

5.1 Conflict at the Activity Level: ERP System and Flexibility

Flexibility, defined as business controllers' discretion to use IS technologies for budget-related decision-making [58], is needed throughout the budgeting process. Based on a normal budgeting cycle, there are two important activities in relation to the flexibility definition: (1) budget construction, and (2) budget reporting. These two activities require business controllers to construct a data model on an IS technology which takes into account the complex environmental conditions [27, 59] to determine the best possible alternatives.

In the first activity of budget construction, this process requires a high level of flexibility because budgets are typically constructed in response to specific activities and conditions presented in each business unit. The ERP system is not called upon for budget construction in any case company because of the following two reasons: (1) the technology is developed in a generic manner such that it cannot be used to support any specific budgeting process. The Vice President Information Technology in Case I mentions: "SAP [ERP] is *too generic*[1] for budgeting. [...] They [SAP ERP developers] have to develop something that perfectly fits with the nature of the business, but I know it is not easy to do because they have to deal with massive accounting codes and a complicated chart of accounts". This suggestion is similar to the reason indicated by the Financial Planning Manager in Case F who explains that her attempt to use an ERP system for budgeting was not successful because "SAP [ERP] has a limitation when it comes to revenue handling. It cannot handle any complicated revenue structure". (2) The technology is not flexible enough to accommodate changes in business conditions which are the keys to forecasting future business operations. The Central Accounting Manager in Case G suggests that the ERP system limits what business controllers can do with their budgeting procedures in connection with volatile environments. She explicitly mentions that: "our [budgeting] requirements change all the time. The ERP system is fixed; you get what the system is configured for. It is almost impossible to alter the system. Our Excel [spreadsheets] can do a lot more than the ERP system. For example, our ERP system does not contain competitor information. In Excel, I can just create another column and put it in".

In the second activity of budget reporting, all cases run basic financial accounting reports from the ERP systems, and then they further edit the reports to fit their managerial requirements and variance analysis in spreadsheets. The practice is also similar in Cases A, B and E, where the ERP systems are utilised for budget monitoring (see more discussion in the next section). For example, the Corporate Accounting Manager in Case D indicates how the ERP system is not flexible for reporting and how he works around it: "When I need to run a report from the ERP

---

[1] This italic shown in the original interview text represents the author's intention to emphasize certain information in the original interview text. This practice is used throughout the paper.

system, I have to run many reports then I mix them all in Excel [spreadsheets] to get exactly what I want". The Business Intelligence Manager in Case K comments on why she sees that the ERP system is not flexible enough for variance analysis: "It is quite hard to analyse budgeting information in the ERP system. It is hard to make any sense out of it because everything is *too standardised*".

In summary, the empirical data suggests the ERP systems are not used to support the flexibility domain in budgeting since that there is a clear conflict between the ERP system and the flexibility required in budgeting activities. The ERP systems put limitations on what business controllers can or cannot do with regard to flexibility in budgeting. For example business controller cannot perform complicated business forecasting which is necessary for budget construction on the ERP system. This conflict is clearly addressed by the Financial Planning Manager in Case F who states: "The SAP [ERP] functions are not flexible enough [for budgeting] but it is quite good for [financial] accounting".

5.2   Conflict at the Activity Level: ERP System and Integration

Integration, defined as the adoption of IS technologies to standardise data definitions and structures across data sources [60], is needed for budget control. Based on a normal budgeting cycle, there are two important activities in relation to the definition of integration: (1) budget consolidation, and (2) budget monitoring. Various departmental budgets are consolidated together at an organisational level, which is subsequently used for comparison with actual operating results generated from financial accounting for monitoring purposes.

In the first activity of budget consolidation, none of the case companies is reported to be using the ERP system for this function. The majority of budgets are constructed and consolidated outside the main ERP system, typically in spreadsheets (except Case B, which uses a mixture of spreadsheets and BI). The CFO in Case H gives an overview of the company budgeting process: "We do budgeting and business planning processes on Excel [spreadsheets]. It is not only us that do it like this. All of the six [Southeast Asian] regional companies also follow this practice. Every company has to submit budgets on spreadsheets to the regional headquarters. The budget consolidation is also completed on spreadsheets". Regardless of a company's choice to bypass the ERP system for budget consolidation, all the case companies are able to use their ERP systems to prepare and consolidate financial statements for a financial accounting purpose at a specific company level, but not necessarily at a group level. These financial accounting statements will be used to support the second activity of budget monitoring.

In the second activity of budget monitoring, three case companies (Cases A, B and E) report that they use their ERP systems for budget monitoring purposes. The Planning Vice President in Case B mentions: "SAP [ERP] is more like a place which we put budgeting numbers into. We use it to control budgets. We prepare budgets outside the system but we put the final budget numbers into it for a controlling purpose so that we can track budget spending in relation to the purchasing function in SAP [ERP]". A similar use of the ERP systems is presented in Cases A and E, where budgets are loaded into SAP ERP Controlling (CO) and Project System (PS) modules for budget spending monitoring. Note that only the final budget numbers (after budget consolidation in spreadsheets) are loaded into the ERP system for a control purpose alone. The ERP system does not play a part in any budget construction processes in these three cases, as it is mentioned in the previous section that budget construction is entirely achieved outside the main ERP system.

In conclusion, the empirical data suggests that the ERP systems are not widely used to support the integration domain in budgeting. However the empirical data suggests that the ERP systems have the potential to support budget integration as it has been shown earlier that all case companies use the ERP system to prepare financial statements and some cases use the ERP systems to monitor budget spending/achievement. Regardless of the potential that the ERP systems offer, these companies have not widely used the ERP systems to support budgeting practice. Companies have yet to realise this hidden potential of the ERP system [18] to integrate currently separated financial accounting (e.g. financial statement preparation) and management accounting (e.g. budgeting) practices.

5.3   Contradiction at the Structural Level

Based on the discussions at the two activity levels presented in earlier sections, this section builds on the concept of contradiction in ST to explain how and why the ERP systems are used or not used in budgeting.

Budgeting as a social practice is deemed to operate in terms of flexibility and integration, while at the same time these contravene each other. It has been shown earlier that the four main budgeting activities in a typical budgeting cycle (budget construction, budget consolidation, budget monitoring and budget reporting) belong equally to both the integration and flexibility domains. With regards to the four budgeting activities, it has been shown that the four main budgeting remain outside the main ERP systems with an exception of the budget monitoring activity alone. In this activity, a minority of case companies use the ERP systems to support this work function. It is also noted that the ERP systems have the potential to consolidate budgeting information but it seems that companies have not yet decided to utilise this capability offered in the systems.

Explanations based on the ulitarian view through the conflict and contradiction concept in ST deem that the ERP systems are not used in the budgeting activities because the systems only have the capabilities to support the integration function alone. Compared with budgeting practice which needs flexibility in decision-making as well as integration in management control, the ERP systems are obviously not suitable to support budgeting. Figure 1 shows the overall discussion about the contradiction between the ERP systems and budgeting at a structural level.   It explains the shifts in the roles of budgeting activities from flexibility in activity one, *budget construction*, to integration in activity two, *budget consolidation,* and so on. It also elaborates how the ERP systems can have the potential to support some particular activities (such as budget consolidation and budget monitoring) but not the others.

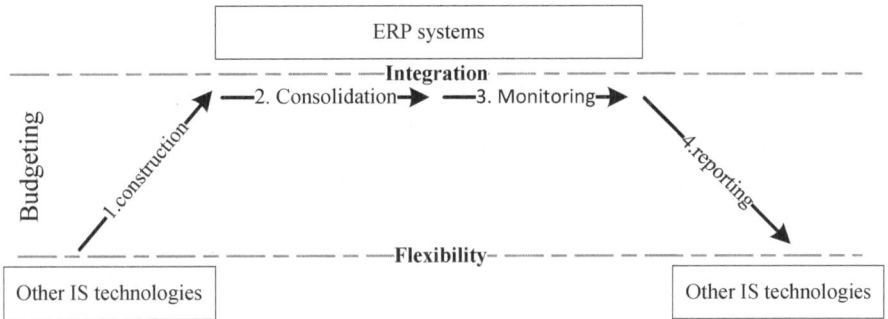

Fig. 1. Contradiction between budgeting and ERP system

So why do the ERP systems support the integration but not the flexibility in budgeting? Despite all the endlessly fancy claims made by numerous ERP vendors, the basic assumptions of the ERP system are a reference model which enforces underlying data, business process and organisational structure. The procedures described by the system must be strictly adhered to throughout organisational task executions [29]. Therefore it is hard or even impossible to alter the systems to change in response to new business requirements or circumstances because such change is contradictory to the most basic principle of the systems.

So how can we readdress the limitations of ERP systems to support the flexibility needs in budgeting? As Figure 1 explains, other types of IS technologies such as spreadsheets and business intelligence (BI) must be called upon to support the activities that the ERP systems cannot accommodate [61]. These technologies are built and designed from different assumptions from those of the ERP systems; therefore they can accommodate the flexibility in budgeting. These systems can be combined to support strategic moves made by top management according to the indication from the LOC framework [26].

6   Conclusions and Implications

This paper investigates how and why the ERP systems are used or not used in budgeting. It builds from the concepts of conflict and contradiction in ST, which is based on the ulitarian view of IS technology use perspective. Budgeting is treated as a social practice which portrays the two consecutive but contradictory roles of flexibility and integration. Using empirical data from eleven case companies in Thailand, the analysis at the activity level reveals that the ERP systems are not used to support the flexibility domain in budgeting because the systems impede business controllers to perform flexibility-related activities in budgeting, namely budget construction and budget reporting. The analysis on the integration-related budgeting function reveals that the ERP are not widely used to support the activities either. However it strongly suggests the system capability to support the integration function in budgeting as the systems are widely used to generate financial reports along with the evidence that some case companies are using the ERP systems for budget monitoring purpose. The analysis at the structuration level concludes why the ERP systems are not widely used to support budgeting. It is deemed that there is a contradictory relationship between the ERP systems and budgeting because the systems operate only in terms of integration, while the budgeting process assumes both roles. For this reason, other types of IS technologies such as spreadsheets and BI are called upon to accommodate tasks that cannot be supported in the main ERP systems.

This research result concurs with previous research conclusion that the ERP systems may post a flexibility issue to organisations because the systems cannot be tailored or changed in respond to business conditions or user requirements [16, 20, 34, 35]. Hence it does not support research findings which conclude the ERP systems promote flexibility in organisations [37]. In addition, it corresponds to previous findings which indicate that the ERP systems may assist integration in organisations [2, 14]. At least, the ERP systems can support a company-wide data integration which is significant in accounting and management control but not necessary a company-wide business process integration [13, 31].

The use of the ulitarian view to generate explanations for ERP system use/non-use is still somewhat limited. There are many aspects that the ulitarian view cannot capture. For example, the ulitarian view cannot provide an explanation as to why the ERP systems are not widely used to support the budget integration functions despite the system capabilities for financial consolidations and budget monitoring. This suggests that other views, such as the social view as well as the contingency view suggested in prior literature, are necessary in explaining the ERP system use/non-use. Therefore future IS use research should employ theories and insights from many perspectives to gain insights into the IS use/non-use phenomena.

The results presented in this study should be interpreted with a careful attention. Case study, by definition, makes no claims to be typical. The nature of case study is based upon studies of small, idiosyncratic and predominantly non-numerical sample set, therefore there is no way to establish the probability that the data can be generalised to the larger population. On the contrary, the hallmark of case study approach lies in theory-building [52] which can be transposed beyond the original sites of study.

The research offers two new insights to the IS research community. First, it explains the ERP system limited use explanation in budgeting from an ulitarian perspective. It holds that the ERP systems have the potential to support only half of the budgeting activities. Explicitly, the systems can support the integration in management control but not the flexibility in decision-making. Second, it shows that business controllers recognise such limitations imposed by the ERP systems and that they choose to rely on other IS technologies especially spreadsheets to accomplish their budgeting tasks. Spreadsheets use is problematic in itself, issues such as spreadsheets errors and frauds are well-documented in the literature. Therefore academia should look for solutions to improve professionally designed IS technologies (e.g., the ERP system or the BI) use in organisations and reduce spreadsheets reliance in budgeting as well as in other business activities.

For practitioners, this research warns them to make informed decisions about IT/IS investments. ERP vendors often persuade prospective buyers to think that their systems are multipurpose. This research shows at least one of the many business functions in which the ERP systems do not excel. Thus any further IT/IS investments must be made with a serious consideration to the business function that needs support, as well the overall business strategies guiding the entire organisation.

References

1. Davenport, T.H.: Putting the enterprise into the enterprise system. Harvard Bus. Rev. 76, 121–131 (1998)
2. Shang, S., Seddon, P.B.: Assessing and managing the benefits of enterprise systems: the business manager's perspective. Information Systems Journal 12, 271–299 (2002)
3. Davis, F.D.: Perceived Usefulness, Perceived Ease of Use, and User Acceptance of Information Technology. MIS Quarterly 13, 319–340 (1989)
4. Granlund, M., Malmi, T.: Moderate impact of ERPS on management accounting: a lag or permanent outcome? Management Accounting Research 13, 299–321 (2002)
5. Walsham, G.: Cross-Cultural Software Production and Use: A Structurational Analysis. MIS Quarterly 26, 359–380 (2002)
6. Taylor, S., Todd, P.A.: Understanding Information Technology Usage: A Test of Competing Models. Information Systems Research 6, 144–176 (1995)
7. Boudreau, M.-C., Robey, D.: Enacting integrated information technology: A human agency perspective. Organization Science 16, 3–18 (2005)
8. Pedersen, P.E., Ling, R.: Modifying adoption research for mobile interent service adoption: Cross-disciplinary interactions. In: Proceedings of the 36th Hawaii International Conference on System Science. IEEE Computer Society, Washington (2003)
9. Scapens, R.W., Jazayeri, M.: ERP systems and management accounting change: opportunities or impacts? A research note. European Accounting Review 12, 201–233 (2003)
10. Granlund, M.: Extending AIS research to management accounting and control issues: A research note. International Journal of Accounting Information Systems 12, 3–19 (2011)
11. Elbashir, M.Z., Collier, P.A., Sutton, S.G.: The role of organisational absorptive capacity in strategic use of business intelligence to support integrated management control systems. The Accounting Review 86, 155–184 (2011)
12. Grabski, S.V., Leech, S.A., Schmidt, P.J.: A review of ERP research: A future agenda for accounting information systems. Journal of Information Systems 25, 37–78 (2011)
13. Dechow, N., Mouritsen, J.: Enterprise resource planning systems, management control and the quest for integration. Accounting, Organizations and Society 30, 691–733 (2005)
14. Quattrone, P., Hopper, T.: A 'time–space odyssey': management control systems in two multinational organisations. Accounting, Organizations and Society 30, 735–764 (2005)
15. Jack, L., Kholeif, A.: Enterprise Resource Planning and a contest to limit the role of management accountants: A strong structuration perspective. Accounting Forum 32, 30–45 (2008)
16. Booth, P., Matolcsy, Z., Wieder, B.: The impacts of enterprise resource planning systems on accounting practice – The Australian experience. Australian Accounting Review 10, 4–18 (2000)

17. Hyvönen, T.: Management accounting and information systems: ERP versus BoB. European Accounting Review 12, 155–173 (2003)
18. Kallunki, J.P., Laitinen, E.K., Silvola, H.: Impact of enterprise resource planning systems on management control systems and firm performance. International Journal of Accounting Information Systems 12, 20–39 (2011)
19. Chapman, C.S., Kihn, L.A.: Information system integration, enabling control and performance. Accounting, Organizations and Society 34, 151–169 (2009)
20. Rom, A., Rohde, C.: Enterprise resource planning systems, strategic enterprise management systems and management accounting: A Danish study. Journal of Enterprise Information Management 19, 50–66 (2006)
21. Rom, A., Rohde, C.: Management accounting and integrated information systems: A literature review. International Journal of Accounting Information Systems 8, 40–68 (2007)
22. Davila, A., Foster, G.: Management control systems in early-stage startup companies. Accounting Review 82, 907–937 (2007)
23. Libby, T., Lindsay, R.M.: Beyond budgeting or budgeting reconsidered? A survey of North-American budgeting practice. Management Accounting Research 21, 56–75 (2010)
24. Abernethy, M.A., Brownell, P.: The role of budgets in organizations facing strategic change: an exploratory study. Accounting, Organizations and Society 24, 189–204 (1999)
25. Covaleski, M.A., Evans, H., Luft, J., Shields, M.: Budgeting reserach: Three theoretical perspectives and criteria for selective integration. In: Chapman, C., Hopwood, A., Shields, M. (eds.) Handbook of Management Accounting Reserach, vol. II, pp. 587–624. Elsevier, Oxford (2006)
26. Simons, R.: How New Top Managers Use Control Systems as Levers of Strategic Renewal. Strategic Management Journal 15, 169–189 (1994)
27. Frow, N., Marginson, D., Ogden, S.: Continuous budgeting: Reconciling budget flexibility with budgetary control. Accounting, Organizations and Society 35, 444–461 (2010)
28. Uppatumwichian, W.: Analysing Flexibility and Integration needs in budgeting IS technologies. In: The Twentith European Conference on Information Systems (2012)
29. Kallinikos, J.: Deconstructing information packages: Organizational and behavioural implications of ERP systems. Information Technology and People 17, 8–30 (2004)
30. Kumar, K., Van Hillegersberg, J.: ERP expiriences and evolution. Communications of the ACM 43, 22–26 (2000)
31. Dechow, N., Granlund, M., Mouritsen, J.: Management Control of the Complex Organization: Relationships between Management Accounting and Information Technology. In: Chapman, C., Hopwood, A., Shields, M. (eds.) Handbook of Management Accounting Research, pp. 625–640. Elsevier, Oxford (2007)
32. Granlund, M., Mouritsen, J.: Introduction: problematizing the relationship between management control and information technology. European Accounting Review 12, 77–83 (2003)
33. Light, B., Holland, C.P., Wills, K.: ERP and best of breed: a comparative analysis. Business Process Management Journal 7, 216–224 (2001)
34. Soh, C., Kien, S.S., Tay-Yap, J.: Cultural fits and misfits: Is ERP a universal solution? Communications of the ACM 43, 47–51 (2000)
35. Akkermans, H.A., Bogerd, P., Yücesan, E., van Wassenhove, L.N.: The impact of ERP on supply chain management: Exploratory findings from a European Delphi study. European Journal of Operational Research 146, 284–301 (2003)

36. Strong, D.M., Volkoff, O.: Understanding organization–Enterprise system fit: A path to theorizing the information technology artifact. MIS Quarterly 34, 731–756 (2010)
37. Brazel, J.F., Dang, L.: The Effect of ERP System Implementations on the Management of Earnings and Earnings Release Dates. Journal of Information Systems 22, 1–21 (2008)
38. Spathis, C.: Enterprise systems implementation and accounting benefits. Journal of Enterprise Information Management 19, 67–82 (2006)
39. Cadili, S., Whitley, E.A.: On the interpretative flexibility of hosted ERP systems. The Journal of Strategic Information Systems 14, 167–195 (2005)
40. Häkkinen, L., Hilmola, O.-P.: Life after ERP implementation: Long-term development of user perceptions of system success in an after-sales environment. Journal of Enterprise Information Management 21, 285–310 (2008)
41. Quattrone, P., Hopper, T.: What is IT?: SAP, accounting, and visibility in a multinational organisation. Information and Organization 16, 212–250 (2006)
42. Daft, R.L., Lengel, R.H.: Organizational Information Requirements, Media Richness and Structural Design. Management Science 32, 554–571 (1986)
43. Fishbein, M., Ajzen, I.: Belief, attitude, intention and behaviour: An introduction to theory and research. Addison-Wesley, Reading (1975)
44. Drazin, R., Van de Ven, A.H.: Alternative Forms of Fit in Contingency Theory. Administrative Science Quarterly 30, 514–539 (1985)
45. Treviño, L.K., Webster, J., Stein, E.W.: Making Connections: Complementary Influences on Communication Media Choices, Attitudes, and Use. Organization Science 11, 163–182 (2000)
46. Robey, D., Boudreau, M.-C.: Accounting for the Contradictory Organizational Consequences of Information Technology: Theoretical Directions and Methodological Implications. Information System Research 10, 167–185 (1999)
47. Giddens, A.: Central problems in social theory. University of California Press, Barkeley (1979)
48. Poole, M.S., DeSanctis, G.: Structuration theory in information systems research: Methods and controversies. In: Whitman, M.E., Woszczynski, A.B. (eds.) The Handbook of Information Systems Research, pp. 206–249. Idea Group Publishing, Hershey (2004)
49. Walsham, G., Han, C.K.: Information systems strategy formation and implementation: The case of a central government agency. Accounting, Management and Information Technologies 3, 191–209 (1993)
50. Orlikowski, W.J.: The Duality of Technology: Rethinking the Concept of Technology in Organizations. Organization Science 3, 398–427 (1992)
51. Walsham, G.: Interpretive Case Studies in IS Research: Nature and Method. European Journal of Information Systems 4, 74–81 (1995)
52. Eisenhardt, K.M., Graebner, M.E.: Theory building from cases: Opportunities and challenges. Academy of Management Journal 50, 25–32 (2007)
53. Gerring, J.: What is a case study and what is it good for? American Political Science Review 98, 341–354 (2004)
54. Eisenhardt, K.M.: Building Theories from Case Study Research. The Academy of Management Review 14, 532–550 (1989)
55. Nicolaou, A.I.: Firm Performance Effects in Relation to the Implementation and Use of Enterprise Resource Planning Systems. Journal of Information Systems 18, 79–105 (2004)
56. Miles, M.B., Huberman, M.A.: Qualitative data analysis: an expanded sourcebook. Sage, Thousand Oaks (1994)

57. Denzin, N.K.: The Reserach Act: A Theoretical Introduction to Sociological Methods. McGraw-Hill, New York (1978)
58. Ahrens, T., Chapman, C.S.: Accounting for flexibility and efficiency: A field study of management control systems in a restaurant chain. Contemporary Accounting Research 21, 271–301 (2004)
59. Chenhall, R.H.: Management control systems design within its organizational context: findings from contingency-based research and directions for the future. Accounting, Organizations and Society 28, 127–168 (2003)
60. Goodhue, D.L., Wybo, M.D., Kirsch, L.J.: The impact of data Integration on the costs and benefits of information systems. MIS Quarterly 16, 293–311 (1992)
61. Hyvönen, T., Järvinen, J., Pellinen, J.: A virtual integration—The management control system in a multinational enterprise. Management Accounting Research 19, 45–61 (2008)

Appendix 1: Interview Guide

How do you describe your business unit information?
What IS technologies are used in relation to budgeting procedure?
What are the budgeting procedures in your organisation?
What are the characteristics of pre-budget information gathering and analysis?
How does your business organisation prepare a budget?
How does your business organisation consolidate budget(s)?
How does your business organisation monitor budgets?
How does your business organisation prepare budget-related reports?
How does your organisation direct strategic management?
How does your organisation control normative management?

Appendix 2: Coding Example

Interview text	Epic (underline) and *Emic (italic)* Coding	Themes emerging from selective coding
Vice President of Information Technology, Case I SAP is too generic for budgeting. From what I understand I think SAP is developing an industrial product line but the budgeting function is very small so they think that it might not worth an investment. First I think that is why they brought in the BI. Second, I think budgeting is something for business students. So they have to develop something that perfectly fits with the nature of the business, but I know it is not easy to do because they have to deal with massive accounting codes and a complicated chart of accounts.	⌐ *Consequences* Budget construction, ERP limitations *Condition* *Consequences*	Comparing this passage to other passages about budgeting construction, a theme (ERP limitations) emerges. Since budgeting is a business activity, ERP developers must develop software which reflects the business processes (*condition*). Anyhow this is not easy to do because of the complexity in real business environments (*consequences*), therefore they just develop a very generic software (*consequences*) instead.

A Decision Support System Based on RCM Approach to Define Maintenance Strategies

Thárcylla Clemente, Adiel Almeida-Filho, Marcelo Alencar, and Cristiano Cavalcante

Federal University of Pernambuco, Production Engineering Departament,
Post Box 7471, 50630971, Recife, Brazil
thnegreiros@ymail.com, atalmeidafilho@yahoo.com.br,
{marcelohazin,cristianogesm}@gmail.com

Abstract. This article presents a Decision Support System which focuses on an important organizational context: maintenance decisions. Usually, a specific management system is required to deal with data on failure, reliability, maintainability and availability regarding equipment. The maintenance context is surrounded by uncertainty and does not provide a clear profit from its activities, and thus requires a tool which fits in with organizational needs. The tool presented in this paper considers the requirements and approaches of an industrial production system, using concepts and methodologies from Reliability Centered Maintenance (RCM) to establish maintenance strategies, such as inspection and preventive maintenance planning, and also takes into consideration sophisticated MCDA and FMECA models for strategic decision making.

Keywords: Decision Support System, Reliability Centered Maintenance, Maintenance Strategies.

1 Introduction

The globalized context requires organizations to formulate a strategic plan to ensure their permanency in the competitive market. Despite the heavy investments that many organizations have been making in communications, operations and negotiations, competitiveness requires organizations to maintain a continuous and updated flow of information within the environment of their organization in order to ensure their survival and to position themselves vis-à-vis constant change [1]. Thus, companies are constantly seeking to improve their performance [2].

Improving performance is linked to both the production function and the business function. Both are associated with the strategic objective of the organization. The activities performed in an organization all contribute to maintenance management, since all activities are related to maintaining the reliability of the operational system at a high level by replacing equipment or parts or maintaining operational conditions [3].

To fulfill its strategic objectives, an organization needs to adopt a management plan that is able to integrate its resources, and its personnel and operational policies. It

G. Poels (Ed.): CONFENIS 2012, LNBIP 139, pp. 122–133, 2013.
© IFIP International Federation for Information Processing 2013

must also acquire engineering capabilities and technologies that enable it to maximize its performance. In this scenario, maintenance actions are part of the production process and can influence the company's position in relation to its competitors as well as to its business strategy. If this is done, maintenance management may be a production activity that adds to profits rather than only an unavoidable business cost [4].

The main objective of maintenance management is to plan the operational system and to manage the product (benefit and/or service). Thus, it is premised on its being deployed to supervise and control the occurrence of failures in a production plant. This task can become complicated and the use of methodologies can facilitate understanding how to analyze the context.

One of the methodologies used for the effective management of failure is preventive maintenance. This methodology specifies maintenance activities to ensure the plant functions for a given period of time, and to avoid production stopping unexpectedly. One of the approaches that adopt this methodology is Reliability Centered Maintenance (RCM).

RCM is understood as a procedure that is able to identify requirements for preventive maintenance in complex systems in order to preserve or maintain materials, people and equipment on the production line in acceptable conditions [5]. When RCM is combined with other approaches, it provides a complete understanding of the operational context, and provides management and financial information throughout the organization.

From this perspective, the use of information technology resources can offer some advantages to organizations worldwide, since they enable complex data to be managed and operations to be planned [6].

The main contribution of this paper is to put forward a Decision Support System for maintenance management. To this end, it will present the methodologies and framework concepts used to model the system as well as a brief study of the system requirements for the maintenance area.

2   Reliability Centered Maintenance

RCM is an approach that considers the economic prioritization and the security function of the production system; thus, its main contribution is to identify opportunities to do preventive maintenance in order to ensure that any physical component continues to fulfill its operational functions [5]. This is why the flow of preventive maintenance activities must be consistently modeled.

In addition, RCM is used to develop and select maintenance alternatives based on the operational, economic and safety criteria of a production system. This method is shown to be a systematic process for managing functional and operational failures [7].

First of all, RCM identifies the appropriate maintenance tasks for maintaining the current reliability level of resources and people in the production environment, which will reduce costs in the maintenance operation [8].

Essentially, RCM presents a methodology based on subjective basic questions that may be extended to any applications [9]:

- Is the cause of failure obvious to the operator?
- What is the consequence of failure?
- What tasks can be selected to prevent this failure?
- What is the reason for selecting a specific task?
- What is the suggested scope of the task?

These simple questions enable extensive knowledge about the operational context of organizations to be gained. While the answers are being given, the system is mapped and relevant information about the occurrence of failures is highlighted. This mapping may be presented in the form of a logical diagram in which the steps correspond to those of the RCM.

2.1   Main Steps of the RCM

Different sequences for implementing the RCM [6,10,11,12] are identified, but the main benefit offered by this methodology, is knowledge about the entire maintenance process, which depends on the detail level given in the process [13].

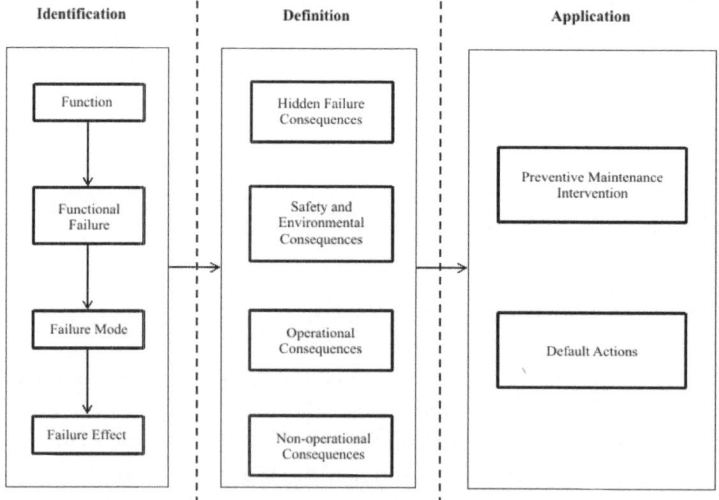

Fig. 1. Simplified representation of the RCM process [17]

In the first instance, the RCM process follows recognizing and identifying the functional requirements of the items in the production context and it establishes the desired reliability levels. For each item, it identifies specified functions and the functional failures associated with them. Then, an analysis is carried out on the failure mode and its effects [14]. This concept is very important for the maintenance context because it analyzes the existing risk in the operational production [15,16]. Then, the process defines the consequence type observed because of the occurrence of the given failure. These consequences are present in four categories: hidden, safety or environmental, operational, and non-operational [12]. Thus, the process identifies the maintenance actions to be put in place in the production system. In general, two profiles of maintenance actions are applied: preventive maintenance and corrective maintenance. Figure 1 presents the simple process of RCM.

The RCM process offers advantages and opportunities to improve the performance and safety of equipment throughout the production process by minimizing waste and machinery downtime [5]. The effort to maintain a consistent assessment process enables accurate and timely information to be obtained, which are important features for maintenance management [18].

In the maintenance area some data are considered strategic, especially those regarding the failure rate, downtime, time to repair and all historic data related to these variables [19]. These data are obtained in general from the performance records of a corrective maintenance service and from experts' knowledge.

The logical structure of the RCM process presents consistency for the specification of an information system that is able to process and provide information for the maintenance area. In this treatment, the focus is placed on the context of industrial production, and aims to extract information from the strategic level for maintenance actions [20].

Strategic level information is characterized by the non-structured data that are presented and therefore the introduction of a Decision Support System (DSS) is timely. The consideration of requirements to shape the system model is important before introducing a DSS.

3   Maintenance Management System Requirements

Using Information Technology resources presents data processing advantages in the business context. Data treatment offers gains in speed and certainty in the decision making process. Thus, the use of information systems adds value to the operational functions of an organization [21].

Adding value in the production context is crucial for acquiring a competitive advantage in the context of current business, since the trend for consumers to require product differentiation is increasing. In light of these arguments, the acquisition of an appropriate information system is essential.

An appropriate information system is one that not only meets the needs of management in the organization as it provides relevant information for decision making but is also an information system that helps the organization achieve its objectives at different levels: operational, tactical and strategic [22].

In general, an information system should meet the development requirements imposed by the user of the service. The user's role is to provide information about his/her preferences and needs with regard to using the information system. Among the requirements are those that refer directly to the characteristics of the information system and the reliability and quality associated with the system.

These groups of requirements are defined by the context in which the information system is inserted. In general, an information system must present values for six crucial aspects [23], which are described in Table 1.

Table 1. Description of the requirements of an information system

Requirement of Information System	Description
System Quality	The information system should meet the client´s needs satisfactorily
Information Quality	The information system should provide relevant and timely information
System Use	The information system should deal with cognition requirements and usability
User Satisfaction	The information system should be easy to operate and/or keep in operation
Individual Impacts	The information system should enable the user to learn, thus encouraging individual development
Organizational Impacts	The information system should have well-informed data on operational performance

For each operation in the organization there is one information system type that is the most appropriate. In the exercise to define maintenance strategies, the appropriate information system is the one that, in addition to providing operational information, supports the decision-making process. A Decision Support System is a type of information system that has specific functions that enable simulations to be conducted and scenarios to be modeled using a structure with a database of the data on thwe requirements/criteria and a database of the model obtained from dialogic interaction with the user [24].

For the context of maintenance management, data processing is essential. It is present at all organizational levels. The demand for maintenance management illustrates different perspectives on implementing an information system. These perspectives take into consideration the goal, purpose, use and user of each organizational level.

At the strategic level, the information system for the maintenance area has the following features: its goal is to ensure the cost-effectiveness of maintenance; its purpose, decision support; its main use is for data output (report generating facility, integrating information technology); and its user is the maintenance manager [21].

The process of identifying the demands on the information system in the maintenance area follows different methodologies. It is important that the steps of the process are outlined so as to meet the real needs of the context.

Implementing a Decision Support System for the maintenance area contributes to structuring the subjectivity of the context. Therefore, the occurrence of failures and interruptions to production are registered consistently and this enables the performance of the maintenance to be maximized with regard to preventing or correcting failures. Thus, it comes to be seen as a management tool that adds value.

The use of specific concepts and specific methodologies of the maintenance area assists in processing knowledge and identifying the several factors and elements involved, in context. The RCM process enables interactions of these factors to be identified. Thus, the logical structure of RCM was used to facilitate the modeling of the DSS presented for maintenance management.

4   A DSS for Maintenance Management

The main goal of this section is to describe and justify a decision support system for the maintenance area. In this perspective, the RCM process was used to outline the application context and the features of the system as per management needs. Thus, the DSS enables the maintenance actions that best suit the scenarios analyzed to be visualized and identified.

4.1   System Architecture

Maintenance actions can be applied to different items belonging to the production system. To this end, what must be known are the several interactions between the components of the system and the equipment in operation. This is a requirement addressed by the DSS proposed, which enables complete knowledge of the production system to be obtained.

To address this consideration, the DSS presents an architecture comprising modules that enable the complete identification of components and their operations in the production system. DSS has two main modules: (i) a physical module and (ii) a functional module. These are described in Table 2

The cognitive aspects considered include the usability of the components and constant access to information. This requirement is critical to the maintenance area, in view of the constant monitoring of changes.

Table 2. Description of the modules of a DSS

Module	Activity	Data
Physical	Registry	Item of production system
		Occurrence of failures
		Failure detection levels
Functional	Registry	Data on the system, subsystem, function, functional failure, equipment and components, failure modes
	Analysis	Criticality of failure modes
	Definition	Maintenance Strategy

Both modules provide a complete view of the context studied in the maintenance area and allow a direct flow to the users of the system. However, the Functional Module provides consistent features to define the maintenance strategies desired by organization.

4.2   Main Flow of the Functional Module

The main flow of the Functional Module of DSS is to insert user data, to validate data by means of the several interactions and to analyze data and, finally, to provide an analysis the results for decision making.

All functional features of the module correspond to steps developed by the RCM process. Thus, there are occurrences of failures analysis and criticality analysis of failure modes that form the foundation to define strategic actions to maintain the items in the analysis of the production system. The process undergone by the Functional Module may be represented in five steps which are illustrated in Figure 2.

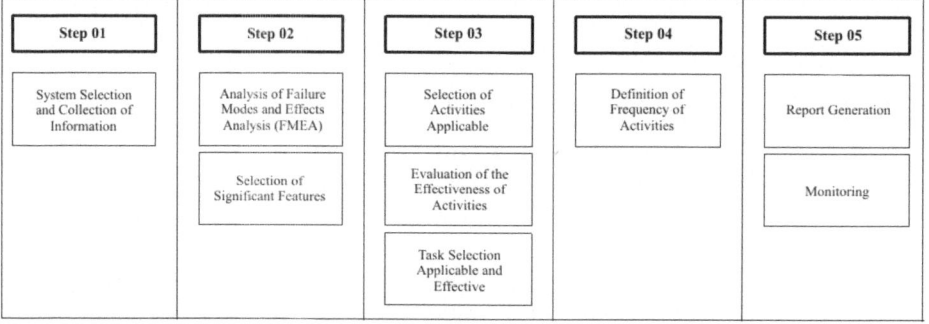

Fig. 2. The structure of the Functional Module consists of five main steps, which are defined by the features of the system

The steps of the Functional Module of DSS enable a sequence designed for a simple navigation in the system to be viewed. It is important that the requirements of the system are obtained so as to construct this sequence. A hierarchy of the functional components was created in order to design a productive context for the DSS.

Thus, consider a productive process. A system is characterized by a set of items that has a higher functionality. This system can consist of subsystems, and those for other subsystems. Each system or subsystem has a function. This function may comprise several potential functional failures that are described by the conditions of operation of the system or subsystem. Each functional failure can occur in an item or a set of items in the production system. For each occurrence of failure on an item there is a failure mode associated with it. This failure mode informs the manner and context that led to the occurrence of a functional failure. Each failure mode presents essential characteristics to determine its criticality as it is important to identify how critical the failure mode for the production system is.

In DSS this sequence is shown in a hierarchy, which facilitates visualizing and compiling elements in the production context. Figure 3 represents the interface of the functional module of the DSS, with emphasis on the evaluation stage of the critical failure mode.

An analysis of the criticality of the failure mode is a very important resource used to define maintenance actions. This issue is closely related to the levels of risk the organization is willing to face. Many studies have been developed to provide a consistent approach so as to obtain the criticality level of the failure modes [14,16].

In the DSS, the criticality analysis is structured by a mathematical model that classifies the severity and risk associated with a failure mode. The information required for this analysis suggests that the user should set qualifying levels of detectability and frequency of failure, as well as levels of severity in line with o the damage: human, environmental, operational and financial, caused by the occurrence of the failure mode in specific equipment the production line, as illustrated in Figure 3.

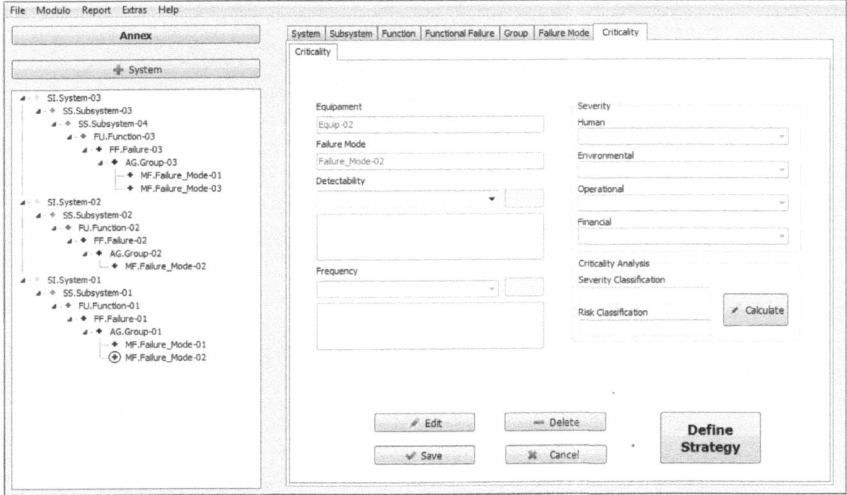

Fig. 3. This is the interface for defining the criticality of failure modes. The hierarchy of the items of the production system is shown on the left. The definition of criticality of failure modes is calculated from the data on detectability, frequency and severity.

After acquiring this information, what follows is to define strategic maintenance actions for the production system, especially for the operations of each piece of equipment/item.

4.2.1 Definition of Maintenance Actions

The information extracted from the DSS depends on the frequency of the occurrence of the failure modes of the production system under study. The information contributes to a summarized analysis of the occurrence of failure, a critical step in defining strategies for maintenance actions.

Classifying the severity and the risks is the basis for defining the critical failure mode. This definition is based on a correlation matrix that identifies how critical the occurrence of a failure is for the production system. In turn, the criticality encourages the mechanism to define the maintenance action.

The process of defining the maintenance action considers several aspects, including cost, timing of maintenance and operational safety in the production system. Thus, to establish the most appropriate strategy for the context under study, the DSS follows a specific logical diagram which is guided by the RCM methodology.

Based on the basic issues of the RCM process, questions are designed to outline the context, given the objects observed (system, subsystem, function failure, and failure mode group) that were selected. The questions are provided in a logical sequence while the maintenance action recommended by the system is being defined. Figure 4 represents the interface to define the maintenance action.

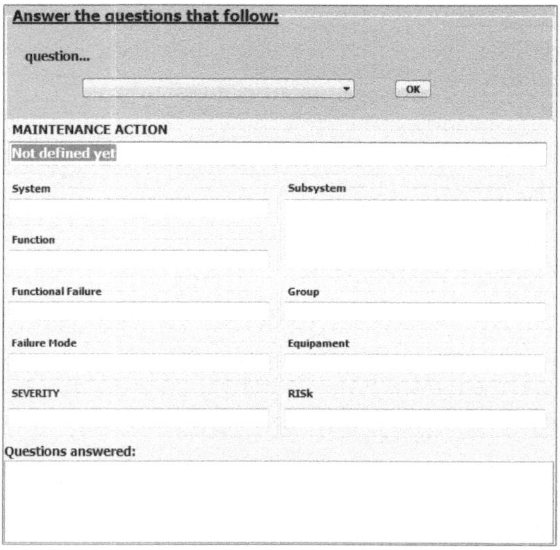

Fig. 4. This is the interface for defining the maintenance strategy. The user must answer the questions by following a sequence diagram. This process will recommend the most appropriate maintenance action for the situation.

It is simple to obtain the process for a maintenance strategy. The questions listed are direct ones and the process enables answers to be categorized. This feature adds value to the process, and aims at the usability of the information system.

Among the alternatives offered by the DSS are: scheduled restoration, scheduled discards, on condition, redesign, failure-finding, not scheduled, combination of tasks and capacity and training of staff. Table 3 gives a description of each maintenance action recommended by the DSS.

The type of maintenance action recommended will depend on the context analyzed. However, it can be helpful to list the aspects considered relevant to define the strategy process: cost, quality and production performance. From this consideration, it can be concluded that there is a relationship between business strategy and maintenance strategy [25].

Table 3. Description of maintenance strategies recommended by the system

Strategy Maintenance	Description
Scheduled restoration	Restoration of the initial production capacity of an item or component
Scheduled discard	Discard of an item or component before the age limit specified
On condition	Is the evaluation of operational conditions and perceptions of potential failures
Redesign	This identifies the need for change in design specifications of the item or component
Failure-Finding	To find hidden failures in regular time intervals
Not scheduled	This is adopted when failure is hidden but does not affect the performance of the production system
Combination of tasks	This is the effective combination of other maintenance activities to solve a problem
Capacity and training of staff	This consists of the organization's ability to invest in training staff to operate the machinery available

The benefits of DSS are moreover based on the type of maintenance action recommended. For these actions that enable the time interval to be analyzed, modeling to estimate the maintenance period based on the inspection and maintenance based on replacing pieces of equipment/items are suggested.

This resource is central to the maintenance strategy, since after learning what to do, it is essential to know when to do it. The results of time analysis are based on mathematical modeling of the specific items of the maintenance area and these are illustrated graphically to the user. Thus, the reports of maintenance activities are consistent since all that needs to be considered doing in the same time period is shown.

Another contribution to define maintenance strategies is the use of multicriteria methods to criticality analysis. The use of multicriteria methods is often in maintenance area in special when complex problems are highlighted in maintenance management systems [26,27]. Some examples these problems in maintenance area include risk evaluation [28,29], outsourcing and logistics [30], project management [31,32] and many others.

5 Conclusion

Investment in information technology in the maintenance area presents is an important resource to strategic position in the competitive context [26]. Since this investment enables value to be added to the decision-making process, it ensures the operational conditions of the organization are satisfactory.

DSS provides a logical sequence for the particular definition of maintenance strategies and provides features that allow a wide understanding of the scenario studied. The application of the DSS satisfies the needs of the maintenance area in the industrial context and is able to deliver results and benefits in any organizational context. Thus, it becomes a tool to support operations management and on which recommends strategic activities.

Thus, this prompts the development of research into the interaction between the concepts involved in the maintenance area with the concepts of decision theory. This article also shows that the multicriteria decision-making process can make a contribution to constructing a new perspective on the occurrence and definition of maintenance actions based on analysis of the criticality failure mode.

References

1. Campos, A.C.S.M., Daher, S.F.D., Almeida, A.T.: New patents on Business Process Management Information Systems and Decision Support. Recent Patents on Computer Science 4, 91–97 (2011)
2. Dekker, R.: Applications of Maintenance Optimization Models: A Review and Analysis. Reliability Engineering & System Safety 51, 240–299 (1996)
3. Pintelon, L.M., Gelders, L.F.: Maintenance management decision making. European Journal of Operational Research 58, 301–317 (1992)
4. Verdecho, M.J., Alfaro-Saiz, J.J., Rodriguez-Rodriguez, R.: Prioritization and management of inter-enterprise collaborative performance. Decision Support Systems 53, 142–153 (2012)
5. Moubray, J.: Reliability-centered Maintenance: RCM II. Ind. Press Inc., New York (1997)
6. Deshpande, V., Modak, J.: Application of RCM for safety considerations in a steel plant. Reliability Engineering and System Safety 78, 325–334 (2002)
7. Jones, R.: Risk-based Maintenance: A Reliability-centered approach. Gulf Professional Publishing, Houston (1995)
8. TM 5-698-2.: Reliability-Centered Maintenance (RCM) for Command, Control, Communications, Computer, Intelligence, Surveillance, and Reconnaissance (C4ISR) Facilities. US Department of the Army, Washington (2006)
9. Jia, X., Christer, A.H.: Case Experience Comparing the RCM Approach to Plant Maintenance with a Modeling Approach. In: Blischke, W.R., Murthy, D.N.P. (eds.) Case Studies in Reliability and Maintenance. John Wiley & Sons, Inc., Hoboken (2003)
10. Rausand, M.: Reliability centered maintenance. Reliability Engineering and System Safety 60, 121–132 (1998)
11. Matteson, T.D.: Airline experience with RCM. Nucl. Engng. Design 89, 385–390 (1985)
12. Nowlan, F.S., Heap, H.: Reliability-centred maintenance. National Technical Information Service, US Department of Commerce, Springfield, VA (1978)
13. Smith, A.M., Hinchcliffe, G.R.: RCM: Gateway to World Class Maintenance. Elsevier Butterworth-Heinemann, Burlington (2004)
14. Alencar, M. H., Almeida-Filho, A. T., Almeida, A. T.: An MCDM model for potential failure causes ranking from FMECA. In: Esrel 2012/PSAM 2011, Helsinki (2012)

15. Braglia, M.: MAFMA: multi-attribute failure mode analysis. Journal of Quality & Reliability Management 17, 1017–1033 (2000)
16. Dong, C.: Failure mode and effects analysis based on fuzzy utility cost estimation. International Journal of Quality & Reliability Management 24, 958–971 (2007)
17. Hipkin, I.B., Lockett, A.G.: A Study of Maintenance Technology Implementation. Omega 23, 79–88 (1995)
18. Abdul-Nour, G., et al.: A reliability based maintenance policy: a case study. Comput. Ind. Eng. 35, 591–594 (1998)
19. Christer, A.H., Whitelaw, J.: An Operation Research Approach to Breakdown Maintenance: Problem Recognition. The Journal of Operational Research Society 34, 1041–1052 (1983)
20. Kans, M.: An approach for determining the requirements of computerised maintenance management systems. Computers in Industry 59, 32–40 (2008)
21. Melville, N., Kraemer, K.L., Gurbaxani, V.: Information technology and organizational performance: an integrative model of IT business value. MIS Quarterly 28, 283–322 (2004)
22. Delone, W.H., Mclean, E.R.: Information systems success: the quest for the dependent variable. Information Systems Research 3, 60–96 (1992)
23. Powell, R.L., Dent-Micallef, A.: Information technology as competitive advantage: the role of human, business, and technology resources. Strategic Management Journal 18, 375–405 (1997)
24. Watson, I.: Case-based reasoning is a methodology, not a technology. Knowl.-Based Syst. 12, 303–308 (1999)
25. Pinjala, S.K., Pintelon, L., Vereecke, A.: An empirical investigation on the relationship between business and maintenance strategies. International Journal of Production Economics 104, 214–229 (2006)
26. Almeida, A.T.: Multicriteria decision making on maintenance: spares and contracts planning. European Journal of Operational Research 129(2), 235–241 (2001)
27. Cavalcante, C.A.V., Ferreira, R.J.P., Almeida, A.T.: A preventive maintenance decision model based on multicriteria method PROMETHEE II integrated with Bayesian approach. IMA Journal of Management Mathematics 21, 333–348 (2010)
28. Brito, A.J., Almeida-Filho, A.T., Almeida, A.T.: Multi-criteria decision model for selecting repair contracts by applying utility theory and variable interdependent parameters. IMA Journal of Management Mathematics 21, 349–361 (2010)
29. Brito, A., Almeida, A.T.: Multi-attribute risk assessment for risk ranking of natural gas pipelines. Reliability Engineering & Systems Safety 94, 187–198 (2009)
30. Almeida, A.T.: Multicriteria modeling of repair contract based on utility and Electre I method with dependability and service quality criteria. Annals of Operations Research 138, 113–126 (2005)
31. Alencar, M.H., Almeida, A.T.: Assigning priorities to actions in a pipeline transporting hydrogen based on a multicriteria decision model. International Journal of Hydrogen Energy 35, 3610–3619 (2010)
32. Mota, C.M.M., Almeida, A.T.: A multicriteria decision model for assigning priority classes to activities in project management. Annals of Operations Research (Online) (2011)

Feedback in the ERP Value-Chain: What Influence Has Thoughts about Competitive Advantage

Björn Johansson

Department of Informatics, School of Economics and Management, Lund University,
Ole Römers väg 6, 223 63 Lund, Sweden
bjorn.johansson@ics.lu.se

Abstract. Different opinions about whether an organization gains a competitive advantage (CA) from an enterprise resource planning (ERP) system exist. However, this paper describes another angle of the much reported competitive advantage discussion. The basic question in the paper concerns how thoughts about receiving competitive advantage from customizing ERPs influences feedback in ERP development. ERP development is described as having three stakeholders: an ERP vendor, an ERP partner or re-seller, and the ERP end-user or client. The question asked is: What influence has thoughts about receiving competitive advantage on the feedback related to requirements in ERP development? From a set of theoretical propositions eight scenarios are proposed. These scenarios are then illustrated from interviews with stakeholders in ERP development. From an initial research, evidence for six of these eight scenarios was uncovered. The main conclusion is that thoughts about competitive advantage seem to influence the feedback, but not really in the way that was initial assumed. Instead of, as was assumed, having a restrict view of providing feedback stakeholders seems to be more interested in having a working feedback loop in the ERP value-chain making the parties in a specific value-chain more interested in competing with other parties in other ERP value-chains.

Keywords: Competitive Advantage, Enterprise Resource Planning (ERP), ERP Development, Resource-Based View, Value-Chain.

1   Introduction

Competitive Advantage (CA) and how organizations gain CA from Information and Communication Technologies (ICTs) are subjects that have been discussed extensively. Different opinions on the answer to the question as to whether ICTs enable organizations to gain CA exist. Some proponents, such as Carr [1], claim that the technology is irrelevant since it can be treated as a commodity. Others, such as Tapscott [2], argue for its importance while still other writers say it depends on how the technology is used and that it is how business processes are managed that are primary for gaining CA [3]. However, in reviewing the academic literature there seems to be a common understanding that it is not the technology as such that

G. Poels (Ed.): CONFENIS 2012, LNBIP 139, pp. 134–148, 2013.
© IFIP International Federation for Information Processing 2013

eventually provides organizations with CA but how the technology is managed and used [4].

However, in this paper another perspective of CA in relation to Enterprise Resource Planning systems (ERPs) is discussed, and that is how the ERP value-chain stakeholders' interests in maintaining or improving their CA may influence feedback related to requirements of ERPs. When distinguishing between the stakeholders in the ERP value-chain and their relative positions, the subject becomes more complex. The research builds on a set of propositions suggesting what gives stakeholders in the ERP value-chain their CA. The propositions are then presented as win-lose scenarios that are discussed using preliminary findings from an empirical study.

The principle question addressed in this paper is: What influence has thoughts about receiving competitive advantage on the feedback related to requirements in ERP development?

The rest of the paper is organized as follows: The next section defines ERPs and describes the ERP value-chain and its stakeholders. Section 3 then define CA and describe ERPs and CA from the resource-based view of the firm perspective. This is followed by a presentation of the propositions and a table suggesting CA scenarios in relation to the different stakeholders in the ERP value-chain. The penultimate section presents eight scenarios together with some preliminary findings from own as well as extant studies. Finally some concluding remarks in addition with directions for future research are presented.

2   ERPs, the ERP Value-Chain and Its Stakeholders

ERPs are often defined as standardized packaged software designed with the aim of integrating the internal value chain with an organization's external value chain through business process integration [5, 6], as well as providing the entire organization with common master data [7]. Wier et al. [8] argue that ERPs aim at integrating business processes and ICT into a synchronized suite of procedures, applications and metrics which transcend organizational boundaries. Kumar and van Hillegersberg [9] claim that ERPs that originated in the manufacturing industry were the first generation of ERPs. Development of these first generation ERPs was an inside-out process proceeding from standard inventory control (IC) packages, to material requirements planning (MRP), material resource planning (MRP II) and then eventually expanding it to a software package to support the entire organization (second generation ERPs). This evolved software package is sometimes described as the next generation ERP and labeled as ERP II which, according to Møller [10], could be described as the next generation enterprise systems (ESs).

This evolution has increased the complexity not only of usage, but also in the development of ERPs. The complexity comes from the fact that ERPs are systems that are supposed to integrate the organization (both inter-organizationally as well as intra-organizationally) and its business processes into one package [11]. It can be assumed that ERPs as well as how organizations use ERPs have evolved significantly from a focus on manufacturing to include service organizations [12]. These changes have created a renewed interest in developing and selling ERPs. Thus, the ERP market is a market that is in flux. This impacts not only the level of stakeholder involvement in an ERP value-chain [13, 14], but also how these different stakeholders gain CA from developing, selling, or using ERPs. It is clear that a user organization no longer achieves CA just by implementing an ERP [15, 16]. Fosser et al., [17] present evidence that supports this and at the same time show that for some organizations there is a need to implement an ERP system for at least achieving competitive parity. They also claim that the way the configuration and implementation is accomplished can enhance the possibility to gain CA from an ERP system, but an inability to exploit the ERP system can bring a competitive disadvantage. This is in line with the assumption from the resource-based view that it is utilization of resources that makes organizations competitive and just implementing ERPs provides little, if any, CA [4]. One reason for this could be that the number of organizations that have implemented ERPs has exploded. Shehab et al. [18] claim that the price of entry for running a business is to implement an ERP, and they even suggest that it can be a competitive disadvantage if you do not have an ERP system. Beard and Sumner [19] argue that through reduction of costs or by increasing organizations revenue, ERPs may not directly provide organizations with CA. Instead, they suggest that advantages could be largely described as value-adding through an increase of information, faster processing, more timely and accurate transactions, and better decision-making.

In contrast to the above analysis, development of ERPs is described as a value-chain consisting of different stakeholders, as shown in Figure 1. The value-chain differs between different business models, however, it can be claimed that the presented value-chain is commonly used in the ERP market. The presented value-chain can be seen as an ERP business model that has at least three different stakeholders: ERP software vendors, ERP resellers/distributors, and ERP end-user organizations (or ERP customers). It can be said that all stakeholders in the value-chain, to some extent, develop the ERP further. However, what it is clear is that the feedbacks, related to requirements, from users are of importance for future development. The software vendors develop the core of the system that they then "sell" to their partners that act as resellers or distributors of the specific ERP. These partners quite often make changes to the system or develop what could be labeled as add-ons to the ERP core. These changes or add-ons are then implemented in order to customize the ERP for a specific customer. In some cases the customer develops the ERP system further either by configuration or customization. At this stage of the value-chain it can be argued that the "original" ERP system could have changed dramatically from its basic design. This ERP development value-chain may result in the ERP software vendors not having as close connection to the end-user that they would choose and they do not always understand what functionalities are added to the end-users' specific ERP systems. Therefore is feedback in the ERP value-chain essential for future development.

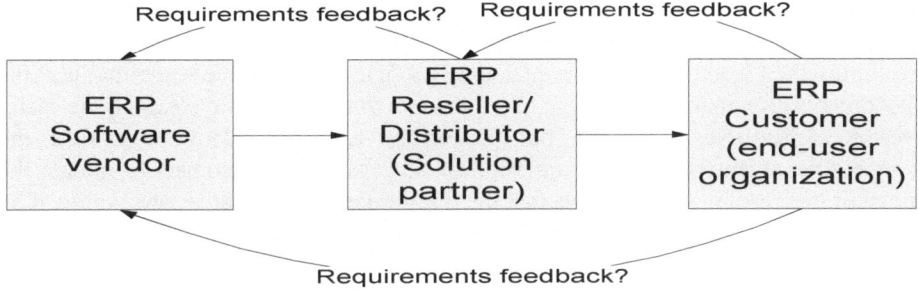

Fig. 1. Stakeholders in the ERP value-chain

The stakeholders in the ERP value-chain have different roles; accordingly, they have different views of CA gained from ERPs. One way of describing this is to use a concept from the resource-based view: core competence [20]. Developing ERPs are normally the ERP software vendor's core competence. The ERP reseller/distributors' core competence should also be closely related to ERPs, but it is unclear if development should be their core competency. Their core competences could or should be marketing and implementing ERPs. However, this probably varies between ERP resellers/distributors; for some it could be development of add-ons that constitute one of their core competences. When it comes to end-user organizations, it can be said that ERP development definitely is not their core competence. However, they are involved in the ERP development value-chain, since it is crucial for an organization to have alignment between its business processes and supporting technology. To further discuss this ERPs and CA are discussed from the resource-based view of the firm in the next section.

3   ERP and Competitive Advantage Seen from the Resource-Based View

Whether an organization (the customer in figure 1) gains CA from software applications depends, according to Mata et al. [4], as well as Kalling [21], on how these resources are managed. The conclusion Mata et al. [4] draw is that among attributes related to software applications – capital requirements, proprietary technology, technical skills, and managerial software applications skills – it is only the managerial software application skills that can provide sustainability of CA. Barney [22] concludes that sources of sustained CA are and must be focused on heterogeneity and immobility of resources. This conclusion builds on the assumption that if a resource is evenly distributed across competing organizations and if the resource is highly mobile, the resource cannot produce a sustained competitive advantage as described in the VRIO framework (Table 1).

The VRIO framework aims at identifying resources with potential for having sustained competitive advantage by answering the questions, is a resource or capability...If all answers are answered affirmative, the specific resource has the potential to deliver sustained competitive advantage to the organization. However, to do that, it has to be efficient and effectively organized. Barney [23] describes this as exploiting the resource. If the organization is a first-mower in the sense that it is the first organization that uses this type of resource in that specific way, it can quite easily receive competitive advantage, but, it can be temporary. How long time the competitive advantage lasts is a question of how hard it is for others to imitate the usage of that resource. This means that the question of how resources are exploited by the organization is the main factor when it comes to if the competitive advantage becomes sustainable or not.

Table 1. The VRIO framework [23]

Is a resource or capability…					
Valuable?	Rare?	Costly to Imitate?	Exploited by Organisation?	Competitive Implications	Economic Performance
No	---	---	No	Competitive Disadvantage	Below Normal
Yes	No	---		Competitive Parity	Normal
Yes	Yes	No		Temporary Competitive Advantage	Above Normal
Yes	Yes	Yes	Yes	Sustained Competitive Advantage	Above Normal

The framework, Table 1, which employs Barney 's [22] notions about CA and ICT in general, has been used extensively [5, 19, 21, 24]. What the conducted research implies is that CA can be difficult but not impossible to achieve if the resource is difficult to reproduce (e.g. the role of history, causal ambiguity and social complexity). Fosser et al., [24] conclude that the real value of the resource is not the ICT in itself, but the way the managers exploit it, which is in line with the resource-based view of the firm and the value, rareness, imitability and organization (VRIO) framework.

Quinn and Hilmer [25] argue that organizations can increase the CA by concentrating on resources which provide unique value for their customers. There are many different definitions of CA; however, a basic definition is that the organization achieves above normal economic performance. If this situation is maintained, the CA is deemed to be sustained. Based on the discussion above and the statement made by Quinn and Hilmer [25], Table 2 suggests what outcome of CA could be and how it potentially could be gained by different stakeholders in the ERP development value-chain including the end-user. There are some conflicts between attributes for gaining

CA, such as developing competitively priced software with high flexibility and developing software that is easy to customize and, at the same time, achieve CA by developing exclusive add-ons.

If the organization is a first mover in the sense that it is the first organization that uses this type of resource in a specific way, it can quite easily gain CA, but it will probably only be temporary. The length of time that the CA lasts depends on how hard or expensive it is for others to imitate the usage of that resource. This means that the question of how resources are exploited by the organization is the main factor when it comes to whether the CA becomes sustainable or not.

Levina and Ross [26] describe the value proposition in outsourcing from a vendor's perspective. They claim that the value derived from vendors is based on their ability to develop complementary core competencies. From an ERP perspective, it can be suggested that vendors, as well as distributors (Figure 1) provide value by delivering complementary core competencies to their customers. The evolution of ERPs has made these resources easier to imitate. However, a major barrier to imitation is the cost of implementation [27, 28].

Table 2. ERP value-chain stakeholders and competitive advantage

Stakeholder	Outcome of Competitive Advantage	Gained through
ERP Software Vendor	High level of market share in the ERP market (e.g. the number software licenses sold)	Competitively priced software Highly flexible software Ease of implementing the software Ease of customizing the software
ERP Resellers/dis tributor	High level of market share in the ERP consultancy market (e.g. consultancy hours delivered)	Knowledge about the customer's business High level of competence in development of add-ons that are seen as attractive by the ERP end-user organization High level of competence at customization
ERP end-user organization	High level of market share in the customer-specific market (e.g. products or services sold; rising market share; lower costs)	Being competitive in its own market Implementing an ERP system that supports its business processes Implementing an ERP system that is difficult for competitors to reproduce

The resource-based view claims that a resource has to be rare or, be heterogeneously distributed, to provide CA. In the case of ERPs, this kind of resource is not rare. There are a lot of possibilities for organizations to implement different ERPs, and the evolution of ICT has made it feasible for more organizations to implement ERPs by decreasing the costs of using ERPs. However, as described by

Barney [23] and Shehab et al. [18], failure to implement an ERP can also lead to an organization suffering competitive disadvantages.

The CA from ERPs would probably be negated by duplication as well as by substitution. If, for instance, the ERP resellers sold their add-ons to the ERP software vendor, the duplication of that add-on would be quicker and the CA that the ERP reseller previously had would be gradually eroded. However, if they kept the add-on as "their" unique solution, other ERP resellers or ERP software vendors would probably find a substitute to the add-on or develop their own.

This implies a conflict between vendors and resellers when it comes to CA and the development of "better" ERPs. This can be explained by realizing that ERP resellers/distributors often develop add-ons which have a specific functionality for solving a particular problem for their customer. This can be seen as one way of customization, where resellers/distributors use their domain knowledge about the customers' industry in addition to their knowledge about the specific customer. This, in effect, allows resellers to increase their CA and earn abnormal returns. Another way is for resellers to sell the add-on to other resellers resulting in the resellers decreasing their CA in the long run. It is probable that resellers who sell their add-on solutions to other resellers would see it as not influencing their CA since they sell the add-on to customers already using the same ERP system and this would not make ERP end-user organizations change resellers. However, the question remains whether the same would apply if the resellers sold the add-on to the software vendor. The answer would depend on the incentives that the resellers had for doing that. If the add-ons were to be implemented in the basic software, the possibility of selling the add-on to client organizations, as well as to other resellers, would disappear.

Beard and Sumner [19] investigate whether a common systems approach for implementing ERPs can provide a CA. The focus of their research was to investigate what happens when a variety of firms within the same industry adopt the same system and employ almost identical business processes. Their conclusion is that it seems that ERPs are increasingly a requirement for staying competitive (i.e. competitive parity), and that ERPs can yield at most a temporary CA. From this it can be suggested that ERP end-user organizations want a "cheap" system that they can use to improve their business processes, thereby making a difference compared with other organizations in the same industry. But, since ERPs encourage organizations to implement standardized business processes (so-called "best practice" Wagner and Newell, [29]), organizations get locked in by the usage of the system and then, depending on whether they are a first mover or not, they receive only a temporary CA. This implies that the ERP end-user organization often implement an ERP with the objective of having a "unique" ERP system. But does the ERP customer want a unique ERP system? If the customer believes they have a unique business model, it is likely they would want a unique ERP system. However, they also want a system with high interoperability internally, as well as one compatible with external organizations systems. It is likely that end-user organizations have a need for a system that is not the same as their competitors. This is congruent with the ERP resellers/distributors. They receive their CA by offering their customers the knowledge of how to customize an ERP using industries' best practices and, at the same time, how to implement functionality that makes ERP system uniquely different from their competitor's system. Based on this discussion the next section presents some propositions on how thoughts about achieving CA from uniqueness of ERP system influence feedback of requirements in the ERP value-chain.

4   Propositions on How Competitive Advantages Thoughts Influence Requirements Feedback

Proposition 1: Both resellers and end-users (encouraged by resellers) in the ERP value-chain see customization as a way of achieving Competitive Advantage (CA). This could result in resistance to providing software vendors with the information necessary for them to develop ERPs further in the direction of standardization and thereby decreasing the resellers' need to customize the system.

Kalling [21] suggested that the literature on resource protection focuses, to a large extent, on imitation, trade and substitution. He proposed that development of a resource can also be seen as a protection of the resource. Referring to Liebeskind [30], Kalling posited that the ability to protect and retain resources arises from the fact that resources are asymmetrically distributed among competitors. The problem, according to Kalling, is how to protect more intangible resources such as knowledge. Relating this to ERPs, it follows that knowledge about a specific usage situation of an ERP would be hard to protect by legal means, such as contracts. Another way of protecting resources is, as described by Kalling, to "protect by development." This means that an organization protects existing resources by developing resources in a way that flexibility is increased by adjusting and managing present resources. In the ERP case this could be described as customizing existing ERPs, thereby sustaining CA gained from using the ERP system. Kalling describes this as a way of increasing a time advantage. From the different ERP stakeholders' perspectives, it could be argued that both protection by development, as well as trying to increase the time advantage, influences the direction in which ERPs are developed.

Proposition 2: The conflict between different parties in the ERP value-chain and how they believe they will gain CA influences the feedback in the ERP value-chain. This tends to increases the cost for both development as well as maintenance of ERP systems.

The discussion and propositions so far suggest that decision-makers in organizations and their beliefs regarding how to gain and sustain CA by customization of ERPs, are a major hindrance to the development of future ERPs. This emanates from the assumption that organizations (end users and resellers) protect what customization they have made. The reason why they do so is based on their belief that they will sustain a CA gained by developing, selling or using customized ERPs. However, returning to Table 2 and the suggestion as to what it is that constitute CA for the different stakeholders, it can be concluded that there are some generic influencing factors. The conflicting goals of the three parties in the ERP value-chain increases complexity in the market place. From a resource-based perspective, first mover advantage could be seen as something that influences all stakeholders and their possibility to gain and to some extent sustain CA.

The same could also be said about speed of implementation. The main suggestion is that even if the role of history, causal ambiguity and social complexity influences the organizations' possibility to gain CA, the management skills that the organizations have is crucial.

When looking at what improves their market share of the three different stakeholders in the ERP value-chain, it can be proposed that there are no direct conflicts amongst stakeholders. The reason is that they all have different markets and different customers; therefore they do not compete directly with one other. In reality, they have each other as customers and/or providers, as described in Figure 1. It is suggested that further development of ERPs carried out by vendors could result in a higher degree of selling directly to end-customers or other ways of delivering ERPs to end-customers so that the partners will be driven to insolvency and replaced by, for instance, application service provision (ASP) [31, 32], or software as a service - SaaS [33] or open source [34, 35]. The first step in this direction would probably be signaled if the add-ons that partners currently deliver to end-customers are implemented in the core product. From this it can be concluded that there is a potential conflict between the different parties in the value-chain when it comes to how different stakeholders gain CA and how that influences future ERP development.

ERP software vendors become competitive if they utilize their resources to develop ERPs that are attractive to the market. ERP resellers/distributors thus need to utilize their resources to become attractive partners when implementing ERPs. Furthermore, ERP end-users need to use the ERP system so that it supports their businesses. In other words, it is how end-user organizations employ the ERP that is of importance, and it could be that having a unique ERP system (Table 1) is not as important as has previously been believed. In other words, while customization is in the interests of the resellers this may not be the case for the end users.

Millman [36] posits that ERPs are the most expensive but least value-derived implementation of ICT support. The reason for this, according to Millman, is that a lot of ERPs functionality is either not used or is implemented in the wrong way. That it is wrongly implemented results from ERPs being customized to fit the business processes, instead of changing the process so that it fits the ERP [36]. However, according to Light [37], there are more reasons for customization than just the need for achieving a functionality fit between the ERP and the organization's business processes. He believes that from the vendor's perspective, customizations might be seen as fuelling the development process. From an end-user' perspective, Light describes customization as a value-added process that increases the system's acceptability and efficiency [37]. He further reasons that customization might occur as a form of resistance or protection against implementation of a business process that could be described as "best practices." One reason why end-user organizations get involved in ERP development is that they want to adjust their ERPs so that they support their core competences.

Proposition 3: End-users of ERPs and their basic assumption about how they receive CA are encouraged by resellers of ERPs. Resellers want to sustain their CA by suggesting and delivering high levels of ERP customization.

The main conclusion so far can be formulated as follows: Highly customized ERPs deliver better opportunities for CA for the resellers in the ERP value-chain while it decreases the opportunity for both ERP software vendors as well as ERP end-user organizations to attain CA.

To discuss this further, in the next section we propose various scenarios supported by some early empirical data.

5   Scenarios Describing ERP Related Competitive Advantage

In this section eight possible scenarios on how thoughts about receiving competitive advantage from a customized ERP system could be described from a CA perspective is presented. The description is based on semi-structured interviews done with an ERP vendor, ERP reseller consultants and ERP customers and recently published studies in two Norwegian companies presented by Fosser et al,.[17, 24]. The interviews with the ERP vendor and the ERP reseller consultants were part of an on-going research project investigating requirements management. The project aimed at gaining knowledge on what factors that influence future development of ERPs. In total there were 11 interviews conducted with different executives at a major ERP vendor organization and three interviews conducted with ERP consultants at a reseller organization. The reseller organization implements and supports different ERP systems, and one of their "products" is the ERP system that is developed by the ERP vendor. The interviews with ERP customers comes from the study done by Fosser et al., [17, 24] (in total 19 interviews) which were part of a research project that aimed at understanding competitive advantage in an ERP context. Citations from interviews done in these different studies are used to illustrate findings and flesh out the content of table 3.

Table 3. Scenarios describing win or lose relationship

Scenario	Vendor	Re-Seller	Client (end user)
A	Win	Win	Win
B	Win	Win	Lose
C	Win	Lose	Win
D	Win	Lose	Lose
E	Lose	Win	Win
F	Lose	Win	Lose
G	Lose	Lose	Win
H	Lose	Lose	Lose

Scenario A: It can be said that this is probably the situation that all stakeholders in a business relationship ideally want. However, to have a win-win-win situation in an ERP development value-chain is not straightforward. From the vendors' perspective it means that they should develop an ERP system that is both so generic that the re-seller could sell it to a lot of different clients to generate revenue from licenses and at the same time be so specific that the end users could gain a CA from the usage of the standardized system. However, if the vendor manages to develop such a generic form of ERP it is likely that end user would demand an extensive customization effort. The result could then be that the re-seller could sell a lot of consultancy hours for adjusting the software to the business processes in the client's organization. A quotation from an ERP consultant at an ERP reseller organization describes a situation when the feedback loop worked as a win-win-win situation. The ERP consultant said: *"Before the ERP vendor merged with a bigger ERP vendor we had a close relationship that actually made it possible to have requests from a specific customer implemented in the system. Now we don't know who to talk with and even if we get a contact with them (the vendor) they are not really interested"*. He (the ERP consultant) continues with stating that: *"We developed a very interesting add-on for a customer, that we then tried to get implemented in the base system but it was impossible. So, we started to sell this add-on to other ERP resellers (of the same system). We did so because we think it will benefit us in the long run if customers feel that the system is interesting – In that way we will probably increase our market"*.

If this continues for some time it probably ends with a situation as in Scenario E. Scenario E is then the situation when vendor loses and the re-seller and clients win. We see this as a possibility if the re-sellers spend so much time with clients developing ERP systems offering CA while generating large consultancy hours but at the cost of not marketing the base ERP system to new clients. Our early data gathering suggests this scenario is common among the stakeholders. One example of support of this situation is the following statement from an executive at the ERP vendor (the same ERP vendor that was mentioned above by the developer at the ERP reseller).

The executive at the ERP vendor said that: *"We don't have enough knowledge about how the system is used and what the user of the system actually wants to have. This makes that future development of the system is extremely hard and it is a fact that there are problems with requirements management in ERP development"* Director of Program Management.

Comparing the citations from consultant with the one from the vendor there seems to be a contradiction. The consultant feels it hard to provide feedback while the vendor feels a lack of feedback. From the CA perspective this is hard to explain, however, what can be said is that this specific consultant see an opportunity in increasing its CA by providing feedback to the vendor. The reason for why it does not happen probably is related to lack of resources at the vendor place or a lack of a clear relationship between the parties. One way for the vendor of dealing with this is to get a closer relationship to some ERP resellers – by a relationship program giving some benefits to reseller that have a close relationship with the vendor. However, it demands that they for instance follow a specific process for implementation of the ERP.

This could then result in the situation described in scenario B, in which both the vendor and the re-seller have a win-win situation while the client has a disadvantaged position especially if they do not customize the software to the extent whereby they gain CA. The following quotations from ERP customers describe this situation.

"An ERP system is something you just need to do business today. But the way we have implemented it and configured it has given us a competitive advantage." Assistant Director of Logistics.

"I believe that it is mostly a system you need to have. But an ERP system can be utilized to achieve a competitive advantage, if you are skillful." Senior Consultant.

"It keeps us on the same level as our competitors. We are focusing on quality products. That is our competitive advantage. An ERP system cannot help us with that". The Quality Manager.

"I don't think we have got any competitive advantage. All our competitors are running such a system, so it is just something we need to have. It is actually a competitive disadvantage because we have not managed to get as far as the others, with the system." Managing Director.

All these citations describe the situation when the customers see ERP implementation as a necessity to avoid competitive disadvantage. To some extent it can be said that they understand customization as something you do to gain CA, which implies that they all are interested in what other customers do and that could be seen as something that hindrance feedback resulting in the scenario B situation. Another reason why the situation could result in scenario B is that it is shown that if clients customize to a high extent, the long-term maintenance costs of the ERP system becomes so great that the benefits are lost. The following statement from a developer at the ERP vendor supports scenario B.

"It is clearly seen that when a customer implement the ERP system for the first time they customize a lot. When they then upgrade with a new version the extensive customization is much less and when they upgrade with version 3 and/or 4 they hardly don't do any customization. The reason is must likely that they have discovered that customization cost a lot at the same time as they have discovered that they are not that unique that they thought when implementing the first version" Program Manager A.

In the long run this could also result in scenario F. Scenario F describes the situation where the vendor starts to lose market share because clients have problems achieving CA resulting in a bad reputation for the ERP product. The situation of less customization and less demand on add-ons could also result in scenario C. In scenario C, we see a vendor by-passing the reseller and working directly with the client enabling them both to gain a CA. This is somewhat supported by an executive at the ERP vendor, who says: *"However, there will probably be a day when the partners not are needed - at least for doing adjustments of ERPs. This is not a problem since the rules of the game always change. And there will still be a need for partners. The partners see themselves as ... they understand the customer's problem."* Program Manager B.

Scenario D is an interesting scenario since it is only the vendor that shows a winning position. It could be explained by the fact that if the vendor manages to develop a generic ERP system and thereby gain a more or less monopoly status they will have the possibility to sell many licenses. It also shows the situation when the vendor not seems to be dependent on feedback from customers in the development of the ERP. A quotation from an ERP customer describes this clearly: *"I try to exploit the available tools in SAP without investing money in new functionality. There are a lot of possibilities in the ERP systems, e.g. HR, which we are working with to utilize our resources more efficiently."* Director of Finance.

It could also be that the client needs to buy and implement the ERP since it more or less a necessity to implement an ERP to obtain competitive parity. This means that ERP end-users use the ERP as standardized software and they do not feel that providing feedback to the vendor is of importance.

With scenario G it is probably a situation that the vendor would not allow to continue. However, from the perspective of an ERP customer one motive for restricting the feedback could be justified from this citation: *"We have a unique configuration of the system that fits our organization and this gives us a competitive advantage. The IS department is very important in this context."* Assistant Director of Logistics. While another citation suggests that providing feedback could be a way of gaining competitive advantage: *"I actually hold lectures about how we do things in our organization. I tell others about the big things, but I think it is the small things that make us good. All the small things are not possible to copy. I think it is a strength that we have a rumor for being good at ERP and data warehouse. It gives [us] a good image. Though, we are exposed to head hunters from other organizations."* Director of IS.

The empirical data so far did not provide any evidence for scenario G or scenario H. Regarding scenario H it can be stated that from a "prisoner dilemma game" [38] it could happen that all lose, however, from research on the prisoners dilemma game it is clear that if the "game" are repeated the involved parties would start to cooperate [38]. This means that it more or less can be assumed that in the ERP value-chain case in the long-run while the stakeholders work in the direction of scenario A. This also to some extent means that neither of the scenarios (B, D, F and H) giving a lose for clients will be sustainable in the long-run.

6   Concluding Remark and Future Research

Using an innovative value chain analysis considering the ERP vendor, reseller and client we developed eight scenarios to examine our research question: "What influence has thoughts about receiving competitive advantage on the feedback related to requirements in ERP development?" From the preliminary empirical research evidence to support six of the eight scenarios were found. As the other two were the least likely to occur, the findings encourages to conduct further systematic research in the future to flesh out the findings and to look particularly at ERP acquisitions in a variety of settings. As ERP systems are ubiquitous in modern corporations it is vital that managers consider the value such systems offer in the long term. Furthermore, the analysis offers a more in-depth understanding of the dynamics of the ERP development value chain, its complexity and its impact on competitive advantage for the different stakeholders.

However, returning to the question about how CA thoughts influence feedback in ERP development, it can be stated that it seems to influence the feedback, but not really in the way that were initial assumed. Instead of, as was assumed, having a restrict view of providing feedback stakeholders seems to be more interested in having a working feedback loop in the ERP value-chain making the parties in a specific value-chain more interested in competing with other parties in other ERP value-chains.

For the future, it will be interesting also to try to reveal the patterns that emerge in the value chain and investigate which scenarios are more sustainable in the long-term and how clients can position themselves more effectively to improve their competitive advantage.

References

1. Carr, N.G.: IT Doesn't Matter. Harvard Business Review 81, 41–49 (2003)
2. Tapscott, D.: The engine that drives success. CIO Magazine (May 1, 2004)
3. Smith, H., Fingar, P.: IT doesn't matter - business processes do: a critical analysis of Nicholas Carr's I.T. article in the Harvard Business Review, 126 p. Meghan-Kiffer, Tampa (2003)
4. Mata, F.J., Fuerst, W.L., Barney, J.B.: Information technology and sustained competitive advantage: A resource-based analysis. MIS Quarterly 19(4), 487–505 (1995)
5. Lengnick-Hall, C.A., Lengnick-Hall, M.L., Abdinnour-Helm, S.: The role of social and intellectual capital in achieving competitive advantage through enterprise resource planning (ERP) systems. Journal of Engineering and Technology Management 21(4), 307–330 (2004)
6. Rolland, C., Prakash, N.: Bridging the Gap Between Organisational Needs and ERP Functionality. Requirements Engineering 5(3), 180–193 (2000)
7. Hedman, J., Borell, A.: ERP systems impact on organizations. In: Grant, G. (ed.) ERP & Data Warehousing in Organizations: Issues and Challenges, pp. 1–21. Idea Group Publishing, Hershey (2003)
8. Wier, B., Hunton, J., HassabElnaby, H.R.: Enterprise resource planning systems and non-financial performance incentives: The joint impact on corporate performance. International Journal of Accounting Information Systems 8(3), 165–190 (2007)
9. Kumar, K., Van Hillegersberg, J.: ERP experiences and evolution. Communications of the ACM 43(4), 22–26 (2000)
10. Møller, C.: ERP II: a conceptual framework for next-generation enterprise systems? Journal of Enterprise Information Management 18(4), 483–497 (2005)
11. Koch, C.: ERP-systemer: erfaringer, ressourcer, forandringer, p. 224. Ingeniøren-bøger, København (2001)
12. Botta-Genoulaz, V., Millet, P.A.: An investigation into the use of ERP systems in the service sector. International Journal of Production Economics (99), 202–221 (2006)
13. Ifinedo, P., Nahar, N.: ERP systems success: an empirical analysis of how two organizational stakeholder groups prioritize and evaluate relevant measures. Enterprise Information Systems 1(1), 25–48 (2007)
14. Somers, T.M., Nelson, K.G.: A taxonomy of players and activities across the ERP project life cycle. Information & Management 41(3), 257–278 (2004)
15. Karimi, J., Somers, T.M., Bhattacherjee, A.: The Impact of ERP Implementation on Business Process Outcomes: A Factor-Based Study. Journal of Management Information Systems 24(1), 101–134 (2007)
16. Kocakulah, M.C., Embry, J.S., Albin, M.: Enterprise Resource Planning (ERP): managing the paradigm shift for success. International Journal of Information and Operations Management Education (IJIOME) 1(2), 125–139 (2006)
17. Fosser, E., et al.: ERP Systems and competitive advantage: Some initial results. In: 3gERP 2nd Workshop. Copenhagen Business School (2008)

18. Shehab, E.M., et al.: Enterprise resource planning: An integrative review. Business Process Management Journal 10(4), 359–386 (2004)
19. Beard, J.W., Sumner, M.: Seeking strategic advantage in the post-net era: viewing ERP systems from the resource-based perspective. The Journal of Strategic Information Systems 13(2), 129–150 (2004)
20. Javidan, M.: Core competence: What does it mean in practice? Long Range Planning 31(1), 60–71 (1998)
21. Kalling, T.: Gaining competitive advantage through information technology: a resource-based approach to the creation and employment of strategic IT resources. Lund studies in economics and management, vol. 55, p. 336. Lund Business Press, Lund (1999); [10], [4]
22. Barney, J.B.: Firm resources and sustained competitive advantage. Journal of Management 17(1), 99–120 (1991)
23. Barney, J.B.: Gaining and sustaining competitive advantage, 2nd edn., 600 p. Prentice Hall, Upper Saddle River (2002)
24. Fosser, E., et al.: Organisations and vanilla software: What do we know about ERP systems and competitive advantage? In: 16th European Conference on Information Systems, Galway, Ireland (2008)
25. Quinn, J.B., Hilmer, F.G.: Strategic Outsourcing. Sloan Management Review 35(4), 43–55 (1994)
26. Levina, N., Ross, J.W.: From the vendor's perspective: Exploring the value proposition in information technology outsourcing(1)(2). MIS Quarterly 27(3), 331–364 (2003)
27. Robey, D., Ross, J.W., Boudreau, M.-C.: Learning to Implement Enterprise Systems: An Exploratory Study of the Dialectics of Change. Journal of Management Information Systems 19(1), 17–46 (2002)
28. Davenport, T.: Holistic management of mega-package change: The case of SAP. Center of Business Innovation, Ernest & Young LLP, Boston (1996)
29. Wagner, E.L., Newell, S.: 'Best' For Whom?: The Tension Between 'Best Practice' ERP Packages And Diverse Epistemic Cultures In A University Context. Journal of Strategic Information Systems 13, 305–328 (2004)
30. Liebeskind, J.P.: Knowledge, strategy, and the theory of the firm. Strategic Management Journal 17, 93–107 (1996)
31. Bryson, K.-M., Sullivan, W.E.: Designing effective incentive-oriented contracts for application service provider hosting of ERP systems. Business Process Management Journal 9(6), 705–721 (2003)
32. Johansson, B.: Deciding on Using Application Service Provision in SMEs. Department of computer and information science, p. 174. Linköping University, Linköping (2004)
33. Jacobs, D.: Enterprise software as service: On line services are changing the nature of software. Queue (July/August 2005)
34. Johansson, B., Sudzina, F.: ERP systems and open source: an initial review and some implications for SMEs. Journal of Enterprise Information Management 21(6), 649 (2008)
35. Johansson, B.: Diffusion of Open Source ERP Systems Development: How Users Are Involved. In: Nuttgens, M., et al. (eds.) Governance and Sustainability in Information Systems. Managing the Transfer and Diffusion of IT, pp. 188–203. Springer, Boston (2011)
36. Millman, G.J.: What did you get from ERP, and what can you get? Financial Executives International 5, 15–24 (2004)
37. Light, B.: Going beyond "misfit" as a reason for ERP package customisation. Computers in Industry 56(6), 606–619 (2005)
38. Tullock, G.: Adam Smith and the Prisoners' Dilemma. The Quarterly Journal of Economics 100(suppl.), 1073–1081 (1985)

Towards a Business Network Management

Daniel Ritter

Technology Development – Process and Network Integration, SAP AG,
Dietmar-Hopp-Allee 16, 69190 Walldorf
daniel.ritter@sap.com

Abstract. Enterprises are part of value chains consisting of cross-enterprise business processes forming large business networks of customers, vendors, partners and competitors. These business process networks run on (technical) integration networks, which are semantically interlinked with the processes, while both are correlated to organizational (social) networks, consisting of technical and business domain experts. The insight into these networks promise a competitive advantage through the visibility into the linked enterprise data. However, this information is hidden in complex, dynamic and heterogeneous enterprise domains.

In this position paper, we introduce the new domain of Business Network Management (BNM), which strives to make business networks visible within network views and sets them into context with each other. For that, we extend the Network Mining (NM) domain by a virtualized network approach towards a BNM. That means automatic discovery, mining and inference capabilities are combined with expert knowledge from different domains to compute the networks and a semantic correlation between entities of different perspectives. We comprehensively define the domain and discuss a system implementation, which we evaluated in a real-world customer case.

Keywords: Business Networks, Business Network Management, Business Network Virtualization, Business Processes, Integration Middleware, Linked (Business) Data, Network Mining.

1 Introduction

Enterprises are part of value chains consisting of business processes with intra and inter enterprise stakeholders. To remain competitive, enterprises need visibility into their business networks and ideally into relevant parts of partner and customer networks and processes. However, currently the visibility often ends at the borders of systems or enterprises. Business Network Management (BNM) helps to overcome this situation and allows companies to get insight into their technical, social and business relations. However, the relevant information is hidden in complex, dynamic and heterogeneous enterprise domains.

In previous work, we introduced the domain of Network Mining (NM) [10], which allows to discover this information from the different business process and integration domains. The extracted raw data contains the information necessary

G. Poels (Ed.): CONFENIS 2012, LNBIP 139, pp. 149–156, 2013.
© IFIP International Federation for Information Processing 2013

to reconstruct the different network perspectives as well as to semantically link them into one business network [11]. An example for a business network is given in Fig. 1, which shows participants in a business process network of a (cross-) enterprise partner network (front) and the corresponding technical network on which these processes are implemented (back). The participants of the business process network represent business artifacts within an enterprise, that are related to participants within a partner network. The participants and relationships are considered complex and contain the underlying business processes, which specify e.g. a business document or goods exchange between related participants. These business processes are actually implemented within the applications and integration capabilities of the enterprises denoting a more technical network, called integration network. This network consists of applications and integration middleware for internal business processes related to processes interacting with business partners like suppliers, transport carriers, dealers.

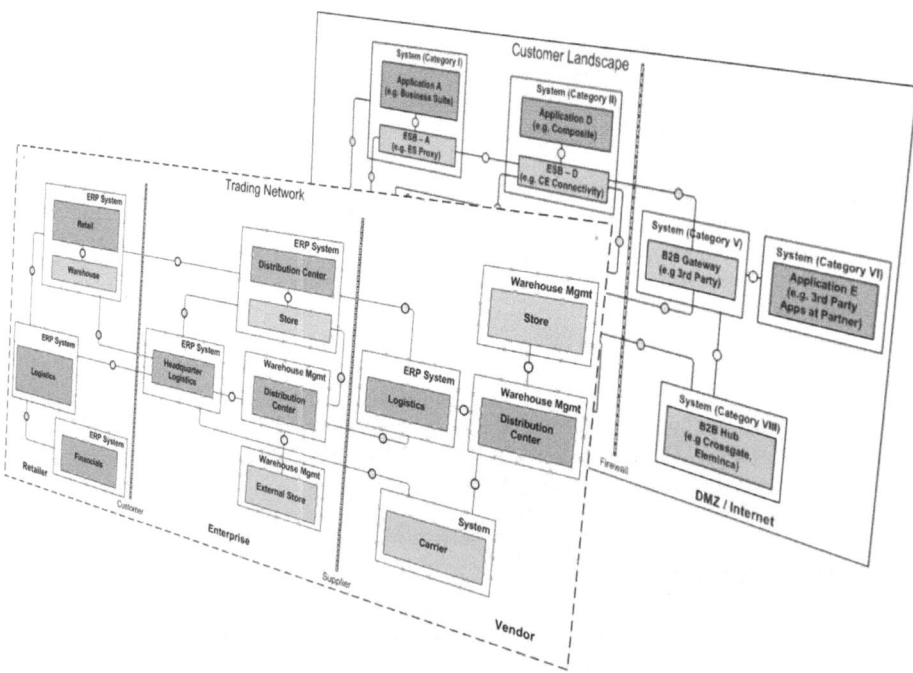

Fig. 1. Sample (cross-) enterprise Business Network showing business participants, denoted as nodes, and business document exchange as edges (front) as well as an integration network perspective (back). Enterprises are characterized by their roles they play within a process.

In this position paper, we introduce a new enterprise and linked data domain, the Business Network Management, which helps enterprises to get insight into their business networks. Based on previous work in the area of Network

Mining [10], we show how to bridge the gap from the NM raw data towards reconstructed business networks. For that, we use the concept of a virtualized business network, which extends the capabilities of NM from discovery to enrichment and re-deployment of information as required for the management of business networks. While developing the domain towards BNM, we discuss relevant areas for research and set them into context with the state-of-the art up to our knowledge. We conclude with a description of customer cases, which state the current progress of our BNM system.

In section 2 we introduce network virtualization to extend the Network Mining approach. On this foundation we define BNM in section 3 and discuss our prototypical application to real-world enterprise landscapes. We conclude with related work and draw conclusions.

2   The Virtualized Business Network

Business Network Virtualization (BNV) is the process of combining network resources and network functionality into a single, software-based administrative entity called (virtual) business network. Within business networks, this allows for efficient utilization, manageability and regulatory compliance. For business networks, we distinguish several levels of virtualization and their options shown in Fig. 2.

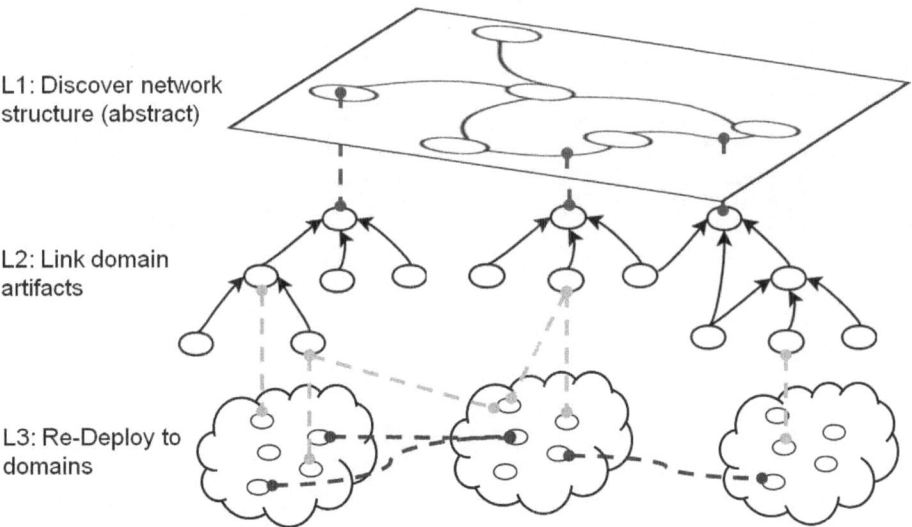

Fig. 2. Sample (cross-) enterprise Business Network showing business participants, denoted as nodes, and business document exchange as edges. Enterprises are characterized by their roles they play within a process.

The first level (L1) specifies the retrieval and interpretation of business process and integration content as well as operation information, which can be extended as second option by runtime artifacts. Therefore, e.g. integration artifacts are implemented in domain or vendor specific tools, but displayed within the business network. The integration or business errors are fixed within the domain-specific tools. To bring this to the second level (L2), application, design time and operation integration content is encapsulated and generated from the business network. For instance, when the business network is visualized, business process and integration artifacts can be defined on the network as expert knowledge and deployed back to the specific integration technology. Based on level 2, the integration content are enriched by process and information flow models (L3). These models allow a drill-down e.g. to the channel, interface, binding or processing level of the integration technology. As second option to L3, the process and integration flow models are interpreted and executed in one system integrated in the heterogeneous applications and integration technology runtimes.

The levels of virtualization conceptually ground an extended definition of mining Business Networks. The virtualization level L1 corresponds to the first two types of Network Mining (NM), i.e. discovery and conformance, in [10] and covers the discovery, extraction and domain specific analysis of relevant data from dynamic, distributed and heterogeneous enterprise landscapes. Fig. 3(a). shows all three types including network enhancement.

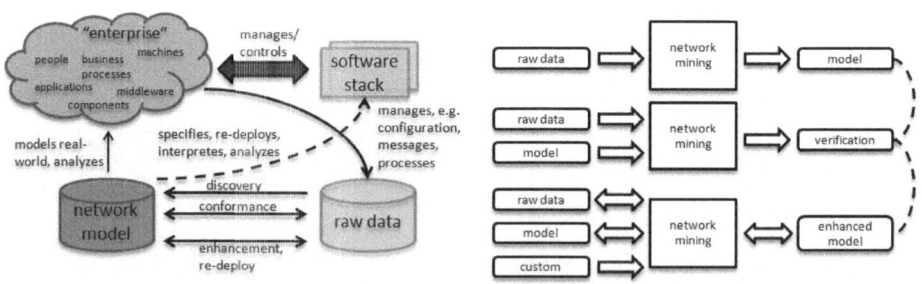

(a) Network Mining as discipline [10]   (b) Network Mining Types as Input/Output

Fig. 3. Business Network Mining extended

The third type of network mining is enhancement, which covers re-deployment. Here, the idea is to extend or improve an existing network model using domain expert knowledge about the actual business network. Whereas conformance measures the alignment between model and reality, this type aims at changing or extending the "as-is" model. For instance, the "as-is" model of the network can be refined and extended by introducing new relationships on the network, which results in an integration channel re-deployment within the specific middleware.

This corresponds to levels L2 and L3 of BNV, which is the most difficult part of NM and requires a bijective mapping between domain-specific and the (virtual) business network model. In case of external linked data, re-deployment would mean to e.g. post messages into dedicated social media or add new connections to a special profile from an abstract social network view.

Fig. 3(b) summarizes the three NM types in terms of input and output. Techniques for discovery take domain-specific raw data and produce a network model. The discovered models are typically completely diverse like configuration, system landscape, business process models. Conformance checking techniques need that raw data and the network model as input. The output consists of verification information showing differences and commonalities between model and data. Techniques for model enhancement and re-deployment, e.g. repair, extension, need the raw data, the model and optionally expert knowledge as input. The output is an improved or extended model. The custom information can come from various personas which are experts in one of the many domains the raw data comes from. Their knowledge and experience is important and is brought into NM through the custom extensions.

3   Business Network Management

The idea of Business Network Management (BNM) is to discover, make visible, monitor (operations) and improve real-world business networks and underlying processes by extracting information from various sources readily available in to-day's (information) systems. The automated data discovery, conformance checking and enhancement is done by NM resulting in a (virtual) network model. This data is input to inference mechanisms which derive the real "as-is" business network and later a business network spanning across enterprises. With that, BNM aims to ease the end-to-end lifecycle behind integration developments and allows collaboration on different information for faster execution. The network gives a generalized view of an enterprise integration and business landscape.

Today this challenge is addressed with documentation and systems management, but leaves manual work for IT administrators and integration experts to gather a consistent view of the network. The basic steps within BNM are depicted in Fig. 4. The real "as-is" network is computed based on the data from NM and visualized showing views on business and integration networks as well as their semantic relationships, e.g. processes implemented by middleware systems or applications. Domain experts work on these views by contextualizing, enriching and adapting the network to their needs, e.g. label or group entities. Thereby the experts analyze the "as-is" network and enhance it by e.g. adding new entities. The enhanced network is closer to the "to-be" network, which influences the general "to-be" business process picture derived from BPM or Process Mining (PM) [2,1]. For that, feedback from the operation on the network is taken into account, e.g. monitoring.

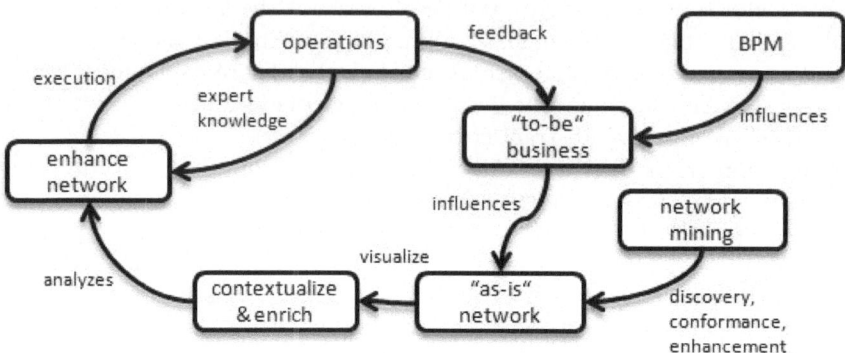

Fig. 4. Business Network Management cycle showing influencing and contributing domains to the "as-is" network computation towards a "to-be" network enhancement

4   The Business Network Management Prototype

To demonstrate the "as-is" network computation and assess the approach with customers, we developed a virtualization level L1 prototype, that auto-discovers and graphically represents integration networks. We applied the system to real-world customer landscapes containing mediated communication through middleware systems, e.g. SAP Process Integration (SAP PI) [12], direct connectivity, e.g. web services, and system landscape information, e.g. [13]. An excerpt of the computed integration network from a big manufacturing company is shown in Fig. 5(a). The network consists of participants representing the logical senders and receivers of messages, e.g. application systems and technical endpoints representing a business partner application/server. On a separate screen detail information is shown, e.g. system descriptions or installed products for an application system (not shown). Moreover, the network shows all message exchanges between the selected participants as drill-in on top-level connections, see Fig. 5(b). For each message exchange additional attributes that constitute and describe the message exchange is shown, e.g. technical information like interfaces and transport protocol used or runtime information like last used time.

This application to real-world enterprise landscapes allowed the evaluation of cross-middleware inference, combination of embedded and mediated communication and fragmented information registered in different domains. With that we showed that the BNM approach is valid and resulted in highly reliable and usable results. Moreover, our system is helpful in the everyday work of integration experts, since it gives an overview of the complete "as-is" network, which is very difficult to identify using existing middleware tools. The system reduces the effort to document integration scenarios and helps to answer questions that are difficult to find today. For instance, when combing configuration and runtime data, it is possible to find unused and possibly obsolete interfaces and flows. Hence, with this system, several customers plan upgrade projects of their middleware content, which will substantially save migration time and effort.

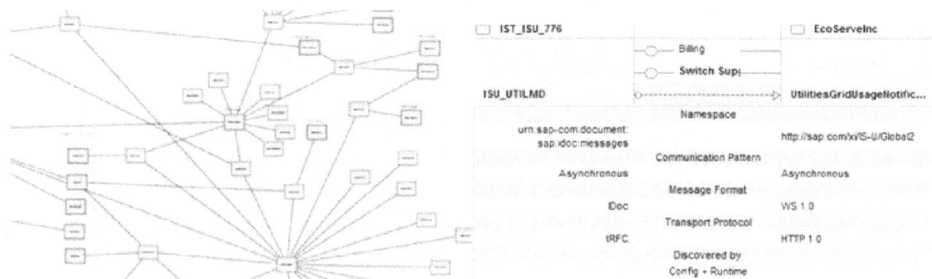

(a) High-level view on an integration network

(b) Conversation details

Fig. 5. Integration network visualization showing a view on the network (left) and details of the conversations (right)

5 Related Work

This work builds on previous work conducted in [10], which discusses how to come from Network Mining to large scale business networks. The contribution of this paper starts with the definition of *Business Network Virtualization*, which is used to extend the definition of *Business Network* towards the Business Network Management.

The most influencing related work is conducted in the area of Process Mining (PM) initiated by [1,2], which is a relatively young research discipline that sits between computational intelligence and data mining. It has similar requirements for data discovery, conformance and enhancement. However, its approach and goals are different. PM strives to derive Business Process Management (BPM) models from process logs. From that, models are automatically generated and checked. PM as well as BNM complement BPM by making it visible through automated discovery and in case of BNM to set the business processes in a broader context to each other.

Similar to Process Mining, Semantic Business Process Management (SBPM) [8] strives to mine business processes semantics mechanically. For that, an ontological approach [7,6] is combined with Semantic Web Services (SWS) and BPM. As in the Process Mining case, SBPM and Business Network Management are complementing approaches with combinable technology stacks.

Gaining insight into the network of physical and logical nodes within companies could be a future extension of BNM, but is not primarily relevant for visualizing and operating business networks. This domain is mainly addressed by the IT service management [9] and virtualization community [5].

The linked (web) data research, conducted by Bizer, and Berners-Lee et al. [3,4], shares similar approaches and methodologies, which have so far neglected linked data within enterprises.

6   Discussion and Future Work

In this position paper, we introduce a new enterprise and linked (business) data domain. We showed how the concept of Business Network Virtualization is used to extend Network Mining towards the Business Network Management. We showed excerpts of a real-world integration enterprise network in our *Business Network Center* to illustrate how BNM systems could look like.

Future work will be conducted especially for the virtualization levels L2 and L3, i.e. re-deployment and operations on the network, as well as discovering, inferring and making visible further aspects of business networks (for L1). Thus letting them grow to cross-enterprise partner networks in one dimension and towards BPM and network virtualization in the other dimension.

References

1. van der Aalst, W., et al.: Process Mining Manifesto. Technical Report, IEEE Task Force (2011)
2. van der Aalst, W.: Process Mining: Discovery, Conformance and Enhancement of Business Processes (2011)
3. Bizer, C., Heath, T., Berners-Lee, T.: Linked Data – The Story so Far. International Journal on Semantic Web and Information Systems 5(3), 1–22 (2009)
4. Bizer, C.: The Emerging Web of Linked Data. IEEE Intelligent Systems 24(5), 87–92 (2009)
5. Chowdhury, N.M.M.K., Boutaba, R.: Network virtualization: state of the art and research challenges. IEEE Communications Magazine (2009)
6. Filipowska, A., Hepp, M., Kaczmarek, M., Markovic, I.: Organisational Ontology Framework for Semantic Business Process Management. In: Abramowicz, W. (ed.) BIS 2009. LNBIP, vol. 21, pp. 1–12. Springer, Heidelberg (2009)
7. Hepp, M., Roman, D.: An Ontology Framework for Semantic Business Process Management. Wirtschaftsinformatik, 423–440 (2007)
8. Hepp, M., Leymann, F., Dominigue, J., Wahler, A., Fensel, D.: Semantic Business Process Management – A Vision Towards Using Semantic Web Services for Business Process Management. In: IEEE International Conference on e-Business Engineering (ICEBE), Beijing (2005)
9. O'Neill, P., et al.: Topic Overview – IT Service Management. Technical Report, Forrester Research (2006)
10. Ritter, D.: From Network Mining to Large Scale Business Networks. In: International Workshop on Large Scale Network Analysis (LSNA), WWW Companion, Lyon (2012)
11. Ritter, D., Westmann, T.: Business Network Reconstruction Using Datalog. In: Barceló, P., Pichler, R. (eds.) Datalog 2.0 2012. LNCS, vol. 7494, pp. 148–152. Springer, Heidelberg (2012)
12. SAP Process Integration (2012),
   http://www.sap.com/germany/plattform/netweaver/components/pi/index.epx
13. Hengevoss, W., Linke, A.: SAP NetWeaver System Landscape Directory – Grundlagen und Praxis. SAP Press (2009)

Towards More Flexible Enterprise Information Systems

Rogerio Atem de Carvalho[1,2] and Björn Johansson[3]

[1] Federal Fluminense Institute, NSI, R. Dr. Siqueira 273, Sala F104, Campos, Brazil
[2] Federal Fluminense University, Latec, R. Passo da Patria 156, Bloco E, Niteroi, Brazil
ratem@iff.edu.br
[3] Department of Informatics, School of Economics and Management,
Lund University, Sweden
bjorn.johansson@ics.lu.se

Abstract. The aim of this paper is to present the software development techniques used to build the EIS Patterns development framework, which is a testbed for a series of techniques that aim at giving more flexibility to EIS in general. Some of these techniques are customizations or extensions of practices created by the agile software development movement, while others represent new proposals. This paper also aims at helping promoting more discussion around the EIS development questions, since most of research papers in EIS area focus on deployment, IT, or business related issues, leaving the discussion on development techniques ill-treated.

Keywords: Enterprise Information Systems, Domain Specific Languages, Design Patterns, Statechart Diagrams, Natural Language Processing.

1 Introduction

In Information Systems, flexibility can be understood as the quality of a given system to be adaptable in a cost and effort effective and efficient way. Although it is usual to hear from Enterprise Information Systems (EIS) vendors that their systems are highly flexible, the practice has shown that customizing this type of system is still a costly task, mainly because there are still based on relatively old software development practices and tools. In this context, the EIS Patterns framework[1] is a research project which aims at providing a testbed for a series of relatively recent techniques nurtured at the Agile methods communities, and ported to the EIS arena.

The idea of suggesting and testing new ways for developing EIS was born from accumulated research and experience on more traditional methods, such as Model Driven Development (MDD), on top of the open source ERP5 system [1]. ERP5 represents a fully featured and complex EIS core, making it hard to test the ideas here presented in their pure form, thus it was decided to develop a simpler framework to serve as a proof of concept of proposed techniques.

---

[1] Initially discussed at the EIS Development blog through a series of posts entitled EIS Patterns, starting in December 2010 (http://eis-development.blogspot.com).

G. Poels (Ed.): CONFENIS 2012, LNBIP 139, pp. 157–164, 2013.
© IFIP International Federation for Information Processing 2013

This paper is organized as follows: the next topic summarizes the series of papers that forms the timeline of research done on top of ERP5; following this, the proposed techniques are presented, and finally some conclusions and possible directions are listed.

2   Background

In order to understand this proposal, it is necessary to know the basis from where it was developed, which is formed by a series of approaches developed on top of ERP5. Following the dominant tendency of the past decade, which was using MDD, the first approach towards a formalization of a deployment process for ERP5 was to develop a high-level modeling architecture and a set of reference models [2], as well as the core of a development process [3]. This process evolved to the point of providing a complete set of integrated activities, covering the different abstraction levels involved by supplying, according to the Geram [4] framework, workflows for Enterprise, Requirements, Analysis, Design, and Implementation tasks [5].

Since programming is the task that provides the "real" asset in EIS development, which is the source code that reflects the business requirements, programming activities must also be covered. Therefore, in "ERP5: Designing for Maximum Adaptability"[6] it is presented how to develop on top of the ERP5's document-centric approach, while in "Using Design Patterns for Creating Highly Flexible EIS"[7], the specific design patterns used to derive concepts from the system's core are presented. Complimentary, in "Development Support Tools for ERP" [8] two comprehensive sets of ERP5's development support tools are presented: (i) Product-related tools that support code creation, testing, configuration, and change management, and (ii) Process-related tools that support project management and team collaboration activities. Finally, in "ERP System Implementation from the Ground up: The ERP5 Development Process and Tools"[9], the whole picture of developing on top of ERP5 is presented, locating usage of the tools in each development workflow, and defining its domain-specific development environment (DSDE).

Although it was possible to develop a comprehensive MDD-based development process for the ERP5 framework, the research and development team responsible for proposing this process developed at the same time an Enterprise Content Management solution [10] and experimented with Agile techniques for both managing the project and constructing the software. Porting this experimentation to the EIS development arena lead to the customization of a series of agile techniques, as presented in "Agile Software Development for Customizing ERPs"[11].

The work on top of ERP5 provided a strong background, on both research and practice matters, enough to identify the types of relatively new software development techniques that could be used on other EIS development projects. Even more, this exploration of a real-world, complex system, has shown that some other advances could be obtained by going deeper into some of the techniques used, as well as by applying them in a lighter framework, where experimentations results could be quickly obtained.

3   Enters EIS Patterns

EIS Patterns is a simple framework focused on testing new techniques for developing flexible EIS. It was conceived having the Lego sets in mind: very basic building blocks that can be combined to form different business entities. Therefore, it was built around three very abstract concepts, each one with three subclasses, representing two "opposite" derived concepts and an aggregator of these first two, forming the structure presented in Fig. 1.

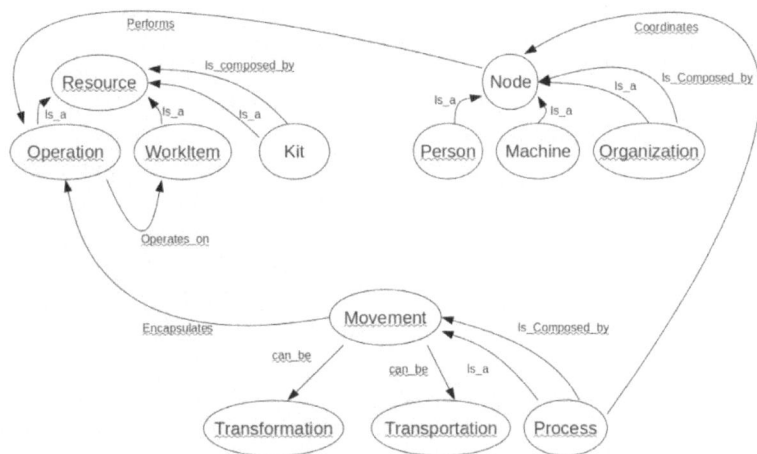

Fig. 1. Ontology representing the EIS Patterns core

Fig 1 is interpreted as follows:

Resource: is anything that is used for production.
-Material: product, component, tool, document, raw material etc.
-Operation: human operation and machine operation, as well as their derivatives.
-Kit: a collective of material and/or immaterial resources. Ex.: bundled services and components for manufacturing.
Node: is an active business entity that transforms resources.
-Person: employee, supplier's contact person, drill operator etc.
-Machine: hardware, software, drill machine, bank account etc.
-Organization: a collective of machines and/or persons, such as manufacturing cell, department, company, government.
Movement: is a movement of a Resource between two Nodes.
-Transformation: is a movement inside a node, in other words, the source and destination are the same node, it represents the transformation by machine or human work of a resource, such as drilling a metal plate or writing a report.

-Transportation: is a movement of resources between two nodes, for example, moving a component from one workstation to another, sending an order from the supplier to the customer.
-Process: a collective of transformations and/or transportations, in other words, a business process.

Besides the obvious "is a" and "is composed by" relationships presented in the ontology in Fig. 1, a chain of relationships denote how business processes are implemented: "a Process *coordinates* Node(s) to *perform* Operation(s) that *operates on* Work Item(s)". The semantic meaning of this chain is that process objects control under which conditions node objects perform operations in order to transform or transport resources. This leads to another special relationship which is "a Movement *encapsulates* an Operation", which means that a movement object will encapsulate the execution of an operation. In practical terms, an operation is the abstract description of a production operation, which is implemented by one or more node objects' methods. When this operation is trigged by a process object, it defers the actual execution to a pre-configured node object's method, and this execution is logged by a movement object, which stores all parameters, date and time, and results of this execution. Therefore, an operation is an abstract concept which can be configured to defer execution to different methods, from different objects, in accordance to the intents of a specific business process instance. In other words, a business process abstraction keeps its logic, while specific results can be obtained by configuration.

Although this execution deference can appear to be complex, it is a powerful mechanism which allows that a given business process model may be implemented in different ways, according to different modeling-time or even runtime contexts. In other words, the same process logic can be implemented in different ways, for different applications, thus leveraging the power of reuse.

It is important to note that in this environment, Processes control the active elements, the Nodes, which in turn operate on top of the passive ones, the Resources. In programming terms, this means that processes are configurable, nodes are extended, and resources are typically "data bag" classes. Therefore, extending the nodes for complying with new business requirements becomes the next point where flexibility must take place.

3.1 Using Decorators to Create a Dynamic System

Usually, class behavior is extended by creating subclasses, however, this basic technique can lead to complex, hard to maintain, and even worse, hard-coded class hierarchies. One of the solutions to avoid this is to use the Decorator design pattern [12], taking into account the following matters:

- While subclassing adds behavior to all instances of the original class, decorating can provide new behavior, at runtime, for individual objects. At runtime means that decoration is a "pay-as-you-go" approach to adding responsibilities.

- Using decorators allows mix-and-matching of responsibilities.
- Decorator classes are free to add operations for specific functionalities.
- Using decorators facilitates system configuration, however, typically, it is necessary to deal with lots of small objects.

Hence, by using decorators it is possible, during a business process realization, to associate and/or dissociate different responsibilities to node objects - in accordance to the process logic, and providing two main benefits: (i) the same object, with the same identifier, is used during the whole business process, there is no need for creating different objects of different classes, and (ii) given (i), auditing is facilitated, since it is not necessary to follow different objects, instead, the decoration of the same object is logged. Moreover, it is possible to follow the same object during all its life-cycle, including through different business processes: after an object is created and validated - meaning that it reflects a real-world business entity - it will keep its identity forever[2].

An important remark is that decorators must keep a set of rules of association, which is responsible for allowing or prohibiting objects to be assigned to new responsibilities. If a given object respects the rules of association of a given decorator, it can be decorated by it. At this point, defining a flexible way of ensuring contracts between decorators and decorated objects is of interest.

Should-dsl: a language for contract checking

Although Should-dsl was originally created as a domain specific language for checking expectations in automated tests [13], in the EIS Patterns framework it is also used to provide highly readable contract verifiers, such as:

```
associated |should| be_decorated_by(EmployeeDecorator)
```

In the case above the rule is auto-explanatory: "the associated object should be decorated by the Employee Decorator", meaning that for someone to get manager's skills he or she should have the basic employee's skills first. Besides being human readable, these rules are queryable, for a given decorator it is possible to obtain its rules, as well as the symmetric: for a given node object, it is possible to identify which decorators it can use. Query results, together with the analysis of textual requirements using Natural Language Processing, are used to help configuring applications built on top of the framework.

Using Natural Language Processing to Find Candidate Decorators

It is also possible to parse textual requirements, find the significant terms and use them to query decorators' documentation, so the framework can suggest possible decorators to be used in accordance to the requirements. Decorators' methods that represent business operations - the components of business processes - are specially

---

[2] A more complete discussion on using decorators, with examples, can be found at
http://eis-development.blogspot.com.br/2011/03/enterprise-information-systems-patterns_09.html

tagged, making it possible to query their documentation as well as obtain their category. Categories are used to classify these operations, for instance, it is possible to have categories such as "financial", "logistics", "manufacturing" and so on. In that way, the framework can suggest, from its base of decorators, candidates to the users' requirements.

3.2   A Domain-Specific and Ubiquitous Language for Modeling Business Process

The ontology presented in Fig. 1, although simple, is abstract enough to represent entities involved in any business process. Moreover, by appropriately using a statechart diagram, it is possible to use a single model to describe a business process, define active entities, as well as to simulate the process.

In order to better describe this proposal, Fig. 2 shows a simple quotation process. Taking into account that a class diagram was used to represent the structural part of the business process[3], by explicitly declaring the objects responsible for the transitions, it is possible to identify the active elements of the process, all of the Person type: sales_rep, verifier, approver, and contractor; as well as how they collaborate to perform the business process, by attaching the appropriate methods calls. Additionally, in some states, a method is declared with the "/do" tag, to indicate that a simulation can be ran when the process enters these states.

To run these state machine models, Yakindu (www.yakindu.org) could be used. By adapting the statechart execution engine, it is possible to run the model while making external calls to automated tests, giving the user the view of the live system running, as proposed by Carvalho *et al.* [14].

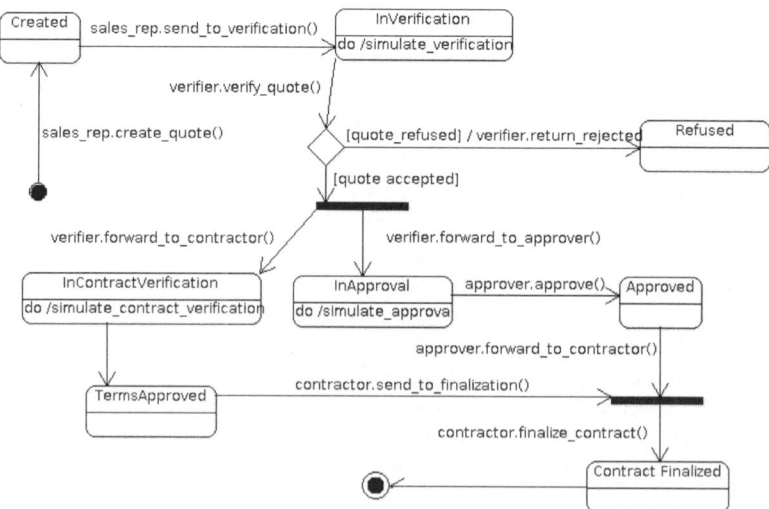

Fig. 2. A simple quotation process using the proposed concepts

---

[3] Not shown here due to the lack of space.

3.3   An Inoculable Workflow Engine

Workflow engines provide the basis for the computational realization of business processes. Basically, there are two types of workflow engines: (i) associated to application development platforms or (ii) implemented as software libraries.

EIS patterns uses Extreme Fluidity (xFluidity), a variation of the type (ii) workflow engine, developed as part of the framework. xFluidity is an inoculable (and expellable) engine that can be injected into any Python object, turning it workflow-aware. Symmetrically, it can be expelled from the object, turning the object back to its initial structure when necessary. It was developed in this way because type (i) engines forces you to use a given environment to develop your applications, while type (ii) forces you to use specific objects to implement workflows, most of times creating a mix of application specific code and workflow specific statements. With xFluidity it is possible to define a template workflow and insert the code necessary to make it run inside the business objects, while keeping the programming style, standards, naming conventions, and patterns of the development team. In EIS Patterns, xFluidity is used to configure Process objects, making them behave as business processes templates.

Currently xFluidity is a state-based machine, however, it can be implemented using other notations, such as Petri Nets. In that case, no changes are necessary in the inoculated objects, given that these objects do not need to know which notation is in use, they simple follow the template.

4   Conclusions and Further Directions

This paper briefly presents a series of techniques that can be applied to turn EIS more flexible, including the use of dynamic languages[4]. Although the EIS Patterns framework is a work in progress, it is developed on top of research and practical experience obtained on the development of the ERP5 framework.

This experience led to the use of an abstract core to represent all concepts, while providing flexibility through the use of the Decorator pattern. On top of this technique, Natural Language Processing (NLP) and automated contract checking is used to improve reuse even more and, as a side effect, enhance system documentation, given that developers are forced to provide code documentation as well as to define association contracts through should-dsl, which is a formal way of defining the requirements for the use of decorators to expand the functionality of Node objects.

The integrated use of an inoculable workflow engine, a domain-specific and ubiquitous language, and should-dsl to check association contracts, is innovative and provides more expressiveness to the models and the source code, by the use of a single language for all abstraction levels, which reduces the occurrence of translation errors through these levels. This is an important point: more expressive code facilitates change and reuse, thus increasing flexibility.

---

[4] For a discussion on this see http://eis-development.blogspot.com.br/2010/09/is-java-better-choice-for-developing.html

Further improvements include the development of a workflow engine based on BPMN, in order to make the proposal more adherent to current tendencies, and provide advances on the use of NLP algorithms to ease identification and reuse of concepts.

References

1. Smets-Solanes, J.-P., Carvalho, R.A.: ERP5: A Next-Generation, Open-Source ERP Architecture. IEEE IT Professional 5, 38–44 (2003)
2. Campos, R., Carvalho, R.A., Ferreira, A.S.: Modeling Architecture and Reference Models for the ERP5 Project. In: Confenis 2006. Research and Practical Issues of Enterprise Information Systems, pp. 677–682. Springer, New York (2006)
3. Carvalho, R.A., Campos, R.: A Development Process Proposal for the ERP5 System. In: IEEE International Conference on Systems, Man, and Cybernetics. IEEE Press, New York (2006)
4. IFIP – IFAC GERAM: Generalized Enterprise Reference Architecture and Methodology, IFIP – IFAC Task Force on Architectures for Enterprise Integration (1999)
5. Monnerat, R.M., Carvalho, R.A., Campos, R.: Enterprise Systems Modeling: the ERP5 Development Process. In: 23rd Annual ACM Symposium on Applied Computing, vol. II, pp. 1062–1068. ACM, New York (2008)
6. Carvalho, R.A., Monnerat, R.M.: ERP5: Designing for Maximum Adaptability. In: Wilson, G., Oram, A. (orgs.) Beautiful Code: Leading Programmers Explain How They Think, pp. 339–351. O'Reilly Media, Sebastopol (2007)
7. Carvalho, R.A., Monnerat, R.M.: Using Design Patterns for Creating Highly Flexible Enterprise Information Systems. In: The III IFIP International Conference on Research and Practical Issues of Enterprise Information Systems. IFIP Series (2009)
8. Carvalho, R.A., Monnerat, R.M.: Development Support Tools for Enterprise Resource Planning. IEEE IT Professional 10, 39–45 (2008)
9. Carvalho, R.A., Campos, R., Monnerat, R.M.: ERP System Implementation from the Ground up: The ERP5 Development Process and Tools. In: Handbook of Research on Software Engineering and Productivity Technologies: Implications of Globalization, pp. 423–438. IGI Global (2009)
10. Carvalho, R.A.: An Enterprise Content Management Solution Based on Open Source. In: Research and Practical Issues of Enterprise Information Systems II, vol. 1, pp. 173–184. Springer, New York (2007)
11. Carvalho, R.A., Johansson, B., Manhaes, R.S.: Agile Software Development for Customizing ERPs. In: Enterprise Information Systems and Implementing IT Infrastructures: Challenges and Issues, pp. 20–39. Information Science Reference, IGI Global, Hershey (2010)
12. Gamma, E., et al.: Design Patterns – Elements of Reusable Object-Oriented Software. Addison-Wesley, Reading (1995)
13. Tavares, H.L., Rezende, G.G., Mota, V., Manhaes, R.S., Carvalho, R.A.: A tool stack for implementing Behavior-Driven Development in Python Language, arXiv:1007.1722v1(cs.SE)
14. Carvalho, R.A., Carvalho e Silva, F.L., Manhaes, R.S.: Business Language Driven Development: Joining Business Process Models to Automated Tests. In: V IFIP International Conference on Research and Practical Issues of Enterprise Information Systems. LNBIP (2011)

A Proposal of a Process Model for Requirements Elicitation in Information Mining Projects

Diego Mansilla[1], M. Pollo-Cattaneo[1,2], Paola Britos[3], and Ramón García-Martínez[4]

[1] Information System Methodologies Research Group,
Technological National University, Buenos Aires, Argentina
[2] PhD Program in Computer Science, Computer Science School,
National University of La Plata, Buenos Aires, Argentina
[3] Information Mining Research Group,
National University of Rio Negro at El Bolson, Río Negro, Argentina
[4] Information Systems Research Group,
National University of Lanus, Buenos Aires, Argentina
dmansilla@educ.ar, fpollo@posgrado.frba.utn.edu.ar,
pbritos@unrn.edu.ar, rgarcia@unla.edu.ar

Abstract. A problem addressed by an information mining project is transforming existing business information of an organization into useful knowledge for decision making. Thus, the traditional software development process for requirements elicitation cannot be used to acquire required information for information mining process. In this context, a process of requirements gathering for information mining projects is presented, emphasizing the following phases: conceptualization, business definition and information mining process identification.

Keywords: Process, elicitation, information mining projects, requirements.

1 Introduction

Traditional Software Engineering offers tools and process for software requirements elicitation which are used for creating automatized information systems. Requirements are referred as a formal specification of what needs to be developed. They are descriptions of the system behaviour [1].

Software development projects usually begin by obtaining an understanding of the business domain and rules that govern it. Understanding business domains help to identify requirements at the business level and at product level [2], which define the product to be built considering the context where it will be used. Models such as Context Diagram, Data Flow Diagrams and others are used to graphically represent the business process in the study and are used as validation tools for these business processes. A functional analyst is oriented to gather data about inputs and outputs of the software product to be developed and how that information is transformed by the software system.

G. Poels (Ed.): CONFENIS 2012, LNBIP 139, pp. 165–173, 2013.
© IFIP International Federation for Information Processing 2013

Unlike software development projects, the problem addressed by information mining projects is to transform existing information of an organization into useful knowledge for decision making, using analytical tools [3]. Models for requirements elicitation and project management, by focusing on the software product to be developed, cannot be used to acquire required information for information mining processes. In this context, it is necessary to transform existing experience in the use of requirements elicitation tools in the software development domain into knowledge that can be used to build models used in business intelligence projects and in information mining process [4] [5] [6].

This work will describe the problem (section 2), it will present a proposal for a process model for requirements elicitation in information mining projects (section 3), emphasizing in three phases: Conceptualization (section 3.1), Business Definition (section 3.2) and Information Mining Process Identification (section 3.4). Then, a study case is presented (section 4), and a conclusion and future lines of work are proposed (section 5).

2   State of Current Practice

Currently, several disciplines have been standardized in order to incorporate best practices learned from experience and from new discoveries.

The discipline of project management, for example, generated a body of knowledge where the different process areas of project management are defined. Software engineering specify different software development methodologies, like the software requirements development process [1]. On the other side, related to information mining projects, there are some methodologies for developing information mining systems such as DM [7], P3TQ [8], y SEMMA [9].

In the field of information mining there is not a unique process for managing projects [10]. However, there are several approaches that attempt to integrate the knowledge acquired in traditional software development projects, like the Kimball Lifecycle [11], and project management framework in medium and small organizations [12]. In [13] an operative approach regarding information mining project execution is proposed, but it does not detail which elicitation techniques can be used in a project.

The found problem is that previously mentioned approaches emphasize work methodologies associated with information mining projects and do not adapt traditional software engineering requirements elicitation techniques. In this situation, it is necessary to understand the activities that should be taken and which traditional elicitation techniques can be adapted for using in information mining projects.

3   Proposed Elicitation Requirement Process Model

The proposed process defines a set of high level activities that must be performed as a part of the business understanding stage, presented in the CRISP-DM methodology, and can be used in the business requirements definition stage of the Kimball Lifecycle. This process breaks down the problem of requirement elicitation in information mining projects into several phases, which will transform the knowledge acquired in the earlier stage. Figure 1 shows strategic phases of an information mining project, focusing on the proposed requirement elicitation activities.

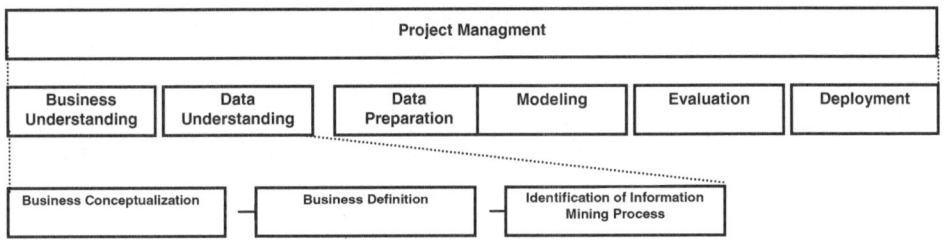

Fig. 1. Information Mining Process phases

The project management layer deals with coordination of different activities needed to achieve the objectives. Defining activities in this layer are beyond this work. This work identifies activities related to the process exposed in [11], and can be used as a guide for the activities to be performed in an information mining project.

3.1   Business Conceptualization Phase

The Business Conceptualization phase is the phase of the elicitation process that will be used by the analyst to understand the language used by the organization and the specific words used by the business. Table 1 summarizes inputs and outputs of the Business Conceptualization phase.

Table 1. Business Conceptualization phase inputs and outputs

Phase	Task	Input product		Transformation technique	Output Product	
		Input	Representation		Output	Representation
Business Conceptualization	Business Understanding	Project Definition	Project KickOff	Project Sponsors Analysis	List of users to be interviewed	List of users to be interviewed template.
	Business Process data gathering	List of users to be interviewed	List of users to be interviewed	Interviews Workshops	Gathered Information	Information gathering template
	Business Model Building	Gathered Information	Information gathering Template	Analysis of gathered information	Use Case Model	Use Case Model template

Interviewing business users will define information related problems that the organization has. The first activity is to identify a list of people that will be interviewed. This is done as part of the business process gathering activity.

In these interviews, information related to business process is collected and modeled in use cases. A business process is defined as the process of using the business on behalf of a customer and how different events in the system occur, allowing the customer to start, execute and complete the business process [14]. The Business Analyst should collect specific words used in business processes in order to obtain both a description of the different tasks performed in each function, as well as the terminology used in each use case.

The Use Case modeling task uses information acquired during business data gathering and, as a last activity of this phase, will generate these models.

3.2   Business Definition Phase

This phase defines the business in terms of concepts, vocabulary and information repositories. Table 2 shows inputs and outputs of this phase

Table 2. Business definition phase inputs and outputs

| Phase | Task | Input product | | Transforma-tion technique | Output Product | |
		Input	Representa-tion		Output	Representation
Business Definition	Build Dictionary of Business Vocabulary	Use Case Model	Use Case Model Template	Use Case Analysis	Concepts Dictionary	Concept Dictionary template
	Establish Concept Relationships	Concepts Dictionary	Concept Dictionary template	Entity Relationship model	Concepts relationships	Concept Relationship Model
	Build a Data Repository Map	Concepts relation-ships	Concept Relationship Model	Documenta-tion Analysis	Data Repository Map	Data Repository Map template

The objective is to document concepts related to business process gathered in the Business Conceptualization Phase and discover its relationships with other terms or concepts. A dictionary is the proposed tool to define these terms. The structure of a concept can be defined as shown in table 3.

Table 3. Concept Structure

Structure element	Description
Concept	Term to be defined
Definition	Description of the concept meaning.
Data structure	Description of data structures contained in the concept
Relationships	A List of Relationships with other concepts
Processes	A list of processes that use this concept

Once the dictionary is completed the map, the analyst begins to analyze the various repositories of information in the organization. It is also important to determinate volume information, as this data can be used to select the information mining processes applicable to the project. The acquired information is used to build a map, or a model, that shows the relationship between the business use cases, business concepts and information repositories. This triple relationship can be used as the start point of any technique of information mining processes.

3.3   Identification of Information Mining Process Phase

The objective of the phase is to define which information mining process can be used to solve the identified problems in the business process. There are several processes that can be used [16], for instance:

— Discovery of behavior rules (DBR)
— Discovery of groups (DOG)
— Attribute Weighting of interdependence (AWI)
— Discovery of membership group rules (DMG)
— Weighting rules of behavior or Membership Groups (WMG)

This phase does not require any previous input, so activities can be performed in parallel with activities related to Business Conceptualization. Table 4 shows inputs and outputs of this phase.

Table 4. Inputs and Outputs of Identification of Information Mining Process Phase

Phase	Task	Input product		Transformation technique	Output Product	
		Input	Representation		Output	Representation
Identification of Information Mining Process	Identify Business Problems	Use Case Model	Use Case Model Template	Documentation Analysis	Problem List	Problem List Template
	Select an information mining process	Problem List Concept Dictionary	Problem List Template Dictionary Template	LEL Analysis	An information Mining process to be applied	

The list of business problems must be prioritized and be written in natural language, using the user's vocabulary. Only important or critical problems are identified.

Analysis of the problems in the list has to be done. This analysis can be done using the model known as "Language Extended Lexicon (LEL)" [17][18] and can be used as a foundation of the work performed in this phase: breaking down the problem into several symbols presented in the LEL model. This model shows 4 general types of symbol, subject, object, verb and state.

To define useful information mining process, a decision table is proposed. The table analyses LEL structures, concepts identified in the Business Conceptualization phase, existing information repositories and problems to be solved. All the information is analyzed together and according to this analysis, an information mining process is selected as the best option for the project. Table 5 shows the conditions and rules identified as foundations in this work. An important remark is that subjects discovery refers to concepts or subject that hasn't been identified as part of the business domain.

Table 5. Information mining process selection decision table

Condition	R01	R02	R03	R04	R05
Does concepts identified as objects exist in some information repository?	Yes	Yes	Yes	Yes	No
Are there any concept identified as an object that are not stored in any information repository?	No	No	No	Yes	Yes
The action represented by a verb. Denotes the discovery of subject concepts?	Yes	No	No	No	Yes
Are there any concept that can be associated with factors?	Yes	Yes	Yes	No	Yes
Have the required factors been identified?	Yes	Yes	No	No	No
Can we deduce factors based on existing information available on repositories?	Yes	Yes	No	No	No
The action represented by a verb. Associates subjects and objects?	Yes	No	No	Yes	Yes
Is Analysis of factors required to obtain a group of subjects or objects?	No	Yes	Yes	Yes	Yes
Actions					
The technique to be applied is:	**DBR**	**DOG**	**AWL**	**DMG**	**WMG**

The objective of the table is to be able to decide, through the analysis of the information gathered about the business, which information mining process can be applied to the project. An important remark is that this decision table will add new knowledge and new rules, with the end of improving the selection technique criteria. With more projects used as input and more experience acquired in these projects, the rules proposed on the table can be adjusted and then we can get a better selection choice.

The Process Information Mining Identification phase is the last phase of the process. The following tasks will depend upon project managing process and tasks defined for the project.

4   Proof of Concept

A case study is presented next to prove the proposed model.

4.1   Business Description

A real estate agency works mainly with residential properties in the suburban area. It's lead by two owners, partners in equal shares. This real state agency publishes its portfolio in different media, mostly local real estate magazines. Published properties are in the mid range value, up to three hundred thousand dollars. It only has one store, where all the employees work. The following business roles are covered: a real estate agent, salesman, administrative collaborators and several consultants.

4.2   Process Execution

The first step of the process consists in two activities: identify project stakeholders and set the list of people to be interviewed. In this case, with the little business information that we have, we can identify three stakeholders: the owners and the real estate agent.

The second step is to set up the interviews of the stakeholders and gather information related to the business in the study. The following paragraph describes information obtained in the interview.

This agency focuses on leasing and selling real estate. Any person can offer a house for sale. If a house is for sale, the real estate agent will estimate the best offer for the property being sold. When a person has an interest in buying a home, they complete a form with the contact details and characteristics that must meet the property. If there are any properties that meet the requested criteria, they are presented to the customer. The real estate agency considered clients as those who have offered a home to sell or have already begun a process of buying a home offered, and considered interested customers, persons who are consulting on the proposed properties or are looking for properties to buy. If interested customers agree on the purchase of a property will be customers of the estate and begins the process of buying property. The customer contact information and the property details are stored in an Excel file.

In this case, we can identify the following Business Use Cases:

— Sell a property Use Case, action of a person selling a property.
— Buy a property Use Case, action of a person buying a property.
— Show a property managed by the real estate agency Use Case, reflects the action of showing a real estate available for sale to interested parties.

For the Business Definition Phase, the business concept dictionary is created. From gathered information, the concepts shown in table 6 can be identified.

Identified concepts are analyzed in order to find relationships between themselves. A class model can show the basic relationships between identified concepts in the case.

Table 6. Identified Business Concepts

Selling Customer: A person who offers a property for sale		**Property Appraisal:** Appraisal of property for sale.	
Structure:	Name and Last Name Contact Information	Structure:	Appraisal value (Number) Property ID Transaction Currency
Relationships:	Property Property appraisal	Relationships:	Property Customer
Busines Process:	Sell a Property	Business Processes	Sell a Property Offer a Property

Table 7. Real Estate agency problems related symbols

Property	[Object]	*Customer*	[Subject]
Idea - It's the object that the real estate agency sells - It has its own attributes		*Idea* - A Person interested in buying a property. - A Person who is selling a property.	
Impact: It is sold to a Customer		*Impact:* Fills a form with buying criteria.	
To Offer a property	[Verb]	*Interested*	[Status]
Idea - The action of showing a property to a customer.		*Idea* - A Customer state achieved when a property meets his or her requirements	
Impact - The property must satisfy the customer requirements.		*Impact* - The property is shown to the interested party.	

From the gathered business information, a problem found is that the real estate agent wants to know, when a property is offered for sale, which customers could be interested in buying the property. Following the identification, a LEL analysis is done with each problem on the list. In this case, the analysis finds the symbols presented in table 7.

With the obtained LEL analysis, information repositories and defined business concepts, the information mining process to apply in the project, will be determined. The decision table presented in section 3.3 is used, checking the conditions against the gathered information. The result of this analysis states that the project can apply the process of Discovery Rules of Conduct.

5   Conclusion

This work presents a proposal of a process model for requirements elicitation in information mining projects, and how to adapt in these projects, existing elicitation techniques. The process breaks down in three phases, in the first phase the business is analyzed (Conceptualization phase), later, a business model is built and defined to understand its scope and the information it manages (Business Definition phase), and finally, we use the business problems found and the information repositories that stores business data as an input for a decision tabke to establish which information mining technique can be applied to a specific information mining project (Identification of an Information Mining Process).

As a future line of work, several cases are being identified to support the empirical case proposed, emphasizing the validation of the decision table presented in section 3.3.

References

[1] Sommerville, I., Sawyer, P.: Requirements Engineering: A Good Practice Guide. John Wiley & Sons, Chichester (1997)
[2] Lauesen, S.: Software Requirements. Styles and Techniques. Pearson Education, London (2002)
[3] Pollo-Cattaneo, F., et al.: Proceso de Educción de Requisitos en Proyectos de Explotación de Información. In: Aguilar, R., Díaz, J., Gómez, G., León, E. (eds.) En Ingeniería de Software e Ingeniería del Conocimiento: Tendencias de Investigación e Innovación Tecnológica en Iberoamérica, pp. 1–11. Alfaomega Grupo Editor (2010) ISBN 978-607-707-096-2
[4] Pollo-Cattaneo, F., et al.: Ingeniería de Proyectos de Explotación de Información. In: Proceedings XII Workshop de Investigadores en Ciencias de la Computación, pp. 172–176 (2010)
[5] Pytel, P., et al.: Ingeniería de Requisitos Basada en Técnicas de Ingeniería del Conocimiento. In: Proceedings XIII Workshop de Investigadores en Ciencias de la Computación, pp. 426–429 (2011) ISBN 978-950-673-892-1
[6] Chapman, P., et al.: CRISP-DM 1.0 Step by step BIguide. Edited by SPSS (2000), http://tinyurl.com/crispdm

[7] Garcia-Martinez, R., et al.: Information Mining Processes Based on Intelligent Systems. In: Proceedings of II International Congress on Computer Science and Informatics (INFONOR-CHILE 2011), pp. 87–94 (2011) ISBN 978-956-7701-03-2

[8] Pyle, D.: Business Modeling and Business Intelligence. Morgan Kauffmann Publishers (2003)

[9] SAS, SAS Enterprise Miner: SEMMA (2011), http://tinyurl.com/semmaSAS

[10] Pollo-Cattaneo, F., et al.: Metodología para Especificación de Requisitos en Proyectos de Explotación de Información. In: Proceedings XI Workshop de Investigadores en Ciencias de la Computación, pp. 333–335 (2009) ISBN 978-950-605-570-7

[11] Kimball, R., et al.: The Data Warehouse Lifecycle Toolkit. John Wiley & Sons (2011)

[12] Vanrell, J., Bertone, R., García-Martínez, R.: Modelo de Proceso de Operación para Proyectos de Explotación de Información (2010)

[13] Britos, P., Dieste, O., García-Martínez, R.: Requirements Elicitation in Data Mining for Business Intelligence Projects. In: Avison, D., Kasper, G.M., Pernici, B., Ramos, I., Roode, D. (eds.) Advances in Information Systems Research, Education and Practice. IFIP Series, vol. 274, pp. 139–150. Springer, Boston (2008)

[14] Jacobson, I., Ericsson, M., Jacobson, A.: The Object Advantage. Business Process Reengineering with Object Technology, p. 98. Addison Wesley Publishing Company (1995)

[15] García-Martínez, R., et al.: Towards an Information Mining Engineering. En Software Engineering, Methods, Modeling and Teaching, pp. 83–99. Universidad de Medellín Editorial (2011) ISBN 978-958-8692-32-6

[16] Pollo-Cattaneo, F., et al.: Ingeniería de Procesos de Explotación de Información. In: Aguilar, R., Díaz, J., Gómez, G., León, E. (eds.) En Ingeniería de Software e Ingeniería del Conocimiento: Tendencias de Investigación e Innovación Tecnológica en Iberoamérica, pp. 252–263. Alfaomega Grupo Editor (2010) ISBN 978-607-707-096-2

[17] Leite, J.C.S.P.: Notas de Aula. Material del curso de Ingeniería de Requisitos (1994)

[18] Fresno, M., et al.: Derivación de objetos utilizando LEL y Escenarios en un caso real (1998), http://wer.inf.puc-rio.br/wer98/artigos/89.html (last access July 2012)

A Financial Perspective on Improving ICT Service Delivery: A Case at the Belgian Railways

Luc Lutin[1], Stijn Viaene[1,2], Nathalie Demeere[3], and Olivier Jolyon[3]

[1] Vlerick Business School, Vlamingenstraat 83, 3000 Leuven, Belgium
[2] KU Leuven, Naamsestraat 69, 3000 Leuven, Belgium
[3] Deloitte Consulting, Berkenlaan 8c, 1831 Diegem, Belgium
{luc.lutin,stijn.viaene}@vlerick.com,
{ndemeere,ojolyon}@deloitte.com

Abstract. This article discusses the financial perspective in a case study at ICTRA[1] that deals with improving ICT service delivery. It outlines the three-step approach taken in the Finance Transformation Project and explains how this approach helped ICTRA in becoming a more business-oriented ICT shared service centre.

Keywords: Finance, ICT, Transformation, Budgeting, Transfer Pricing, Service Costing, Service Levels.

1 Introduction: Challenges and Strategic Intent

This section zooms in on the external (market, evolution…) and internal (company vision, internal projects…) factors relevant to the context of the case study in this article.

1.1 External Challenges

Run as a government monopoly, NMBS/SNCB[2], the national railway company of Belgium, was used to evolving at its own pace. With the upcoming liberalisation and privatisation of Europe's railway system, it needed to prepare for a more demanding environment. This required a clear strategy to cope with increased competition. The company would need to be able to respond more quickly and accurately to rapidly changing market demands. Internal reorganisation was therefore a must.

Consequently, in 2005 NMBS/SNCB was reorganized into three separate entities (see Fig. 1). The railway operator (NMBS/SNCB) would be responsible for freight

---

[1] This article was written as the basis for discussion, rather than to illustrate either effective or ineffective handling of a business situation.

[2] The NMBS/SNCB was founded in 1926. NMBS/SNCB stands for "Nationale Maatschappij der Belgische Spoorwegen" (NMBS) in Dutch and "Société Nationale des Chemins de fer Belges" (SNCB) in French.

G. Poels (Ed.): CONFENIS 2012, LNBIP 139, pp. 174–181, 2013.
© IFIP International Federation for Information Processing 2013

and passenger services as well as the management of all rolling stock. Infrabel would be responsible for maintaining, renovating and developing the Belgian railway network infrastructure. NMBS/SNCB Holding, the umbrella organisation and owner of the operator NMBS/SNCB and Infrabel, would be responsible for asset management, human resources, strategy, finance and ICT. The above three entities together formed the Belgian Railways Group.

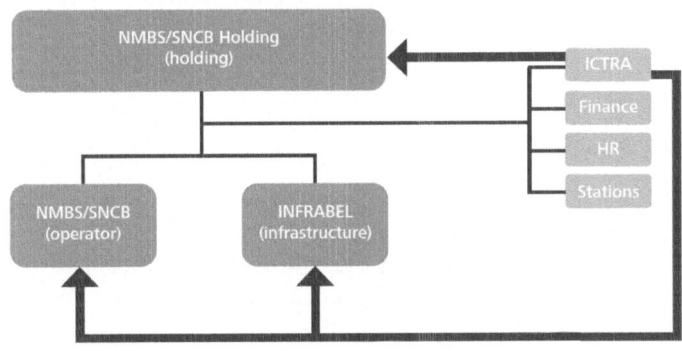

Deliver ICT development & support services

Fig. 1. Structure of the Belgian Railways Group since 2005 (situation 2010)

1.2   Internal Challenges

Following the reorganisation in 2005, ICTRA[3], as a division of NMBS/SNCB Holding, became the preferred supplier of ICT services to the three business entities of the Belgian Railways Group (the Group). Its activities could be divided into three categories: (1) standard operational/supply activities, such as the ICT helpdesk and hardware support; (2) development and maintenance of applications, such as e-ticketing; and (3) implementation of strategic projects, e.g. real-time passenger information systems and ERP (Enterprise Resource Planning) applications.

Over the years, the Group's business entities grew dissatisfied with ICTRA's services as well as the transfer pricing mechanism. They felt ICTRA's services did not meet their needs. As for the budgets, they had the impression they were signing a blank cheque at the start of each financial year. Although the ICT budgets were discussed as part of the budget cycle, ICTRA charged actual costs with almost no explanation. The business wanted to be notified of changes and their impact on the actual budget in advance, instead of having to learn about them through the invoice. The business entities also wanted to have a say in the make-or-buy decision, i.e. in the choice between ICTRA and external service providers. This meant that they wanted ICTRA to submit a formal offer, detailing scope, timing and pricing. In short: the business entities wanted to be treated as a customer, receiving high-quality services at a fair price.

---

[3] ICTRA is short for Information and Communication Technology (ICT) for Rail. Operating as a shared services centre, it provides ICT development and support services to the entire Belgian Railways Group.

1.3   Strategic Intent

In 2008, ICTRA formulated a new vision to address the external and internal challenges. As a support organisation, ICTRA wanted to be recognised for its strong technological know-how and experienced ICT employees. It would seek to continuously improve the productivity of its services, while matching supply to demand [1]. ICTRA therefore had to become a partner who understands the needs of the business. To ensure optimal delivery of business value, it would have to deliver total solutions, from development to utilisation.

2   Transforming ICTRA

2.1   Starting from the Vision

To achieve its vision, ICTRA embarked on a transformation path. At the heart of ICTRA's transformation was a fundamental review of its internal financial processes. In 2008, ICTRA launched its Finance Transformation Project. This project would help address the following major issues that had contributed to the dissatisfaction felt by ICTRA's internal customers:

- ICTRA's service catalogue was not aligned with the requirements of the business entities.
- ICTRA's services lacked the transparent pricing mechanisms of external providers.
- ICTRA's internal financial business processes were cumbersome, lacked structure and tools, and did not involve stakeholders sufficiently.
- There was an overall lack of cost awareness within the ICTRA organisation.

The Finance Transformation Project would increase operational process effectiveness in order to ensure a more customer-oriented service delivery [2]. It consisted of three phases: (1) establish commitment, (2) gain credibility and (3) prove competence. The project was led by Sammie Courtens, ICTRA's Head of Finance. Giovanni Palmieri, ICTRA's General Manager and Group CIO, was the project's sponsor.

2.2   Adopting a New ICT Operating Model

To support optimal delivery of business value, ICTRA adopted a new operating model, in parallel with the Finance Transformation Project. This target operating model clearly distinguished between demand-oriented and supply-oriented responsibilities. By adapting its organisation to this model, ICTRA would be able to put the right focus on the business. ICTRA therefore decided to migrate from a functional structure to a matrix organization (see Fig. 2.). This new organisational structure was designed to support business-oriented servicing and divided the ICTRA organisation in "shared operations supply units" on the one hand and "business entity solution units" on the other. These units would be supported by a number of "support departments", such as Finance.

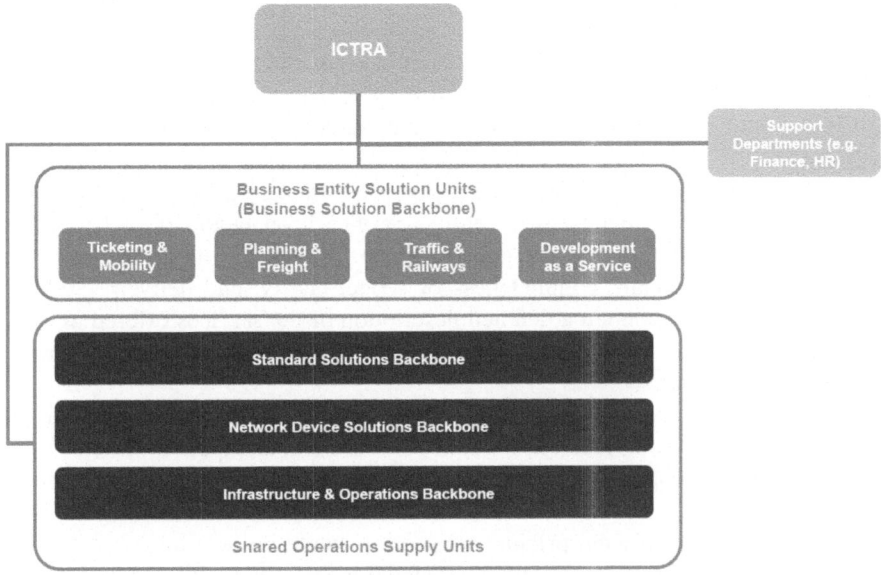

Fig. 2. New organizational structure

The shared operations supply units, or supply units, were structured around broad capabilities and transversal processes (network device & solutions, infrastructure & operations, and standard solutions). Their focus would be on cost efficiency and quality.

The business entity solution units, or demand units, were in charge of service and solution development for the respective Group business entities. These demand units were supported by account managers, performing a liaison role between ICTRA and the business. Together, they would drive process improvement and project design. Their aim was to be as close to the business as possible, increase ICT effectiveness and improve customer satisfaction.

3   Finance Transformation Project

The finance transformation and organisational restructuring went hand in hand with a formal change management (see Fig. 3.). This section outlines the three-step approach taken by ICTRA: 1) Establish Commitment, 2) Gain Credibility and 3) Prove Competence.

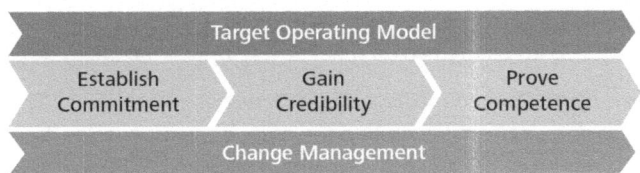

Fig. 3. Transforming ICTRA: building blocks

3.1   Establish Commitment

Getting the business on board was essential to the success of the finance transformation. Therefore, ICTRA initiated discussions with the business entities of the Group, which resulted in the joint development of a business-specific service catalogue.

This catalogue then served as a basis for establishing service level agreements (SLAs) per service and per business entity. Service level negotiations between the business entities and ICTRA were guided by the following values: customer focus, appropriate level of detail, completeness of scope, clarity, and delivery credibility. SLAs would typically contain a detailed description of the services offered as well as a specification of the required service levels, a pricing per service item, and key performance indicators.

Business entities could choose their desired service levels. For example, a "gold package" for the ticketing machines would include 24-hour support, while a "bronze package", more appropriate for less critical applications, would only offer support during working hours.

It was also agreed that the pricing per service would be determined using a cost chargeback model (see next section). This model would enable ICTRA to accurately charge costs made for the delivery of its services to the consumers of these services, based on actual consumption.

When engaging with the business in this first phase, ICTRA was guided by the motto "Deliver what you promise". The collaborative development of the service catalogue and service level agreements was aimed at gaining the necessary commitment from all stakeholders - both ICTRA and the business.

3.2   Gain Credibility

To become a trusted business partner, ICTRA needed to determine a fair price for its services. Also, it had to communicate clearly and explain its invoices and any deviations from the budget to its customers, i.e. the business entities of the Group.

A key step in gaining credibility with the business was the development of the cost chargeback model [3]. This model would:

- make ICT costs more predictable and transparent as they would be based on the actual quantity of services delivered. Through the model ICTRA would also provide more details on the cost drivers of its services.
- increase cost awareness and help understand service profitability for the purpose of cost control.
- be benchmarked regularly with internal and external alternatives and offer the flexibility to change costing according to new business developments.

There are many ways to recoup the cost of delivering a service [4]. The approach followed by ICTRA was to first calculate the cost per service item ("service costing"), then set a service unit transfer price to cover the costs and stimulate desirable demand for their services, and finally multiply the unit price by the quantity of service delivered ("transfer pricing"). Then using the most appropriate transfer pricing strategy for ICTRA's services has allowed them to influence business decisions.

The steps of ICTRA's cost chargeback model are outlined in more detail in Fig. 4.

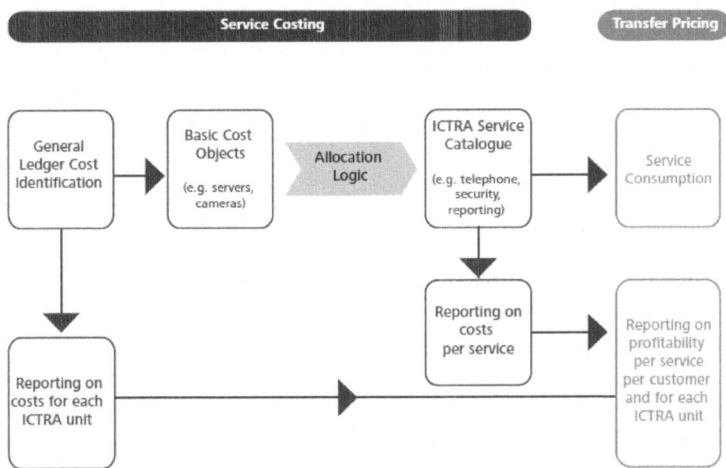

Fig. 4. Cost chargeback model

First, the costs identified in the "general ledger" were allocated to "basic cost objects" (e.g. servers, cameras, IP). These costs were then allocated to "ICTRA service catalogue items" (e.g. application hosting, connectivity, telephone, security, reporting) according to an allocation logic. The result was a service unit cost for each item in the service catalogue. The service unit transfer price resulted from adjusting the service unit cost according to four pricing strategy principles:

- Commercial strategy: transfer prices were compared with market prices and set competitively.
- Technological strategy: the use of technology supported by ICTRA was favoured in terms of transfer price. Unsupported technology, which would be more expensive to service, was penalised.
- Service level agreements: the difference in service levels (e.g. gold, silver and bronze) was reflected in the transfer price.
- Transfer pricing of prior years: to avoid excessive differences between the old transfer prices and transfer prices calculated with the new cost chargeback model, it was decided that transfer prices should only gradually change.

The cost chargeback model was developed, tested and fine-tuned iteratively by ICTRA and extensively explained to the Group's business entities. To support this effort, ICTRA's Finance department made sure to provide the necessary cost management training to ICTRA's non-financial staff. Not only did this improve the understanding of financial issues, it also helped to create a shared language, which in turn optimised the alignment of all parties involved.

The cost chargeback model was also used for reporting: (1) on the cost of service delivery for each ICTRA supply and demand unit and (2) on the profitability per service, per ICTRA supply and demand unit and per customer (Group business entity).

3.3   Prove Competence

The ultimate test for the new cost chargeback model was whether it would survive the budget cycle.

The existing budgeting process had already caused a lot of frustration for the Group's business entities. ICT budgets only seemed to increase year after year and could not be questioned. The Group's business entities felt like signing a blank cheque, authorising ICTRA to spend without trying to improve its operating efficiency. Another cause of frustration was the time needed to determine the budget.

ICTRA had also identified inefficiencies in the existing budgeting process: it lacked formal guidelines, standard templates and definitions, as well as validation opportunities. Neither business requirements nor cost trend analyses were taken into account. From ICTRA's point of view, ICT budgets often seemed inconsistent and lacked ownership. To overcome these shortcomings, a new budgeting process was designed combining a top-down and a bottom-up approach. An innovation to ICTRA in this new budgeting process was the interaction between business and ICT to match their demand and supply planning and associated budgets. With the help of ICTRA's Finance department information processing was streamlined to enable a constructive dialogue.

Benefits of the new budgeting process included: (1) an improved financial accuracy and transparency. Budgets had become more predictable at the different levels as ICTRA's non-financial managers and the Group's business entity managers had improved their understanding of financial and service delivery concepts. (2) Credibility was no longer subjective but objective and quantifiable. Managers who were unable to adapt supply to demand would end up with non-rechargeable costs that they would have to explain to ICTRA's General Manager and ICTRA's Head of Finance. (3) The standardised budget cycle resulted in more reliable budget-setting. Because the jointly-developed service catalogue offered services responding to real business needs rather than standard services defined by ICTRA, the Group's business entities and ICTRA felt they were working as a team. The result: well thought-through services and projects, and improved business satisfaction.

4   Outcome and Conclusion

ICTRA's Head of Finance, Sammie Courtens, concluded as follows: "With the help of this finance transformation ICTRA is now better prepared for the liberalised market. Our service catalogue has enabled us to map and understand our offering to the business. Managers at ICTRA's demand and supply units have changed their mind-set completely. Not only do they now understand the real business requirements for ICT, they also focus more on cost effectiveness and operational efficiency."

For other organisations facing a similar challenge, ICTRA's finance transformation can serve as a blueprint. The following highlights conclude the three-step approach.

1. Establish Commitment: start building your service catalogue and negotiate service levels early in the process. One single, all-encompassing service catalogue would be ideal, but if this is too ambitious, better leave it for later and start off with the services for which there is buy-in from the business.
2. Gain Credibility: use your cost insights to set your transfer prices and use it as a vehicle to steer business behaviour and to stimulate desired demand for ICT services.
3. Prove Competence: integrate your work of the previous step in your business and put it to the test of your business counterparts, not only to gain buy-in, but also to show what you are capable of offering.

Acknowledgments. The authors wish to thank Deloitte Consulting Belgium for the financial support to the research effort, as well as Mr Sammie Courtens and his ICTRA colleagues who participated in our case study research.

References

1. Mark, D., Rau, D.P.: Splitting demand from supply in IT. McKinsey on IT, 22–29 (2006)
2. Viaene, S., De Hertogh, S., Jolyon, O.: Engaging in Turbulent Times - Direction Setting for Business and IT Alignment. International Journal of IT/Business Alignment and Governance 2(1), 1–15 (2011)
3. Kaplan, R.S., Cooper, R.: Cost & effect: using integrated cost systems to drive profitability and performance. Harvard Business Press (1998)
4. Drury, D.H.: Assessment of chargeback systems in IT management. Information Systems & Operational Research 38, 293–313 (2000)

Looking for a Fit for Purpose: Business Process Maturity Models from a User's Perspective

Amy Van Looy[1,2]

[1] University College Ghent, Faculty of Business Administration & Public Administration,
Department of Management & ICT, Ghent, Belgium
`amy.vanlooy@hogent.be`
[2] Ghent University, Faculty of Economics & Business Administration,
Department of Management Information Science & Operations Management, Ghent, Belgium
`Amy.VanLooy@UGent.be`

Abstract. Many books and articles have been written about the importance of business process management. However, in practice, improving business processes remains challenging. Therefore, business process maturity models (BPMMs) have been developed to assist organizations in their search for business process excellence (e.g. CMMI or OMG-BPMM). However, given their importance, a BPMM proliferation exists and practitioners are left without overview. Moreover, BPMMs differ in approach. An organization wishing to start with a BPMM thus risks selecting a model that does not fully fits its needs. The BPMM literature and the general literature on maturity models are mainly restricted to the design perspective. To our knowledge, the user's perspective is largely neglected. Based on an international Delphi study, this article introduces 14 criteria that (potential) BPMM users must consider to obtain a fit for purpose. The findings will be used to build a decision tool for BPMM selection.

Keywords: business process maturity, maturity model, selection, decision criteria, design research.

1 Introduction

Two paradigms dominate the research on business processes [1], and information systems (IS) [2,3]: (1) behavioral-science paradigm (i.e. building and testing theories to explain and predict situations), and (2) design-science paradigm (i.e. building and testing artefacts to solve problem situations). Research on BPMMs and maturity models in general is mostly situated in the second paradigm. For instance, the IS design research cycle has been translated towards maturity models [4,5]. It typically covers pre-design, design and post-design phases. Furthermore, Hevner et al. [2] formulate seven guidelines to evaluate the design of IS artefacts, which have also been translated towards maturity models [4]. The design-science paradigm thus examines maturity models as artefacts. March and Smith [3] distinguish four IS artefact types:

- *construct*: a conceptualization or vocabulary to describe problems and solutions;
- *model*: a description of problems and solutions, based on the conceptualization;

G. Poels (Ed.): CONFENIS 2012, LNBIP 139, pp. 182–189, 2013.
© IFIP International Federation for Information Processing 2013

- *method*: a set of steps (i.e. algorithms or guidelines) to perform a task;
- *instantiation*: the realization of constructs, models and methods into a tool.

Translated towards maturity models, Mettler and Rohner [5] confirm that a common *conceptualization* is lacking. Consequently, for this research, we describe a BPMM as '*a model to assess and/or to guide best practice improvements in organizational maturity and process capability, expressed in lifecycle levels, by taking into account an evolutionary road map regarding (1) process modeling, (2) process deployment, (3) process optimization, (4) process management, (5) the organizational culture, and/or (6) the organizational structure*' [6, p.1132-1133]. A BPMM assesses (AS-IS) and improves (TO-BE) maturity. The latter is a collection of capabilities (e.g. skills or competences) that are needed for a business process to perform excellently. For instance, how capable is your organization to model its business processes in a graphical design, or to run them without errors? Maturity levels indicate the overall growth through all capabilities together, whereas capability levels indicate the growth per capability. The business process itself may consist of several sub processes, and defines how an organization operates. Furthermore, BPMMs are both *models* and *methods*, as they combine descriptions (e.g. maturity levels) with key practices (e.g. to achieve higher levels) [5]. Finally, *instantiations* can be documents or websites to assist organizations in using a BPMM.

To our knowledge, the BPMM literature is mainly restricted to a design perspective, i.e. by creating a design theory or by designing particular BPMMs, e.g. [7]. The research cycles, guidelines, and artefact types constitute a theory on the design of maturity models. When designed accordingly, BPMMs are supposed to have a sound methodological foundation. However, not all design criteria are relevant when choosing a BPMM. Moreover, also non-design criteria may come to the foreground during BPMM selection, such as financial or practical considerations. Consequently, this article takes a user's perspective. Particularly, we focus on the BPMM selection phase, which increases in importance as the number of BPMMs continues to increase. For instance, in the second quarter of 2010, we already collected a sample of 69 BPMMs regarding generic processes, supply chains and collaboration processes. We are of the opinion that investing in the BPMM selection phase pays off by saving money and efforts afterwards, i.e. for the corrective actions needed if a used BPMM turns out to be no fit for purpose.

Furthermore, the BPMM proliferation [8] raises questions about the substantial differences between BPMMs. Some comparative overviews have been made, albeit with a small number of BPMMs [9]. Mettler [10] also presents criteria for designing maturity models from a user's perspective, but not specific to the BPMM context and without an overview of existing models. On the other hand, Röglinger, Pöppelbuss and Becker [11] present a limited BPMM overview while proposing BPMM design criteria, but without practical advice on BPMM selection. Consequently, organizations have no comprehensive overview of academic and industry-owned BPMMs and an incomplete state of knowledge on how to select a BPMM that best fits their needs.

This article is a work-in-progress which elaborates on the decision criteria that (potential) BPMM users must consider when selecting a BPMM. It is based on a thorough methodological approach, explained in section 2. The criteria and their trade-offs are discussed in section 3, followed by the future research steps in section 4. Finally, the preliminary research findings are summarized in the conclusion section.

2   Methodology

The decision criteria for BPMM selection were obtained by consulting independent subject matter experts in an international Delphi study. A Delphi study is an established consensus-seeking decision-making method using '*a series of sequential questionnaires or rounds, interspersed by controlled feedback, that seek to gain the most reliable consensus of opinion of an expert panel*' [12, p.458]. We have chosen a Delphi study as its iterative approach enhances validity, compared to a single questionnaire. Furthermore, according to Van De Ven and Delbecq [13], it generally results in a higher quantity and quality of ideas than other group decision-making methods. The experts are also anonymous, which minimizes group pressures. Moreover, a Delphi study is widely used for exploring ideas and structuring group communication on framework development and rating. Delphi examples are also present in IS research in general [14] and business processes in particular [7].

In November 2011, the Delphi study started with 22 BPM experts, i.e. 11 academics and 11 practitioners, each from five different continents. The academics had credible BPM(M) publications in academic journals, and the practitioners designed a BPMM, applied BPM(M), or were interested in BPMM selection. The selection procedure conforms to [14], introducing different backgrounds to minimize bias. Consensus conditions were a priori defined for a 7-point Likert scale, based on measures of location (i.e. frequencies) and spread (i.e. interquartile range) [15]: (1) 50% of the experts must agree on the two most extreme scores (i.e. either 1-2 or 6-7), (2) 75% must agree on the three most extreme scores (i.e. either 1-2-3 or 5-6-7), (3) the interquartile range must be 1.50 or less, and (4) no opposite extreme score given by any expert (i.e. either 7 for the first case or 1 for the second). Per round, the responses were anonymously analyzed by four coders, of which one independent coder was from another university. This codification panel stopped iterating when the consensus conditions were met, or when results became repetitive. Hence, a Delphi study typically takes three to four rounds [7,15].

After three Delphi rounds, consensus was reached for 14 decision criteria. Other criteria had no trend towards consensus due to condition 4, i.e. at least one expert with an opposite extreme score in multiple rounds. In all rounds, the response rates exceeded the minimum value of 70%, enhancing research rigor and validity [15]. Moreover, 95% of the respondents in the third round (N=17) agreed that the set of final criteria is very to extremely important for BPMM selection (i.e. scores 6 or 7), with a median of 6 and an interquartile range of 0. In subsequent Delphi rounds, the experts were asked to determine which of these 14 decision criteria are more important in pairwise comparisons (i.e. Analytical Hierarchy Process). Besides ranking, it allows calculating weightings for assigning evaluation scores to existing BPMMs. As this article concerns a work-in-progress, the subsequent rounds are out-of-scope.

3   Preliminary Results

We hereby present the criteria that a user must consider when selecting a BPMM. For reasons of comprehensiveness, they are grouped: (1) assessment criteria, i.e. how maturity is measured and by whom, (2) improvement criteria, i.e. what is measured as maturity, particularly the capabilities and their improvements to reach successive levels, and (3) non-design criteria, i.e. other criteria not directly related to assessment and improvement. Table 1 alphabetically shows the decision criteria per group.

Table 1. An alphabetical overview of the 14 decision criteria for BPMM selection

Assessment criteria	Improvement criteria	Non-design criteria
1. Availability	7. Architecture details	12. Costs
2. Data collection	8. Architecture type	13. Purpose
3. Duration	9. Capabilities	14. Validation
4. Nr. of questions	10. Nr. of processes	
5. Rating scale	11. Type of processes	
6. Respondents		

3.1   Assessment Criteria

Availability. Whether the assessment questions and corresponding level calculation are publicly available (instead of only known to the assessors). BPMMs do not always provide full details. This particularly counts for non-academic models, e.g. in consultancy. The user must decide whether this limited availability is an issue for the organization. For instance, fully known BPMMs (i.e. either free or charged) can be used for educating process team members or for earning credibility.

Data Collection. The way information is collected during an assessment. Objective techniques involve document reviews, and give an idea of how organizations work, without interrupting individuals or activities. They minimize biased results of (particularly internal) assessors and respondents. On the other hand, subjective techniques gather information about how organizations actually work, e.g. by questionnaires, interviews or observations. As it rather concerns personal beliefs, some precautions can be taken, e.g. a third party lead assessor, multiple assessors and respondents, data collection training, or a combination with objective techniques.

Duration. The maximal duration of a particular assessment. Some BPMMs only take one day (e.g. a quick scan within 15 minutes), whereas other BPMMs present a more profound analysis of one week or longer. As time is money, the user must consider how much time he wants to spent on the assessment alone.

Number of Questions. The maximal number of questions to be answered during an assessment. More questions provide more insight to develop a road map, but may be less feasible and/or take longer. Less than 20 questions are rather used as a teaser or a quick scan.

Rating Scale. The type of data that is collected during an assessment. Quantitative data (i.e. discrete, interval or ratio scales) can be statistically analyzed and compared, independent of the assessors' interpretation. On the other hand, qualitative data (i.e. nominal or ordinal scales) provide more in-depth descriptions by delving into details. However, they depend more on the assessors' skills. Also a combination of rating scales is possible, depending on which data and skills are available.

Respondents. The explicit recognition to include people from outside the assessed organizations as respondents. If only internal respondents (i.e. managers and/or staff of the assessed organizations) are questioned, the user assumes that they fully know their stakeholders' needs. However, also involving stakeholders recognizes the need for an outside-in perspective by explicitly listening to stakeholders.

3.2   Improvement Criteria

Architecture Details. The degree of guidance that a BPMM gives on your journey towards higher maturity. It concerns the extent to which the road map (i.e. step-by-step plan) explains which criteria (i.e. goals and best practices) must be satisfied before reaching each particular level: (1) descriptive, (2) implicit prescriptive or (3) explicit prescriptive. A descriptive road map is limited to high-level descriptions. As it gives less support, it is suited for organizations wishing to become acquainted with BPMMs, or for organizations which are highly experienced with process improvements. An implicit prescriptive road map has criteria interwoven in the assessment questions, i.e. with an ordinal scale or a matrix, that explain all capabilities per level. Assessors can derive the criteria from the assessment questions. Finally, an explicit prescriptive road map gives most guidance by separately listing criteria from the assessment questions.

Architecture Type. The possibility to define a road map per capability, a road map for overall maturity, or both. It concerns linking (maturity of capability) levels to capabilities in a step-by-step plan, which explains how to reach each consecutive level. A continuous architecture provides capability levels per capability, i.e. one road map per capability. It allows organizations to assess and improve each capability separately, and thus to improve capabilities at a different pace or to limit their scope to only those capabilities they are interested in. As not all capabilities are necessarily taken into account, there is a risk for suboptimal optimizations (in terms of overall maturity). On the other hand, a staged architecture provides maturity levels linked to all capabilities together, i.e. one road map for overall maturity. The emphasis is on simultaneous advancements, instead of individual capability advancements.

Capabilities. The capabilities to be assessed and improved. BPMMs differ in the capabilities they actually address. They generally vary from basic capabilities related to the traditional business process lifecycle, i.e. modeling, deployment, optimization, and management, to the addition of organizational capabilities, i.e. to create a process-oriented culture and structure. In theory, all presented capabilities are required for fully mature business processes. However, in practice, an organization can opt for only a subset of capabilities, e.g. depending on the degree of top management support, IT background of the user, prior BPM experience, organization size, etc. For instance, organizations with local, bottom-up initiatives or with limited BPM experience might wish to start with the basic capabilities, limited to the traditional business process lifecycle. Additionally, the culture capability requires a minimum level of management support to promote business processes and granting (financial) rewards to process performance. Finally, structural configurations inherently require top management support. The latter is particularly recommended if you already have some BPM experience or if your ambition is to standardize processes across large departments or divisions. As capabilities are core to BPMMs, the user must select a set of capabilities that best fits its organizational needs.

Number of Processes. The number of business processes to be assessed and improved: (1) one, (2) more or (3) all. For BPMMs focusing on a single business process, the process boundaries must be defined by the user, e.g. is a business process assessed and improved as a sub process or as a separate process. BPMMs can also focus on more than one, but not all business processes within the assessed organizations. Assessment questions then deal with a particular business domain or value chain and all its (sub) processes. Furthermore, BPMMs can cope with all business processes in the assessed organizations. As such, assessment questions take a management perspective by focusing on how organizations deal with business processes in general, without focusing on particular processes. However, by improving the BPM mastery, it is likely that particular processes are indirectly improved too. Only few BPMMs combine specific processes (i.e. one or more) with the overall BPM mastery.

Type of Processes. Whether the BPMM is generic (i.e. for business processes in general) or domain-specific (e.g. for business processes in supply chains or collaboration situations). The terminology used in generic BPMMs, e.g. in the assessment questions, is likely to be more holistic. Benchmarking is possible across business domains. Accordingly, domain-specific BPMM use terminology adapted to their domain, which are likely to be less abstract to respondents and thus better understandable. However, benchmarking remains limited to organizations within the same domain. Hence, also this choice requires strategic considerations.

3.3   Non-design Criteria

Costs. The direct costs to access and use a BPMM. Not all BPMMs are free of charges. Particularly non-academic models may ask a one-off access fee or a required training to be followed. Recurring costs rather serve to pay a third party lead assessor, certification or benchmarking. The user must decide which budget can be spent, and adapt his expectations accordingly: you often get what you pay for. However, academic models can be free if they use your data for enhancing their research.

Purpose. The purpose for which a BPMM is intended to be used. The basic purpose of any BPMM is assessing and identifying process improvements, i.e. raising awareness. The key is recognizing deficiencies, creating willingness to act and to follow-through on the findings. Besides raising awareness, BPMMs can also allow benchmarking with other organizations (i.e. for comparing with competitors and sharing best practices) or certification (i.e. for external recognition of the assessment results, in line with the ISO quality certificates).

Validation. Whether or not empirical evidence is given that the BPMM helps to enhance the efficiency and effectiveness of business processes. Most BPMMs do not provide any proof of validity (or success). If they do, evidence is frequently limited to enumerating other organizations applying the model. Only few BPMM give evidence for the performance outcomes. The user must decide whether some proof of validity is required, depending on the planned investments. However, we strongly discourage the use of non-validated BPMMs. They can result in frustrations, time and money losses afterwards, i.e. if they appear to be flawed or unusable after you start using it.

4   Future Work

The decision criteria will be used to build a decision tool for BPMM selection, based on an online questionnaire and a decision table design. Particularly, by answering the questionnaire, the user will be guided to existing BPMMs that best fit his answers. Therefore, we will rely on a sample of 69 BPMMs. The final decision tool will be of practical use for organizations interested in assessing and improving their business processes, and for scholars who want to create or apply BPMMs. The next steps are:

1. Ranking and weighing decision criteria, and calculating evaluation scores for existing BPMMs.
2. Translating decision criteria and their options into a questionnaire.
3. Coupling the questionnaire to a decision table which comprises a mapping to existing BPMMs. BPMMs with low evaluation scores are omitted to guarantee quality.
4. Automating the questionnaire and the decision table in a proof-of-concept.
5. Conducting case studies. Managers will be asked to evaluate the tool and its output, i.e. by rating their satisfaction with the criteria and the proposed BPMMs.

5   Conclusion

This article discussed 14 criteria and their trade-offs that users must consider when selecting a BPMM, i.e. six assessment criteria, five improvement criteria, and three non-design criteria. They result from an international Delphi study with 22 BPM experts, both practitioners and academics from five continents, and will serve as input for a decision tool on BPMM selection. The novelty of this work-in-progress is that BPMMs are examined from a user's perspective, i.e. as a search for BPMMs that best fit the user's needs ('fit for purpose'). To our knowledge, it contrasts to current literature on maturity models which mainly takes a design perspective. Furthermore, the final decision tool will rely on a large sample of 69 BPMMs. At present, the criteria are alphabetically introduced. In future research, the experts will rank and weigh them to obtain a more refined overview and to grant evaluation score to existing BPMMs.

References

1. Houy, C., Fettke, P., Loos, P.: Empirical Research in Business Process Management. Business Process Management Journal 16(4), 619–661 (2010)
2. Hevner, A.R., et al.: Design Science in Information Systems Research. MIS Quarterly 28(1), 75–105 (2004)
3. March, S.T., Smith, G.F.: Design and Natural Science Research on Information Technology. Decision Support Systems 15(4), 251–266 (1995)
4. Becker, J., Knackstedt, R., Pöppelbuss, J.: Developing Maturity Models for IT Management. Business & Information Systems Engineering 1(3), 213–222 (2009)
5. Mettler, T., Rohner, P.: Situational Maturity Models as Instrumental Artifacts for Organizational Design. In: 4th DESRIST Conference, pp. 1–9. ACM, Malvern (2009)
6. Van Looy, A., De Backer, M., Poels, G.: Defining Business Process Maturity. A Journey towards Excellence. TQM & Business Excellence 22(11), 1119–1137 (2011)
7. de Bruin, T., Rosemann, M.: Using the Delphi Technique to Identify BPM Capability Areas. In: 18th ACIS Conference, Toowoomba, pp. 642–653 (2007)
8. Sheard, S.A.: Evolution of the Frameworks Quagmire. IEEE Computer 34(7), 96–98 (2001)
9. Maier, A.M., Moultrie, J., Clarkson, P.J.: A Review of Maturity Grid based Approaches to Assessing Organizational Capabilities. In: Academy of Management Meeting (2008)
10. Mettler, T.: A Design Science Research Perspective on Maturity Models in Information Systems. Report BE IWI/HNE/03. Institute of Information Management, St. Gallen (2009)
11. Röglinger, M., Pöppelbuss, J., Becker, J.: Maturity Models in Business Process Management. Business Process Management Journal 18(2), 7 (2012)
12. Dalkey, N., Helmer, O.: An Experimental Application of the Delphi Method to the Use of Experts. Management Science 9(3), 458–467 (1963)
13. Van De Ven, A.H., Delbecq, A.L.: The Effectiveness of Nominal, Delphi, and Interacting Group Decision Making Processes. The Academy of Management Journal 17(4), 605–621 (1974)
14. Okoli, C., Pawlowski, S.D.: The Delphi Method as a Research Tool: an Example, Design Constructions and Applications. Information & Management 42, 15–29 (2004)
15. Hasson, F., Keeney, S., McKenna, H.: Research Guidelines for the Delphi Survey Technique. Journal of Advanced Nursing 32(4), 1008–1015 (2000)

Hype or Reality: Will Enterprise Systems as a Service Become an Organizing Vision for Enterprise Cloud Computing in Denmark?

Per Svejvig[1], Torben Storgaard[2], and Charles Møller[3]

[1] Department of Business Administration, Aarhus University, Denmark
psve@asb.dk
[2] HerbertNathan & Co, Copenhagen, Denmark
ts@herbertnathan.com
[3] Center for Industrial Production, Aalborg University
Charles@business.aau.dk

Abstract. Cloud computing is at "the peak of inflated expectations" on the Gartner Hype Cycle from 2010. Service models constitute a layer in the cloud computing model and Software as a Service (SaaS) is one of the important service models. Software as a Service provides complete business applications delivered over the web and more specific when delivering enterprise systems (ES) applications such as ERP, CRM and others we can further categorize the model as an Enterprise Systems as a Service (ESaaS) model. However it is said that ESaaS is one of the last frontier for cloud computing due to security risk, downtime and other factors. The hype about cloud computing and ESaaS made us speculate about our local context, Denmark, what are the current situation and how might ESaaS develop. We are asking the question: Will ESaaS become an organizing vision in Denmark? We used empirical data from a database with more than 1150 Danish organizations using ES, informal contacts to vendors etc. The result of our study is very surprising as none of the organizations in the database apply ESaaS although recent information from vendors indicates more than 50 ESaaS implementations in Denmark. We discuss the distance between the community discourse and current status of real ESaaS implementations.

Keywords: Cloud computing, software as a service (SaaS), enterprise systems, organizing vision, institutional theory.

1 Introduction

Cloud computing is on everybody's lips today and is promoted as a silver bullet for solving several of the past problems with IT by offering pay per use, rapid elasticity, on demand self-service, simple scalable services and (perhaps) multi-tenancy [1]. Cloud computing is furthermore marketed as a cost saving strategy appealing well to the post financial crisis situation for many organizations with cloud's *"Opex over Capex story and ability to buy small and, if it works, to go big"* [2]. Cloud computing has even been named by Gartner *" as the number one priority for CIOs in 2011"* [3].

G. Poels (Ed.): CONFENIS 2012, LNBIP 139, pp. 190–197, 2013.
© IFIP International Federation for Information Processing 2013

Gartner position in addition cloud computing at the "peak of inflated expectations" at the Gartner Hype Cycle predicting 2 to 5 years to mainstream adoption [4].

Service models constitute a layer in the cloud computing model and Software as a Service (SaaS) is one of the important types of service models. Software as a Service provides complete business applications delivered over the web and more specific when delivering enterprise systems (ES) applications such as ERP, CRM and others we can further categorize the model as an Enterprise Systems as a Service (ESaaS) model. In this paper we use ESaaS interchangeable with SaaS but also as a more specific concept. As cloud computing is still an evolving paradigm, its definitions, use cases, underlying technologies, issues, risks, and benefits can be refined [5].

Software as a Service (SaaS) embraces cloud applications for social networks, office suites, CRM, video processing etc. One example is Salesforce.com, a business productivity application (CRM), which relies completely on the SaaS model [6] consisting of Sales Cloud, Service Cloud and Chatter Collaboration Cloud [7] residing on "*[Salesforce.com] servers, allowing customers to customize and access applications on demand*" [6].

However enterprise wide system applications and especially ERP has been considered the last frontier for SaaS where companies has put forward the following reasons preventing them from considering ESaaS (prioritized sequence): (1) ERP is too basic and strategic to running our business, (2) security concerns, (3) ability to control own upgrade process, (4) downtime risk, (5) greater on-premise functionality, (6) require heavy customizations, and finally (7) already invested in IT resources and don't want to reduce staff [8]. A very recent example shows the potential problem with cloud and ESaaS where Amazon had an outage of their cloud services lasting for several days and affecting a large number of customers [9].

Despite these resisting factors there seems to be a big jump in ESaaS interest with 39% of respondents willing to consider ESaaS according to Aberdeen's 2010 ERP survey, which is a 61% increase in willingness from their 2009 to 2010 survey [10], this a furthermore supported by a very recent report from Panorama Consulting Group [11] stating the adoption rate of ESaaS to be 17%.

The adoption pattern of ESaaS varies in at least two dimensions company size and application category. Small companies are more likely to adopt SaaS followed by mid-size organizations [8], which might be explained by large companies having a more complex and comprehensive information infrastructure [as defined in 12] compared to small and mid-size companies. CRM applications are more frequent than ERP application [8] where a possible explanation can be the perception of ERP as too basic and strategic to run the business in a ESaaS model.

Most recently, the Walldorf German based ERP vendor SAP have launched an on demand ERP (SaaS) solution: SAP Business By Design that can be seen as prototype ESaaS model[13]. SAP Business By Design is a fully integrated on-demand Enterprise Resource Planning (ERP) and business management software solution for small and medium sized enterprises (SME). It is a complete Software as a Service (SaaS) offering for 10-25 users available on most major markets. However, the real cases are actually hard to locate.

The previous trends, numbers [e.g. 11] and the statements from Gartner are referring to the global landscape for cloud computing and ESaaS operating at this rather abstract global level. This made us speculate about our local context, Denmark, what is the current situation and how might ESaaS develop specifically in our landscape – this framed our research question: *Will Enterprise Systems as a Service become an organizing vision in Denmark?*

2   Enterprise Systems as a Service – Global and Local Context

Cloud computing appears to have emerged very recently as a subject of substantial industrial and academic interest, though its meaning, scope and fit with respect to other paradigms is hotly debated. For some researchers, Clouds are a natural evolution towards full commercialization of Grid systems, while for others they may be dismissed as a mere rebranding of the existing pay-per-use or pay-as-you-go technologies [14].

Cloud computing is a very broad concept and an umbrella term for refined on demand services delivered by the cloud [6]. The multiplicity in understanding of the term is probably fostered by the "beyond amazing hype level" [1] underlining the peak in Gartner's Hype Cycle [4]. Many stakeholders (vendors, analysts etc.) jump on the bandwagon inflating the term and "if everything is a cloud, then it gets very hard to see anything" [1], so we need to be very explicit about using the term. We follow the US National Institute of Standards and Technology (NIST) definition [5]:

Cloud computing is a model for enabling convenient, on-demand network access to a shared pool of configurable computing resources (e.g., networks, servers, storage, applications, and services) that can be rapidly provisioned and released with minimal management effort or service provider interaction.

This cloud model promotes availability and is composed of five essential characteristics, three service models, and four deployment models as illustrated in figure 1 below [15].

The notion of the "cloud" as a technical concept is used as a metaphor for the internet and was in the past used to represent the telephone network as an abstraction of the underlying infrastructure [16]. There are different deployment models for cloud computing such as private clouds operated solely for an organization, community clouds shared by several organizations, public clouds and hybrid clouds as a composition of two or more clouds (private, community or public) [17]. The term virtual private clouds have also entered the scene analogous to VPN. There is a controversy about whether private clouds (virtual or not virtual) really is cloud computing [1].

Cloud computing can be divided into three layers namely [6]: (1) Infrastructure as a Service (IaaS), (2) Platform as a Service (PaaS) and (3) Software as a Service (SaaS). The focus in this paper is on the enterprise systems as a service (ESaaS) where *"SaaS is simply software that is delivered from a server in a remote location to your desktop, and is used online"* [18]. ESaaS usage is expected to expand in 2011 [19].

The air is also charged with cloud computing and SaaS in Denmark. Many of the issues discussed in this paper apply to the local Danish context, but there are also additional points to mention. *First*, Denmark has a lot of small and medium sized organizations (SME's) which are expected to be more willing to adapt ESaaS [8].

Second, the Local Government Denmark (LGDK) (an interest group and member authority of Danish municipalities) tried to implement a driving license booking system based on Microsoft's Azure PaaS, but ran into technical and juridical problems. The technical problems were related to the payment module, logon and data extract from the cloud based solution [20]. The legal issue was more serious as LGDK (and the municipalities) was accused by the Danish Data Protection Agency to break the act on processing of personal data, especially about location of data [21]. LGDK decided to withdraw the cloud solution and replaced it with an on premise solution with the comments *"cloud computing is definitely more difficult, and harder, than what is mentioned in the booklets"* [20].

Finally, the CIO from "The LEGO Group", a well-known Danish global enterprise within toy manufacturing, stated in news media that *"cloud is mostly hot air"*. Cloud can only deliver a small fraction of the services that LEGO need and cannot replace their *"customized SAP, Microsoft, Oracle and ATG [e-commerce] platforms with end to end business process support"*. LEGO are using cloud to specific point solutions such as "spam and virus filtering", "credit card clearing" and load-testing of applications but *"[t]o put our enterprise-platform on the public cloud is Utopia"* [22].

This section has described the global and local context for ESaaS and both contexts will probably influence Danish organizations and their willingness to adopt these solutions. In the next section we will look into a theoretical framing of the cloud computing impact on the enterprise systems in Denmark.

3   IS Innovations as Organizing Visions

An Organizing Vision (OV) can be considered a collective, cognitive view of how new technologies enables success in information systems innovation. This model is used to analyze ESaaS in Denmark.

Swanson and Ramiller (1997) takes institutional theory into IS research and propose the concept of *organizing vision in IS innovation*, which they define as *"a focal community idea for the application of information technology in organizations"* [23]. Earlier research has argued that early adoption of a technological innovation is based on rational choice while later adoption is institutionalized. However Swanson and Ramiller suggest that institutional processes are engaged from the beginning. Inter-organizational communities create and employ organizing visions of IS innovations. Examples are CASE tools, e-commerce, client server [24] and Application Service Providers (ASP) [25] and comparable to management fads like BPR, TQM and quality circles [25, 26]. The organizing vision is important for early and later adoption and diffusion. The vision supports interpretation (to make sense of the innovation), legitimation (to establish the underlying rationale) and mobilization (to activate, motivate and structure the material realization of innovation) [23, 25].

The OV model presents different institutional forces such as community discourse, community structure and commerce and business problematic, which are used in the analysis of ESaaS in Denmark.

4   Research Methodology

The research process started early 2011 where we applied different data collection methods: (1) Queries into HNCO database with ERP, CRM systems, (2) Informal dialogue with ES vendors, and finally (3) Literature search of cloud computing and SaaS (research and practitioner oriented). The second author is employed at a Herbert Nathan & Co (HNCO), a Danish management consulting company within area of ERP, they maintains a database of top 1000 companies in Denmark and their usage of enterprise systems. However we did not find any customers in the database using ESaaS, which were surprising. We repeated our study in spring 2012 and surprisingly got the same result as one year ago. ES as a Service is apparently not used by Top 1000 companies in Denmark. However informal talk with vendors indicates that there might be about 50 references in Denmark, but we have only been able to confirm a small number of these claimed references.

5   Analysis

The table below shows the analysis concerning ESaaS as an organizing vision (adapted from Figure 3):

Table 1. Analysis of ESaaS as an organizing vision

Institutional forces	Global Context	Local Context
Community discourse	Cloud computing has been named by Gartner "as the number one priority for CIOs in 2011" [3]	The global discourse are part of the local Danish discourse, but local stories does also shape the local context
	Gartner position cloud computing at the "peak of inflated expectations" at the Gartner Hype Cycle predicting 2 to 5 years to mainstream adoption [4]	Denmark has a lot of small and medium sized organizations (SME's) which are expected to be more willing to adapt ESaaS [8]. That might fertilize the ground for faster adoption of ESaaS
	Aberdeen survey and Panorama Consulting Group report shows a big jump in interest in ESaaS / SaaS [10, 11]	
	Amazon had an outage of their cloud services lasting for several days and affecting a large number of customers [9]. This case received very much press coverage and it would be natural to expect it to have a negative impact on the perception of cloud computing	The Local Government Denmark (LGDK) tried to implement a driving license booking system based on Microsoft's Azure PaaS, but ran into technical and juridical problems [20]. The CIO from "The LEGO Group" stated in news media that "*cloud is mostly hot air*". Cloud can only deliv-

Institutional forces	Global Context	Local Context
		er a small fraction of the services that LEGO need [22]
Community structure and commerce	Computer press, newspaper articles, white papers, websites, technology vendors, consultants, industry analysts, IT management books, trade publications, trade shows etc.	There is no big difference in the community structure at global and local level
Business problematic	Cloud computing is on everybody's lips today and is promoted as a silver bullet for solving several of the past problems with IT by offering pay per use, rapid elasticity, on demand self-service, simple scalable services and (perhaps) multi-tenancy [1] Cloud computing is furthermore marketed as a cost saving strategy appealing well to the post financial crisis situation for many organizations with cloud's *"Opex over Capex story and ability to buy small and, if it works, to go big"* [2]	The business problematic is the same at the global and local level However as Denmark has a lot of small and medium sized companies the business conditions might be different, and the arguments in favor of cloud computing and ESaaS / SaaS might be more prevailing

Table 1 above shows the conditions for ESaaS to become an organizing vision although it would be too early to claim it is an organizing vision especially because the link to practice appears to be uncertain. Our knowledge about the 50 implementations in Denmark is very limited and we do not know the status of the implementations (pilots, just started, normal operation, abandoned etc.).

5.1 Discussions

First of all the research indicate that the organizing vision of ESaaS in Denmark is perhaps on a too preliminary stage to make sense. The evidence are scarce or inaccessible which indicate that the idea is either not existing or at an immature state. Given the vast amount of interest, we assume that the concept is either immature or that the ideas will emerge under a different heading that we have not been able to identify.

In any cases we can use the idea of the organizing vision as a normative model for the evolution of the cloud computing concept in an enterprise systems context. This is comparable to Gartner's hype cycle: After the initial peak of inflated expectations we will gradually move into the slope of enlightenment. The organizing vision could be a normative model for making sense of the developments. But only future research will tell.

As a final comment to the organizing vision of ESaaS the following quote from Larry Ellison, the CEO of Oracle from September 2008 sum up the experiences:

The interesting thing about cloud computing is that we've redefined cloud computing to include everything that we already do. I can't think of anything that isn't cloud computing with all of these announcements. The computer industry is the only industry that is more fashion-driven than women's fashion. Maybe I'm an idiot, but I have no idea what anyone is talking about. What is it? It's complete gibberish. It's insane. When is this idiocy going to stop?

6   Conclusion

This paper has sought to further our understanding of cloud computing, SaaS and with special focus on ESaaS. We described the global and local context for cloud computing and ESaaS / SaaS. We furthermore presented institutional theory extended by the work of Swanson and Ramiller about their concept of organizing visions. We asked the question: Will ESaaS become an organizing vision in Denmark. The paper can give some initial and indicative answers to the question that the community discourse support ESaaS as an organizing vision but the current status of real ESaaS implementations is uncertain.

The paper has only been able to scratch the surface and to give some initial thoughts about ESaaS in the local context. However the paper sets the stage for a longer-term research challenges about ESaaS. *First,* an obvious extension of this paper is to study the Danish market in much more detail by interviewing the actors in the community structure especially ESaaS customers. *Second,* comparative studies between countries would also be interesting, does such an organizing vision as ESaaS diffuse similarly or differently and what shapes the diffusion and adoption. *Finally,* the theoretical framework by Swanson and Ramiller are appealing to study the adoption and diffusion of technology possible extended by this paper's approach with the global and local context.

References

1. Wohl, A.: Cloud Computing. In: Simon, P. (ed.) The Next Wave Technologies - Opportunities in Chaos, pp. 59–78. John Wiley & Sons, Hoboken (2010)
2. Schultz, B.: Enterprise Cloud Services: the agenda. CIO Magazine (2011), http://www.cio.com/article/print/662607 (cited March 14, 2011)
3. Golden, B., Cloud CIO: 5 Key Pieces of Rollout Advice. CIO Magazine (2011), http://www.cio.com/article/print/679070 (cited April 11, 2011)
4. Fenn, J.: Hype Cycle for Emerging Technologies, Gartner, p. 10 (2010)
5. Mell, P., Grance, T.: The NIST Definition of Cloud Computing (2009), http://www.nist.gov/itl/cloud/upload/cloud-def-v15.pdf (cited April 25, 2011)

6. Voorsluys, W., Broberg, J., Buyya, R.: Introduction to Cloud Computing. In: Buyya, R., Broberg, J., Goscinski, A.M. (eds.) Cloud Computing Principles and Paradigms, pp. 3–42. Wiley, New Jersey (2011)
7. Salesforce.com. The leader in customer relationship management (CRM) & cloud computing (2011), http://www.salesforce.com (cited April 22, 2011)
8. Aberdeen Group, SaaS ERP: Trends and Observations, A. Group (ed.) (2009)
9. Thibodeau, P.: Amazon Outage Sparks Frustration, Doubts About Cloud. CIO Magazine (2011), http://www.cio.com/article/print/680329 (cited March 14, 2011)
10. Subramanian, K.: Big Jump in SaaS ERP Interest (2010), http://www.cloudave.com/8058/big-jump-in-saas-erp-interest/ (cited March 13, 2011)
11. Panorama Consulting Group, 2011 ERP Report, Panorama Consulting Group (2011)
12. Hanseth, O., Lyytinen, K.: Design theory for dynamic complexity in information infrastructures: the case of building internet. Journal of Information Technology 25(1), 1–19 (2010)
13. SAP. SAP Business ByDesign (2012), http://www.sap.com/solutions/technology/cloud/business-by-design/highlights/index.epx (cited April 28, 2011)
14. Antonopoulos, N., Gillam, L.: Cloud Computing: Principles, Systems and Applications. Springer-Verlag London Limited (2010)
15. Williams, M.I.: A quick start guide to cloud computing: moving your business into the cloud. Kogan Page Limited (2010)
16. Baan, J.: Business Operations Improvement, The New Paradigm in Enterprise IT. Cordys Holding B.V. (2010)
17. Beck, K., et al.: Agile Software Development Manifesto (2001), http://agilemanifesto.org/ (cited July 1, 2009)
18. Wohl, A.: Software as a Service (SaaS). In: Simon, P. (ed.) The Next Wave Technologies - Opportunities in Chaos, pp. 97–113. John Wiley & Sons, Hoboken (2010)
19. O'Neill, S.: Cloud Computing in 2011: 3 Trends Changing Business Adoption. CIO Magazine (2011), http://www.cio.com/article/print/663316 (cited March 14, 2011)
20. Elkær, M.: Derfor gik kommunernes cloud-forsøg i vasken. In: Computerworld (2011)
21. Elkær, M.: Datatilsynet farer i flæsket på KL over cloud-flop. In: Computerworld (2011)
22. Nielsen, J.: LEGO: Skyen er mest varm luft. In: Comon (2011)
23. Swanson, E.B., Ramiller, N.C.: The Organizing Vision in Information Systems Innovation. Organization Science 8(5), 458–474 (1997)
24. Ramiller, N.C., Swanson, E.B.: Organizing Visions for Information Technology and the Information Systems Executive Response. Journal of Management Information Systems 20(1), 13–50 (2003)
25. Currie, W.L.: The organizing vision of application service provision: a process-oriented analysis. Information and Organization 14(4), 237–267 (2004)
26. Abrahamson, E., Fairchild, G.: Management Fashion: Lifecycles, Triggers, and Collective Learning Processes. Administrative Science Quarterly 44(4), 708–740 (1999)

Effect of ERP Implementation on the Company Efficiency – A Macedonian CASE

Jan Devos[1], Jasmina Rajcanovska[1], Hendrik Van Landeghem[2],
and Dirk Deschoolmeester[3]

[1] ELIT Lab, University College West Flanders, Ghent University Association,
Graaf Karel de Goedelaan 5, 8500 Kortrijk, Belgium
[2] Technologiepark Zwijnaarde 903, 9052 Zwijnaarde, Belgium
[3] Reep 1, 9000 Gent, Belgium
{jang.devos,hendrik.vanlandeghem,dirk.deschoolmeester}@ugent.be,
rajchanovska@yahoo.com

Abstract. Enterprise Resource Planning (ERP) is slowly find its place in many organizations in Macedonia. The primary goal of an ERP implementation is managing and coordinating all resources, information, and business processes from shared data stores. This paper elaborates on an ERP solution implementation in the Macedonian production sector and the effect it has on the company efficiency. A case study was conducted in a small or medium-sized manufacturing company in Macedonia during a period of seven years and compared to empirical findings of ERP systems implementations in developed countries. Findings show almost similar results. ERP systems implementations require time, money and management commitment and the effect to improve efficiency is embryonic. However it was also noticed that ERP system implementation helps in the transformation of the ownership of the company and in establishing better market competitiveness.

Keywords: ERP systems, case study, implementation, SME, developing countries.

1   Introduction

Globalization has driven companies to invest most of their resources and time in trying to maintain a competitive level. ERP systems present companies with a opportunity to increase efficiency of existing business processes as well as enabling entirely new business processes throughout organization, thus increasing productivity and reducing cycle time [1]. Motivated by the actuality of ERP implementations in Macedonia, the main goal of this research is to find out whether the implementation of such systems affects the organizational efficiency, and to what extent. The main research questions this research concentrates on are: 1) What is the situation with ERP usage in Macedonia?, 2) What was the reason for decision to implement ERP?, 3) What were the objectives of the ERP implementation? 4) What was the effect of the ERP system implementation on the company?, and 5) How the company changes its efficiency after ERP system implementation?

G. Poels (Ed.): CONFENIS 2012, LNBIP 139, pp. 198–205, 2013.
© IFIP International Federation for Information Processing 2013

The contribution of this work is the analysis of a ex-socialistic enterprise (previously state owned, now privatized) which implemented an ERP solution very early compared to companies similar in size and transformation of ownership. The paper itself is organized in six parts: the first part follows the situation with ERP implementation in Macedonia. The second part begins with a review of literature about the impact of ERP systems on performance of organizations. It continues with presenting the operational (financial) performance measures for ERP impact and the time for experiencing benefits. The third part presents the research methodology beginning with the description of the research framework. Next we bring our findings preceded by a short description of the company and the final part presents the conclusions of the research.

2   The Situation in Macedonia

The Republic of Macedonia is located in the central Balkans and gained independence from the former Socialist Federal Republic of Yugoslavia in 1991. The country became a member state of the United Nations in 1993 under the temporary title of "the Former Yugoslav Republic of Macedonia" (FYROM). The turbulent period, in the wake of the break-up of Yugoslavia inevitably impacted the Macedonian economy. In the first years after the independence, the Macedonian economy suffered the loss of large and protected market resulting in steep falls in GDP. Privatizations of state owned enterprises together with foreign investments have been performed quickly since the 90's [2]. Although the above has enabled the development of a stable macro-economic environment, the country has not been as successful in restarting its economic growth [3]. Irrespective of the size, if Macedonian companies want to operate on foreign markets, if their intention is sustainable development and durable success, they should have more efficient organizations and more competing products and services. These attributes are claimed to be achieved through ERP solutions usage. All in all, Macedonian companies in general are more interested in the implementation of software adapted to their work and needs. There is a visible awareness rising among them about the need of investment in software as a business tool. This rise is mostly due to the investments in the telecommunication and banking sector, while the growth of SMEs interest is still not satisfying.

3   Research Methodology

The objective of this study was to explore in detail the process of implementation and usage of ERP systems in a developing country and interpret the significance of factors that lead to successful implementations. Due to they nature, our research questions can be answered using the case study method [4]. We focused this research at one company and choose for a case study research model [5]. Yin defines the scope of a case study as follows: 'A case study is an empirical inquiry that: investigates a contemporary phenomenon within its real-life context, especially when the boundaries between phenomenon and context are not clearly evident' [4]. Myers stress that the case study research method is particularly well-suited to IS research, since the object of study are information systems in organizations, and "interest has shifted to organizational rather than technical issues" [6]. The research follows certain indicators of the company prior and after ERP implementation and from the other side it is a typical case among large ex-socially owned Macedonian companies which implemented ERP system solution very early compared to companies similar to it in size and ownership. Development of this case study was established by analysis of the archival data of the organization as well as analysis of the data gained during the interviews. This particular research relies on a triangulation of the following three techniques: 1) semi-structured interviews with managers (IT and CEO) within the organization, 2) employees' survey intended to test employees' perceptions about the effect of the implemented ERP system, and 3) secondary data analysis of existing organizational data comprising annual financial reports. The financial indicators movement was followed in the period before and after the system implementation. Between- (or across-) method triangulation is where two or more distinct methods are employed to measure the same phenomenon, but from different angles. The rationale is that cumulatively the weaknesses of one research method are offset by the strengths of the others [7]. The questionnaires of the semi-structured interviews and the survey are not included in this paper but can be obtained by the authors. Before continuing with the research it is essential to give a definition for the word "efficiency", as is the basic word that this work relies on. The term used here be explained with the definition from "The Concise Encyclopedia of Economics" which says: 'economic efficiency is measured not by the relationship between the physical quantities of ends and means, but by the relationship between the value of the ends and the value of the means'.

4   Findings

4.1   The Case Study Company

The shareholder company Komuna in Skopje is one of the oldest and leading producers for paper and cardboard boxes in the Republic of Macedonia. The computerization of the company started in 1998 when they bought their first computers. Regarding the software, that period the company used several separate applications in finance, accounting and material working. The rest of the processes were performed with no automation, using human hand, machines, paper and telephone. This way of organization of the work produced a lot of inefficiency and errors. Due to misunderstanding and having no control of the work, a lot of mistakes appeared and very often wrong orders were produced that laid in inventory. The company was also receiving complaints by the clients about not respecting of promised deadlines. Perceiving the current situation at that time (1998) and having a long term oriented vision, the company IT team suggested the company management implementation of an ERP system. The reason behind this proposal was implementation of new solution that will offer new functionality. According to IT manager: "the basic need for redesign and reengineering of business software solution build with technology and knowledge 15-20 years ago and in completely different economic climate, led our company to implementation of an integrated information system".

4.2   Findings from the Interviews with the CIO and the CEO

The CIO stressed that the company had milieu of goals with the implementation of the ERP system: "gaining of technological benefits, effectiveness, consistency, reaching integrated system, control, efficiency, preciseness, timeliness, operating costs reduction, rationalization within certain departments, providing quality finished work, respecting of proposed deadlines". Realization of all these goals was envisaged with implementation of customized ERP solution from Macedonian vendor Artisoft. The implementation (phased approach) started with the implementation of the financial module in April 2000. After this implementation, the complete financial work was transferred to this module. Phase by phase the following modules were added: material accounting, warehouse accounting, sales, assets, production (technical preparation of working orders), HR, personnel files, payroll and internal security data flow with consistency. Due to internal management restructuring, the second and the third phase of the implementation which perceived detailed functionalities within the production module as well as implementation of Decision Support System (DSS) tools (graphical presentations, trends, and data mining tools) were not realized. Due to the same factors Komuna also continues to use an old independent payroll application, besides having that functionality in the ERP system. Technical acceptance of the system was made in January 2003. The employees were also partially involved during the implementation phase, because of the opinion that "being detail oriented they didn't have vision of the whole system". Still they were consulted about the specific processes/procedures of their work. After the implementation, trainings for the users were conducted several times during the implementation phase and partially on departments' level after the implementation. Manuals were prepared by Artisoft and distributed to the users.

User comments afterwards were various. They went from satisfaction to complete dissatisfaction. Some reaction on department level was evident, which aroused by the fear that the work can be controlled: control of how much is produced, how long it stands in the warehouse. This is very much connected to the socio-political approach to user resistance proposed by Markus [8]. According to Markus, users resist to a system if they perceive that the project could reduce their official or unofficial power in the organization e.g. people show resistance if they feel loss of power and do not show resistance if they feel they gain power. The CEO explained during the interview that there were no metrics established prior to ERP implementation for determining how well the company achieved ERP implementation objectives and no cost benefit analysis was performed after. According to him, implementing the ERP system, the following business processes of the company became more competitive: marketing including sales and supply, production process in terms of better organization and monitoring of the financial management. Regarding the benefits brought by the system, they are reflected in improved monitoring level of strategic information about Komuna's activities. The system provides information regarding monitoring of activities that did not existed before the implementation, such as instant access to customized information to every user regardless of location and time (on 24/7 bases). Most significant monitoring information is about sales, financial flow, supply of materials for production, work orders and production itself. Other benefits that Komuna gained due to the system implementation include better visibility on creditors and debtors which increased up to 25%, improvement of the history data management up to 75%, reduction of the delivery time to 33% from average 15days to 10days reducing errors in planning process, decrease of the production cycle, optimization of the administration cycle with cutting of the overlapping functions and concurrently decreasing the administration cycle which was all the time needed to monitor, measure plan and trigger the corrective measures. The latter was one of the areas where the impact was the biggest.

4.3   Findings from the Employees' Survey

The influence of the system to employees work and their perception about the changes it brought was measured through a survey. The survey was based on a questionnaire consisted of six single answer questions. In total, 50 questionnaires were delivered through different sectors of the company. Out of them only 35 were received back, meaning that technically the survey was conducted on a sample of 35 employees. According to the answers, the respondents belonged: 8.6% to the management/operations sector, 14.3% to the finance sector, 8.6% to the material accounting, 11.4% to the warehouse, 14.3% to the sales, marketing 11.4%, production 25.7% and HR 5.7%.

The first question they were asked was "if their work position requires use of the software system (Q2)". 62.9% of them answered that it does require, 22.9% that it doesn't require, and 14.3% that "it is up to them". To the question "How much do you use the system (Q3)" 51.4% of them responded "Often", 25.7% "Sometimes", 11.4% "Never" and 11.4% "Rarely". If a cross tabulation is made between these two questions the following result in table 1 is received.

Table 1. Cross tabulation of question 2 and question 3

Cross tabulation of question 2 and 3		Question 3 (How much do you use it?)				
		Often	Some-times	Rarely	Never	Total
Question 2 (Does your work position require use of the software system?)	Yes	77.3%	22.7%			100.0%
	No		25.0%	37.5%	37.5%	100.0%
	It is up to me	20.0%	40.0%	20.0%	20.0%	100.0%
Total		51.4%	25.7%	11.4%	11.4%	100.0%

When asked the question to which extent did the system affect the difficulty of accomplishing of your tasks (question 5), 62.9% answered "it made it easier", 2.9%"it made it more complicated" and 34.3% "didn't change anything". Almost 73% of the employees, whose work position requires using of the software system and 80% of the ones saying that using of the system is up to them, answered that the system made the accomplishing of their tasks easier for them. A cross tabulation of question 5 with question 2 is shown in table 2.

Having in mind the answers per work position requirement of usage of the software system, a cross tabulation is shown in table 3 and the conclusion can be made that employees feel fairly empowered about accomplishing of their tasks.

Table 2. Cross tabulation of question 2 and question 5

Cross tabulation of question 2 and 5		Question 5 (To which extend did the system affect the difficulty of accomplishing your tasks?			
		It made it more easier	It made it more complicated	Didn't change anything	Total
Question 2 (Does your work position require use of the software system?)	Yes	72.7%	4.5%	22.7%	100.0%
	No	25.0%		75.0%	100.0%
	It is up to me	80.0%		20.0%	100.0%
Total		62.9%	2.9%	34.3%	100.0%

Table 3. Cross tabulation of question 2 and question 6

Cross tabulation of question 2 and 5		Question 6 (Does the system make you feel more empowered about accomplishing your tasks?				
		Feel more confident about the quality of my job	It is interesting for my tasks	I feel the same	No	Total
Question 2 (Does your work position require use of the software system?)	Yes	31.8%	40.9%	22.7%	4.5%	100.0%
	No		25.0%	75.0%	37.5%	100.0%
	It is up to me	40.0%	40.0%	20.0%	20.0%	100.0%
Total		25.7%	37.1%	34.3%	14.3%	100.0%

Change of the speed in doing the work compared to before the system implementation is evidenced by 34.3% of the respondents as "a lot faster", 45.7% say that they do their work "a bit faster" compared to before the system implementation and 20% say that there is "no change". All in all 80% of the respondents say that the system gave effect in speeding the process of doing the work.

4.4   Findings from the Company's Annual Reports

As third source of information, Komuna's annual reports (2001-2008) received from the Macedonian Stock Exchange were used. After extracting and processing the data from the reports and converted to financial indicators, the results are shown in table 4.

The only indicator which shows characteristic movement through the years is Labor Productivity. Following this indicator constant inclination can be noticed which indicates increasing of the employee productiveness. Employees' number declines from 473 in 2001 to 305 in 2008; however the results show that they are becoming more productive. All in all in this case financial indicators do not give good information for making firm conclusions about the effect of the ERP system implementation of the company efficiency.

Table 4. Financial indicators

	2001	2002	2003	2004	2005	2006	2007	2008
Inventory/Sales	0.17	0.12	0.15	0.14	0.15	0.14	0.14	0.14
Inventory/Total Assets	0.18	0.13	0.16	0.14	0.14	0.13	0.14	0.15
Labour Productivity	1.41	1.58	1.53	1.49	1.71	2.03	2.17	2.44
ROS	2.07	1.91	3.21	3.95	2.22	2.28	4.75	3.54
ROA	-2.04	3.02	3.85	2.01	0.55	0.71	2.96	2.22
Profit Margin	-2.01	2.68	3.73	2.08	0.61	0.76	2.96	2.06
Inventory Turnover	4.75	7.01	5.75	6.49	6.05	6.61	6.39	6.84
Assets Turnover	1.01	1.13	1.03	0.97	0.90	0.94	1.00	1.08
AR Turnover	5.49	4.64	5.36	4.96	4.36	4.55	4.92	4.85

5   Conclusion

Implementation of Enterprise Resources Planning (ERP) systems in organizations in developed countries is an issue that has been in focus of interest over decade ago. The situation in Macedonia even though a bit time delayed is following the same path. The research of the ERP implementation by the factory "Komuna" chronologically followed through the period of seven years lead to conclusion that determining the ERP implementation effect on the company efficiency is rather complex task.As the ERP system is not isolated from the rest of the influences on organization, it is very complicated to assign certain advantages and disadvantages solely to its introduction. More precisely, using three different techniques for the case study method the results showed the following:

The conducted interviews with the managerial stuff revealed the changes that the system brought: different processes gained on competitiveness, the organization gained better visibility and monitoring of activities, improved decision making, improved serving of the customers, organization and optimization of the processes and of the production cycle.

On the other side the interview with the employees showed that employees see benefit in using the system and fair percentage of them use it even though their work position does not require that. The largest percent of them state that using of the system is very important for their work. Some reactions have been evident within the departments where the system reduced the previously existing privileges- taking of the power. The employees also state that the system made accomplishing of their tasks easier, as well as it brought speed in accomplishing of their work. The largest percent of the respondents don't feel that the system made them more confident about accomplishing of their tasks, but feel that it is interesting for their tasks. Regarding the financial indicators, their movement does not give good information for making conclusions. The only indicator which shows characteristic movement through the years is Labor productivity. Following this indicator constant inclination can be noticed which indicates increasing of the employee productiveness. Employees' number declines from 473 in 2001 to 305 in 2008; whilst the results show that they are becoming more productive. Summarizing all this effects it can be said that ERP systems implementation like in the case presented require time, money and will of management, but the effect is improvement of the company's efficiency, which further on helps in transformation of the ownership capital and more than all better market competitiveness. Generalization of the results should be given careful consideration, because the research is done for single case. According to (Garson, 2008), no generalization to a population beyond cases similar to those studied should be made. This means that the results of this research are applicable to the companies of similar size, production oriented. For this kind of companies it is justifiable to be said that if properly conducted, the implementation of ERP solutions will bring efficiency improvement.

References

1. Shanks, G., Seddon, P.: Enterprise resource planning (ERP) systems. J. of Information Technology 15, 243–244 (2000)
2. Bah, E., Brada, J.C., Yigit, T.: With a little help from our friends: The effect of USAID assistance on SME growth in a transition economy. J. of Comparative Economics 39, 205–220 (2011)
3. PWC, Guide to Doing Business and Investing in Macedonia (2008)
4. Yin, R.K.: Case Study Research: Design and Methods, 3rd edn., vol. 5. Sage Publications, Inc., Thousand Oaks (2003)
5. Sarker, S., Lee, A.S.: Using a case study to test the role of three key social enablers in ERP implementation. Inf. & Man. 40, 813–829 (2003)
6. Myers, M.D.: Qualitative research in information systems. MISQ 21, 241–242 (1997)
7. Arksey, H.P.T., Knight, P.T., Knight, P.: Interviewing for social scientists: an introductory resource with examples. SAGE (1999)
8. Markus, M.L.: Power, Politics, and MIS Implementation. Comm. of the ACM 26, 430–444 (1983)

Enterprise Information Systems Security: A Case Study in the Banking Sector

Peggy E. Chaudhry[1], Sohail S. Chaudhry[1], Kevin D. Clark[1], and Darryl S. Jones[2]

[1] Department of Management and Operations/International Business,
Villanova School of Business, Villanova University, Villanova, PA 19085 USA
{peggy.chaudhry,sohail.chaudhry,kevin.d.clark}@villanova.edu
[2] MBA Program, Villanova School of Business, Villanova University, Villanova, PA 19085
djones21@villanova.edu

Abstract. One important module of Enterprise Information System (EIS) is the development and implementation of the security component of EIS. Furthermore, this EIS Security structure needs to be monitored through the corporate governance of the firm. Based on a literature review and our previous work, we identified four key pillars of a model for EIS Security. These pillars are Security Policy (e.g., set rules for employee behavior), Security Awareness (e.g., continued education of employees), Access Control (e.g., access linked to employee job function), and Top Level Management Support (e.g., engrain information security into the company's culture). We explore the relevance of this model using a case study approach by way of interviewing top-level information systems mangers in the banking sector. We validate the model through using key informant in-depth interviews and qualitative research methods.

Keywords: Enterprise information systems, security, conceptual model, banking sector, case study.

1   Introduction

Enterprise Information Systems (EIS) are companywide Information Technology (IT) systems that companies use to combine multiple business functions information into one data warehouse. They "enable a company to integrate the data used throughout its entire organization [1]." The plethora of information technologies developed and improved over the last few decades has made business decisions easier for managers who now have all of the relevant information available from one access point without the fear of missing or overlapping information. A problem that results from this convenience is that all company information is now available in one location. This centrality makes a company's intellectual property, one of its core competitive advantages, more vulnerable. Security breaches (malicious or unintentional) can result in continuity disruption, poor reliability of information, lowered effectiveness and efficiency of processes, and can even have legal implications. The current events of *external* information security problems related to information access, such as the

G. Poels (Ed.): CONFENIS 2012, LNBIP 139, pp. 206–214, 2013.
© IFIP International Federation for Information Processing 2013

hacker who obtained the personal information of 77 million consumers at Sony's PlayStation Network is testimony to the problems that companies will continue to face with security breaches [2]. However, in this paper, we are not addressing so-called "Hack attacks" but will be evaluating the risk of *internal* information security dilemmas, such as employees of the firm either intentionally or unintentionally compromising the data stored. Overall, firms must safeguard their employee access to the "keys to the kingdom" (e.g., accounts and passwords) [3]. Until recently, most of the concern regarding security in enterprise information systems was more of a technical nature (e.g., viruses, worms, Trojans, etc.), however, more research is finding that human interaction with the systems is the real cause of most breaches [4], [5], and [6]. In fact, Sachlar Paulus, Senior Vice-President of Product and Security Governance of SAP (a global EIS provider) has stated that "The weakest link is still people … the biggest problems occur wherever technology comes into contact with people who need to administer, manage, or even use IT security functionality [7]."

2   Literature Review

Up until the last few years, most of the research done on corporate dealings with security in EIS focused mainly on the technical aspect of IT such as firewalls and anti-virus software which rely more on technology than the employees using the systems. In fact, as recent as 2005, Siponen believed "the importance of the socio-organizational nature of (E)IS is not recognized seriously enough by traditional Information Systems Security methods" [8]. Researchers are now starting to realize that the human interaction with the EIS of the firm is just as important, if not more, than the technical -and that information security cannot be achieved solely through these technological tools [9]. Many researchers now believe the biggest threat to information security remains *internal* [4], [10], and [11]. Swartz [12] outlined several cases in which employees stole data while still working for their company, yet the majority of employee security breaches occur accidently or unintentionally [5] and [6]. There are currently many theories on the best way to combat these issues. These range from the importance of cultivating an information security policy to significance of employee training and awareness. Overall, just a few researchers have developed frameworks to help companies secure their systems [11], [13], and [14].

2.1   Information Security Policy

An information security policy is the set of rules, standards, practices, and procedures that the company employs to maintain a secure IT system. It has been said that the "credibility of the entire information security program of an organization depends upon a well-drafted information security policy [15]." Many experts now think that the development of an information security policy is one of the most practical ways to preserve protected systems [14] and [16]. Knapp et al. [14] believe that "the development of an information security policy is the first step toward preparing an organization against attacks from internal and external sources." They actually developed an information security policy process that companies can use to develop and analyze their current programs.

2.2   Employee Awareness

"Creation and maintenance of security awareness include both individual and collective activities, i.e. education and awareness-raising initiatives, e.g. emails, pamphlets, mouse pads, formal presentations, and discussion groups" [17]. Many researchers now believe that employee awareness is one of the best ways to protect a company's data [13] and [18]. In fact, empirical research found that awareness creation is the most effective information security measure [17]. Security training and education programs should aim to make employees recognize the legitimacy of information security policy to safeguard the firm [19].

2.3   Access Control

Access control is defined as the process a company takes to limit the access an employee has to various functions of the business; particularly functions not relevant to their position or containing more information than they should have access to [20]. She and Thuraisingham [20] stated that many companies now use Role Based Access Control (RBAC), which is a way to limit employee access by permissions, roles, users, and constraints. Access control requirements can be driven by a need for customer, stockholder, and insurer confidence; privacy of personal information; prevention of unauthorized financial asset distribution and adherence to professional standards, among others [21].   In addition, so long as information is stored and consumed within one organization, security policy and access controls can be optimized for internal use, and access by people from outside of the company can be prevented [22]. However most enterprise information systems are connected to the internet, which can blur the boundaries of enterprise information systems, leads organizations to face new attack threats [23].

2.4   Top Level Management Support

One important factor that most researchers agree must be adhered to in policy development is the support of top level management [24] and [25]. The best way to get employees to comply with information security policies is to engrain the policy into the organizational culture of the company. The overarching objective of information security management is to convert the organization's security policy into a set of requirements that can be communicated to the organization, measured, and imposed [26].   Basically, the better the top management support of information security, the greater the preventative efforts a firm (and its employees) will make [11]. Overall, top management support is essential to security governance success [27].

2.5   Corporate Governance

The research of Weill and Ross [28] on IT governance in 300 companies found that "IT governance is a mystery to key decision-makers at most companies" and that only about one-third of the managers' surveyed understood how IT is governed at his or her company (p. 26). Engulfing all of these methods for security protection is the idea of corporate governance. For information security, corporate governance is the way top level management and the board decide to run the IT department, and in turn, information system security. This is where the true decisions on how to attack a possible weakness are made. Solms [29] posits that "Information Security Governance is now accepted as an integral part of good IT and Corporate Governance (Information Security Governance)." Khoo et al. [30] stated that information security governance is a subset of corporate governance that relates to the security of information systems, and because the board of directors is ultimately in charge of corporate governance information security must start at the top.

2.6   Implementation

The careful selection and implementation of security policies, standards and procedures will determine if the overall security program will support the organization's mission [31]. So important is the implementation of these systems that national and international standards have been developed including ISO 27001, ISO 13569, GAISP (Generally Accepted Information Security Practices), and the Gramm-Leach Bliley (GLB) Act, among others [31]. Sengupta et al. [32] affirms that ineffective implementation of security policy leads to weaknesses in enterprise information systems security.

3   Conceptual Framework

We have developed a conceptual model in Fig. 1 for EIS security that encompasses the major themes found in our literature review. This model is a slightly revised version of the conceptual model that was developed earlier [33], [34]. In its simplest form, we draw the analogy that the company's EIS security is the roof that protects four main pillars: security policy, security awareness, access control, and top level management support (TLMS). Each of these pillars has an element of implementation required for sound EIS Security. The basic solid foundation of this 'house' is the company's corporate governance. These four pillars are the processes that management and the board of directors can choose to implement to make the system as secure as possible. Having all four pillars is the best way to make the enterprise information system secure, however removing any one of these columns can truly diminish the stability/security of the entire system. Below is a pictorial representation of the model.

4   Information Security in the Banking Sector

MWR Labs identified three banking sector security risks facing the industry and two of these, data loss prevention and identity & access management, are closely related to our model [35].The banking sector is governed by a regulatory framework to safeguard information. To highlight the regulatory governance of financial institutions to implement their information security, we briefly describe the role of the Federal Financial Institutions Examination Council (FFIEC) and the GLB Act.

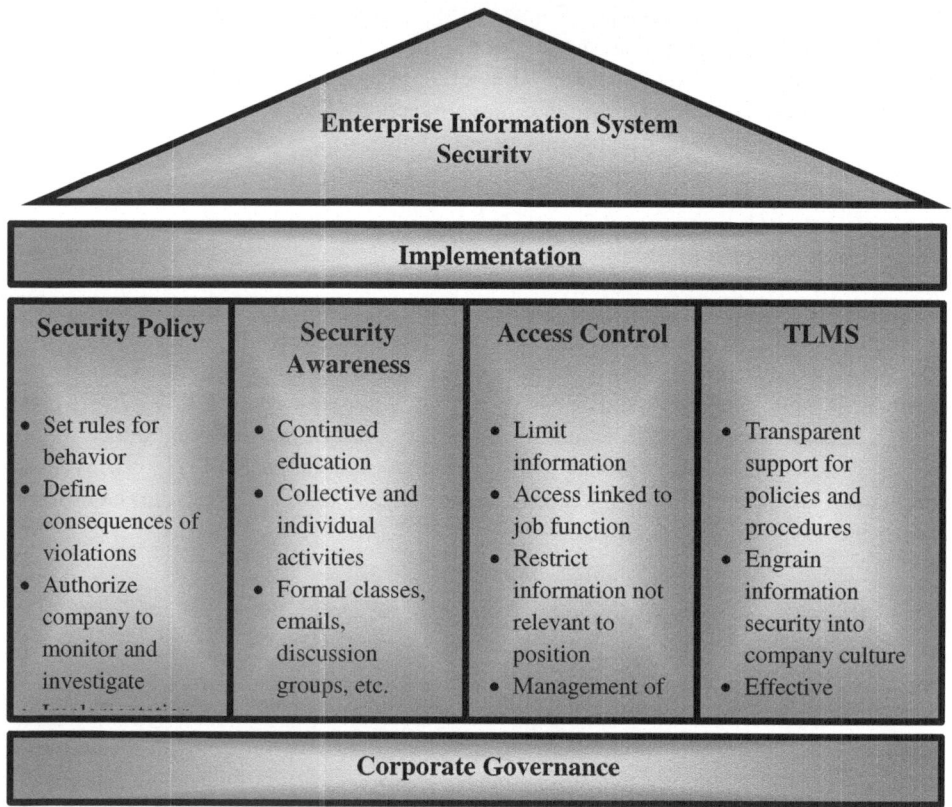

Fig. 1. Conceptual model for enterprise information system security

4.1   The Federal Financial Institutions Examination Council

The FFIEC was established in 1979 and its primary goal is "[A]a formal interagency body empowered to prescribe uniform principles, standards, and report forms for the federal examination of financial institutions by the Board of Governors of the Federal Reserve System, the Federal Deposit Insurance Corporation, the National Credit Union Administration, the Office of the Comptroller of the Currency, and the Consumer Financial Protection Bureau" [36]. The FFIEC key areas to be addressed by financial institutions to implement information security measures [37] as 1) security process (e.g. governance issues); 2) information security risk assessment (e.g., steps in gathering information); 3) information security strategy (e.g., architecture considerations);

4) security controls implementation (e.g., access control); 5) security monitoring (e.g., network intrusion detection systems); and 6) security process monitoring and updating.

4.2   The Gramm-Leach-Bliley Act

The FDIC provides an outline of compliance issues related to the development and implementation of Information Security Program governed by the GLB Act in three key areas: involvement of the board of directors, assessment of risk, and managing and controlling risk [38]. The detailed security guidelines that banks are given to comply with the GLB Act center on [39]: 1) access controls on customer information systems; 2) access restrictions at physical locations containing customer information; 3) encryption of electronic customer information; 4) procedures to ensure that system modifications do not affect security; 5) dual control procedures, segregation of duties, and employee background checks; 6) monitoring systems to detect actual attacks on or intrusions into customer information systems; 7) response programs that specify actions to be taken when unauthorized access has occurred; and 8) protection from physical destruction or damage to customer information.

5   Qualitative Analysis of Personal Interviews with Senior Information Officers in the Banking Sector

We validate the model through using key informant in-depth interviews and qualitative research methods.   We interviewed senior information officers dealing with security aspects at four banking institutions in the Philadelphia area.   Next, we present the highlights of these interviews with the senior information officers based on a content analysis of the themes in the interviews.

It was quite surprising to learn from the interviews that all the four senior information officers in the banking industry agreed with the proposed conceptual security model. In addition, they all rated the four pillars of security policy, security awareness, access control, and top level management support as being extremely important for their organizations.

Under the security policy pillar, three of the four officers stated that another key element is the training of the employees. Other key elements related to security mentioned by the senior information officers include the training of top-level management and simplifying the communication of the policy to all levels of the organization.

Some of the most important aspects associated with security awareness mentioned by the senior information officers were using third-party audits to test the system and to provide training with minimal technical jargon during the training sessions.

For access control, the overarching element mentioned by all four senior information officers was the development of sophisticated measures to limit access. In addition, other key elements included avoiding carte blanche access to any employee and requiring the employees to 'sign off' on greater security privileges.

In regards to the most important elements of top level management support, all four senior information officers stated that top level management involvement is required due to stipulations imposed by the regulatory bodies in the banking sector. One manager stressed that overseeing the implementation of the system was a key role of top management at his financial institution.

6   Conclusions and Future Research

We identified four major themes that impact the security issues within firms. These four factors are identified as security policy documentation, access control, employee awareness, and top level management support. Based on these factors, a conceptual framework based on relevant literature was presented within the context of corporate governance for enterprise information systems. To test the framework, in-depth interviews with IT officers using a cross-section of companies in the banking sector were used to confirm the model. In the future, we will administer a survey instrument to a larger population of IT officers to further study the various issues that have been exposed in this research within the context of enterprise information systems security.

References

1. Davenport, T.: Putting the Enterprise into the Enterprise System. Harvard Business Review 76(4), 121–131 (1998)
2. Sherr, I.: Sony Faces Lawsuit Over PlayStation Network Breach (April 28, 2011), http://online.wsj.com/article/BT-CO-20110428-720452.html (accessed on April 30, 2011)
3. Cyber-Ark Snooping Survey (April 2011), http://www.cyber-ark.com/downloads/pdf/2011-Snooping-Survey-data.pdf (accessed on April 30, 2011)
4. Boss, S., Kirsch, L., Angermeier, I., Shingler, R., Boss, R.: If Someone is Watching, I'll Do What I'm Asked: Mandatoriness, Control, and Information Security. European Journal of Information Systems 18(2), 151–164 (2009)
5. Keller, S., Powell, A., Horstmann, B., Predmore, C., Crawford, C.: Information Security Threats and Practices in Small Businesses. Information Systems Management 22(2), 7–19 (2005)
6. Sumner, M.: Information Security Threats: A Comparative Analysis of Impact, Probability, and Preparedness. Information Systems Management 26(1), 2–12 (2009)
7. Walsh, K.: The ERP Security Challenge (January 8, 2008), http://www.cio.com/article/216940/The_ERP_Security_Challenge (accessed on April 30, 2011)
8. Siponen, M.T.: An Analysis of the Traditional IS Security Approaches: Implications for Research and Practice. European Journal of Information Systems 14(3), 303–315 (2005)
9. Herath, T., Rao, H.R.: Protection Motivation and Deterrence: A Framework for Security Policy Compliance in Organisations. European Journal of Information Systems 18(2), 106–125 (2009)
10. Vroom, C., von Solms, R.: Towards Information Security Behavioural Compliance. Computers & Security 23(3), 191–198 (2004)

11. Kankanhalli, A., Teo, H.H., Tan, B.C.Y., Wei, K.K.: An Integrative Study of Information Systems Security Effectiveness. International Journal of Information Management 23(2), 139–154 (2003)
12. Swartz, N.: Protecting Information from Insiders. Information Management Journal 41(3), 20–24 (2007)
13. D'aubeterre, F., Singh, R., Iyer, L.: Secure Activity Resource Coordination: Empirical Evidence of Enhanced Security Awareness in Designing Secure Business Processes. European Journal of Information Systems 17(5), 528–542 (2008)
14. Knapp, K., Morris, R., Marshall, T., Byrd, T.: Information Security Policy: An Organizational-Level Process Model. Computers & Security 28(7), 493–508 (2009)
15. Kadam, A.W.: Information Security Policy Development and Implementation. Information Systems Security 16(5), 246–256 (2007)
16. Myyry, L., Siponen, M., Pahnila, S., Vartiainen, T., Vance, A.: What Levels of Moral Reasoning and Values Explain Adherence to Information Security Rules? An Empirical Study. European Journal of Information Systems 18(2), 126–139 (2009)
17. Hagen, J.M., Albrechtsen, E., Hovden, J.: Implementation and Effectiveness of Organizational Information Security Measures. Information Management & Computer Security 16(4), 377–397 (2008)
18. Chang, A.J.T., Yeh, Q.J.: On Security Preparations against Possible IS Threats across Industries. Information Management & Computer Security 14(4), 343–360 (2006)
19. Son, J.: Out of Fear or Desire? Toward a Better Understanding of Employees' Motivation to follow IS Security Policies. Information and Management 48, 296–302 (2011)
20. She, W., Thuraisingham, B.: Security for Enterprise Resource Planning Systems. Information Systems Security 16, 152–163 (2007)
21. Sandhu, R., Cope, E.J., Feinstein, H.L., Youman, C.E.: Role Based Access Control Models. IEEE (1996) 0018-9162
22. Sinderen, M.: Challenges and Solutions in Enterprise Computing. Enterprise Information Systems 2(4), 341–346 (2008)
23. Wang, J.W., Gao, F., Ip, W.H.: Measurement of Resilience and its Application to Enterprise Information Systems. Enterprise Information Systems 4(2), 215–223 (2010)
24. von Solms, R., von Solms, S.H.B.: Information Security Governance: A Model based on the Direct-Control Cycle. Computers & Security 25(6), 408–412 (2006)
25. Doughty, K.: Implementing Enterprise Security: A Case Study. Computers & Security 22(2), 99–114 (2003)
26. Tracey, R.P.: IT Security Management and Business Process Automation: Challenges, Approaches, and Rewards. Information Systems Security 16, 114–122 (2007)
27. Da Veiga, A., Eloff, J.: An Information Security Governance Framework. Information Systems Management 24(4), 361–372 (2007)
28. Weill, P., Ross, J.: A Matrixed Approach to Designing IT Governance. Sloan Management Review 46(2), 26–34 (2005)
29. von Solms, S.H.B.: Information Security Governance: Compliance Management vs. Operational Management. Computers & Security 24, 443–447 (2005)
30. Khoo, B., Harris, P., Hartman, S.: Information Security Governance of Enterprise Information Systems: An Approach to Legislative Compliant. International Journal of Management and Information Systems 14(3), 49–55 (2010)
31. Peltier, T.R.: Information Security Policies, Procedures, and Standards: Guidelines for Effective Security Management. Auerbach Publications, Florida (2002)

32. Sengupta, A., Mazumdar, C., Bagchi, A.: A Formal Methodology for Detecting Managerial Vulnerabilities and Threats in an Enterprise Information System. Journal of Network System Management 19(3), 319–342 (2011)
33. Chaudhry, P.E., Chaudhry, S.S., Reese, R., Jones, D.S.: Enterprise Information Systems Security: A Conceptual Framework. In: Møller, C., Chaudhry, S. (eds.) CONFENIS 2011. LNBIP, vol. 105, pp. 118–128. Springer, Heidelberg (2012)
34. Chaudhry, P., Chaudhry, S.S., Reese, R.: Developing a Model for Enterprise Information Systems Security. Journal of Academic Research in Economics 3(3), 243–254 (2011)
35. Banking Sector Security, A Report by MWR Labs, http://labs.mwrinfosecurity.com/assets/130/mwri_annual-research-banking-review-2010-08.pdf (accessed on April 24)
36. About the FFIEC, http://www.ffiec.gov/about.htm (accessed on April 24, 2012)
37. Federal Financial Institutions Examination Council, Information Security (2006), http://ithandbook.ffiec.gov/ITBooklets/FFIEC_ITBooklet_InformationSecurity.pdf (accessed on April 24, 2012)
38. FDIC Law, Regulations, Related Acts, http://www.fdic.gov/regulations/laws/rules/2000-8660.html (accessed on April 24, 2012)
39. Langin, D.J.: Gramm-Leach-Bliley Security Requirements: Keeping Robbers and Regulators from the Door, http://www.securitymanagement.com/archive/library/gramm_tech 0902.pdf (accessed on April 24, 2012)

Group Preference Aggregation
Based on ELECTRE Methods
for ERP System Selection

Suzana de França Dantas Daher and Adiel Teixeira de Almeida

Federal University of Pernambuco, Management Engineering Department
Cx. Postal 7462, Recife, PE, 50.630-970, Brazil
{suzanadaher,almeidaatd}@gmail.com

Abstract. The ability of enterprise information systems, such as enterprise resource planning (ERP), manufacturing executive systems (MES) and customer relation management (CRM), to improve production and business performance are demanding more attention from enterprises, since increase in competitive advantages is a goal to be reached. Integration of all the information flowing through a company is a key characteristic of ERP systems. Enterprise systems are not developed in-house and so, in order to implement an ERP project successfully, organizations must purchase ERP systems which can be aligned with their needs. In a group decision context where all opinions and preferences must be taken into account, choosing the most suitable alternative may be a hard work. In this study, a group preference aggregation approach based on a combination of ELECTRE II and ELECTRE IV method is presented within the context of ERP project selection.

Keywords: Group preferences, multicriteria decision aid, ELECTRE II, ELECTRE IV, ERP selection.

1 Introduction

It is well known that market competition transforms the way in which companies deal with their business and organizational environments. Companies are looking for tools, methodologies and operational policies that support them to reduce total costs, maximize return on investment, shorten lead times and be more responsive to customer demand [1]. An Enterprise Resource Planning (ERP) system is an Enterprise Information System (EIS) designed to improve operational efficiency and enhance organizational performance. An ERP improves operational efficiency by integrating business processes and providing better access to integrated data across the entire enterprise, while to enhance business efficacy, means that a company may review (or redesign) its business practices by using an ERP [2]. Integrating business processes means fostering a seamless integration of all the information flowing through a company, including financial and accounting; human resource information; supply chain information and customer information [3,4].

G. Poels (Ed.): CONFENIS 2012, LNBIP 139, pp. 215–222, 2013.
© IFIP International Federation for Information Processing 2013

Deciding which is the most suitable ERP solution is often a difficult task for many companies. Therefore, decide among preselected alternatives using criteria that sometimes conflict with each other, based on the enterprise's needs, has led researchers to investigate better ways to evaluate and select ERP systems. Several studies have been conducted to identify models and methodologies to support decision makers in making technology acquisitions, including in the selection of software packages. Within the context of using a multicriteria decision making for this, some papers use analytic network process (ANP) and analytic hierarchy process (AHP) approaches [1,5,6] to select an ERP. For the same purpose, it is possible to find combinations of these methods with Delphi Methods and goal programming [7] and by using an artificial neural network and an ANP [8]. A combination of a quality function deployment (QFD), fuzzy linear regression and zeroone goal programming to develop a framework for an ERP system selection can be found in [9]. Fuzzy approaches [10] some of which are combined with rough set and TOPSIS methods [11] have been adopted for a selection problem. Data Envelopment Analysis (DEA) approach has also been applied to the process of selecting an ERP system [12]. Outranking methods such as ELECTRE [13] and PROMETHEE [14] are also found in the literature.

Organizations select and implement ERP systems so as to obtain a variety of tangible and intangible benefits and for strategic reasons. The evaluation process of ERP systems needs to take many criteria into account [15] which include organizational factors such as the complexity of the business; dealing with change management, cost drivers, its functional requirements, system flexibility, system scalability, and also external factors such as its relationship with supply chain partners, and the pressure of value networks may affect the ERP selection process [16]. A multicriteria decision making must consider such diversity in order to better evaluate the alternatives.

Although most studies are conducted based on a single decision maker (DM), there is a strong possibility that in several organizations, an ERP system will be selected by a group. Multicriteria group decision making involves individuals who provide their preferences for a set of alternatives with respect to a set of attributes [17]. Diverging opinions may arise since DMs have their own unique characteristics with regard to their knowledge, skills, and personality. Group decision making involves two or more decision makers who take responsibility for the choice. This study deals with how support a group of individuals to achieve a collective decision when selecting an ERP system. The methodology adopted considered that DMs act in accordance with their own interests and there is no information about their relative importance to each other [18]. Group decision making has a wide diversity of applications and has been the study focus of several research studies which is indicative of its relevance [19,20,21,22].

This study sets out the methodology proposed by [18] based on a combination of ELECTRE II and ELECTRE IV methods. The most widely used method in outranking methods is ELECTRE [23]. Outranking methods are particularly suitable for decision-making through the notion of weak preference and incomparability [24].

The remainder of this paper is organized as follows. Section 2 presents the model proposed and Section 3 describes a numerical application to illustrate the applicability of the model in the context of selecting an ERP system. The final section gives the conclusions of the study.

2 Model Proposed

ELECTRE is a family of multicriteria decision analysis methods and its acronym stands for ELimination Et Choix Traduisant la REalité [23]. This family seeks to obtain a set of N alternatives that outrank those which do not belong to the subset N. ELECTRE assumes that DMs are able to provide intercriteria information, which reflect the relative importance among the k objectives (criteria weights).

The model proposed assumes that the decision problem is well structured and a set A of n alternatives and a set C of k evaluation criteria are also prior defined. A decision matrix $D = [d_{ij}]_{nxk}$ can be defined for each DM, in which the element dij represents the performance evaluation of the alternative a_i in accordance with criterion C_j. Note that if m DM exists, m decision matrices (n x k) are established.

This model includes the aggregation of individual priorities and a combination of ELECTRE II and ELECTRE IV methods [18] and is organized in three steps. The first step involves ELECTRE II so as to generate individual rankings of alternatives. The outranking relation is built by using concordance and discordance indices. A concordance index $C(a,b)$ represents the coalition of arguments in favor of the statement "a is at least as good as b" or in other words "a outranks b". A discordance index $D(a,b)$ is used to measure the arguments that may cast some doubt upon the latter statement. These indices are used to construct two pre-orders based on a strong ($a\ S^S b$) outranking relation and a weak outranking relation ($a\ S_w\ b$). Finally strong and weak rankings are deduced to obtain the final ranking for each DM. The outranking relations (strong and weak) between two alternatives a and b are presented as follows [23]:

$$a\ S^s b \iff \begin{cases} C(a,b) \geq c^+ \\ D(a,b) \leq d^+ \\ \sum_{j:gj(a)>gj(b)} w_j > \sum_{j:gj(a)<gj(b)} w_j \end{cases} \quad (1)$$

$$a\ S_w b \iff \begin{cases} C(a,b) \geq c^- \\ D(a,b) \leq d^- \\ \sum_{j:gj(a)>gj(b)} w_j > \sum_{j:gj(a)<gj(b)} w_j \end{cases} \quad (2)$$

Where $g_j(a)$ denote the evaluation of action a on criterion g_j, for all $a \in A$ and $j \in C$. In the second step of the evaluation, all individual rankings are brought together to create a global matrix of preferences (n x m) and, the third step is for aggregating all individual preferences by using the ELECTRE IV method. According to [25], ELECTRE IV was developed so as to rank actions without introducing any weighting of the criteria. This method is suitable for the last step of the model proposed since all DMs are considered to have the same weight. Note that ELECTRE IV is used in cases in which there is a pseudo-criterion family and its main feature is the absence of a weighting related to the relative importance of the criteria.

3 Selecting an ERP System: A Numerical Application

In this section, a fictitious case study was drawn up using ERP characteristics found in the literature to illustrate how the proposed model can be applied to selecting an ERP system for a Brazilian airline. Air services for the transport of passengers and freight is a highly competitive market and the need for useful tools and techniques to reduce costs and improve operational efficiency seems absolutely vital if an organization is to be competitive.

This company has to deal with inefficient operational procedures and an IT/IS legacy system. In order to improve its competitiveness, senior managers have announced the launch of several projects including an ERP system and the reengineering of complex business processes with a view to enhancing the effectiveness of its operational procedures and to responding better to its customers' demands.

Four decision makers are involved in the ERP selection process: the financial manager (DM1), the IT/IS manager (DM2), the operational manager (DM3) and the customer relation manager (DM4). These DMs are also responsible for deciding on and accepting the evaluation criteria for the selection process. An analyst should conduct the evaluations of the criteria.

ISO/IEC 9126-1 is a standard that addresses quality model definition and its use as framework for software evaluation. Therefore criteria for software projects are usually established based on this standard. However it is possible to organize criteria according to other aspects and a more complete list of criteria can be found at [6]. Table 1 presents the selected criteria for this case study. Four ERP system alternatives (A1, A2, A3 and A4) are considered for this problem. All criteria and alternatives are acceptable to all DMs.

Decision model first step: individual rankings. The first step of the model comprises defining individual preferences by obtaining a preorder from each DM. The evaluation matrix is the same for all DMs since there is no modification as to evaluating the ERP products in each criterion for each DM. The evaluation matrix is shown in Table 2 and the concordance and discordance coefficients with their corresponding parameters for each DM are presented in Table 3.

The criteria weights (inter-criteria information) of each DM are shown in Table 4.

ELECTRE II is run using the data from the above tables. Table 5 summarizes the preorders obtained for each DM after the application of the method.

Decision model second step: obtaining a matrix of global evaluation. In this step, the analyst must collect all individual rankings and compile them in a global evaluation matrix. For this matrix, DMs are considered as criteria and their rankings correspond to the evaluations of the alternatives. The higher the

Table 1. Criteria adopted for selecting an ERP system

	Criteria	Criteria group	Meaning of the criterion
C1	Completeness	Functional	This is defined as the degree to which the software satisfies the functional requirements (uses a 5-level ordinal scale)
C2	Number of simultaneous users	Functional	Number of simultaneous users that can be linked to and served by the system
C3	DBMS Standards	Portability	Breadth of database management systems that can be accessed by the software package
C4	Number of modules	Maintainability	Average size of independent code units
C5	Time behavior	Efficiency	Ability of the software package to produce results in a reasonable amount of time relative to the size of the data (in milliseconds)
C6	Length of experience	Vendor	Experience of vendor in developing software products (uses a 5-level ordinal scale)
C7	License cost	Cost	License cost of the product in terms of number of users (in monetary units)
C8	Installation and implementation Cost	Cost	Cost of installing and implementing the product (in monetary units)

Table 2. Decision matrix

	C1	C2	C3	C4	C5	C6	C7	C8
A1	4	5000	4	8	0.3	4	0.7	1.8
A2	5	3000	5	12	0.6	5	0.5	1.3
A3	3	4500	4	10	0.2	4	0.6	1.7
A4	5	4000	3	5	0.7	5	0.4	2.0

Table 3. Concordance and discordance coefficients for each DM

	c^+	c^-	d^+	d^-
DM1	0.8	0.6	0.4	0.5
DM2	0.7	0.5	0.3	0.4
DM3	0.8	0.5	0.3	0.4
DM4	0.9	0.6	0.3	0.5

Table 4. Normalized weights of each DM's criteria

	C1	C2	C3	C4	C5	C6	C7	C8
DM1	0.175	0.175	0.082	0.221	0.043	0.117	0.093	0.094
DM2	0.081	0.101	0.086	0.333	0.005	0.081	0.188	0.125
DM3	0.102	0.004	0.005	0.200	0.136	0.149	0.370	0.034
DM4	0.035	0.035	0.198	0.167	0.056	0.232	0.211	0.066

Table 5. Table of preorders for each DM

Ranking	DM1	DM2	DM3	DM4
1st	A2	A2	A2,A4	A2
2nd	A3	A3	A3	A3
3rd	A1	A1	A1	A1,A4
4th	A4	A4		

numerical evaluation of an alternative is, the better its position in the preorder, as shown in Table 6.

Table 6. Matrix of global evaluation

	DM1	DM2	DM3	DM4
A1	2	2	2	2
A2	3	3	4	3
A3	1	1	3	1
A4	4	4	1	4

Decision model third step: obtaining a group ranking. Given that there is no intercriteria information, ELECTRE IV could be applied and the following ranking is obtained (Table 7). Note that since the evaluation of an alternative corresponds to its position, any difference between alternatives implies a strict preference. Some incomparability occurred among A1, A3 and A4. Therefore,

Table 7. Global ranking of alternatives

Ranking	Alternatives
1st	A2
2nd	A1, A3, A4

alternative A2 which was ranked in first place is the one selected. Actually in this numerical problem, alternative A2 is a consensual alternative since it is considered as the best option by all DMs. If two or more alternatives are ranked equal first in the ranking, the DMs must review their preferences in order to achieve a group final recommendation for only one of them.

4   Final Remarks and Conclusions

ERP Systems have an extremely important role in helping organizations to realize their corporative strategic planning goals. Companies are looking for tools, methodologies and operational policies that support them to reduce total costs, maximize return on investment, shorten lead times and which will help them be more responsive to customers demands. However, during the ERP selection and implementation process they may well also incur high costs and face potential high risks.

This study presents an approach to support a group of decision makers to select an ERP system for a Brazilian airline. The model proposed combines two ELECTRE methods (ELECTRE II and ELECTRE IV). ELECTRE II was used to provide individual rankings of alternatives and ELECTRE IV to generate a global ranking using an approach that aggregates individual priorities.

An important observation to be made is that different results could appear if in the last step of the model proposed, the ELECTRE IV method should be changed to another other method such as the Borda Count or Condorcet. This modification is possible since it is not necessary to evaluate weights given by DMs. However, the analyst must consider the fact that these methods are based only on positions in the ranking (the Borda Count is a positional voting method while Condorcet performs a pairwise comparison of alternatives to identify the preference of the majority of the DMs) and consequently provides less information to the selection process.

Acknowledgment. This study is part of a research project funded by the Brazilian Research Council (CNPq). The authors also acknowledge the financial support given by CAPES.

References

1. Wei, C.-C., Chien, C.-F., Wang, M.-J.J.: An AHP-based approach to ERP system selection. Int. J. Production Economics 96, 47–62 (2005)
2. Chou, S.-W., Chang, Y.-C.: The implementation factors that influence the ERP (enterprise resource planning) benefits. Decision Support Systems 46(1), 149–157 (2008)
3. Nah, F.F.-H., Lau, J.L.-S., Kuang, J.: Critical factors for successful implementation of enterprise systems. Business Process Management Journal 7(3), 285–296 (2001)
4. Davenport, T.: Putting the enterprise into the enterprise system. Harvard Business Review 76(4), 121–131 (1998)
5. Liang, C., Li, Q.: Enterprise information system project selection with regard to BOCR. International Journal of Project Management 26, 810–820 (2008)
6. Jadhav, A.S., Sonar, R.M.: Evaluating and selecting software packages: A review. Information and Software Technology 51, 555–563 (2009)
7. Lee, J.W., Kim, S.H.: An integrated approach for interdependent information system project selection. International Journal of Project Management 19, 111–118 (2001)
8. Yazgan, H.R., Boran, S., Goztepe, K.: An ERP software selection process with using artificial neural network based on analytic network process approach. Expert Systems with Applications 36, 9214–9222 (2009)
9. Karsak, E.E., Ozogul, C.O.: An integrated decision making approach for ERP system selection. Expert Systems with Applications 36, 660–667 (2009)

10. Lee, H., Shen, P., Chih, W.: A fuzzy multiple criteria decision making model for software selection. In: IEEE International Conference on Fuzzy Systems, pp. 1709–1713 (2004)
11. Huiqun, H., Guang, S.: ERP software selection using the rough set and TOPSIS methods under fuzzy environment. Advances in Information Sciences and Service Sciences 4(3), 111–118 (2012)
12. Lall, V., Teyarachakul, S.: Enterprise Resource Planning (ERP) System Selection: A Data Envelopment Analysis (DEA) Approach. Journal of Computer Information Systems 47(1), 123–128 (2006)
13. Wu, J.-H., Tai, W.-C., Tsai, R.J., Lu, I.-Y.: Using multiple variables decision-making analysis for ERP selection. International Journal of Manufacturing Technology and Management 18(2), 228–241 (2009)
14. Rao, R.V., Rajesh, T.S.: Software Selection in Manufacturing Industries Using a Fuzzy Multiple Criteria Decision Making Method, PROMETHEE. Intelligent Information Management 1, 159–165 (2009)
15. Olson, D.L., Johansson, B., de Carvalho, R.A.: A Combined Method for Evaluating Criteria When Selecting ERP Systems. In: Møller, C., Chaudhry, S. (eds.) CONFENIS 2011. LNBIP, vol. 105, pp. 64–74. Springer, Heidelberg (2012)
16. Haddara, M., Zach, O.: ERP Systems in SMEs: A Literature Review. In: Proceedings of the 44th Hawaii International Conference on System Sciences (2011)
17. Daher, S.F.D., Almeida, A.T.: The use of ranking veto concept to mitigate the compensatory effects of additive aggregation in group decisions on a water utility automation investment. Group Decision and Negotiation 21(2), 185–204 (2012)
18. Alencar, L.H., Almeida, A.T., Morais, D.C.: A Multicriteria Group Decision Model Aggregating the Preferences of Decision-Makers Based on ELECTRE Methods. Pesquisa Operacional 30(3), 687–702 (2010)
19. Brito, A.J., de Almeida-Filho, A.T., de Almeida, A.T.: Multi-criteria Decision Model for Selecting Repair Contracts by applying Utility Theory and Variable Interdependent Parameters. IMA Journal of Management Mathematics 21(4), 349–361 (2010)
20. Daher, S.F.D., Almeida, A.T.: A combination of ranking veto concept and distance measures to minimize conflicts in a group decision problem. In: IEEE International Conference on Systems, Man, and Cybernetics (IEEE SMC 2011), pp. 3195–3200 (2011)
21. Morais, D.C., Almeida, A.T.: Group decision making on water resources based on analysis of individual rankings. Omega (Oxford) 40, 42–52 (2011)
22. Leyva-López, J.C., Fernández-Gonzalez, E.: A new method for group decision support based on ELECTRE III methodology. European Journal of Operational Research 26(3) (2003)
23. Roy, B.: The outranking approach and the foundations of ELECTRE methods. Theory and Decision 31(1), 49–73 (1991)
24. Figueira, J., Greco, S., Ehrgott, M.: Multiple criteria decision analysis: state of the art surveys. Springer, New York (2005)
25. Vincke, P.: Multicriteria decision-aid. John Wiley & Sons, Bruxelles (1992)

ERP System Implementations vs. IT Projects: Comparison of Critical Success Factors

Christian Leyh and Lars Crenze

Technische Universität Dresden,
Chair of Information Systems, esp. IS in Manufacturing and Commerce
Christian.Leyh@tu-dresden.de

Abstract. The aim of our study was to gain insight into the research field of critical success factors (CSFs) of enterprise resource planning (ERP) implementation projects and of IT projects and to compare the different CSFs. Therefore, we conducted two literature reviews, more specifically systematic reviews of relevant articles in different databases and among several international conference proceedings. Ultimately, we identified 241 relevant papers (111 single or multiple case studies, 82 surveys, and 48 literature reviews or articles from which CSFs can be derived). From these existing studies, we discovered 31 different CSFs for ERP implementation and 24 different CSFs for IT projects. The top two factors identified are equal in both reviews – Top management support and involvement and Project management. However, there are nine CSFs that seem to be relevant only for ERP implementations and two factors that could be found only in the review of IT projects.

Keywords: ERP systems, IT projects, implementation, critical success factors, CSF, literature review, comparison.

1 Introduction

Today's enterprises are faced with the globalization of markets and fast changes in the economy. In order to be able to cope with these conditions, the use of information and communication systems as well as technology is almost mandatory. Specifically, the adoption of enterprise resource planning (ERP) systems as standardized systems that encompass the actions of whole enterprises has become an important factor in today's business. Therefore, during the last few decades, ERP system software represented one of the fastest growing segments in the software market; indeed, these systems are one of the most important recent developments within information technology [1], [2].

The demand for ERP applications has increased for several reasons, including competitive pressure to become a low-cost producer, expectations of revenue growth, and the desire to re-engineer the business to respond to market challenges. A properly selected and implemented ERP system offers several benefits, such as considerable reductions in inventory costs, raw material costs, lead time for customers, production time, and production costs [3]. The strong demand for ERP applications resulted in a

G. Poels (Ed.): CONFENIS 2012, LNBIP 139, pp. 223–233, 2013.
© IFIP International Federation for Information Processing 2013

highly fragmented ERP market and a great diffusion of ERP systems throughout enterprises of nearly every industry and every size [4], [5]. This multitude of software manufacturers, vendors, and systems implies that enterprises that use or want to use ERP systems must strive to find the "right" software as well as to be aware of the factors that influence the success of the implementation project. Remembering these so-called critical success factors (CSFs) is of high importance whenever a new system is to be adopted and implemented or a running system needs to be upgraded or replaced. Errors during the selection, implementation, or maintenance of ERP systems, incorrect implementation approaches, and ERP systems that do not fit the requirements of the enterprise can all cause financial disadvantages or disasters, perhaps even leading to insolvencies. Several examples of such negative scenarios can be found in the literature (e.g. [6], [7]).

However, it is not only errors in implementing ERP systems that can have negative impact on enterprises; errors within other IT projects (e.g., implementations of BI, CRM or SCM systems, etc.) can be damaging as well. Due to the fast growing and changing evolution of technology, it is especially necessary for enterprises to at least keep in touch with the latest technologies. For example, buzz words like "Cloud computing" or "Software as a Service (SaaS)" can be read throughout managerial magazines very often. Therefore, to cope with implementations of these and other systems it is mandatory for the enterprises to be aware of the CSFs for these IT projects as well.

In order to identify the factors that affect ERP system implementations or IT projects, several case studies, surveys, and even some literature reviews have already been conducted by various researchers. However, a comparison of the factors affecting ERP implementation or IT project success has only rarely been done. To be aware of the differences within the CSFs for ERP and IT projects, it is important for the enterprises to be sure to have / to acquire the "right" employees (project leader, project team members, etc.) with adequate know-how and experience.

To gain insight into the different factors affecting ERP implementation and IT project success, we performed a CSF comparison. We conducted two literature reviews, more specifically, systematic reviews of articles in different databases and among several international conference proceedings. This also served to update the existing reviews by including current literature.

The CSFs reported in this paper were derived from 185 papers dealing with ERP systems and from 56 papers referring to factors affecting IT projects' success. The frequency of the occurrence of each CSF was counted. The aggregated results of these reviews as well as the comparison of the reviews will be presented in this paper.

Therefore, the paper is structured as follows: Within the next section our literature review methodology will be outlined in order to render our reviews reproducible. The third section deals with the results of the literature reviews and the comparison of the reviews. We will point out the factors that are the most important and those that seem to have little influence on the success of ERP implementations and IT projects. Finally, the paper concludes with a summary of the results as well as a critical acclaim for the conducted literature reviews.

2   Research Methodology – Literature Review

Both literature reviews to identify the aforementioned CSFs were performed via several steps, similar to the approach suggested by Webster & Watson [10]. In general, they were systematic reviews based on several databases that provide access to various IS journals. For the ERP system CSFs, we performed an additional search in the proceedings of several IS conferences. During the review of the ERP papers we identified 185 papers with relevant information concerning CSFs within five databases and among proceedings of five international IS conferences. However the overall procedure for the ERP system review will not be part of this paper. It is described in detail in [8], [9].

The steps of the IT projects' CSF review procedure are presented below. These steps are similar to the ERP CSF review [8], [9]. An overview of the steps is given in Figure 1. However, due to our experience during the first review (duplicates, relevant papers per database and/or proceedings), we reduced the number of databases and did not perform a review among conference proceedings.

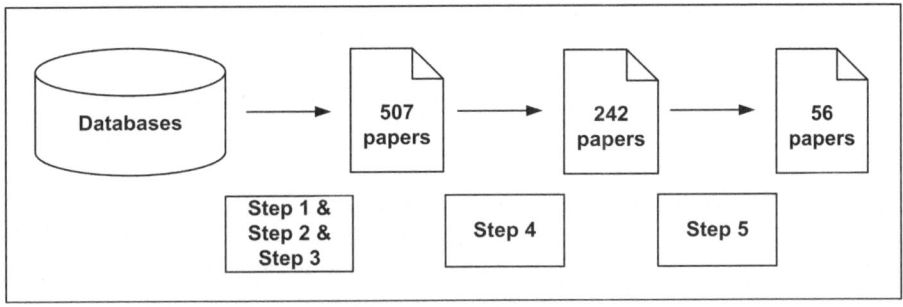

Fig. 1. Progress of the IT projects literature review

Step 1: The first step involved defining the sources for the literature review. For this approach, as mentioned, due to our earlier experience in the review procedure, two databases were identified – "Academic Search Complete" and "Business Source Complete." The first contains academic literature and publications of several academically taught subjects with specific focus on humanities and social sciences. The second covers more practical topics. It contains publications in the English language from 10,000 business and economic magazines and other sources.

Step 2: Within this step, we had to define the search terms for the systematic review. Keywords selected for this search were primarily derived from the keywords supplied and used by the authors of some of the relevant articles identified in a preliminary literature review. It must be mentioned that the search term "CSF" was not used within the Academic Search Complete database since this term is also predominantly used in medical publications and journals. As a second restriction, we excluded the term "ERP" from the search procedure in the Business Source Complete database to focus on IT projects other than ERP projects. However, this restriction could not be used within the first database due to missing functionality.

Step 3: During this step, we performed the initial search according to steps 1 and 2 and afterwards eliminated duplicates. Once the duplicates were eliminated, 507 articles remained.

Step 4: The next step included the identification of irrelevant papers. During the initial search, we did not apply any restrictions besides the ones mentioned above. The search was not limited to the research field of IS; therefore, papers from other research fields were included in the results as well. These papers had to be excluded. This was accomplished by reviewing the abstracts of the papers and, if necessary, by looking into the papers' contents. In total, this approach yielded 242 papers that were potentially relevant to the field of CSFs for IT projects.

Step 5: The fifth and final step consisted of a detailed analysis of the remaining 242 papers and the identification of the CSFs. Therefore, the content of all 242 papers was reviewed in depth for the purpose of categorizing the identified success factors. Emphasis was placed not only on the wording of these factors but also on their meaning. After this step, 56 relevant papers that suggested, discussed, or mentioned CSFs remained. The results of the analysis of these 56 papers are described in the following section. A list of these papers will not be part of this article but it can be requested from the first author.

3   Results of the Literature Review – Critical Success Factors Identified

The goal of the performed reviews was to gain an in-depth understanding of the different CSFs already identified by other researchers. As stated previously, 185 papers that referred to CSFs of ERP implementation projects were identified, as were 56 papers referring to CSFs of IT projects. The identified papers consist of those that present single or multiple case studies, survey results, literature reviews, or CSFs conceptually derived from the chosen literature. They were reviewed again in depth in order to determine the various concepts associated with CSFs. For each paper, the CSFs were captured along with the publication year, the type of data collection used, and the companies (i.e., the number and size) from which the CSFs were derived.

To provide a comprehensive understanding of the different CSFs and their concepts, we described the ERP implementation CSFs in [8] and [9]. There, the detailed definitions of the ERP implementation CSFs can be found. Since most of those CSFs can be matched with CSFs of IT projects (as shown later) we will not describe them within this paper.

3.1   Critical Success Factors for ERP System Implementations

Overall, 31 factors (as described in [8], [9]) were identified referring to factors influencing the ERP system implementation success. In most previous literature reviews, the CSFs were grouped without as much attention to detail; therefore, a lower number of CSFs was used (e.g., [3], [11], [12]). However, we took a different approach in our review. For the 31 factors, we used a larger number of categories than other researchers, as we expected the resulting distribution to be more insightful. If more broad definitions for some CSFs might be needed at a later time, further aggregation of the categories is still possible.

All 185 papers were published between the years 1998 and 2010. Table 1 shows the distribution of the papers based on publication year. Most of the papers were published between 2004 and 2009. Starting in 2004, about 20 papers on CSFs were published each year. Therefore, a review every two or three years would be reasonable in order to update the results of previously performed literature reviews.

Table 1. Paper distribution of ERP papers

Year	2010	2009	2008	2007	2006	2005	2004
Papers	6	29	23	23	25	18	23
Year	2003	2002	2001	2000	1999	1998	
Papers	11	12	5	6	3	1	

The identified CSFs and each factor's total number of occurrences in the reviewed papers are shown in the Appendix in Table 4. Top management support and involvement, Project management, and User training are the three most-named factors, with each being mentioned in 100 or more articles.

Regarding the data collection method, we must note that the papers we analyzed for CSFs were distributed as follows: single or multiple case studies – 95, surveys – 55, and literature reviews or articles in which CSFs are derived from chosen literature – 35.

3.2   Critical Success Factors for IT Projects

In the second literature review, 24 factors were identified referring to the success of IT projects. Again, we used a larger number of categories and did not aggregate many of the factors since we had good experience with this approach during our first CSF review. All 56 papers were published between the years 1982 and 2011. Table 2 shows the distribution of the papers based on publication year. Most of the papers were published between 2004 and 2011. It must be stated that some of the papers are older than 15 years. However, we included these papers in the review as well.

Table 2. Paper distribution of IT project papers

Year	2011	2010	2009	2008	2007	2006	2005	2004	2003
Papers	4	5	6	6	3	10	4	5	1
Year	2002	2001	1998	1995	1993	1987	1983	1982	
Papers	2	1	1	2	2	2	1	1	

Table 3 shows the results of our review, i.e., the identified CSFs and each factor's total number of occurrences in the reviewed papers. Project management and Top management support are the two most often named factors, with each being mentioned in some 30 or more articles. These factors are followed by Solution fit, Organizational structure, and Resource management, all mentioned in nearly the half of the analyzed articles. As shown in Table 3, due to the smaller number of relevant papers, the differentiation between the separate CSFs is not as clear as with the ERP CSFs. Most differ by only small numbers.

Table 3. IT projects CSFs in rank order based on frequency of appearance in analyzed literature

Factor	Number of instances	Factor	Number of instances
Project management	31	Commitment and motivation of the employees	17
Top management support	30	Implementation approach	17
Organizational structure	26	Communication	15
Solution fit	26	Strategy fit	15
Resources management	25	Change management	14
User involvement	24	Team organization	14
Knowledge & experience	23	Corporate environment	10
Budget / available resources	20	Monitoring	10
Stakeholder management	19	Project scope	10
Leadership	18	Risk management	8
User training	18	Corporate culture	6
Working conditions	18	Legacy systems and IT structure	3

Regarding the data collection method, in this review the papers we analyzed for IT projects' CSFs were distributed as follows: single or multiple case studies – 16, surveys – 27, and literature reviews or articles where CSFs are derived from chosen literature – 13.

3.3   Comparison of the Critical Success Factors

As mentioned earlier, we identified 31 CSFs dealing with the success of ERP system implementations and 24 factors affecting IT projects' success. The factors are titled according to the naming used most often in the literature. Therefore, we had to deal with different terms in both reviews. However, most of the CSFs (despite their different naming) can be found on both sides. Here, Table 4 in the Appendix provides an overview of the CSF matching.

As shown, there are nine CSFs that occur only in the review of ERP literature. Therefore, these factors are specifically affecting only for ERP implementation projects. However, most of these nine factors are not cited very often, so they seem to be less important than other CSFs mentioned in both reviews. Hence, two of these nine – Business process reengineering (BPR) and ERP system configuration – are in the top 10. Since ERP implementation has a large impact on an enterprise and its organizational structures, BPR is important for adapting the enterprise to appropriately fit the ERP system. On the other side, it is also important to implement the right modules and functionalities of an ERP system and configure them so they fit the way the enterprise conducts business. As not all IT projects have as large an impact on an organization as do ERP implementations, their configuration (or the BPR of the organization's structure) is a less important factor for success.

Within the review of IT project literature, two factors – Resource management and Working conditions – have no match within the ERP implementation CSF list, but here, the first lands in the top five of this review and seems to be an important factor for IT projects' success.

Comparing the top five, it can be found that the two most-often cited factors are the same in both reviews (see Table 3 and Table 4). These top two are followed by different factors in each review. However, it can be stated that project management and the involvement and support of the top management is important for every IT project and ERP implementation. Solution fit (rank #3) and Organizational fit of the ERP system (rank #8), which are matched, are both important factors, but are even more important for IT projects. This is also supported by Organizational structure. This factor is #4 for IT projects but only #27 for ERP implementation. For IT projects, a fitting structure within the enterprise is important since BPR (as mentioned above) is not a factor for those projects. For ERP implementations, the "right" organizational structure is less important, since BPR is done during almost every ERP implementation project and, therefore, the structure is changed to fit the ERP system.

4   Conclusion and Limitations

The aim of our study was to gain insight into the research field of CSFs for ERP implementations and for IT projects and to compare those CSFs. Research on the fields of ERP system implementations and IT projects and their CSFs is a valuable step toward enhancing an organization's chances for implementation success [12]. Our study reveals that several papers, i.e., case studies, surveys, and literature reviews, focus on CSFs. All in all, we identified 185 relevant papers for CSFs dealing with ERP system implementations. From these existing studies, we derived 31 different CSFs. The following are the top three CSFs that were identified: Top management support and involvement, Project management, and User training. For factors affecting IT projects' success, we identified 56 relevant papers citing 24 different CSFs. Here, Project management, Top management support, and Solution fit are the top three CSFs.

As shown in Table 1 and Table 2, most of the papers in both reviews were published after 2004. Within the ERP paper review, in particular, about 20 or more CFS-papers have been published each year since 2004. Thus, one conclusion suggests that new literature reviews on the CSFs of ERP systems and even on the CSFs for IT projects should be completed every two or three years in order to update the results.

Due to the quickly evolving technology, it becomes more and more important for companies to be up to date and to at least keep in touch with the latest developments. This is also important for smaller and medium-sized enterprises (SMEs). Especially in the ERP market that became saturated in the segment for large companies at the beginning of this century, many ERP manufacturers have shifted focus to the SMEs segment due to low ERP penetration rates within this segment. Therefore, large market potential awaits any ERP manufacturers addressing these markets. This can be transferred to other software and IT solutions as well. To cooperate with larger enterprises with highly developed IT infrastructure, SMEs need to improve their IT systems and infrastructure as well. Therefore, CSF research should also focus on SMEs due to the remarkable differences between large-scale companies and SMEs. ERP implementation projects and IT projects must be adapted to the specific needs of SMEs. Also, the importance of certain CSFs might differ depending on the size of the organization. Thus, we have concluded that an explicit focus on CSFs for SMEs is necessary in future research.

Regarding our literature reviews, a few limitations must be mentioned as well. We are aware that we cannot be certain that we have identified all relevant papers published in journals and conferences since we made a specific selection of five databases and five international conferences, and set even more restrictions while conducting the IT projects' review. Therefore, journals not included in our databases and the proceedings from other conferences might also provide relevant articles. Another limitation is the coding of the CSFs. We tried to reduce any subjectivity by formulating coding rules and by discussing the coding of the CSFs among several independent researchers. Hence, other researchers may code the CSFs in other ways.

References

1. Deep, A., Guttridge, P., Dani, S., Burns, N.: Investigating factors affecting ERP selection in the made-to-order SME sector. Journal of Manufacturing Technology Management 19(4), 430–446 (2008)
2. Koh, S.C.L., Simpson, M.: Change and uncertainty in SME manufacturing environments using ERP. Journal of Manufacturing Technology Management 16(6), 629–653 (2005)
3. Somers, T.M., Nelson, K.: The impact of critical success factors across the stages of enterprise resource planning implementations. In: Proceedings of the 34th Hawaii International Conference on System Sciences (HICSS 2001), Hawaii, USA, January 3-6 (2001)
4. Winkelmann, A., Klose, K.: Experiences while selecting, adapting and implementing ERP systems in SMEs: a case study. In: Proceedings of the 14th Americas Conference on Information Systems (AMCIS 2008), Paper 257, Toronto, Ontario, Canada, August 14-17 (2008)

5. Winkelmann, A., Leyh, C.: Teaching ERP systems: A multi-perspective view on the ERP system market. Journal of Information Systems Education 21(2), 233–240 (2010)
6. Barker, T., Frolick, M.N.: ERP implementation failure: A case study. Information Systems Management 20(4), 43–49 (2003)
7. Hsu, K., Sylvestre, J., Sayed, E.N.: Avoiding ERP pitfalls. The Journal of Corporate Accounting & Finance 17(4), 67–74 (2006)
8. Leyh, C.: Critical success factors for ERP system implementation projects: A literature review. In: Møller, C., Chaudhry, S. (eds.) Advances in Enterprise Information Systems II. CRC Press (2012)
9. Leyh, C.: Critical success factors for ERP system selection, implementation and post-implementation. In: Léger, P.-M., Pellerin, R., Babin, G. (eds.) Readings on Enterprise Resource Planning, ch. 5, pp. 63–77. ERPSim Lab, HEC, Montreal (2011)
10. Webster, J., Watson, R.T.: Analyzing the past, preparing the future: Writing a literature review. MIS Quarterly 26(2), 13–23 (2002)
11. Loh, T.C., Koh, S.C.L.: Critical elements for a successful enterprise resource planning implementation in small-and medium-sized enterprises. International Journal of Production Research 42(17), 3433–3455 (2004)
12. Finney, S., Corbett, M.: ERP implementation: A compilation and analysis of critical success factors. Business Process Management Journal 13(3), 329–347 (2007)

Appendix

Table 4. Matching of the identified CSFs (CSFs in rank order based on frequency of appearance in analyzed literature)

Rank [Number of instances]	CSFs for ERP system implementations	CSFs for IT projects	Rank [Number of instances]
1 [128]	Top management support and involvement	Top management support	2 [30]
2 [104]	Project management	Project management	1 [31]
3 [99]	User training	User training	10 [18]
4 [86]	Change management	Change management	17 [14]
5 [85]	Balanced project team	Team organization	17 [14]
6 [83]	Clear goals and objectives	Project scope	19 [10]
7 [78]	Communication	Communication	15 [15]

8 [77]	Organizational fit of the ERP system	Solution fit	3 [26]
8 [77]	**ERP system configuration**	No match	
10 [73]	**Business process reengineering**	No match	
11 [68]	Involvement of end-users and stakeholders	User involvement	6 [24]
		Stakeholder management	9 [19]
12 [62]	**External consultants**	No match	
13 [53]	Project champion	Leadership	10 [18]
13 [53]	IT structure and legacy systems	Legacy systems and IT structure	24 [3]
15 [48]	**Vendor relationship and support**	No match	
16 [47]	Skills, knowledge, and expertise	Knowledge & experience	7 [23]
17 [42]	ERP system acceptance / resistance	Commitment and motivation of employees	13 [17]
18 [41]	Project team leadership / empowered decision makers	Leadership	10 [18]
19 [39]	Vendor's tools and implementation methods	Implementation approach	13 [17]
20 [38]	Monitoring and performance measurement	Monitoring	19 [10]
21 [34]	**Data accuracy**	No match	
22 [33]	Available resources	Budget / available resources	8 [20]
23 [31]	Organizational culture	Corporate culture	23 [6]
24 [23]	**ERP system tests**	No match	

25 [22]	Troubleshooting	Risk management	22 [8]
26 [21]	Environment	Corporate environment	19 [10]
27 [17]	Organizational structure	Organizational structure	3 [26]
28 [16]	**Interdepartmental cooperation**	**No match**	
28 [16]	Company's strategy / strategy fit	Strategy fit	15 [15]
30 [15]	**Use of a steering committee**	**No match**	
31 [8]	**Knowledge management**	**No match**	
	No match	**Resource management**	5 [25]
	No match	**Working conditions**	10 [18]

Understanding the Role of Knowledge Management during the ERP Implementation Lifecycle: Preliminary Research Findings Relevant to Emerging Economies

Anjali Ramburn, Lisa F. Seymour, and Avinaash Gopaul

Information Systems Department, University of Cape Town, Private Bag,
Rondebosch 7700, South Africa
{Anjali.Ramburngopaul,Lisa.Seymour}@uct.ac.za

Abstract. This work in progress paper presents a preliminary analysis on the challenges of knowledge management (KM) experienced in the ERP implementation phase. This paper is an integral section of an ongoing research focusing on the role of KM during the ERP implementation lifecycle in both large and medium organizations in South Africa. One of the key research objectives is to investigate the core challenges of KM in large and medium organizations in South Africa. A review of the existing literature reveals a lack of comprehensive KM research during the different ERP implementation phases and particularly, in emerging economies. Initial findings include lack of process, technical and project knowledge as key challenges. Other concerns include poor understanding of the need for change, lack of contextualization and management support. This paper closes some of the identified research gaps in this area and should benefit large organizations in the South African economy.

Keywords: Knowledge Management, ERP Implementation, ERP Implementation Phase, Emerging Economy.

1 Introduction

1.1 Background and Context

Organizations are continuously facing challenges, causing them to rethink and adapt their strategies, structures, goals, processes and technologies in order to remain competitive [1], [2]. Many large organizations are now dependent on ERP systems for their daily operations. An increasing number of organizations are investing in ERP systems in South Africa. There have been many implementations in the South African public sector such as the SAP implementations at the City of Cape Town and Tshwane Metropolitan Council. The implementation process is however described as costly, complex and risky whereby firms are not able to derive benefits of the systems despite huge investments. Half of all ERP implementations fail to meet the adopting organizations' expectations [4]. This has been attributed to the disruptive and threatening nature of ERP implementations [5], [6]. This process however can be less challenging and more effective through proper use of knowledge management (KM)

G. Poels (Ed.): CONFENIS 2012, LNBIP 139, pp. 234–241, 2013.
© IFIP International Federation for Information Processing 2013

throughout the ERP lifecycle phases. Managing ERP systems knowledge has been identified as a critical success factor and as a key driver of ERP success [7]. An ERP implementation is a dynamic continuous improvement process and "a key methodology supporting ERP continuous improvement would be knowledge management" [8].

1.2   Research Problem, Objective and Scope

There has been very little work conducted to date that assesses the practices and techniques employed to effectively explain the impact of KM in the ERP systems lifecycle [9], [10]. Current research in the context of KM focuses mostly on knowledge sharing and integration challenges during the actual ERP adoption process, offering only a static perspective of KM and ERP implementation [11], [12], [13]. A number of organizations see the ERP GO Live as the end of the cycle, and very little emphasis has been given to the post implementation phases.

This research seeks to explore the ERP implementation life cycle from a KM perspective within a South African context and aims at providing a comprehensive understanding of the role of KM practices during the ERP implementation lifecycle. One of the key objectives is to investigate the KM challenges faced by organizations while implementing ERP systems. This paper therefore presents the findings of KM challenges experienced during the implementation phase of an ERP system. It should be noted that the results, discussed in this paper, are an interpretation of the initial findings which is still under review. This analysis will be further developed and elaborated in the subsequent research phases.

2   Literature Review

2.1   Enterprise Resource Planning Systems

An ERP system can be defined as "an information system that enables the integration of transaction-based data and business processes within and across functional areas in an enterprise" [9]. Some of the key enterprise functions that ERP systems support include supply chain management, inventory control, sales, manufacturing scheduling, customer relationship management, financial and cost management and human resources [10], [14]. Despite the cost intensive, lengthy and risky process, the rate of implementation of ERP systems has increased over the years. Most of the large multinational organizations have already adopted ERPs as their de facto standard with the aim of increasing productivity, efficiency and organizational competitiveness [15].

2.2   Role and Challenges of Knowledge Management

KM is defined as an on-going process where knowledge is created, shared, transferred to those who need it, and made available for future use in the organization [16]. Effective use of KM in ERP implementation has the potential to improve organizational efficiency during the ERP implementation process [7]. Successful transfer of knowledge between different ERP implementation stakeholders such as the client, implementation partner and vendor is important for the successful implementation an ERP system.

Use of KM activities during the ERP implementation phase ensures reduced implementation costs, improved user satisfaction as well as strategic and competitive business advantages through effective product and process innovation during use of ERP [10]. Organizations should therefore be aware of and identify the knowledge requirement for any implementation. However, a number of challenges hindering the proper diffusion of KM activities during the ERP implementation phase have been highlighted. The following potential knowledge barriers have been identified by [15].

Knowledge Is Embedded in Complex Organizational Processes. ERP systems' capabilities and functionalities span across different departments involving many internal and external users, leading to a diversity of interest and competencies in specific knowledge areas. A key challenge is to overcome any conflicting interest in order to integrate knowledge in order to promote standardization and transparency.

Knowledge Is Embedded in Legacy Systems. Users are reluctant to use the new systems, constantly comparing the capabilities of the new systems to legacy systems. This is a prevalent mindset which needs to be anticipated and [15] suggest the ERP system looks outwardly similar to the legacy system through customization. This can be achieved by "integrating knowledge through mapping of the information, processes, and routines of the legacy system into the ERP systems with the use of conversion templates" [15].

Knowledge Is Embedded in Externally Based Processes. ERP systems link external systems to internal ones, as a result external knowledge from suppliers and consultants needs to be integrated in the system. This can be a tedious process and the implementation team needs to ensure that essential knowledge is integrated from the initial implementation phases through personal and working relationships.

2.3   Gaps in the Literature

The literature review indicates that most of the studies performed in the context of KM and ERP implementation offer a one dimensional static view of the actual ERP adoption phases without emphasizing the overall dynamic nature of ERP systems. Furthermore, previous studies have failed to provide a holistic view of the challenges, importance, different dimensions and best practices of KM during the whole ERP implementation cycle.

3   Research Method

3.1   Research Paradigm and Approach

This research employs an interpretive epistemology which is ideal for this research as this study focuses on theory building, where the ERP implementation challenges faced by organizations are explored using a knowledge perspective [17]. A qualitative research method is deemed suitable as opposed to a quantitative one, as qualitative research emphasizes on non- positivist, non-linear and cyclical forms of research, allowing the scientist to gain new insights of the research area through each iteration whilst aiming to provide a better understanding to the social world [18], [21].

Grounded theory seems particularly applicable in the current context as there has been no exhaustive analysis on, barriers, dimensions and role of KM focusing on the whole ERP implementation life cycle in organizations. Grounded theory used in this research is an "inductive, theory-discovering methodology that allows the researcher to develop a theoretical account of the general features of a topic, while simultaneously grounding the account in empirical observations of data" [19], [20].

Semi-Structured interviews targeting different ERP implementation stakeholders are being conducted in an organization currently in their ERP implementation phase. The aim is to interview as many participants as possible until theoretical saturation is achieved. Approval for this research has been obtained from the University of Cape Town's ethical committee. Participants have been asked to sign a voluntary participant consent form and their anonymity has been assured.

All the interviews have been recorded and transcribed. Iterative analysis of the collected data has enabled the researcher to understand and investigate the main research problems posed. The transcripts of the interviews have been read a number of times to identify, conceptualise, and categorise emerging themes.

3.2   Case Description

This section provides a brief overview of the case organization. Founded in 1923, the company has a number of branches throughout South Africa, employing over 39 000 people. The organization is currently launching the SAP Project Portfolio Management module throughout its different branches across the country. Currently in the implementation stage, an organization wide initial training, involving the employees, has already been conducted. The interviews have been carried out in one of organization's division in Cape Town and purposive sampling has been used to select the interviewees. All the chosen participants had been through the training and were impacted by the SAP implementation process.

4   Preliminary Findings

Preliminary research findings indicate several challenges with regards to KM in the ERP implementation phase. Most of the barriers identified were either directly or indirectly related to the inadequacies and inefficiencies of knowledge transfer. The section below provides a comprehensive account of the major challenges that have been identified.

4.1   Knowledge Management Challenges

Trainer's Lack of Process Knowledge. Interviewees mentioned the training provided was inadequate in various ways. The trainers were not knowledgeable enough; they lacked key SAP skills and did not understand the process from the users' perspective. Since none of the trainers had any experience as end users of the system, there were some inconsistencies in their understanding of the new system from a user perspective. Ownership of roles and tasks were not clearly defined. They also lacked the expertise to engage with the different problems that surfaced during the training and there was no clarification on the information and process flow between the different departments and the individuals as per their role definition. *"However what makes it difficult is that the trainers do not work with the project. They do not know the process entirely and are not aware of what is happening in the background, they only collect data."*

Trainer's Lack of Technical Knowledge. The technical knowledge and qualification of the trainers were put into question. The trainers were the admin support technicians who are experts in the current system the interviewees use but did not have enough expertise to deal with the upcoming ERP system. *"I think they did not know the system themselves, I had been in training with them for the current program we use and they were totally 100% clued up. You could have asked them anything, they had the answers."*

Interviewees' Lack of Technical Knowledge. Interviewees also struggled with use and understanding of the ERP system. They found the user interface and navigation increasingly complex as opposed to their existing system. As a result, they were overcome with frustration and they did not see the importance of the training. *"I have not used the system before, so I do not understand it. We struggled with the complexity of the system. The number of steps we had to do made it worse. No one understood what and why we were doing most of the steps."*

Lack of Knowledge on Need for Change. The interviewees did not understand the benefits of using SAP from a strategic perspective. They questioned the implementation of the new system as they felt their previous system could do everything they needed it to. They had never felt the need for a new system.

Lack of Project knowledge. Interviewees were unaware of the clear project objectives, milestones and deployment activities. The interviewees did not have any information regarding the status of the project activities. They were only aware of the fact that they had to be trained in SAP as this would be their new system in the future but did not exactly know by when they were required to start using the system. Some of them believed they were not near the implementation stage, and the training was only a pilot activity to test whether they were ready for implementation. However, others hoped that the implementation had been cancelled due to the number of problems experienced in the training sessions.

Poor Project Configuration Knowledge. Another key concern voiced related to the complexity of the ERP system as opposed to the existing system the participants are using. They have been working with the current system for a number of years and believed it operated in the most logical way, the same way as to how their minds would function. On the other hand, the ERP system was perceived as complex, the number of steps required to perform for a task seem to have increased drastically. This may be attributed to the lack of system configuration knowledge which could have been essential in substantially decreasing the number of steps required to perform a particular task.

Lack of Knowledge on Management Initiatives. The interviewees felt they did not have to use or understand the system until they got the 'go ahead' from top and middle management. Interviews indicated that top and middle management had not supported the initiative as yet. Interviewees had received no information or communication on planning, adoption and deployment of the new system from management; hence they showed no commitment towards using the new system.

Lack of Knowledge on Change Management Initiatives. Managing change is arguably one of the primary concerns of ERP implementation. The analysis show the lack of importance attributed to this area. Lack of proper communication channels and planning coupled with the absence of change management initiatives resulted in employees' confusion, instability and resistance as shown by quotes below. *"We should not have used SAP at all, they should scrap it...If someone new came and asked me whether they should go for the training, I would tell them, try your best to get out of it."*

Knowledge Dump (Information overload). Information overload was another identified challenge. The training included people from different departments who are associated with different aspects of the process. As a result, the trainers covered various tasks related to various processes in one training session as opposed to focusing on the specific processes that the interviewees understood and were involved with. The participants got confused with regards to their role definition and the ownership of the different activities. The trainers were unable to clear this confusion. This caused a certain level of panic amongst the group; subsequently they lost interest in the training and attributed it as an unproductive process.

Poor Contextualization of Knowledge. Another concern raised was with reference to the lack of customization of the training materials and exercises used resulting in a poor focus on local context. Interviewees could not relate to the training examples given as they were based on the process flow from a different suburb. Interviewees said each suburb has its own way of operating and has unique terms and terminologies. The fact that the examples used came from Johannesburg and not from Cape Town made it harder for the interviewees to understand the overall process. *"The examples they used were from Joburg, so they work in a different way to us. The* *examples should have been customised to how we work in order for us to better understand the process."*

5   Conclusions and Implications

This paper reports on the preliminary findings based on the implementation activities of an ERP system in a large engineering company in Cape Town. The findings of this study show a number of intra-organizational barriers to efficient knowledge transfer. Inadequate training, lack of technical and project knowledge, lack of management support and change management initiatives have been cited as the major KM challenges. Other fundamental KM challenges include process knowledge, customization and contextualization of knowledge. Seemingly, in a large organization with multiple branches throughout South Africa, understanding the process, contextualization and customization of the training content from the users' perspective is a key aspect to consider during an ERP implementation process.

This research is still ongoing and the subsequent research phases focus on providing a holistic view of the role, different dimensions and best practices of KM during the entire ERP implementation cycle. Upon completion, this research will be of immediate benefit to both academics and practitioners.

From an academic perspective, this study will explore the whole ERP implementation lifecycle from a KM perspective, hence contributing to the existing body of knowledge in this area by attempting to offer a better explanation of the existing theories and frameworks. Since there has not been any study that looked at the entire lifecycle of ERP implementation through a KM perspective in South Africa, this research is unique in nature and is expected to break some new ground in South Africa, aiming to provide an advancement of knowledge in this particular field. Through a practical lens, this research should be of immediate benefit to large and medium organizations. The results of this study can also be useful and applicable to international companies with global user bases.

References

1. Bhatti, T.R.: Critical Success Factors for the Implementation of Enterprise Resource Planning (ERP): Empirical Validation. In: 2nd International Conference on Innovation in Information Technology, Zayed University, College of Business, Dubai, UAE (2005)
2. Holland, C.P., Light, B.: A critical success factors model for ERP implementation. IEEE Software 16(3), 30–36 (1999)
3. Seethamraju, R., Seethamraju, J.: Adoption of ERPs in a Medium-sized Enterprise - A Case Study. In: 19th Australasian Conference on Information Systems Adoption of ERPs for Medium-sized Enterprise, Christchurch, December 3-5 (2008)
4. Jasperson, J.S., Carter, P.E., Zmud, R.W.: Conceptualization of Post-Adoptive Behaviours Associated with Information Technology Enabled Work Systems. MIS Quarterly 29(3), 525–567 (2005)
5. Zorn, T.E.: The Emotionality of Information and Communication Technology Implementation. Journal of Communication Management 7(2), 160–171 (2002)

6. Robey, D., Ross, J., Boudreau, M.: Learning to Implement Enterprise Systems: An Exploratory Study of the Dialectics of Change. Journal of Management Information Systems 19(1), 17–46 (2002)
7. Leknes, J., Munkvold, B.E.: The role of knowledge management in ERP implementation: a case study in Aker Kvaerner. In: 14th European Conference on Information Systems (ECIS 2006), Göteborg, Sweden, June 12-14 (2005)
8. McGinnis, T.C., Huang, Z.: Incorporating of Knowledge Management into ERP continuous improvement: A research framework. Issues in Information Systems 2, 612–618 (2004)
9. Parry, G., Graves, A.: The importance of knowledge management for ERP systems. International Journal of Logistics Research and Applications 11(6), 427–441 (2008)
10. Sedera, D., Gable, G., Chan, T.: Knowledge Management for ERP success. In: 7th Pacific Asia Conference on Information Systems, Adelaide, South Australia, July 10-13 (2004)
11. Suraweera, T., Remus, U., Wakerley, S.: Dynamics of Knowledge Leverage in ERP Implementation. In: 18th Australasian Conference on Information Systems, Toowoomba, Australia, December 5-7 (2007)
12. Gable, G.: The enterprise system lifecycle: through a knowledge management lens. Strategic Change 14, 255–263 (2005)
13. Markus, M.L.: Towards a Theory of Knowledge Reuse: Types of Knowledge Reuse Situations and Factors in Reuse Success. Journal of Management Information Systems 18(1), 57–93 (2001)
14. Soffer, P., Golany, B., Dori, D.: ERP modeling: a comprehensive approach. Journal of Information Systems 28, 673–690 (2002)
15. Pan, S.L., Huang, J.C., Newell, S., Cheung, A.W.K.: Knowledge Integration as a key problem in an ERP Implementation. In: 22nd International Conference on Information Systems, December 16-19, New Orleans, Louisiana (2004)
16. Chan, R.: Knowledge management for implementing ERP in SMEs. In: 3rd Annual SAP Asia Pacific Institutes of Higher Learning Forum Maximizing the Synergy Between Teaching, Research and Business, Singapore, November 1-2 (1999)
17. Walsham, G.: Interpretive case studies in IS research: Nature and method. European Journal of Information Systems 4, 74–81 (1995)
18. Leedy, P.D.: Practical research: planning and design, 6th edn. Prentice-Hall, Upper Saddle River (1997)
19. Glaser, B.G., Strauss, A.L.: The Discovery of Grounded Theory: Strategies for Qualitative Research, Chicago. Aldine Publishing Company, Hawthorne (1967)
20. Orlikowski, W.J.: CASE tools as organisational change: Investigating incremental and radical changes in systems development. MIS Quarterly 17, 309–340 (1993)
21. Strauss, A., Corbin, J.: Basics of Qualitative Research: Grounded Theory Procedure and Techniques. Sage, Newbury Park (1990)
22. Fang, L., Patrecia, S.: Critical Success Factors in ERP Implementation. Master thesis. Jànkàping International Business School (2005)
23. Huang, Z.: A compilation research of ERP implementation Critical Success Factors. Issues in Information Systems 11(1), 507–512 (2010)
24. Somers, T.M., Nelson, K.: The impact of critical success factors across the stages of enterprise resource planning implementations. In: 34th Hawaii International Conference on Systems Sciences, Maui (2001)

Implementing Behavior Driven Development
in an Open Source ERP

Rogerio Atem de Carvalho, Fernando Luiz de Carvalho e Silva,
Rodrigo Soares Manhães, and Gabriel Lima de Oliveira

Federal Fluminense Institute, NSI, R. Dr. Siqueira 273, Sala F104, Campos, Brazil
{ratem,fernando.carvalho,rmanhaes,gabriel.oliveira}@iff.edu.br

Abstract. A typical problem in Software Engineering is how to guarantee that all system's requirements are correctly implemented through source code. Traditionally, requirement tracing is a manual task comprised of keeping links from requirements to source code, going through different modeling artifacts, including models. However, these techniques cannot guarantee that requirements are always correctly implemented by source code. Aiming at solving this problem, Behavior-Driven Development (BDD) is a specification technique that automatically checks if all functional requirements are treated properly by source code through the connection of the textual description of requirements to automated tests. Given that for Enterprise Information Systems, requirements are usually identified by analyzing business process models, and these processes are implemented through workflows, connecting workflows to automated tests through BDD specifications can provide automated requirements traceability. The aim of this paper is to briefly present this proposal and show how it was implemented for the open source ERP5 system.

Keywords: Behavior Driven Development, Automated Tests, ERP.

1   Introduction

Requirement tracing is a typical Software Engineering matter that can be described as how to guarantee that all functional requirements are implemented correctly by the source code. Many techniques were developed to address requirement tracing, such as the use of the Requirements Traceability Matrix [1], which keeps track of the source code elements that realize the requirements. These artifacts require that developers determine by hand, for each functional requirement, which classes collaborate to implement it. This technique is time consuming and error prone, given that the traceability work is done manually and through the introduction of an additional artifact - the matrix. The ideal way of keeping track of requirements is directly linking them to source code.

Behavior-Driven Development (BDD) [2] is a specification technique that links functional requirements to source code, through the connection of the textual representation of the requirements to automated tests. BDD extends Test-Driven Development (TDD) [3], which in turn is a technique that consists of writing test

G. Poels (Ed.): CONFENIS 2012, LNBIP 139, pp. 242–249, 2013.
© IFIP International Federation for Information Processing 2013

cases for every programming task, before these implementations are performed. TDD is intended to achieve the correct solution that exactly matches the business problem at unit and integration levels [4] – while BDD takes care of the acceptance level, where requirements reside.

For Enterprise Information Systems, identify requirements by analyzing business process models facilitates the participation of the domain experts [5]. Business processes, in turn, are implemented through workflows. Therefore, connecting workflows to automated tests through BDD specifications can provide an end to end traceability of requirements, as well as facilitate communication among developers and domain experts. This paper aims at presenting the application of BDD to the Open Source ERP (FOS-ERP) ERP5 [6], as a way of showing how this technique can drive the development of high quality business systems. The proposal here presented is a simpler variation of the Business Language Driven Development (BLDD) technique [7], which extends BDD by using business process models to drive the testing process. This paper is organized as follows: after this introduction, BDD main characteristics are briefly presented; followed by the description of the application of it to ERP5, and finally conclusive remarks are commented.

2   Introducing BDD

BDD starts by defining requirements using specific keywords that tag the type of the sentence, indicating how it is going to be treated in the subsequent development phases. These descriptions are written in an Ubiquitous Language (UL), which is a language structured around the domain model and used by all team members to connect all the activities of the team with the software [8]. In summary, requirements are described sets of Given-When-Then constructs (GWT) [9]:

```
Given a Context (or a system State)
When an Event happens (or an user Action)
Then an Action is taken (or a system Reaction)
```

From this point onwards, a story runner maps the natural language sentences into the underlying programming language equivalent calls, while keeping the same abstraction level. The next step is to write acceptance tests to the generated steps, pieces of code that excite the source code that implements the system. By wrapping all implementation code with tests, which in turn are automatically tied to the business requirements using the GWT constructs, the need for requirement documentation is fulfilled, having the advantage of making the whole system verifiable automatically at any time. Therefore, the use of BDD allows reducing the risks and effort to implement a given change in an information system; hence the system can be continuously improved without making the cost of change grow exponentially, avoiding Boehm's Cost of Change Curve phenomena [10]. Moreover, the *Then* constructs represent the tests' acceptance criteria, stating an objective method to validate if a given requirement is *done*.

According to [7], BDD provides an automated and cost effective way of keeping requirements traceability, addressing each of the challenges introduced by Kannenberg and Saiedian [11]:

- Cost: it is able to provide full tracing in a way that is even cheaper than Value-based requirement tracing [12]. Requirements are tied to tests, so that if tests return non-expected values or simply are not implemented, the tool will automatically point out the problem.
- Managing change: there is no need to impose "strong discipline in maintaining the accuracy of traceability", instead, BDD tools make all the necessary checks automatically. Whenever a requirement changes, the tests will not run until the code is also changed accordingly. Moreover, by changing a requirement and immediately running a complete build, errors will pop-up in specific places where the system must be changed, easing effort estimation.
- Different stakeholder viewpoints: standards provide no guidance to traceability [11], through BDD, it is possible for any stakeholder to check system consistency, since it is based on executable documentation. Even end users can push a button and check its higher level error messages.
-Organizational problems: according to [11], "the easiest way to correct organizational problems related to traceability is through the use of policy and training". BDD provides a proper policy for traceability because it enforces the connection between code and requirements.
- Poor tool support: the correct combination and use of BDD and TDD testing tools results in a development environment which monitors and alerts about inconsistencies introduced in the code.

3   BDD in ERP5

ERP5 is an open source ERP that offers an enterprise-wide system based on the open source Zope platform. This platform integrates an object database, a workflow engine, a content management framework, and rapid GUI scripting [6]. ERP5 has different variants for industry, governments, and services, including CRM, MRP, SCM, Sales, Payroll, and others modules.

The motivation to use BDD in an ERP that works on top of a workflow engine is to connect tests directly to the workflows, thus joining the business logic represented by the workflows to the requirements comprehension represented by automated tests, or, in other words, checking the validity of the mapping from the business experts' definitions to the developers' definitions.

The first step to use BDD in ERP5 was to map GWT constructs to state-based business process models, given that ERP5's workflow engine is state-based. This task was facilitated by the fact that GWT constructs represent a state machine, connecting the human concept of cause and effect, to the software concept of input-process-output. According to [13], this convention "is simply a state transition, and that BDD is really just a way to describe a finite state machine. Clearly *Given* is the current state of the system to be explored, *When* describes an event or stimulus to that system, and

Then describes the resulting state of the system." Therefore, the set of all scenarios of a given business requirement can be represented by a Finite State Machine.

Following this reasoning, and using the mappings from the most common business process patterns to GWT constructs provided by [14], it was developed an ERP5 module which connects the system's workflows to their automated tests through detailed definitions described using GWT.

The sequence of steps for using the Feature Module for implementing a given business process is as follows:

a) Represent the business process in the system using a state-based workflow.
b) Describe the feature's goal and its business value.
c) Define each scenario (state change) supplying examples.
d) Using the values defined in the *Given* and *When* clauses, write the automated tests. Tests success will be checked by comparing their results to the acceptance criteria defined in the *Then* tags.
e) Write the source code that implements the workflow, and that will be excited by the tests.
f) Run the tests and check for their correctness.

In order to exemplify this process, the ERP5's Basic Sale Opportunity business process, showed in Fig.1, is used.

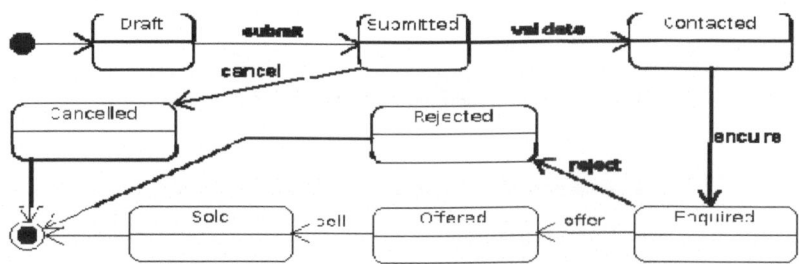

Fig. 1. ERP5's Basic Sales Opportunity process

Fig. 2 shows the Module's main form used to describe the feature, as well as to list its scenarios. Features are described for the sake of defining their business value. The arrow in the figure indicates the icon to create a new scenario.

Following BDD's incremental and test-first process, the following sequence of steps is performed for each state change on the workflow: (i) create a scenario defining the example values for the tests and the acceptance criteria, (ii) write automated acceptance tests, (iii) write the equivalent source code, (iv) run the tests until there are successful. In order to support this incremental process, the Feature Module allows the execution of each scenario independently. The result of running the scenario "Sale Opportunity is Submitted" is shown in Fig. 3. The first four lines prepare the environment for the test, creating the workflow object, while the fifth and the sixth lines are responsible, respectively, for firing the transition, and checking if the workflow is in the expected state - *submitted*.

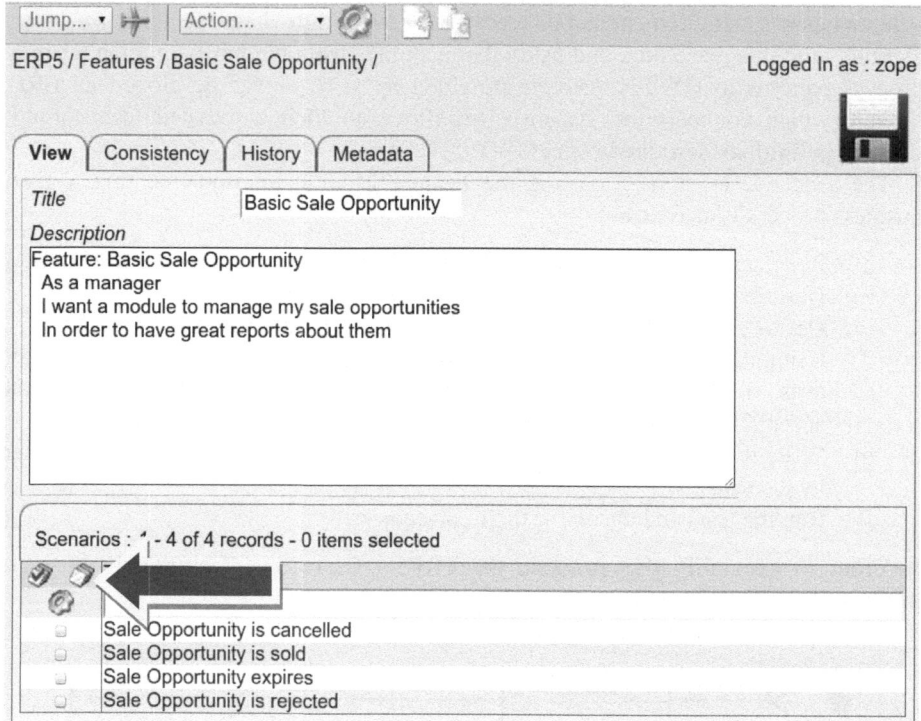

Fig. 2. Creating the Feature and defining its value

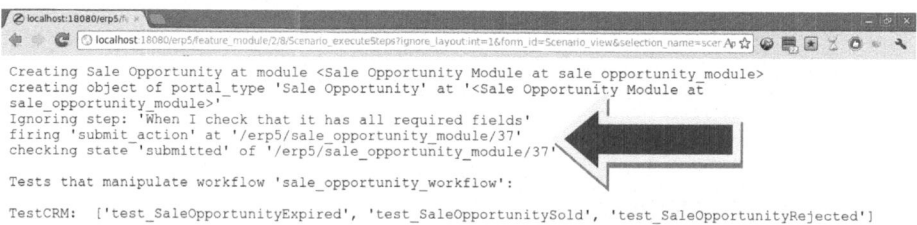

Fig. 3. Results of running the scenario "Sale Opportunity is Submitted." The red arrow marks the firing of the transition and the checking of the workflow state.

After defining all scenarios, it is possible to run the workflow's different paths. Fig. 4 shows the "happy path" of the sale opportunity, ending in the sold state.

Fig. 5 shows what happens if the test fails for a given scenario, for demonstration purposes, a wrong expected state called "not enquired" was used as acceptance criterion, while the source code changes the state to "enquired", raising an assertion error. In that way it is possible to identify which specific part of the workflow is not

```
Terminal                                        _  +  ×
Arquivo  Editar  Ver  Pesquisar  Terminal  Ajuda
Running Unit tests of CRM
{'edit_workflow': [{'action': 'edit',
                    'new_state': 'current',
                    'old_state': 'current'}],
 'sale_opportunity_workflow': [{'action': '',
                    'new_state': 'draft',
                    'old_state': 'draft'},
                   {'action': 'submit_action',
                    'new_state': 'draft',
                    'old_state': 'draft'},
                   {'action': 'submit',
                    'new_state': 'submitted',
                    'old_state': 'draft'},
                   {'action': 'validate_action',
                    'new_state': 'draft',
                    'old_state': 'submitted'},
                   {'action': 'validate',
                    'new_state': 'contacted',
                    'old_state': 'submitted'},
                   {'action': 'enquire_action',
                    'new_state': 'draft',
                    'old_state': 'contacted'},
                   {'action': 'enquire',
                    'new_state': 'enquired',
                    'old_state': 'contacted'},
                   {'action': 'offer_action',
                    'new_state': 'draft',
                    'old_state': 'enquired'},
                   {'action': 'offer',
                    'new_state': 'offered',
                    'old_state': 'enquired'},
                   {'action': 'sell_action',
                    'new_state': 'draft',
                    'old_state': 'offered'},
                   {'action': 'sell',
                    'new_state': 'sold',
                    'old_state': 'offered'}]}
----------------------------------------------------------------
Ran 1 test in 4.272s

OK
```

Fig. 4. Sales opportunity's happy path tests successfully ran

in accordance to the acceptance criteria, and even a business expert can identify what is the problem by checking the test log. If other errors were present they would be raised one by one.

Although the workflow logic already provides, by nature, the current state (Given), the event and its conditions (When), and the new state (Then), the textual representation of the workflow provided by the GWT constructs is necessary for two reasons: (i) provide example values for the automated texts and (ii) describe internal changes in the information system, such as the creation of objects.

4   Conclusions

This paper aimed at briefly presenting the first implementation of the BDD technique into an ERP, in this case, the open source ERP5. Moreover, it showed an ERP5 module specifically developed to integrate the BDD's features with ERP5's workflows. In that way, the goal of joining the advantages of using BDD to keep track of all requirements while using an underlying workflow engine was reached.

A future direction is making the Feature Module able of, by checking a given workflow's configuration, generating the GWT constructs, guaranteeing that all transitions will be implemented. By changing the generation of GWT constructs to a specific language that reflects a state-based workflow, as proposed by [7], it is possible to use a single a unique language for describing both business process and testing details.

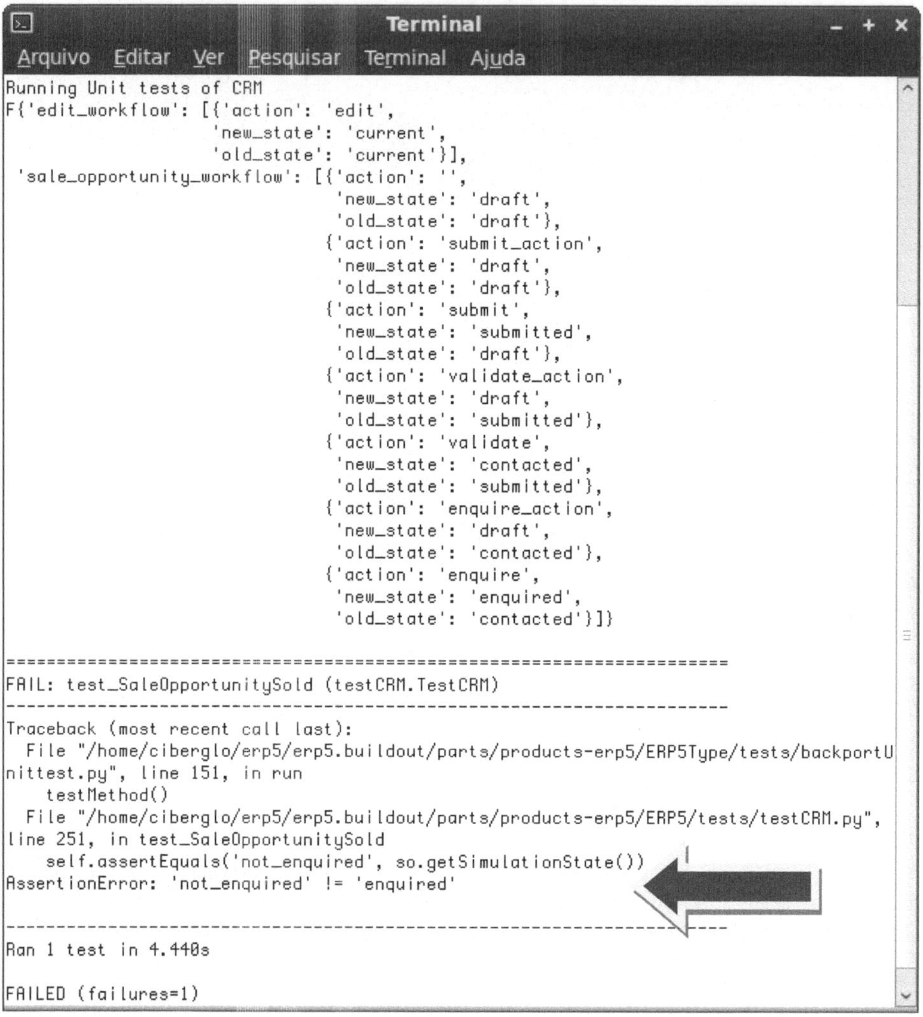

Fig. 5. Test failed while trying to transit to a wrong state

References

1. Carlos, T.: Requirements Traceability Matrix - RTM,
   http://www.pmhut.com/requirements-traceability-matrix-rtm
2. North, D.: Introducing Behavior-Driven Development,
   http://dannorth.net/introducing-bdd
3. Beck, K.: Test-Driven Development by Example. Addison-Wesley (2003)
4. Koskela, L.: Test-Driven: TDD and Acceptance TDD for Java Developers. Manning (2007)

5. Heinecke, A., Bruckmann, T., Griebe, T., Gruhn, V.: Generating Test Plans for Acceptance Tests from UML Activity Diagrams. In: 17th IEEE International Conference and Workshops on Engineering of Computer-Based Systems, pp. 57–66 (2010)
6. Smets-Solanes, J., Carvalho, R.A.: ERP5: A Next-Generation, Open-Source ERP Architecture. IEEE IT Professional 5(4), 38–44 (2003)
7. Carvalho, R.A., Carvalho e Silva, F.L., Manhaes, R.S.: Business Language Driven Development: Joining Business Process Models to Automated Tests. In: V IFIP International Conference on Research and Practical Issues of Enterprise Information Systems. LNBIP (2011)
8. Evans, E.: Domain-Driven Design - Tackling Complexity in the Heart of Software. Addison-Wesley (2004)
9. Behavior Driven Development.org: Behavior Driven Development, http://behaviour-driven.org
10. Carvalho, R.A., Johansson, B., Manhaes, R.S.: Agile Software Development for Customizing ERPs. In: Parthasarathy, S. (Org.) Enterprise Information Systems and Implementing IT Infrastructures: Challenges and Issues, pp. 20–39. Information Science Reference, IGI Global, Hershey, USA (2010)
11. Kannenberg, A., Saiedian, H.: Why Software Requirements Traceability Remains a Challenge. CrossTalk 22(5), 14–21 (2009)
12. Heindl, M., Stefan, B.: A Case Study on Value-Based Requirements Tracing. In: Proc. of the 10th European Software Engineering Conference, Lisbon, Portugal, pp. 60–69 (2005)
13. Martin, R.C.: The Truth About BDD, http://blog.objectmentor.com/articles/2008/11/27/the-truth-about-bdd
14. Carvalho, R.A., Silva, F.L.C., Manhaes, R.S.: Mapping Business Process Modeling constructs to Behavior Driven Development Ubiquitous Language, arXiv: 1006.4892v1 (cs.SE) (2010)

Adoption of Standard ERP Solution in Health Care Sector: Is SAP ERP All-in-One Capable to Meet Specific Requirements?

Adnan Kraljić, Tarik Kraljić, and Denis Delismajlović

{akraljic,tkraljic}@ibu.edu.ba, denisdelismajlovic@gmail.com

Abstract. Objective of this experience report is to address specific issues regarding standard SAP ERP implementation in a medical institution. Target Company is a state owned health care institution from Bosnia and Herzegovina. Report will treat selected issues which could trouble standard SAP ERP implementation trough predefined ERP implementation methodology for SAP ERP. This report presents observations/remarks based on experience of authors in particular SAP ERP implementation project in health care institution. Author's goal is to provide useful insight into "real life" standard ERP implementation and problems that arise. Also, it should provide useful information for all stakeholders involved in the process of ERP implementation in public health care sector.

Keywords: SAP ERP All-in-One, Health care information systems, Inventory management, Health care billing system.

1 Introduction

This industry report provides insight into an implementation of SAP ERP solution in a major medical institution in Bosnia and Herzegovina with several thousands of employees. The project was initiated by management of the hospital with purpose to eliminate the ineffectiveness of the current information system. Analysis of the current financial system and the list of new system requirements have been prepared by an external consulting company. This was required for announcing a public tender for selection of the ERP software solution integrator. After several months of tender procedure and assessment of the best vendor (price was eliminatory criteria, in accordance with the law), software integrator was selected. At the end, SAP All-in-One solution [1] was the preferred one. Relevant project information is presented in next sections.

As recommended by external consultants the main goals of the project were:

- To centralize the information system (create/provide a centralized database);
- To increase data integrity and consistency;
- To focus on accounting and financial department processes;

G. Poels (Ed.): CONFENIS 2012, LNBIP 139, pp. 250–257, 2013.
© IFIP International Federation for Information Processing 2013

- To improve drug warehouse management and billing system;
- To provide comprehensive and accurate reports for top management;

The project incorporated five SAP modules: FI (Finance), CO (Controlling), MM (Material management), SD (Sales and Distribution) and HR (Human resources). SAP integrator offered a team of seven SAP solution consultants, including one SAP system administrator. In addition, two consultants (ABAP programmers) were teamed up for specific ABAP developments. During the implementation it became clear that the number of consultant was inadequate, given the project scope and specific demands in medical service industry.

2   Situation before SAP Implementation

The hospital is an institution that devotes considerable resources in upgrading its primary domain and activities by investing in specialized diagnostic and medical equipment. However, this is not the case with ICT. No substantial investments were made in information system improvements in the last twenty years. Moreover, parts of existing hospital IT infrastructure were damaged during the war (1992-1995).The example which reflects this initial situation is that network between Clinics was non-existent of network infrastructure between Clinics which is the basic assumption for any SAP implementation

Due to the law regulations, the hospital was obliged to have certain software solutions, mainly disintegrated applications aimed at specific business domain. This software landscape contained dozen applications developed by one or few individuals. There was no recognized company behind them. All applications were technically isolated instances, mostly installed only on local machines with no server-client architecture. All master and transactional data were stored on a single machine. Only network connected application was accounting (General ledger) application (terminals), which was implemented in the eighties. The final (consolidated) reports, made by manual data collecting from various applications, were presented to the steering committee. The process of preparing reports took between five to ten days. Microsoft Excel sheets were being (physically on USB) passed from department to department. The most representative example of their legacy IT architecture was the billing system. Each PC machine had application installed for specific billing types (7 types/scenarios of billing); there were seven local machines each responsible for the specific billing scenario.

3   Implementation and Its Specific Features

The implemented system was standard SAP ERP All-in-One. Since it was not specialized health care solution, additional industry-specific functionalities needed to be developed to fulfill basic client's needs. They were mostly related to the processes of Materials Management and Sales and Distribution.

In the following sections we will discuss main issues faced during SAP ERP implementation in two mentioned modules: MM (Materials Management) and SD (Sales and Distribution).

3.1   Sales and Distribution Functionality and Obstacles

Standard functionalities of SAP ERP SD include handling of sales and distribution. The main activities are the sales order handling, and the distribution of shipments to customers. In addition the billing process, customer invoice, delivery, and risk management   are responsibility of the SD module. The Sales and Distribution (SAP SD) consists of all master data, system configuration, and transactions to complete the Order. The billing process is important for every Health Institution, hence it was recognized that SD module is necessary to be installed in the hospital.

Particular attention was paid on the billing department which bills all medical and non-medical services provided by the institution. Billing department employs of 20 people, who create over 15 000 invoice documents (billing documents) each month. This number of invoices does not pose a problem for SAP SD module. The real issue was the complexity of the invoicing process. As the previous billing software was outdated, complex billing affected process of collecting receivables negatively, as billing department was constantly in delay of two months when invoicing services provided to patient.

The process of invoicing can be divided into three stages, as shown in the Figure 1:

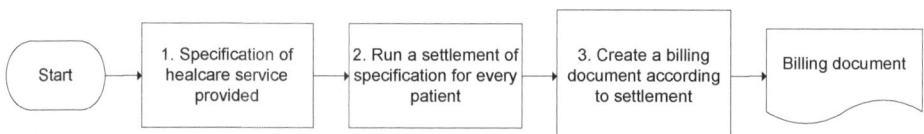

Fig. 1. Process of invoicing in the hospital

All processes shown in the diagram above were conducted in separate programs (software). This meant that for each operation, point cleric was required to re-enter data. The reliability of information over this life cycle was not guaranteed as the process was manual. In addition, billing of health services was carried out separately for different types / groups of patients; 7 types in total. All these different types have a special logic of calculation for health services, which was necessary to be realized and implemented through the implementation of the SAP SD module.

Issues and problems arose during SAP SD implementation:

a) The first detected problem was that the standard SAP system does not contain functionalities which would adequately handle the first process in billing system's life cycle – creation of specifications for health services provided to a patient. The suggestion given by SD consultants was not implementing this particular process with SAP system, and leaving it for the eventual second phase of the project, which was the implementation of the full SAP Healthcare solution. This suggestion was rejected by the steering committee. The decision was to develop this functionality using ABAP programming. . Add-on for standard SAP SD module had to be made, which would cause a number of changes in core SD processes (sales orders creation and billing documents creation).

At first, decision seemed reasonable, but later it proved to be one of the biggest mistakes made by SAP project manager. This generated other problems, such as dramatic increase in number of new users and SAP licenses needed for employees who would work on the data input for specification of health services and billing. It became apparent that the project cost was very close to violate the budget.

b) Another big issue raised was that the process of specification orders of healthcare services and pricing calculation was not standardized. The procedures and rules for price calculation differed between the clinics, so there were over 10 "QS procedures" which greatly hampered the first phase of SAP project – creation of Blueprints. Blueprint phase, which was planned to last for maximum of one month, was extended to a 80 days, due to unsynchronized billing processes and defined billing procedures in the hospital (once again – each clinic has its own procedure). Also, each clinic has its own working practice, which put additional strain on system integrator. Although the Blueprints phase represents the very first phase of the SAP project according to the ASAP methodology, it was clear that the period of 4 months for full implementation and go live were insufficient. All of this put enormous pressure on consultants.

c) The process of master data migration, and import preparation on the test system, discovered a lot of irregularities of the previous billing system procedure. It was possible for the same patient to have four different codes (system ID) depending on the type of service for which he was billed.

By the end of the project, along the standard ones, the following non-standard functionalities were implemented (developed as add-on):

1. Creation of specification of healthcare services (two type and transactions – for ambulant and hospital use);
2. Creation of advance payment for hospital and ambulant use;
3. Automated process for creation of sales order referenced on healthcare specification;
4. Automation of price calculation depending on a patient's status;
5. Development of many Z reports (add on development on standard SAP).

3.2   Material Management Functionality and Obstacles

From the beginning of the project it was apparent that the drug warehouse of the hospital will be the most demanding part of the whole project. With annual turnover around 40 million EUR it was the major consumer of the hospital's budget. New, efficient inventory management system was essential to the "profitability" of the drug warehouse.

SAP ERP All-in-One was chosen to replace the old legacy system that was in use. This existing system was specifically designed and developed for the drug warehouse with features adjusted to their specific needs. The system was in use for over 12 years and was improved/upgraded during this time. However, the system operated only in this organizational unit. At the end of each month, accounting department was provided with the reports (goods receipt, goods issue, goods transfer, inventory status etc.) from the system, which contained no detailed analytics in itself.

The SAP module which covers processes of clinical drug warehouse is called SAP MM (Material management) module. All the issues that standard SAP MM module faces during implementation phase are stated in the rest of this section.

a) Adequate inventory is generally defined as basic stock plus safety stock. Inventory which is to big is a leading cause for unsatisfactory cash flow. On regular basis, hospital's drugstore had to put more of its cash into the purchase of medicaments in order to meet its obligations, especially in the case of the wholesaler who was located outside of Bosnia and Herzegovina. In theory, SAP ERP All-in-One solution provides the MRP function which covers the safety stock. The idea is to alert the responsible person when a group of materials or a material is close to the minimum of inventory stock, and suggest the number of units that should be purchased in order to meet the optimal stock. However, in practice, system provided alerts only when the responsible employee wanted to order particular material. Unfortunately, it was possible that the material is already under the safety stock red line. This was frustration for both, SAP consultants, and hospital warehouse management.

b) The complete database of pharmacy's inventory needed to be implemented according to the generic molecules, as it ensures standardization across health systems.

c) Even though it was not defined in the scope of the project, it was necessary to fulfill all pharmacy standards regarding pharmacy business proposed by law. All generics & their particular brands, batches, used by the hospital had to be maintained in a database with the appropriate commercial terms (commercial name, pharmacy agency approval number etc). At first, the main challenge for the SAP integrator and consultants was implementation of ATC/DDD standardization for medicaments. The ATC/DDD system classifies all therapeutic drugs and provides a tool for drug utilization research in order to improve quality of drug use. In the ATC classification system, drugs are divided into different groups according to the organ or the system on which they act and their chemical, pharmacological and therapeutic properties. Drugs are classified into 14 main groups / classes [2], [3]. Each of the main classes contains hundreds of subgroups which include hundreds of groups itself. At the end, there was a need for thousands of predefined material groups in SAP MM. This approach was overly complicated so the integrator decided to implement the SAP Classification system for clinic drug warehouse.

The Classification system in SAP for clinical drug warehouse was, at the beginning, seen as blueprint of ATC/DDD classification. However, implementation/situation became more complex. The Classification system in SAP does not only depend on the definition of the ATC/DDD, but also on costing procedures and reporting (which was wanted to get as reports from classification). In addition, assuming that SAP classification needs to meet all, by law, proposed legislation, SAP integrator defined set of characteristics for each material. After few kick off meetings integrator came up with those classification characteristics; presentation/package (box, pills, mg etc.), aggregate state, product hierarchy grouping (ATC/DDD) and profit centers. All of these had to be set as characteristics of the material classification. After months of preparation of all materials (over 30 000 records) for import into the system with all the necessary classification characteristics, it became apparent that such a big number of characteristics would be hard to maintain. Performance of drugstore as whole was seriously jeopardized by the time required to complete the entire process of maintaining material master data. At the end, this SAP classification system was refused by the hospital's drugstore.

d) The lack of batch management and shelf life – The main and very important point of any drug warehouse is the batch management. All pharmacy products are managed by the batch and the shelf life. Those are critical factors for managing the inventory efficiently. The standard SAP ERP provides fields (after activation) for those material attributes, but, once again, it did not work properly in practice. The standard SAP ERP does not provide ad-hoc integration of bar code reader technology, so the only option was to extend the project's scope and to develop the specific solution for bar code technology. Moreover, integrator was required to build up good receipt transaction in SAP (MIGO transaction) in order to support goods receipt process supported by code readers. This particular development increased the project's costs.

Another issue was the shelf life of materials. The proposition from hospital drug warehouse management was to create inventory management system where medicaments with closest expire date would be suggested for goods issue. However, this was not a feature of the standard SAP ERP All-in-One. It was only possible to create a new report where all medicaments would be listed by the expiry date criteria. However, this was not satisfactory for clinical drug management because their employees required too much time to operate with particular report.

e) Standardization hierarchy for equipment (medical as well as non- medical) – The complete database of non-pharmacy inventory like equipment, linen, stationary, sundry items etc. was imported in SAP. Also, the database of the approved suppliers for each item was maintained with relevant commercial terms & specifications. However, as with the ATC/DDD standardization, the proposed solution for standardization of the equipment (class/subclass/group) was impractical for daily usage.

f) Goods issue of material was not linked to the specification of healthcare services for a patient (SAP SD module) – One of the major issues for the SAP integrator was implementation of fully automated goods issue process. At the beginning the idea was to blueprint the real life scenario. That is, medicament was supposed to be issued when given to patient. However, in reality, due to the lack of infrastructure (no available network) and because of the license issue (management of clinic found it too expensive SAP), process was delayed 7 days at average. So, medicament was issued to a patient from the department drug storage location, but transaction was written on a paper. After 7 days, when the list of medicaments issued is usually over 50 pages long, it is provided to employees in central hospital drugstore, and then imported into SAP. This was undesirable process for employees who import those lists weekly into SAP. In addition, dozens of mistake were made each week due to manual data import into SAP system.

4   Conclusion

Implementation of the standard SAP system in health care environment results in specific issues and problems during the implementation of SAP ERP SD and MM modules. The main problems encountered explained for SD and MM module are:

- Standard SAP SD module does not fit health care institution billing needs - too much development is needed, which is not good for maintenance and support;
- SAP ERP SD is not intended to cope with patient master date (huge load of data);
- The Standard material group in MM is not sufficient to describe ATC/DDD standardization;
- SAP material classification is too complex when it respects all attributes needed for maintaining drug material master data.

This leads to the general conclusions regarding implementation of standard SAP system in health care institution:

- Standard SAP ERP system does not support specific Healthcare processes, so a lot of custom development (i.e. "Z" programs) must be made to fulfill customer's requirements. It is a risky decision, because it boosts system maintenance cost;
- SAP All-in-One is not capable to meet all the health care institution requirements in a satisfactory way without SAP Healthcare solution, i.e. SAP ERP is tailored to fit standard business processes present in majority of business domains. However, only SAP Healthcare industry specific solution addresses all specific requirements for healthcare institution.

References

1. SAP Business All-in-One,
   http://www.sap.com/sme/solutions/businessmanagement/
   businessallinone/index.epx
2. WHO: The Anatomical Therapeutic Chemical Classification System with Defined Daily
   Doses (ATC/DDD), http://www.who.int/classifications/atcddd/en/
3. Anatomical Therapeutic Chemical Classification System,
   http://en.wikipedia.org/wiki/Anatomical_Therapeutic_
   Chemical_Classification_System

An Application of the ψ-Theory to the Analysis of Business Process Models[*]

Artur Caetano[1,2,3], Aurélio Assis[1,3], José Borbinha[1,2], and José Tribolet[1,3]

[1] Instituto Superior Técnico, Technical University of Lisbon,
Avenida Rovisco Pais 1, 1049-001 Lisboa, Portugal
[2] Information Systems Group, INESC-ID, Lisboa, Portugal
[3] Centre for Organizational Design and Engineering, INESC INOV, Lisboa, Portugal
{artur.caetano,aurelio.assis,jose.borbinha,
jose.tribolet}@ist.utl.pt

Abstract. This paper presents a method to analyse the consistency and completeness of process models according to the principles of the ψ-theory and the underlying concept of business transaction. Transactions specify the collaborative behaviour between actors while services are being requested and provided. The method assesses the consistency of a process in terms of the business transactions that can be inferred from it. To do so, it takes as input a process model that is converted to a transactional model. The transactional model is then analysed and revised so that all transactions become consistent and complete according to the transactional pattern. This enables to identify the problems on the original process model and to prompt areas of improvement.

Keywords: business process modelling, business transaction, ψ-theory, DEMO, BPMN.

1   Introduction

Business process modelling techniques can be used to analyse and communicate inter- and intra-organizational business processes as well as to develop business support information systems [1-5]. The project reported in this paper is motivated by the need to analyse the consistency of business process models. This capability is lacking in process modelling techniques since their focus is on the constructs required to define the models and not on methods to assess the actual quality of the models. Moreover, the lack of semantics behind process modelling languages and the unclear specification of their constructs contributes to the design of ambiguous models [6, 7]. An example of such ambiguity is the usage of natural language as the means to specify a process. These problems become evident when models or views need to be integrated or when the services to support a business process need to be consistently identified. On the other hand, methods to design business processes mainly focus on aligning business with technological concepts and do not prescribe the principles to design

---

[*] This work is partially supported by the EU-FP7 grant 269940, project TIMBUS, "Digital Preservation for Timeless Business Processes and Services".

G. Poels (Ed.): CONFENIS 2012, LNBIP 139, pp. 258–267, 2013.
© IFIP International Federation for Information Processing 2013

consistent business process [6]. The combination of these factors creates the need to define techniques to design new business processes or to provide the means to analyse existing process models with the goal of continuously improving their consistency while responding to the stakeholder's needs.

To address this problem, this paper uses the principles set forth by the ψ-theory to analyse the consistency of business processes. We consider a process model to be *consistent* if its activities comply with the business transaction pattern. This pattern, which is part of the ψ-theory, defines communication steps that a requester and a producer perform while responding to a request. If a process complies with the transaction pattern then its specification describes who is responsible for the execution of its activities and why each activity is being performed. However, a business process can be consistent but still be missing activities required to fully produce the intended transactional results. This means that a *complete* process must not only be consistent but also specify all transactional activities. Thus, a process model that is both consistent and complete is a process that fully specifies an end-to-end collaboration pattern between a service requester and a service provider.

The next section of the paper introduces the ψ-theory along with the concept of business transaction. Section 3 describes the method to analyse business processes along with a running example. Finally, section 4 concludes the paper.

2   The ψ -Theory

The ψ-theory (ψ is pronounced as PSI, standing for Performance in Social Interaction) is a theory about the ontological essence of organizations. It clarifies and explains the construction and operation of organizations. The operating principle of enterprises is that the employees, together with representatives of the customers and the suppliers, enter into and comply with commitments regarding the products that they cooperatively produce. This very basic understanding makes enterprises primarily social systems, of which the elements are human beings in their role of social individuals, bestowed with appropriate authority and bearing the corresponding responsibility. The ψ-theory is rooted in speech act theory [8], in social action theory [9, 10], and in information systems theory [11]. It is extensively discussed in [12]. The ψ-theory provides an effective notion of Enterprise Ontology, defined as the fully implementation independent understanding of the essence of an enterprise's organization. The Design & Engineering Methodology for Organizations [12] is a methodology for the engineering and implementation of organizations that is formally grounded on the ψ-theory . Some authors state that DEMO defines a robust enterprise engineering approach as it provides a formal yet simple conceptualization of an organization that can be used a point of departure for its implementation [1, 13]. DEMO can also deliver models which can be formally assessed and executed on DEMO automata [14]. DEMO can be used to assess existing BPMN models with the purpose of verifying their consistency [1]. The main contribution is thus combining the representational capability of the BPMN standard with the formal correctness of the DEMO principles. However, DEMO ends where BPMN and other transformational business process modelling languages start. Thus, this paper proposes using DEMO to help construct-ing consistent and complete BPMN process models [15]. The ψ-theory consists of four axioms [1, 12]. We briefly describe two of these axioms due to their significance to the method put forward in this paper.

2.1 The Operation Axiom

The operation axiom states that the operation of an enterprise results from the per-formance of actor roles. An *actor role* is an element of *authority* and *responsibility* which is fulfilled by a subject. A subject performs two kinds of acts: *production acts* (P-acts) and *coordination acts* (C-acts). By performing P-acts, subjects contribute to bringing about the function of the organization. By performing C-acts, the subjects enter into and comply with commitments regarding P-acts. So C-acts are the way in which cooperation between subjects is accomplished and made explicit. An actor role is defined as the *authority* to perform one particular kind of P-act. A subject in its fulfilling of an actor role is called an actor.

P-acts and C-acts produce results. The result of a production is a production fact (P-fact) and the result of coordination act is a coordination fact (C-fact). For instance, the action of packing an order (a material P-act) results in a package with the order items (the corresponding P-fact).

2.2 The Transaction Axiom

The transaction axiom states that C-acts and P-acts occur in a particular pattern and consists of an *order* followed by a *result* conversation. A conversation is a sequence of coordination acts between two actor roles required to achieve a result. A transac-tion evolves in three phases: the order phase (O-phase) where the request is made, the execution phase (E-phase) that produces the result, and the final result phase (R-phase) where the initiator is notified of the result. The actor role that starts the order conversation is the *initiator* or *requestor*. The role that executes the request, produces the fact and responds to the initiator is the *executor* or *provider*. The basic transaction pattern consists of the following steps:

1. Order phase
    1.1. The initiator makes a *request* (rq) to the executor to produce a specific P-fact. This P-fact will be the result of the transaction.
    1.2. The executor then *promises* (pm) the initiator that he agrees with the request and that he is committed to produce the result. Thus, the order phase defines the initial contract or commitment between the initiation and executor.
2. Execution phase: the executor produces the P-fact as promised.
3. Result phase
    3.1. The executor *states* (st) to the initiator that the result is complete.
    3.2. The initiator *accepts* (ac) the result, thus successfully ending the transaction.

The basic transaction pattern assumes that all conversations have a successful out-come. DEMO also defines a standard transaction pattern that extends the basic pattern with four additional cancellation patterns. The standard transaction pattern is considered complete as it covers all possible communicative and rollback actions [12].

3   The Analysis Method

This section describes an iterative method to analyse the consistency and completeness of business process models. A business process model is *consistent* if the order of its actions complies with the transactional axiom. A business process model is *complete* if all transactional pattern steps can be mapped to its activities. Therefore, a process that is consistent and complete specifies all the actions that are required to produce a specific result and does so according to the transactional axiom. Note that consistency applies to any level of detail of the process. Therefore, if a business process is functionally decomposed then each level must also comply with the transactional axiom.

Throughout this paper we will consider the input model to be a BPMN process diagram, although other transformational modelling techniques could be used [16]. Thus, a process is specified as a flow of named activities that are performed by actors. The method comprises five steps. The first steps identify the production and coordination acts embedded in the input process model. The next steps assess the completeness and consistency of the process model according to the ψ-theory axioms. The input process model can then be reviewed according to the assessment. This enables the process model to be incrementally analysed and reviewed. The remainder of this section describes these steps along with an example of application.

3.1   Analyse the Input Process Model (Step 1)

The method starts with a BPMN process model and produces a DEMO process structure diagram that abstracts the coordination and production acts depicted on the input model. The goal of the first step is to analyse the design artefacts used to represent the business process model. It analyses the activities and classifies them according to the operation axiom and distinction axiom. As a result each activity is classified as a production or coordination act (operation axiom) and also as a *performa, informa,* or *forma* speech act (distinction axiom). Furthermore, the operation axiom also discriminates the actor roles involved in the process. The result of this step is a traceable list that maps the coordination and production acts and actors to the original process model from where they were sourced.

Consider the following examples: an activity that sends an electronic message is classified as a coordination act since it involves communication between actors and as a *forma* act because it represents a source uttering a message to a recipient. An activity that archives that message is classified as *forma* but it is a production act because it is generating a new production fact (the archived message). An activity that counts the number of messages archived on a given date is a production act as it generates a new production fact (the message count) but it is classified as an *informa* speech act since it is computing a result.

Next, each *performa* coordination act is classified as a *request, promise, state, accept* coordination act according to the transaction pattern. Using the standard transaction pattern implies further identifying the *decline, reject, stop, quit* acts. . For instance, an activity Place Order is as a *request* coordination act as it is performed by the initiator to start a new transaction. The activity Receive Ordered Product is an *accept* coordination act as it indicates the initiator acknowledged and accepted the result of the transaction.

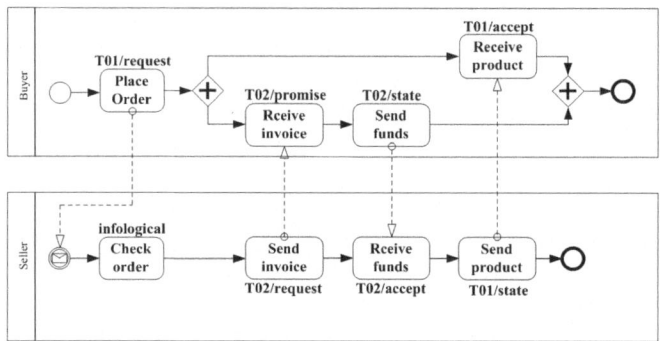

Fig. 1. Input business process model after application of steps 1

Figure 1 depicts a business process represented in BPMN describing the selling of a product to a buyer. The buyer places an order to a seller who checks its validity. Then the seller sends an invoice to the buyer. After receiving the payment the seller sends the buyer the product. This process is intentionally being specified at a high level of functional detail and it excludes error conditions and compensation actions due to space limitations.

The application of step 1 classifies the activity Check Order as infological (*informa*) according to the distinction axiom. The remaining activities are ontological (*performa*) acts. The coordination acts are further classified according to the transaction axiom (e.g. Place Order is classified as T01/request and Receive Invoice as T02/promise). The result is shown in Figure 1.

3.2   Generate the DEMO Models (Step 2)

This step takes the classifications produced in step 1 and generates the corresponding DEMO process structure diagram. The classification of the coordination acts along with the control and data flow restrictions that are specified on the input process model are used to generate the DEMO process model.

Step 2 of the bottom-up phase derives a DEMO process from the labelled business process model. The initial resulting model is shown in the left-hand side of Figure 2. It can be observed that this model is incomplete as several acts are missing.

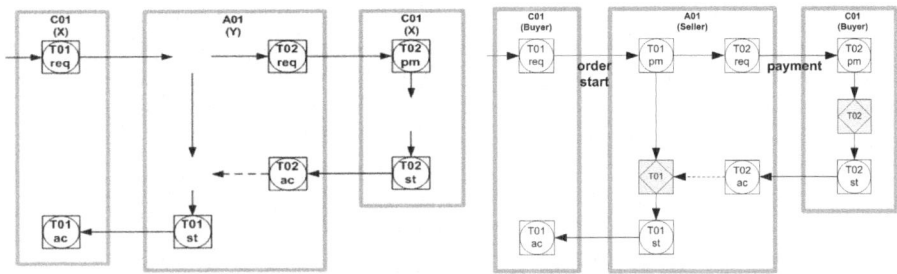

Fig. 2. Incomplete process structure diagram after step 2 (left) and revised model after step 3 (right)

3.3   Revise the DEMO Models (Step 3)

This step adds acts found to be missing during the previous step to the process model. These acts are the ontological acts that are not described explicitly in the input business process. The model is revised according to the transaction axiom so that each transaction goes through all the steps defined in the O-, E-, and R-phases. Next, the application of the composition axiom ensures that all of the transaction steps follow a logical sequence according to the pattern. The results of step 3 are process structure diagram (process model) and an actor-transaction diagram (construction model).

The result is the process model shown in in the right-hand side of Figure 2. This step has added the acts T01/pm, T01, T02 according to the transaction pattern. This revised model is now complete and consistent with the Ψ-theory axioms.

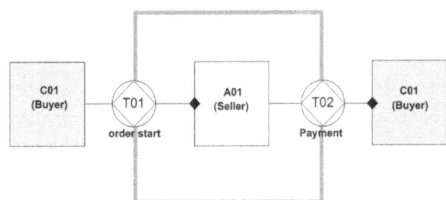

Fig. 3. Construction model

The actor-transaction diagram (ATD) depicted in Figure 3 shows the actors responsible for initiating and executing a transaction. The buyer is responsible for initiating the transaction T01 (Order) which is executed by the seller (the executor role is depicted by a black diamond on the association end). Conversely, the seller initiates transaction T02 (Payment) which is executed by the buyer.

3.4   Revise the Input Process Model (Step 4)

This step performs a gap analysis that identifies the ontological acts in the revised DEMO model that are missing from the input business process model. Based on the results, the original BPMN process model is revised so that its activities match the missing ontological acts. The revised process becomes ψ-theory compliant, meaning it is now consistent with the transaction pattern and complete as it contains all transaction steps.

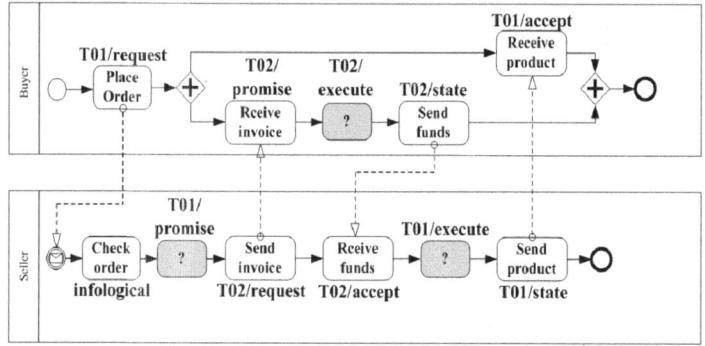

Fig. 4. Identification of missing steps according to the transaction pattern (step 4)

This step identifies the missing activities on the original process model that derive from the missing acts. The revised process is depicted in Figure 4. The changes imply adding three activities, one for each missing ontological act: T01/promise, T01/execute and T02/execute. The name of these activities is actually irrelevant at this stage. The revised process is now consistent and complete with the ψ-theory axioms since all essential speech acts are explicit.

The missing promise act (T01/promise) means the seller is implicitly accepting the buyer's request. Such decision may either be a design decision or the result of an incomplete specification. In either case, such an implicit promise makes this model ambiguous because it is not clear when the order is actually being accepted by the seller. It may be the case that the seller commits to selling the product to the buyer immediately after checking the order. But it may also be the case that the seller is only committed to the transaction if he sends the invoice. This makes the responsibility of the actors involved in the transaction to be ambiguous. For instance, if the buyer places an order and the seller does not send the invoice in a timely manner (e.g. as defined on a service-level agreement), the model does not make explicit if the seller was already committed to send the invoice or not. The revised process makes such decision clear.

However, it is important to note that the revised process may not be ideal because there are usually several variations that are consistent and complete. Thus, the revised process primarily serves as a means to emphasize problem areas and to point the architects towards possible solutions. A definite solution can only be found after an iterative analysis and revision of the process model according to the overall architecture of the organization in such a way that it suits the needs of its stakeholders and the overall architectural alignment principles.

3.5   Results of Application

This method was applied to the analysis of two core business processes at a large organization (+2000 employees) that handles legal and judicial procedures. This was done using a software tool that fully automates parts of the method and supports the remaining semi-automated parts. The two processes total approximately 500 activities and cross 10 inter-organizational boundaries and involve more than 60 actor roles. The activities of these processes were already modelled and were detailed up to 4 or 5 levels of depth. The method was applied to these processes and the results were discussed and validated with the stakeholders. The application of the method took 20 person-days and was performed by a team process modelling experts who analysed the processes and met regularly with groups of stakeholders from the organization. Note that the example presented on the previous section is similar to this case study except in terms of complexity and extent. The following results were observed. The original processes lacked 25% of *production acts,* meaning that the original processes included activities that were not explicitly producing any tangible results. The following observations apply to the missing *coordination acts*:

- Missing 25% of request acts. Results are being produced without an explicit request being made and thus it is not possible to identify an accountable service initiator. This is particularly important in processes that are executed by multiple actors, especially inter-organizational actors.
- Missing 50% of promise acts. Requests are implicitly confirmed, often without any governing contract. The service performer starts producing a result without agreeing with the initiator and thus it is not formally accountable for the production.
- Missing 25% of state coordination acts. Production results are not explicitly communicated. The implication is that is not clear whether the responsibility of checking the completion of a result lies on the initiator or on the executor.
- Missing 40% of accept acts. Production results are not being accepted by the initiator. There is no formal acceptance and therefore the initiator does not confirm that the results comply with the request. Moreover, the executor cannot assess the quality of its results since there is no formal acceptance of the product.

4   Conclusions

This paper presents a method to analyse the consistency of a process model based on the ψ-theory. A business transaction specifies a pattern that describes how actors collaborate. The method takes as input a process model that is converted to a transactional model. The transactional model is then revised so that all transactions comply with the ψ -theory axioms. Finally, the original process model is revised to become consistent and complete in the sense it expresses all transactional steps. The method was illustrated through the analysis and revision of a simple business process. We have also used this method to analyse a set of detailed business processes comprising several hundred activities at a large public institution. The method identified a set of implicit and missing acts from the original processes and prompted their revision so that the areas of responsibility and the contracts between the organizational actors became clear.

Nevertheless, the successful application of this method implies a sound understanding of the original process as well as working closely with its stakeholders so that it can be iteratively revised. This also means each step could end up be repeated several times until we get to the point where the input model satisfies the stakeholder's needs and is consistent and complete at the same time. Despite such shortcomings, such analysis will raise questions about the contents of the process models. The main question that tends to surface is about the actual meaning of the activities specified in the process model. Answering these questions contributes to reducing the ambiguity of the original specification and to clarifying implicit responsibilities. This means that a process model should clarify the areas of responsibility and the chain of accountability. We believe the method proposed in this paper is a contribution to this complex undertaking.

References

1. Van Nuffel, D., Mulder, H., Van Kervel, S.: Enhancing the Formal Foundations of BPMN by Enterprise Ontology. In: Albani, A., Barjis, J., Dietz, J.L.G. (eds.) CIAO!/EOMAS 2009. LNBIP, vol. 34, pp. 115–129. Springer, Heidelberg (2009)
2. Dijkmana, M., Dumas, M., Ouyang, C.: Semantics and analysis of business process models in BPMN. Information and Software Technology 50(12), 1281–1294 (2008)
3. Zimmermann, O., Schlimm, N., Waller, G., Pestel, M.: Analysis and Design Techniques for Service-Oriented Development and Integration. In: INFORMATIK 2005, Bonn, Germany (2005)
4. Sousa, P., Caetano, A., Vasconcelos, A., Pereira, C., Tribolet, J.: Enterprise architecture modeling with the UML 2.0. In: Rittgen, P. (ed.) Enterprise Modeling and Computing with UML, pp. 67–94. Idea Group Inc. (2006)
5. Caetano, A., Rito Silva, A., Tribolet, J.: A Role-Based Enterprise Architecture Framework. In: 24th Annual ACM Symposium on Applied Computing, Hawaii, USA (2009)
6. Barjis, J.: Automatic business process analysis and simulation based on DEMO. In: Enterprise Information Systems, vol. 1(4). Taylor & Francis (2007)
7. Recker, J., Indulska, M., Rosemann, M.: How Good is BPMN Really? Insights from Theory and Practice. In: Ljungberg, J., Andersson, M. (eds.) Proceedings of the 14th ECIS, Goeteborg, Sweden (2006)
8. Searle, J.: Speech Acts: An Essay in the Philosophy of Language. Cambridge University Press, Cambridge (1969)
9. Dignum, F., Dietz, J.: Communication Modelling: The Language/Action Perspective. In: Second International Workshop on Communication Modeling (LAP 1997), The Netherlands (1997)
10. Habermas, J.: The theory of communicative action - reason and the rationalization of society. Beacon Press, Boston (1984)
11. Langefors, B.: Information System Theory. Information Systems 2, 207–210 (1977)
12. Dietz, J.: Enterprise Ontology: Theory and Methodology, p. 244. Springer, New York (2006)

13. Ettema, R., Dietz, J.L.G.: ArchiMate and DEMO – Mates to Date? In: Albani, A., Barjis, J., Dietz, J.L.G. (eds.) CIAO!/EOMAS 2009. LNBIP, vol. 34, pp. 172–186. Springer, Heidelberg (2009)
14. Nuffel, D.V., Huysmans, P., Bellens, D., Ven, K.: Translating Ontological Business Transactions into Evolvable Information Systems. In: International Conference on Software Engineering Advances, France, pp. 58–63 (2010)
15. OMG, Business Process Model and Notation (BPMN), version 2.0 (2011)
16. Carlsen, S.: Comprehensible Business Process Models for Process Improvement and Process Support. In: Constantopoulos, P., et al. (eds.) Advances on Information Systems Engineering. Springer (1996)

Transition from Process- to Product-Level Perspective
for Business Software

Nuno Ferreira[1], Nuno Santos[2], Pedro Soares[2],
Ricardo J. Machado[3], and Dragan Gašević[4]

[1] I2S Informática, Sistemas e Serviços S.A., Porto, Portugal
nuno.ferreira@i2s.pt
[2] CCG - Centro de Computação Gráfica, Campus de Azurém, Guimarães, Portugal
{nuno.santos,psoares}@ccg.pt
[3] Centro ALGORITMI, Escola de Engenharia, Universidade do Minho, Guimarães, Portugal
rmac@dsi.uminho.pt
[4] School of Computing and Information Systems, Athabasca University, Canada
dgasevic@acm.org

Abstract. When there are insufficient inputs for a product-level approach to requirements elicitation, a process-level perspective is an alternative way for achieving the intended base requirements. We define a V+V process approach that supports the creation of the intended requirements, beginning in a process-level perspective and evolving to a product-level perspective trough successive models derivation with the purpose of creating context for the implementation teams. The requirements are expressed through models, namely logical architectural models and stereotyped sequence diagrams. Those models alongside with the entire approach are validated using the architecture validation method ARID.

Keywords: Enterprise logical architecture, Information System Requirement Analysis, Design, Model Derivation.

1   Introduction

A typical business software development project is coordinated so that the resulting product properly aligns with the business model intended by the leading stakeholders. The business model normally allows for eliciting the requirements by providing the product's required needs. In situations where organizations focused on software development are not capable of properly eliciting requirements for the software product, due to insufficient stakeholder inputs or some uncertainty in defining a proper business model, a process-level requirements elicitation is an alternative approach. The process-level requirements assure that organization's business needs are fulfilled. However, it is absolutely necessary to assure that product-level (IT-related) requirements are perfectly aligned with process-level requirements, and hence, are aligned with the organization's business requirements.

One of the possible representations of an information system is its logical architecture [1], resulting from a process of transforming business-level and technological-level decisions and requirements into a representation (model). It is necessary to promote an

G. Poels (Ed.): CONFENIS 2012, LNBIP 139, pp. 268–275, 2013.
© IFIP International Federation for Information Processing 2013

alignment between the logical architecture and other supporting models, like organizational configurations, products, processes, or behaviors. A logical architecture can be considered a view of a system composed of a set of problem-specific abstractions supporting functional requirements [2].

In order to properly support technological requirements that comply with the organization's business requirements, we present in this paper an approach composed by two V-Models [3], the V+V process. The requirements are expressed through logical architectural models and stereotyped sequence diagrams [4] in both a process- and a product-level perspective. The first execution of the V-Model acts in the analysis phase and regards a process-level perspective. The second execution of the V-Model regards a product-level perspective and enables the transition from analysis to design trough the execution of the product-level 4SRS method [5]. Our approach assures a proper compliance between the process- and the product-level requirements through a set of transition steps between the two perspectives.

This paper is structured as follows: section 2 presents the V+V process; section 3 describes the method assessment through ARID; in section 4 we present an overview of the process- to product-level transition; in section 5 we compare our approach with other related works; and in section 6 we present the conclusions.

2   A V+V Process Approach for Information System's Design

At a macro-process level, the development of information systems can be regarded as a cascaded lifecycle, if we consider typical and simplified phases: analysis, design and implementation. We encompass our first V-Model (at process-level) within the analysis phase and the second V-Model (at product-level) in the transition between the analysis and the design. One of the outputs of any of our V-Models is the logical architectural model for the intended system. This diagram is considered a design artifact but the design itself is not restricted to that artifact. We have to execute a V+V process to gather enough information in the form of models (logical architectural model, *B-type* sequence diagrams and others) to deliver, to the implementation teams, the correct specifications for product realization.

Regarding the first V-Model, we refer that it is executed at a process-level perspective. How the term *process* is applied in this approach can lead to inappropriate interpretations. Since the term *process* has different meanings depending on the context, in our process-level approach we acknowledge that: (1) real-world activities of a business software production process are the context for the problem under analysis; (2) in relation to a software model context [6], a software process is composed of a set of activities related to software development, maintenance, project management and quality assurance. For scope definition of our work, and according to the previously exposed acknowledgments, we characterize our process-level perspective by: (1) being related to real-world activities (including business); (2) when related to software, those activities encompass the typical software development lifecycle. Our process-level approach is characterized by using refinement (as one kind of functional decomposition) and integration of system models. Activities and their interface in a process can be structured or arranged in a process architecture [7].

Our V-Model approach (inspired in the "Vee" process model [3]) suggests a road-map for product design based on business needs elicited in an early analysis phase. The approach requires the identification of business needs and then, by successive artifact derivation, it is possible to transit from a business-level perspective to an IT-level perspective and at the same time, aligns the requirements with the derived IT artifacts. Additionally, inside the analysis phase, this approach assures the transition from the business needs to the requirements elicitation.

In this section, we present our approach, based on successive and specific artifacts generation. In the first V-Model (at the process-level), we use *Organizational Configurations* (OC) [8], *A-type* and *B-type* sequence diagrams [4], (business) *Use Case* models (UCs) and a process-level logical architectural model. The generated artifacts and the alignment between the business needs and the context for product design can be inscribed into this first V-Model.

The presented approach encompasses two V-Models, hereafter referred as the V+V process and depicted in Fig. 1. The first V deals with the process-level perspective and its vertex is supported by the process-level 4SRS method detailed in [9]. The process-level 4SRS method execution results in the creation of a validated architectural model which allows creating context for the product-level requirements elicitation and in the uncovering of hidden requirements for the intended product design. The purpose of the first execution of the V-Model regards eliciting requirements from a high-level business level to create context for product design, that can be considered a business elicitation method (like the Business Modeling discipline of RUP).

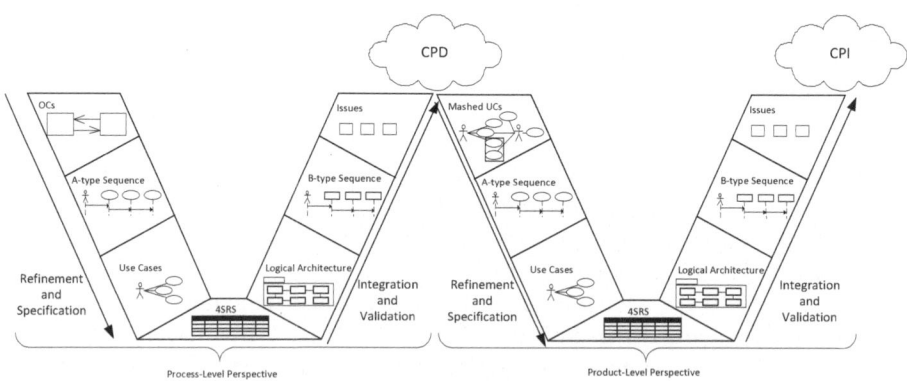

Fig. 1. The V+V process approach

The second execution of the V-Model is done at a product-level perspective and its vertex is supported by the product-level 4SRS method detailed in [5]. The product-level V-Model gathers information from the context for product design (*CPD*) in order to create a new model referred as *Mashed UCs*. Using the information present in the *Mashed UCs* model, we create *A-type* sequence diagrams, detailed in [4]. These diagrams are input for the creation of (software) *Use Case Models* that have associated textual descriptions of the requirements for the intended system. Using the 4SRS method in the vertex, we derive those requirements into a *Logical Architectural model*. Using a process identical to the one used in the process-level V-Model, we create *B-type* sequence diagrams and assess the *Logical Architectural Model*.

The V-Model representation provides a balanced process representation and, simultaneously, ensures that each step is verified before moving into the next. As seen in Fig. 1, the artifacts are generated based on the rationale and in the information existing in previously defined artifacts, i.e., *A-type* diagrams are based on OCs, (business) use case model is based on *A-type* sequence diagrams, the logical architecture is based on the (business) use case model, and *B-type* sequence diagrams comply with the logical architecture. The V-Model also assures validation of artifacts based on previously modeled artifacts (e.g., besides the logical architecture, *B-type* sequence diagrams are validated by *A-type* sequence diagrams). The aim of this manuscript is not to detail the inner execution of the V-Model, nor is it to detail the rules that enable the transition from the process- to the product-level, but rather to present the overall V+V process within the macro-process of information systems development.

In both V-Models, the assessment is made using an adaption of ARID (presented in the next section) and by using *B-type* sequence diagrams to check if the architectural elements present in the *Logical Architectural Model* produced by the models are contained in the scenarios depicted by the *B-type* sequence diagrams.

The first V produces a process-level logical architecture (that can be considered the information system logical architecture); the second V produces a product-level logical architecture (that can be considered the business software logical architecture). Also, for each of the V-Models, in the descending side of the V (left side), models created in succession represent the refinement of requirements and the creation of system specifications. In the ascending side (right side of the V), models represent the integration of the discovered logical parts and their involvement in a cross-side oriented validating effort contributing for the inner-validation for macro-process evolution.

3   V-Model Process Assessment with ARID

In both V-Models execution, the assessments that result from comparing *A-* and *B-type* sequence diagrams produce *Issues* documents. These documents are one of the outputs of the Active Reviews for Intermediate Designs (ARID) method [10, 11] used to assess each V-Model execution. The ARID method is a combination of Architecture Tradeoff Analysis Method (ATAM) [11] with Active Design Review (ADR) [11]. By its turn, ATAM can be seen as an improved version of Software Architecture Analysis Method (SAAM) [11]. These methods are able to conduct reviews regarding architectural decisions, namely on the quality attributes requirements and their alignment and satisfaction degree of specific quality goals. The ADR method targets architectures under development, performing evaluations on parts of the global architecture. Those features made ARID our method of choice regarding the evaluation of the in-progress logical architecture and in the assistance to determine the need of further refinements, improvements, or revisions before assuming that the architecture is ready to be delivered to the teams responsible for implementation. This delivery is called context for product implementation (*CPI*).

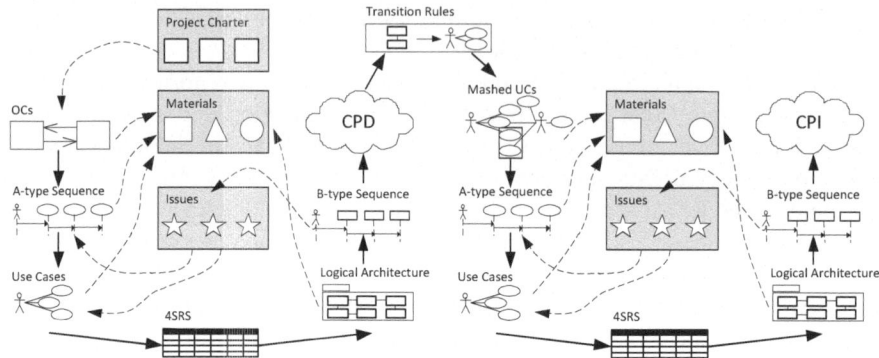

Fig. 2. Assessment of the V+V execution using ARID

In Fig. 2, we present the simplified interactions between the ARID-related models in the V+V process. In this figure, we can see the macro-process associated with both V-Models, the transition from one to the other (later detailed) and the ARID models that support the assessment of the V+V execution.

The *Project Charter* regards information that is necessary for the ongoing project and relates to project management terminology and content [12]. This document encompasses information regarding the project requirements in terms of human and material resources, skills, training, context for the project, stakeholder identification, amongst others. It explicitly contains principles and policies of the intended practice with people from different perspectives in the project (analysis, design, implementation, etc.). It also allows having a common agreement to refer to, if necessary, during the project execution.

The *Materials* document contains the necessary information for creating a presentation of the project. It regards collected seed scenarios based on *OCs (or Mashed UCs)*, *A-type* sequence diagrams and (business or software) *Use Case Models*. Parts of the *Logical Architectural* model are also incorporated in the presentation that will be presented to the stakeholders (including software engineers responsible for implementation). The purpose of this presentation is to enlighten the team about the logical architecture and propose the seed scenarios to discussion and create the *B-type* sequence diagrams based on presented information.

The *Issues* document supports information regarding the evaluation of the presented logical architecture. If the logical architecture is positively assessed, we can assume that we reached consensus to proceed into the macro-process. If not, using the *Issues* document it is possible to promote a new iteration of the corresponding V-Model execution to adjust the previously resulting logical architecture to make the necessary corrections to comply with the seed scenarios. Main causes for this adjustment are: (1) bad decisions that were made in the corresponding 4SRS method execution; (2) *B-type* sequence diagrams not complying with all the *A-type* sequence diagrams; (3) created *B-type* sequence diagrams not comprising the entire *logical architecture*; (4) the need to explicitly placing a design decision in the logical architectural model, usually done by using a common architectural pattern and injecting the necessary information in the use case textual descriptions that are input for the 4SRS.

The adjustment of the logical architectural model (by iterating the same V-Model) suggests the construction of a new use case model or, in the case of a new scenario, the construction of new *A-type* sequence diagrams. The new use case model captures user requirements of the revised system under design. At the same time, through the application of the 4SRS method, it is possible to derive the corresponding logical architectural model.

Our application of common architectural patterns include business, analysis, architectural and design patterns as defined in [13]. By applying them as early as possible in the development (in early analysis and design), it is possible to incorporate business requirements into the logical architectural model and at the same time assure that the resulting model is aligned with the organization needs and also complies with the established non-functional requirements. The design patterns are used when there is a need to detail or refine parts of the logical architecture and, by itself, to promote a new iteration of the V-Model.

In the second V, after being positively assessed by the ARID method, the business software logical architectural model is considered a final design artifact that must be divided into products (applications) for latter implementation by the software teams.

4   Process- to Product-Level Transition

As stated before, a process-level V-Model can be executed for business requirements elicitation purposes, followed by a product-level V-Model for defining the software functional requirements. The V+V process is useful for both stakeholders, organizations and technicians, but it is necessary to assure that they properly reflect the same system. In order to assure an aligned transition between the process- and product-level perspectives in the V+V process we propose the execution of a set of transition steps whose execution is required to create the *Mashed UC* model referred in Fig. 1 and in Fig. 2. The detail of the transition rules is subject of future publications.

Like in [2, 14], we propose the usage of the 4SRS by recursive executions with the purpose of deriving a new logical architecture. The transition steps are structured as follows: (1) Architecture Partitioning, where the Process-level Architectural Elements (AEpc's) under analysis are classified by their computation execution context with the purpose of defining software boundaries to be transformed into Product-level (software) Use Cases (UCpt's.); (2) Use Case Transformation, where AEpc's are transformed into software use cases and actors that represent the system under analysis through a set of transition patterns that must be applied as rules; (3) Original Actors Inclusion, where the original actors that were related to the use cases from which the architectural elements of the process-level perspective are derived (in the first V execution) must be included in the representation; (4) where the model is analyzed for redundancies; and (5) Gap Filling; where the necessary information of any requirement that is intended to be part of the design and that is not yet represented, is added, in the form of use cases.

By defining these transition steps, we assure that product-level (software) use cases (UCpt) are aligned with the architectural elements from the process-level logical architectural model (AEpc); i.e., software use case diagrams are reflecting the needs of the information system logical architecture. The application of these transition rules to all the partitions of an information system logical architecture gives origin to a set of *Mashed UC* models.

5   Comparison with Related Work

An important view considered in our approach regards the architecture. What is architecture? In the literature there is a plethora of definitions but most agree that an architecture concerns both structure and behavior, with a level of abstraction that only regards significant decisions and may be in conformance with an architectural style, is influenced by its stakeholders and the environment where it is intended to be instantiated and also encompasses decisions based on some rationale or method.

It is acknowledged in software engineering that a complete system architecture cannot be represented using a single perspective [15, 16]. Using multiple viewpoints, like logical diagrams, sequence diagrams or other artifacts, contributes to a better representation of the system and, as a consequence, to a better understanding of the system. Our stereotyped usage of sequence diagrams adds more representativeness value to the specific model than, for instance, the presented in Krutchen's 4+1 perspective [16]. This kind of representation also enables testing sequences of system actions that are meaningful at the software architecture level [17]. Additionally, the use of this kind of stereotyped sequence diagrams at the first stage of analysis phase (user requirements modeling and validation) provides a friendlier perspective to most stakeholders, easing them to establish a direct correspondence between what they initially stated as functional requirements and what the model already describes.

6   Conclusions and Outlook

We presented an approach to create context for business software implementation teams in contexts where requirements cannot be properly elicited. Our approach is based on successive models construction and recursive derivation of logical architectures, and makes use of model derivation for creating use cases, based on high-level representations of desired system interactions. The approach assures that validation tasks are performed continuously along the modeling process. It allows for validating: (1) the final software solution according to the initial expressed business requirements; (2) the *B-type* sequence diagrams according to *A-type* sequence diagrams; (3) the logical architectures by traversing it with *B-type* sequence diagrams. These validation tasks, specific to the V-Model, are subject of a future publication.

It is a common fact that domain-specific needs, namely business needs, are a fast changing concern that must be tackled. Process-level architectures must be in a way that potentially changing domain-specific needs are local in the architecture representation. Our proposed V+V process encompasses the derivation of a logical architecture representation that is aligned with domain-specific needs and any change made to those domain-specific needs is reflected in the logical architectural model through successive derivation of the supporting models (OCs, *A-* and *B-type* sequence diagrams, and use cases). Additionally, traceability between those models is built-in by construction, and intrinsically integrated in our V+V process.

Acknowledgments. This work has been supported by project ISOFIN (QREN 2010/013837).

References

1. Castro, J., Kolp, M., Mylopoulos, J.: Towards requirements-driven information systems engineering: the Tropos project. Information Systems (2002)
2. Azevedo, S., Machado, R.J., Muthig, D., Ribeiro, H.: Refinement of Software Product Line Architectures through Recursive Modeling Techniques. In: Meersman, R., Herrero, P., Dillon, T. (eds.) OTM 2009 Workshops. LNCS, vol. 5872, pp. 411–422. Springer, Heidelberg (2009)
3. Haskins, C., Forsberg, K.: Systems Engineering Handbook: A Guide for System Life Cycle Processes and Activities; INCOSE-TP-2003-002-03.2. 1. INCOSE (2011)
4. Machado, R., Lassen, K., Oliveira, S., Couto, M., Pinto, P.: Requirements Validation: Execution of UML Models with CPN Tools. International Journal on Software Tools for Technology Transfer (STTT) 9, 353–369 (2007)
5. Machado, R.J., Fernandes, J.M., Monteiro, P., Rodrigues, H.: Transformation of UML Models for Service-Oriented Software Architectures. In: Proceedings of the 12th IEEE ECBS 2005, pp. 173–182. IEEE Computer Society (2005)
6. Conradi, R., Jaccheri, M.L.: Process Modelling Languages. In: Derniame, J.-C., Kaba, B.A., Wastell, D. (eds.) Software Process. LNCS, vol. 1500, pp. 27–52. Springer, Heidelberg (1999)
7. Browning, T.R., Eppinger, S.D.: Modeling impacts of process architecture on cost and schedule risk in product development. IEEE Trans. on Eng. Management 49, 428–442 (2002)
8. Evan, W.M.: Toward a theory of inter-organizational relations. Management Science, 217–230 (1965)
9. Ferreira, N., Santos, N., Machado, R.J., Gašević, D.: Derivation of Process-Oriented Logical Architectures: An Elicitation Approach for Cloud Design. In: Dieste, O., Jedlitschka, A., Juristo, N. (eds.) PROFES 2012. LNCS, vol. 7343, pp. 44–58. Springer, Heidelberg (2012)
10. Clements, P.C.: Active Reviews for Intermediate Designs. Technical Note CMU/SEI-2000-TN-009 (2000)
11. Clements, P., Kazman, R., Klein, M.: Evaluating software architectures: methods and case studies. Addison-Wesley (2002)
12. Project Management Institute: A Guide to the Project Management Body of Knowledge (PMBOK® Guide) (2008)
13. Azevedo, S., Machado, R.J., Bragança, A., Ribeiro, H.: Systematic Use of Software Development Patterns through a Multilevel and Multistage Classification. In: Model-Driven Domain Analysis and Software Development: Architectures and Functions, vol. 304 (2010)
14. Machado, R.J., Fernandes, J.M., Monteiro, P., Rodrigues, H.: Refinement of Software Architectures by Recursive Model Transformations. In: Münch, J., Vierimaa, M. (eds.) PROFES 2006. LNCS, vol. 4034, pp. 422–428. Springer, Heidelberg (2006)
15. Sungwon, K., Yoonseok, C.: Designing logical architectures of software systems. In: SNPD/SAWN 2005, pp. 330–337 (2005)
16. Kruchten, P.: The 4+1 View Model of Architecture. IEEE Softw. 12, 42–50 (1995)
17. Bertolino, A., Inverardi, P., Muccini, H.: An explorative journey from architectural tests definition down to code tests execution. In: Proceedings of the 23rd International Conference on Software Engineering, pp. 211–220. IEEE CS, Toronto (2001)

Author Index